T0389221

"Many of the world's leading organizations create social value and simultaneously aim at reducing their environmental footprint. Metrics and measurements can become transformation enablers, when they make people more aware of what works and where progress has been achieved. Drawing on numerous disciplinary fields and real-life case studies, this anthology, Measuring and Controlling Susdtainability, provides a thought-after compilation of how to put this in practice. The editors and authors have done a superb job!"
— *Dr. Peetra Kuenkel*, Co-Founder,
Executive Director, Collective Leadership Institute

"This new book is a very welcome addition to the international literature on CSR performance and measurement. The book presents a lively and broad variety of approaches to CSR measurement and impact which allows readers to obtain a more comprehensive and in-depth understanding of this important topic. The book is particularly relevant at a time when many CSR academics and practitioners are concerned about whether CSR claims can indeed be back up by sufficient empirical evidence. I strongly recommend the book to students, practitioners, and academics interested in reflecting more deeply ongoing CSR developments and debates."
— *Dr. Peter Lund-Thomsen*, Professor in Corporate Social
Responsibility in Developing Countries, Copenhagen Business School

"The idea that 'If you can measure it, you can manage it' is often associated with the great management guru Peter Drucker, but as an idea it can be traced back at least to the 1500s and Rheticus. When sustainability moved from the fringes of the debate in management scholarship and practice towards the mainstream in the late 1980s, there was a widespread perception that it was somehow a 'soft' set of issues, difficult to get to grips with. This book demonstrates how far we have come in the last 30 years in recognising sustainability as a very 'hard' set of issues, both in the sense of being challenging to tackle, and in having very direct and measurable impacts on all aspects of business organisations. The 17 chapters in this book combine to demonstrate how the challenge of measuring and managing sustainability varies across different types of organisation, and cuts across traditional disciplinary boundaries. For those wishing to understand the vital importance of managing sustainability issues, and how to do it effectively in ways that protect the value of companies, their brands and their contribution to society, this book will be invaluable."

— *Prof. Ken Peattie*, Head of Marketing
and Strategy Section, Cardiff University

"For organizations wanting to gain and maintain a competitive edge in today's marketplace, corporate sustainability is a necessary practice. This collection of chapters puts forward a comprehensive view of challenges in connection with the sustainable value-creation process and of opportunities resulting from innovations in this process. Written in an accessible language, this anthology offers a fine mix of theoretical, integrative, and empirical perspectives on key dimensions in sustainability. As such, the anthology represents an important resource for researchers, as well as a source of key insights and inspiration for practitioners willing to engage strategically with sustainability questions and ideas."

— *Prof. Valérie Swaen*, Louvain School
of Management, Université catholique de Louvain

Measuring and Controlling Sustainability

Efforts to establish the measurement and control of sustainability have produced notable tools, but those instruments lack applicability in practice. Increasing the level of standardization of such tools also seems difficult to achieve, because the contexts surrounding the focal organizations differ considerably. Therefore, what we need is a systematic, interdisciplinary assessment of how to measure and control sustainability, so that we can establish an essential definition and up-to-date picture of the field.

Measuring and Controlling Sustainability attempts to provide such an assessment in 17 chapters, organized into four main topic sections: (a) organizations and social value creation: concepts, responsibilities, and barriers; (b) accounting, measurement, performance, and diffusion of social value; (c) practical and managerial insights from real-life cases; and (d) choices, incentives, guidance, and ethics.

This research anthology provides a comprehensive collection of cutting-edge theories and research that will further the development and advancement of measuring and controlling sustainable efforts in theory and managerial practice.

Dr. Adam Lindgreen is Professor of Marketing at Copenhagen Business School where he heads the Department of Marketing and Extra Ordinary Professor at University of Pretoria's Gordon Institute of Business Science. Dr. Lindgreen received his PhD from Cranfield University. He has published in *California Management Review, Journal of Business Ethics, Journal of Product and Innovation Management, Journal of the Academy of Marketing Science*, and *Journal of World Business*, among others.

Dr. Christine Vallaster is Professor of Marketing and Relationship Management at the University of Applied Sciences in Salzburg. Dr. Vallaster received her post-doctoral qualification from the University of Innsbruck. She has published in *California Management Review, Journal of Business Research, European Journal of Marketing*, and *Journal of World Business*, among others.

Dr. Shumaila Yousafzai is Associate Professor at Cardiff University. Her research focuses on the contextual embeddedness of entrepreneurship, institutional theory, and entrepreneurial orientation. She is an Associate Editor with *Journal of Small Business Management* and has published extensively in various international journals. She has edited research anthologies on women's entrepreneurship with Edward Elgar and Routledge.

Dr. Bernhard Hirsch is Professor of Management Accounting at Bundeswehr University Munich. He received his post-doctoral qualification (Dr. rer. pol. habil.) from WHU – Otto Beisheim School of Management and his doctoral degree (Dr. rer. pol.) from Witten/Herdcke University. He has published in *Management Accounting Research, Journal of Accounting and Organizational Change, Business Strategy and the Environment, International Journal of Physical Distribution & Logistics Management,* and *Financial Accountability & Management,* among others.

Measuring and Controlling Sustainability

Spanning Theory and Practice

Edited by Adam Lindgreen, Christine Vallaster, Shumaila Yousafzai, and Bernhard Hirsch

Routledge
Taylor & Francis Group

LONDON AND NEW YORK

First published 2019
by Routledge
2 Park Square, Milton Park, Abingdon, Oxon OX14 4RN

and by Routledge
711 Third Avenue, New York, NY 10017

Routledge is an imprint of the Taylor & Francis Group, an informa business

British Library Cataloguing-in-Publication Data
A catalogue record for this book is available from the British Library

Library of Congress Cataloging-in-Publication Data
Names: Lindgreen, Adam, editor.
Title: Measuring and controlling sustainability : spanning theory and
   practice / edited by Adam Lindgreen [and three others].
Description: Abingdon, Oxon ; New York, NY : Routledge, 2018. |
   Includes bibliographical references and index.
Identifiers: LCCN 2018014883 (print) | LCCN 2018017903
   (ebook) | ISBN 9781315401904 (eBook) | ISBN
   9781138224636 (hardback : alk. paper)
Subjects: LCSH: Sustainable development reporting. | Sustainable
   development–Evaluation.
Classification: LCC HD60.3 (ebook) | LCC HD60.3 .M43 2018
   (print) | DDC 338.9/27–dc23
LC record available at https://lccn.loc.gov/2018014883

ISBN: 9781138224636 (hbk)
ISBN: 9781315401904 (ebk)

Typeset in Bembo
by Swales & Willis Ltd, Exeter, Devon, UK

Printed and bound in Great Britain by
TJ International Ltd, Padstow, Cornwall

For Valérie, who convinced me that corporate social responsibility and sustainability would be interesting topics — Adam

For my family — Christine

For my father, Deedi, who believed in me and always gave me confidence disproportionate to my abilities, which is what all fathers should do — Shumaila

For my family — Bernhard

Contents

List of figures	xii
List of tables	xiv
About the editors	xvi
About the contributors	xix
Foreword and acknowledgements	xxvi

PART 1
Organizations and social value creation: concepts,
responsibilities, and barriers — 1

1.1 The Responsible Care initiative as an enabler
of implementing corporate social responsibility
concepts in the chemical industry — 3
PETER LETMATHE AND ILJA RABINOVITCH

1.2 Mind the gap! Existing barriers to standardizing
the measurement of social value creation — 18
CECILIA GRIECO AND LAURA MICHELINI

PART 2
Accounting, measurement, performance, and diffusion
of social value — 31

2.1 The sustainability balanced scorecard: an introduction to the
SBSC and its links to accounting and reporting — 33
FLORIAN LÜDEKE-FREUND AND STEFAN SCHALTEGGER

2.2 Sustainability accounting standards in the USA –
procedural legitimacy: governance, participation,
and decision-making processes — 54
DELPHINE GIBASSIER

2.3 **Adapting the measuring rod for social returns in advanced welfare states: a critique of SROI**   71
KONSTANTIN KEHL, GORGI KRLEV, VOLKER THEN,
AND GEORG MILDENBERGER

2.4 **Measuring the impact of strategic corporate social responsibility (S-CSR): finding the right approach**   89
FABIAN HERKENRATH AND CHRISTINE VALLASTER

2.5 **A performance tool for policy-makers to monitor the dual objective of social enterprises: a data envelopment analysis approach**   102
MATTHIAS STAESSENS, PIETER JAN KERSTENS, JOHAN BRUNEEL,
AND LAURENS CHERCHYE

2.6 **Diffusion of sustainability: a road map for developing corporate compliance programmes with high diffusion potential**   122
DUYGU TÜRKER AND CEREN ALTUNTAŞ VURAL

PART 3
Practical and managerial insights from real-life cases   139

3.1 **The impact of environmental and social practices on the triple bottom line: a mediated model**   141
CRISTINA GIMENEZ, VICENTA SIERRA, CRISTINA SANCHA, JOAN RODÓN,
AND STEFAN MARKOVIC

3.2 **Disclosing the invisible: measurement and disclosure pitfalls of carbon dioxide emissions**   166
NILS NIEHUES AND ANDREAS DUTZI

3.3 **Social entrepreneurship and social impact assessment: the case of euforia**   179
FLORIAN HOOS

3.4 **Mechanisms and tools for measuring and reporting sustainability in the hotel industry: a practical dimension**   189
PIOTR ZIENTARA AND PAULINA BOHDANOWICZ-GODFREY

3.5 **The growth of social banks: a new measurement approach**   206
NIKOLAS HÖHNKE AND SUSANNE HOMÖLLE

PART 4
Choices, incentives, guidance, and ethics   223

4.1 An experimental study on corporate social responsibility in junior managers' project choice in an energy-producing company   225
MATTHIAS SOHN, DOMINIK FISCHER, AND WERNER SOHN

4.2 Design options for sustainability-oriented incentive systems   240
ROBERT HUBER, BERNHARD HIRSCH, AND MATTHIAS SOHN

4.3 Sustainability reporting: do the Global Reporting Initiative Guidelines provide clear guidance?   253
RÜDIGER W. WALDKIRCH AND BERNHARD HIRSCH

4.4 Sustainability and ethics in financial reporting: an empirical study of German, Austrian, and Swiss groups   269
PETER G. KIRCHSCHLÄGER AND MICHAELA M. SCHAFFHAUSER-LINZATTI

Index   284

Figures

1.1.1	Framework of the CSR outcome variables	12
2.1.1	Basic perspectives of the balanced scorecard concept	35
2.1.2	Example of a cause-and-effect chain in a simple strategy map	36
2.1.3	Basic layout of an SBSC with a fifth, non-market perspective	39
2.1.4	Process and steps of formulating an SBSC	40
2.1.5	Strategy map of Hamburg Airport's SBSC	46
2.1.6	Integrated framework for sustainability performance measurement, management, and reporting	47
2.2.1	The non-financial corporate reporting landscape	59
2.4.1	The calculation of the Social Return on Investment	95
2.5.1	The social enterprise spectrum	104
2.5.2	Industry best practice frontier	106
2.5.3	Graphical representation of efficiency score	109
2.5.4	Malmquist index	111
2.5.5	Efficiency change	112
2.6.1	A road map for developing codes and compliance programmes: critical questions	131
3.1.1	Hypothesized model of the impact of environmental and social practices	147
3.1.2	Results of the direct effects	164
3.2.1	Carbon dioxide disclosure options	170
3.2.2	Overview of carbon dioxide emissions by scope	171
3.3.1	The impact dimensions of euforia	183
3.5.1	Intermediation approach	211
3.5.2	CAP_{Loa} and CAP_{Dep}	217
3.5.3	Relative growth G_r	218
3.5.4	Relative growth of TA, CD, and CV	218
4.1.1	Average number of cell openings per attribute and participant	231
4.1.2	Relative subjective weighting (mean) of project information	232
4.1.3	Percentage of employees who have rated the project as the most attractive/unattractive	233
4.1.4a	Percentage of projects rated as the most attractive one for male and female managers	234

4.1.4b	The distribution of workload among the projects	235
4.3.1	Trust game	255
4.4.1	Average percentage of economic, ecologic, and social content	277
4.4.2	Results of empirical study	278

Tables

1.1.1	Frameworks used for the analysis of the interplay between responsible care and corporate social responsibility concepts	4
1.1.2	Extract of chemical industry disasters from the 1970s to the 1990s	5
1.1.3	Descriptive statistics of rc and rc_delay	10
1.1.4	Descriptive statistics of the CSR outcome variables	13
1.1.5	Overview of the Wilcoxon rank sum tests significances	13
1.2.1	Topics and items included in the interviews	23
2.1.1	Examples of generic categories of lagging and leading indicators	36
2.1.2	Methods of developing an SBSC	38
2.1.3	Template for the identification of the environmental exposure	41
2.1.4	Template for the identification of the social exposure	42
2.1.5	Template for the determination of environmental and social aspects' strategic relevance	43
2.1.6	Strategic core aspects and performance drivers of Hamburg Airport	45
2.2.1	Data collected to analyse the SASB's procedural legitimacy	60
2.2.2	The SASB standard-making process	61
2.2.3	SASB versus GRI multi-stakeholder processes	66
2.3.1	Five approaches to measuring the impact of multi-faceted organizations	82
2.4.1	Categories and aspects of the Global Reporting Initiative	93
2.4.2	Common good matrix	96
2.4.3	Comparison of GRI, ISO 26000, SROI, and GWÖ	98
2.5.1	Input and outputs of social enterprises	114
2.5.2	Efficiency scores over time	115
2.5.3	Efficiency scores and ranking at $t0$	116
2.5.4	Efficiency change between $t0$ and $t1$	117
2.5.5	Technical change between $t1$ and $t2$	118
2.6.1	The shortened version of Whirlpool Corporation's supplier code of conduct	124
2.6.2	The diffusion of sustainability across the suppliers of Apple (2011–2015)	127
2.6.3	The diffusion of sustainability across the suppliers of H&M (2011–2015)	128

3.1.1   Descriptive statistics of the companies studied   149
3.1.2   Hypotheses: results   151
3.1.3   Measurement features for reflective indicators   162
3.1.4   Pearson correlation between factors   163
3.1.5   Measurement features for formative indicators   163
3.1.6   Marker variable   163
3.1.7   VIF between constructs   164
3.1.8   Results of the mediation effects   165
3.3.1   Schedule for imp!act 2013 in Geneva (Switzerland)   181
3.3.2   Questionnaire for euforia   184
3.4.1   A comparison of selected initiatives and tools available within
        the hotel sector   195
3.5.1   Requirements for growth measures   210
3.5.2   Variables and balance sheet items   215
3.5.3   Differences between conventional growth measures and G_r 218
4.1.1   Decision scenario and stimuli values   230
4.2.1   Options to create sustainability-oriented incentive systems   244
4.2.2   Assessment of the options available for creating
        sustainability-oriented incentive systems   247

About the editors

Adam Lindgreen

After studies in chemistry (Copenhagen University), engineering (the Engineering Academy of Denmark), and physics (Copenhagen University), Adam Lindgreen completed an MSc in food science and technology at the Technical University of Denmark. He also finished an MBA at the University of Leicester. Professor Lindgreen received his PhD in marketing from Cranfield University. His first appointments were with the Catholique University of Louvain (2000–2001) and Eindhoven University of Technology (2002–2007). Subsequently, he served as Professor of Marketing at Hull University's Business School (2007–2010); University of Birmingham's Business School (2010), where he also was the research director in the Department of Marketing; and University of Cardiff's Business School (2011–2016). Under his leadership, the Department of Marketing and Strategy at Cardiff Business School ranked first among all marketing departments in Australia, Canada, New Zealand, the United Kingdom, and the United States, based upon the hg indices of senior faculty. Since 2016, he has been Professor of Marketing at Copenhagen Business School, where he also heads the Department of Marketing. He also is Extra Ordinary Professor with University of Pretoria's Gordon Institute of Business Science (since 2018) and a visiting professor at Northumbria University's Newcastle Business School (since 2017).

Professor Lindgreen has been a visiting professor with various institutions, including Georgia State University, Groupe HEC in France, and Melbourne University. His publications have appeared in *Business Horizons, California Management Review, Entrepreneurship and Regional Development, Industrial Marketing Management, International Journal of Management Reviews, Journal of Advertising, Journal of Business Ethics, European Journal of Marketing, Journal of Business and Industrial Marketing, Journal of Marketing Management, Journal of the Academy of Marketing Science, Journal of Product Innovation Management, Journal of World Business, Psychology & Marketing,* and *Supply Chain Management: An International Journal,* among others.

Professor Lindgreen's books include *A Stakeholder Approach to Corporate Social Responsibility* (with Kotler, Vanhamme, and Maon), *Managing Market Relationships, Memorable Customer Experiences* (with Vanhamme and Beverland), and *Sustainable Value Chain Management* (with Maon, Vanhamme, and Sen).

The recipient of the "Outstanding Article 2005" award from *Industrial Marketing Management* and the runner-up for the same award in 2016, Professor Lindgreen serves on the board of several scientific journals; he is co-editor-in-chief of *Industrial Marketing*

Management and previously was the joint editor of the *Journal of Business Ethics'* section on corporate responsibility. His research interests include business and industrial marketing management, corporate social responsibility, and sustainability. Professor Lindgreen has been awarded the Dean's Award for Excellence in Executive Teaching. Furthermore, he has served as an examiner (for dissertations, modules, and programmes) at a wide variety of institutions, including the Australian National University, Unitec, University of Amsterdam, University of Bath's Management School, University of Lethbridge, and University of Mauritius.

Professor Lindgreen is a member of the International Scientific Advisory Panel of the New Zealand Food Safety Science and Research Centre (a partnership between government, industry organizations, and research institutions), as well as of the Chartered Association of Business Schools' Academic Journal Guide (AJG) Scientific Committee in the field of marketing.

Beyond these academic contributions to marketing, Professor Lindgreen has discovered and excavated settlements from the Stone Age in Denmark, including the only major kitchen midden – Sparregård – in the south-east of Denmark; because of its importance, the kitchen midden was later excavated by the National Museum and then protected as an historical monument for future generations. He is also an avid genealogist, having traced his family back to 1390 and published widely in scientific journals (*Personalhistorisk Tidsskrift, The Genealogist,* and *Slægt & Data*) related to methodological issues in genealogy, accounts of population development, and particular family lineages.

Christine Vallaster

Christine Vallaster studied international business and management at the University of Innsbruck (Austria), where she also received her post-doctorial qualification (habilitation) in 2009 and earned research support from DFG Deutsche Forschungsgemeinschaft (Germany) and Humboldt Stiftung (Germany). Throughout her academic career, she has worked for various firms in Austria and Liechtenstein, as well as engaging in visiting professorships at University of Bolzano (Italy), University of Würzburg (Germany), and IAE Buenos Aires (Argentina). Currently, as a professor at the University of Applied Sciences Salzburg in Austria, she heads the Department of Marketing and Relationship Management and conducts mostly qualitative research pertaining to strategic corporate brand management and corporate social responsibility/sustainability in an entrepreneurial context, with a focus on aligning internal processes. She has published in leading international academic journals including *Journal of World Business, Journal of Business Research, California Management Review, European Journal of Marketing, Industrial Marketing Management,* and *Journal of Marketing Management.* Furthermore, Professor Vallaster serves on the editorial board of *Corporate Social Responsibility and Environmental Management.* Her book *Connective Branding* has been widely endorsed by leading academics and business-people working for global companies. For her latest research, seeking to measure the impact of sustainability practices, she is working as a research associate at the University of Armed Forces (Munich), Department of Controlling. As a corporate brand management consultant, Professor Vallaster has helped companies in China, Austria, and Germany develop and implement their marketing and brand strategies, after starting her consulting career with Bain & Co. in Hong Kong.

Shumaila Yousafzai

Shumaila Yousafzai is Associate Professor (reader) at Cardiff Business School, Cardiff University (UK), where she teaches entrepreneurship, marketing, and consumer behaviour. After completing her undergraduate studies in physics and mathematics (University of Balochistan) and an MSc in electronic commerce (Coventry University, UK), she finished her PG diploma in research methods from Cardiff University, then a doctoral degree in 2005, also from Cardiff University. In her research, Professor Yousafzai focuses mainly on topics linked to the contextual embeddedness of entrepreneurship, firm performance, institutional theory, and entrepreneurial orientation. She has published articles in various international journals, such as *Entrepreneurship Theory & Practice, Journal of Small Business Management, Industrial Marketing Management, Technovation, Journal of Business Ethics, Psychology & Marketing, Journal of Applied Social Psychology*, and *Computers in Human Behavior*. She co-edited a special issue on women's entrepreneurship for *Entrepreneurship & Regional Development*.

Bernhard Hirsch

Bernhard Hirsch studied business administration at the Catholic University of Eichstaett-Ingolstadt (Germany) and Svenska Handelshögskolan in Helsinki (Finland). He received his doctoral degree from Witten/Herdecke University (Germany) and his post-doctoral qualification (habilitation) from WHU–Otto Beishem School of Management (Germany). Since 2007, he has served as a Professor of Management Accounting at Bundeswehr University Munich (Germany). In his research, Professor Hirsch focuses on behavioural aspects of management accounting and sustainability accounting. His publications have appeared in *Management Accounting Research, Business Strategy and the Environment, Journal of Applied Accounting Research, International Journal of Physical Distribution and Logistics Management, Journal of Accounting & Organizational Change, Financial Accountability & Management, Journal of Management Control*, and *Journal of Business Economics*, among others.

About the contributors

Paulina Bohdanowicz-Godfrey

Paulina Bohdanowicz-Godfrey is a visiting researcher at the School of Hospitality and Tourism, University of Surrey, UK. She has a PhD in sustainable energy engineering from the Royal Institute of Technology, Stockholm, Sweden, and in social sciences from the University of Gdańsk, Poland. Her research interests include environmental issues and corporate responsibility in the hospitality industry, with focus on efficiency, benchmarking, and engagement. She is an author, reviewer, and an editorial board member for a number of international tourism and hospitality-focused journals. She has co-authored a book with Rebecca Hawkins entitled *Responsible Hospitality: Theory and Practice* (Goodfellow, 2011).

Johan Bruneel

Johan Bruneel is currently Assistant Professor of Innovation and Entrepreneurship at KU Leuven and also senior researcher at the Chair of Entrepreneurship at ETH Zurich. From 2005 to 2009, Johan worked towards a PhD in management science with a fellowship from the Intercollegiate Center for Management Science. His research focuses on gaining a better understanding of the performance of social enterprises and also the governance challenges in organizations pursuing multiple goals.

Laurens Cherchye

Laurens Cherchye holds a PhD in economics (Leuven, 2001). He has been teaching at the University of Leuven and Tilburg University; topics cover microeconomics, operations research, and econometrics. He is currently a full professor at the University of Leuven, an extramural fellow of CentER (Tilburg University), an honorary senior research associate of University College London (UCL), an international research fellow of the Institute for Fiscal Studies (IFS), and an associate editor of *Economic Journal* and *Journal of Productivity Analysis*. He has been a full professor at Tilburg University (2009–2011), a visiting professor at ECARES (Université Libre de Bruxelles) (2008–2009), and was a post-doctoral fellow of the Fund for Scientific Research, Flanders (2002–2008).

Andreas Dutzi

Andreas Dutzi is Professor of Management, Accounting, and Corporate Governance and Vice Dean at the School of Economic Disciplines, University of Siegen, Germany. He holds a doctorate in business administration from Johann Wolfgang Goethe-University, Frankfurt, and supports entrepreneurs and distressed firms. His current research interests include forensic accounting, corruption, and social media reporting.

Dominik Fischer

Dominik Fischer is research assistant at the Leadership Excellence Institute Zeppelin (LEIZ) at Zeppelin University. He obtained his masters degree in management from the University of Sydney and CEMS. His research covers institutional economics, leadership, strategy, and corporate social responsibility.

Delphine Gibassier

Delphine Gibassier is Associate Professor of management control and sustainability accounting at Toulouse Business School, France. Her PhD thesis at HEC Paris, entitled "Environmental Management Accounting Development: Institutionalisation, Adoption and Practice", obtained the Highly Commended rating of the 2014 Emerald/EFMD Outstanding Doctoral Research Award. Her main research interests are environmental management accounting and innovations in social and environmental accounting, with a specific interest in carbon accounting, water accounting, and biodiversity accounting creation and practices. Her research obtained the Highly Commended rating of the Laughlin/Broadbent Research Award at APIRA in 2016. She is on the editorial board of *Sustainability Accounting, Management and Policy Journal*, and has published her research in *Critical Perspectives on Accounting* and *Accounting, Auditing and Accountability Journal*.

Cristina Gimenez

Cristina Gimenez is Professor in the Department of Operations, Innovation and Data Sciences in ESADE Universitat Ramon Llull, Barcelona, Spain. She obtained her PhD in business administration at Universitat de Barcelona. Her research outlets have been published in different leading journals in the supply chain and operations management fields. Her research interests include sustainable supply chain management and supply chain integration.

Cecilia Grieco

Cecilia Grieco is post-doctoral fellow in management at the University of Rome Tor Vergata. She holds a PhD in communication, interculturality and organizations from LUMSA University (2015), with a thesis about social impact assessment in social enterprises. She was also a visiting scholar at the Erasmus University of Rotterdam during her doctoral studies. Her research interests also include business model innovation, sharing economy, marketing and communications. She is lecturer of business model innovation at the University of Rome Tor Vergata and lecturer of marketing game (*Markstrat* simulation) at LUMSA University of Rome.

Fabian Herkenrath

Fabian Herkenrath, BSc and Lieutenant, is a research student at the department of Management Accounting at the Bundeswehr University Munich, Germany. His research interests are corporate sustainability and measurement.

Nikolas Höhnke

Nikolas Höhnke is a PhD student and research assistant at the Chair of Banking and Finance, Faculty of Economic and Social Sciences, University of Rostock, Germany. His research interests include social banking, impact investing, and entrepreneurship.

Susanne Homölle

Susanne Homölle is Professor of Banking and Finance at the Faculty of Economic and Social Sciences, University of Rostock, Germany. She obtained her PhD in business administration from the University of Münster in 1998 and finished her habilitation in 2004. Her research interests include bank regulation, risk management and risk reporting of banks, as well as bank customers' behaviour.

Florian Hoos

Florian Hoos is Affiliate Professor in the Department of Accounting and Management Control at HEC Paris (France). He earned his PhD from HEC Lausanne (Switzerland) in 2010. He has published articles in international journals such as the *Journal of Business Ethics and Accounting* and *Business Research*. His research interests include social entrepreneurship, impact assessment, entrepreneurship pedagogy, and ethical decision-making.

Robert Huber

Robert Huber was research associate at Bundeswehr University Munich and is now working as global project manager in the chemical industry. He obtained his doctoral degree (Dr. rer. pol.) from Bundeswehr University Munich. His research interests include behavioural management accounting and corporate sustainability.

Konstantin Kehl

Konstantin Kehl is a lecturer at the Institute of Management and Social Policy, School of Social Work, ZHAW Zurich University of Applied Sciences. Before joining the Institute, he was Head of Transfer and Advisory Services of the Centre for Social Investment, Heidelberg University, Berlin office. His research focuses on social policy, non-profit organizations, and impact measurement.

Pieter Jan Kerstens

Pieter Jan Kerstens is a PhD student in economics at KU Leuven, Belgium. He obtained master degrees in economics and mathematical engineering. His research interests cover microeconomics, operations research, and behavioural economics. The focus of his PhD is on efficiency and productivity analysis and its applications. In October 2017, he will join IFRO at the University of Copenhagen as a post-doctoral researcher.

Peter G. Kirchschläger

Peter G. Kirchschlaeger is Professor of Theological Ethics and Director of the Institute of Social Ethics ISE at the Faculty of Theology of the University of Lucerne. He obtained his PhD – including a research stay at the University of Chicago – from the University of Zurich, his habilitation in theological ethics from the University of Fribourg, and he was visiting fellow at Yale University. His research interests include business ethics, human rights ethics, and digitalization, robotization, and the use of artificial intelligence from an ethical perspective.

Gorgi Krlev

Gorgi Krlev is a research associate at the Centre for Social Investment of the University of Heidelberg. He is also a DPhil candidate at the University of Oxford and a member of Kellogg College. His research focuses on social impact measurement, social innovation, social entrepreneurship, and related subjects.

Peter Letmathe

Peter Letmathe holds the Chair of Management Accounting at RWTH Aachen University since 2011. He received his PhD from University GH Essen, Germany, and completed his post-doctoral stage with his habilitation on "Flexible Standardization" at Ruhr-University Bochum, Germany. His research interests include behavioural management accounting, value chain management, managerial accounting for innovative business models.

Florian Lüdeke-Freund

Florian Lüdeke-Freund, PhD, is Interim Professor for Corporate Sustainability at ESCP Europe Business School, Berlin, Germany, and Research Fellow at the Centre for Sustainability Management (CSM) and Copenhagen Business School (CBS). His research interests are corporate sustainability, sustainable business models, and values-based innovation.

Stefan Markovic

Stefan Markovic is an assistant professor in the Department of Marketing at Copenhagen Business School, Denmark. He is also a member of the Brand Meaning Research Cluster at Copenhagen Business School. He received his PhD in management sciences from ESADE Business School in 2016. His research focuses on the areas of brand management and business ethics, and he has published several articles in leading international academic journals, including *Journal of Business Ethics*, *Journal of Brand Management*, and *Journal of Business Research*.

Laura Michelini

Laura Michelini is Associate Professor in Management at LUMSA University of Rome, where she teaches management and social entrepreneurship. She holds a PhD in communication science, with a thesis on business–NGO alliances, a topic she has largely addressed in several years spent at UNICEF managing profit/non-profit global partnerships. She has been visiting professor of corporate social responsibility at ISCEM, Instituto Superior de Comunicação Empresarial, in Lisbon. Her main research interests involve: social and inclusive innovation management, social entrepreneurship, and corporate social responsibility. On these topics, she has authored and co-authored over forty national and international publications. She is member of the Steering Committee in the ERASMUS+ project "European Incubator for Business Ideas" (2015–2017).

Georg Mildenberger

Georg Mildenberger is Head of Research at the Centre for Social Investment of the University of Heidelberg. His research focuses on social innovation, civil society organizations, civic engagement, and impact measurement. At the moment, he is preparing research on indicators for social innovativeness and social innovation activities.

Nils Niehues

Nils Niehues is a PhD student at the University of Siegen, Germany. He studied business administration in Karlsruhe, Vlissingen, and Business Informatics in Berlin. He is an experienced practitioner in the field of carbon dioxide accounting for a Dax 30 company. He is ad-hoc reviewer for the sustainability accounting *Management and Policy Journal*.

Ilja Rabinovitch

Ilja Rabinovitch, MSc, has been a research assistant at the Chair of Management Accounting at RWTH Aachen University since 2016. He obtained his masters degree in business chemistry from the University of Münster, Germany. His research interests include resource efficiency and sustainability accounting.

Joan Rodón

Joan Rodón is Associate Professor in the Department of Operations, Innovation and Data Sciences in ESADE, Universitat Ramon Llull, Barcelona, Spain. His research focuses mainly on the processes of emergence and evolution of digital infrastructures. His research has been published in journals such as the *Journal of the Association for Information Systems, International Journal of Production Economics, European Journal of Information Systems, Communications of the ACM, Journal of Information Technology, Information Systems Journal,* and *Decision Support Systems.*

Cristina Sancha

Cristina Sancha is Academic Director of Systems and Operations Management in OBS Business School, Barcelona, Spain. She obtained her PhD in management sciences from ESADE Business School and has published in different journals in the supply chain management and sustainability fields. Her research interests include sustainable supply chain management, buyer–supplier relationships, and higher education.

Michaela M. Schaffhauser-Linzatti

Michaela M. Schaffhauser-Linzatti is Professor for Financial Accounting at the Department of Business Administration, University of Vienna, Austria. Her research interests comprise accounting in non-profit management and critical review of the current economic directions. Being author of several textbooks, she publishes in international journals as well as collective volumes, in which she publishes mainly on health care and educational issues such as efficiency of universities.

Stefan Schaltegger

Stefan Schaltegger, PhD, is Professor for Sustainability Management at the Centre for Sustainability Management (CSM) and head of the MBA Sustainability Management at Leuphana University Lüneburg, Germany. His research interests are in corporate sustainability management, accounting, and entrepreneurship.

Vicenta Sierra

Vicenta Sierra is Professor in the Department of Operations, Innovation and Data Sciences in ESADE Universitat Ramon Llull, Barcelona, Spain. She obtained her PhD in psychology at Universitat de Barcelona. Her research interests lie in the areas of psychometrics, statistical analysis of single-case design, analysis of social systems, and quantitative methods. She has several publications in leading journals in the management field.

Matthias Sohn

Matthias Sohn is research associate at the Leadership Excellence Institute Zeppelin (LEIZ) at Zeppelin University and at Bundeswehr University Munich. He obtained his doctoral degree (Dr. rer. pol.) from Bundeswehr University Munich. His research interests include behavioural management accounting and behavioural business ethics.

Werner Sohn

Werner Sohn was visiting professor of logistics and transportation at the Berlin School of Economics and Law. Currently, he is lecturing at the Duale Hochschule Baden Württemberg (DHBW) with focus on logistics controlling. He obtained his PhD (Dr. rer. nat.) in physics from the Technical University Kaiserslautern. His research focuses on the influence of corporate social responsibility on business and operations management.

Matthias Staessens

Matthias Staessens is a PhD student in business economics at KU Leuven, Belgium. He obtained a masters degree in business economics (Leuven, 2015). His research interests cover social entrepreneurship, sustainability, and governance. The aim of his PhD research is to advance quantitative research on social entrepreneurship by developing an appropriate measure of the dual bottom-line performance of social enterprises.

Volker Then

Volker Then is the Executive Director of the Centre for Social Investment of the University of Heidelberg. His research focuses on social investment, philanthropy, and civil society, namely on strategy development of organizations, organizational governance, and social impact measurement. He has published extensively on these issues and currently prepares the English-language edition of the handbook on *Social Return on Investment: Measuring the Impact of Social Investment.*

Duygu Türker

Duygu Türker is Associate Professor of Management and Organization at the Faculty of Business, Yasar University. Her research interests include social responsibility, business ethics, sustainability, entrepreneurship, and social innovation.

Ceren Altuntaş Vural

Ceren Altuntaş Vural is Associate Professor at the International Trade Department of Dokuz Eylul University and also a post-doc at Chalmers University of Technology. She gained her master's degree in total quality management and PhD in business administration at Dokuz Eylul University. She worked for the transportation and logistics industry from 2002 to 2009. Her research interests include industrial marketing, sustainability, corporate social responsibility, supply chain management, logistics, and logistics centres. Ceren has published in journals such as *European Management Journal, International Marketing Review, Journal of Business* and *Industrial Marketing,* and *International Journal of Logistics Research and Applications.*

Rüdiger W. Waldkirch

Ruediger W. Waldkirch is Professor for Management Accounting and Control at South Westfalia University of Applied Sciences in Meschede, Germany. He holds a doctorate degree from Catholic University of Eichstaett-Ingolstadt.

Piotr Zientara

Piotr Zientara is Associate Professor of Economics at the Faculty of Economics, the University of Gdańsk, Gdańsk, Poland. He obtained his PhD in economics from the University of Gdańsk in 2005. His research interests include sustainability and corporate social responsibility in hospitality and tourism, industrial relations, and human resource management. He has published in the *Journal of Sustainable Tourism, Journal of Business Ethics, Scandinavian Journal of Hospitality and Tourism, Eastern European Economics,* and *Industrial Relations: A Journal of Economy and Society.*

Foreword and acknowledgements

The notion of sustainability has enjoyed greater popularity in recent decades. In essence, sustainable efforts are those that firms undertake to capture and create social value, while also reducing their environmental footprint. Such efforts often coincide with attempts to capture and create economic value. These overlapping frameworks produce combined notions, such as shared value (Porter and Kramer, 2011; Pfitzer et al., 2013), corporate social entrepreneurship (Austin et al., 2006), corporate social innovation (Kanter, 1999), and strategic corporate social responsibility (Husted and Allen, 2007; McElhaney, 2009). Sustainable actions offer new responses to societal challenges, such that they affect social interactions and have implications for a wide range of stakeholders. Many initiatives in this field accordingly build on cross-sector collaboration. But because civil society, business, and the public sector have different structural logics, the measures and controls for success differ across these cooperating actors.

Efforts to measure and control for sustainability thus are active across Europe, engaging social innovators, policy-makers, and investors, as well as the academic community, in the discussion. One of the most used methodologies for measuring social impacts relies on social returns on investment (SROI), described by the SROI Network (2012) as a framework for measuring and accounting for a broad notion of value. The SROI measures, which aim to be relevant to the people or firms affected by the underlying factors, tell the story of how change comes about by measuring social, environmental, and economic outcomes, and using monetary values to represent them. Despite the widespread acceptance of SROI, though, it remains underused and undervalued, for several reasons. Studies show that the SROI methodology is perceived as time and resource intensive, as well as complicated to implement. The SROI methodology includes ecological together with social value, yet in practice, few SROI analyses take ecological impacts into consideration (Jönsson, 2013). Finally, the SROI concept acknowledges the uniqueness of the content and context of each project being investigated, such that the values these measures produce are difficult to compare. Attempts to increase standardization often lead to reduced relevance for specific projects.

Therefore, efforts to establish the measurement and control of sustainability have produced notable tools, but those instruments lack applicability in practice. Increasing the level of standardization of such tools also seems difficult to achieve, because the contexts surrounding the focal organizations differ considerably. Therefore, what we need is a systematic, interdisciplinary assessment of how to measure and control sustainability, so that we can establish an essential definition and up-to-date picture of the field. This research anthology attempts to provide such an assessment in seventeen chapters, organized into four main topic sections:

- Organizations and social value creation: concepts, responsibilities, and barriers
- Accounting, measurement, performance, and diffusion of social value
- Practical and managerial insights from real-life cases
- Choices, incentives, guidance, and ethics

Organizations and social value creation: concepts, responsibilities, and barriers

In this anthology's first chapter, Peter Letmathe and Ilja Rabinovitch take a closer look at the Responsible Care Initiative, a reaction to the 1985 Bhopal disaster, which has attracted the participation of many firms, especially from the chemical industry. In proposing "The Responsible Care Initiative as an enabler of implementing corporate social responsibility concepts in the chemical industry", they argue that corporate social responsibility and the need to integrate social and environmental considerations voluntarily into business operations should be combined with the notions of responsible care. Therefore, this chapter examines how responsible care influences corporate social responsibility (CSR) activities, such as by sparking earlier adoption of CSR initiatives and prompting better environmental performance by chemical firms that participate. The findings reveal that earlier adoption of the Responsible Care Initiative benefits firms' environmental CSR activities, such that it functions like an enabling platform and can help companies operate more sustainably.

Next, in "Mind the gap! Existing barriers to standardizing the measurement of social value creation", Cecilia Grieco and Laura Michelini assert that even as increasing numbers of models emerge to help organizations measure generated value, in terms of social impact, the uses of these models remain limited. Common concerns include potential biases in existing, standardized measurement tools, which must address the conflict between the efficient processes that organizations prefer and the need to quantify the qualitative social impacts. With this assessment, this chapter provides an in-depth analysis of the main barriers, as perceived by managers, to efforts to derive and apply a standardized tool to measure social value created through their sustainability activities.

Accounting, measurement, performance, and diffusion of social value

Starting off a more measurement-oriented section of the anthology, Florian Lüdeke-Freund and Stefan Schaltegger offer an overview of the foundations of the sustainability balanced scorecard (SBSC) and its use in sustainability accounting and reporting in "The sustainability balanced scorecard: an introduction to the SBSC and its links to accounting and reporting". The basis of the SBSC is the original balanced scorecard (BSC), and the authors outline its conceptual elements, including its key perspectives, leading and lagging indicators, and use of strategy maps that reflect cause-and-effect chains. Yet, because it was open to various modifications, the BSC could be extended and specified to support corporate sustainability management, in the form of the SBSC, which deals with relevant environmental and social inputs to the strategy that business units or firms implement and execute. This chapter highlights the case of the Hamburg Airport Corporation to demonstrate how to use the SBSC to support sustainability accounting and reporting.

Delphine Gibassier examines a different process for developing sustainability accounting standards in her chapter, "Sustainability accounting standards in the USA – procedural legitimacy: governance, participation, and decision-making processes". By performing a qualitative analysis of public documents pertaining to the Consumption I group of standards, as developed by the US-based Sustainability Accounting Standards Board (SASB), she details due processes and stakeholders' participation to clarify the procedural legitimacy of this multi-stakeholder process. It comprises governance, participation, transparency, and accountability. In this sense, the SASB's approach relies on expert-based procedural legitimacy, in direct contrast with the Global Reporting Initiative's inclusive model. The troubling implications of this contrast involve excluding some key voices with regard to which standards should be applied in the future and whether those applications should be voluntary or mandatory.

Another measurement tactic, the social return on investment (SROI) approach, links the positive value created for society with costs associated with any such intervention. In principle, Konstantin Kehl, Gorgi Krlev, Volker Then, and Georg Mildenberger argue that SROI is appropriate for various social agencies. But an overly simplistic interpretation of its impact creates comparability and legitimacy problems. Therefore, in "Adapting the measuring rod for social returns in advanced welfare", these authors propose ways to address both existing capabilities and deficiencies with an integrated SROI version that can assess individual initiatives while also detailing the impacts of large service providers (e.g., networks) in developed welfare regimes.

In their chapter, "Measuring the impact of strategic corporate social responsibility (S-CSR): finding the right approach", Fabian Herkenrath and Christine Vallaster argue that organizations must pursue social and ecological responsibility, in addition to their economic activities, whether mandated by law or due to their internal motivation. To facilitate measures of the consequences of their problematic actions (e.g., environmental pollution, employee exploitation, wage inequality), as well as their strategic corporate social responsibility, which will actually be adopted in practice, this chapter reviews four popular instruments: the Global Reporting Initiative, ISO 26000, SROI, and *Gemeinwohlökonomie* (GWÖ). The evaluation of these instruments covers their thematic focus, target group, level of detail, transparency, legal status, and addressees.

With a novel perspective on social entrepreneurship, Matthias Staessens, Pieter Jan Kerstens, Johan Bruneel, and Laurens Cherchye similarly cite the need for accurate performance measures of social enterprises as a prominent challenge, because existing efforts suffer from both practical and methodological issues, primarily due to the dual objectives of such enterprises. In "Performance tool for policy-makers to monitor the dual objective of social enterprises: a DEA approach", they propose a methodological basis for a new approach to measuring social enterprises' performance, according to data envelopment analysis. With this grounding, policy-makers in the social sector might assess both the performance of the social enterprises themselves and the impact of specific policy choices on this performance.

The final chapter in this section, "Diffusion of sustainability: a road map for developing corporate compliance programmes with high diffusion potential", acknowledges that a global supplier network can benefit firms, by decreasing their costs and increasing efficiencies, but its management also creates challenges related to standardization and sustainability requirements for members in developing countries. Codes of conduct and compliance programmes are common responses to scandals in the supply chain; many companies establish their own unique codes or programmes that demand suppliers adopt identical production standards. Yet understanding of the characteristics and roles of these codes remains limited. Duygu Türker and Ceren Altuntaş Vural therefore review literature that details how codes of conduct can help diffuse sustainability standards and which questions inform their development. By noting the effectiveness of actual examples and analysing important factors identified in prior literature, this chapter provides a code of conduct road map for researchers and practitioners.

Practical and managerial insights from real-life cases

Real-world examples are pivotal. Therefore, the third section in the anthology focuses on real-life cases, such as in the opening analysis of "The impact of environmental and social practices on the triple bottom line: a mediated model". With a survey of 120 Spanish manufacturers, Cristina Gimenez, Vicenta Sierra, Cristina Sancha, Joan Rodón, and Stefan Markovic gather data on sustainable practices and their performance implications, then test predicted relationships of environmental and social practices with the triple bottom line (TBL: environmental, social, economic). Environmental practices emerge with positive, direct effects on social and environmental dimensions; their influence on the economic dimension is meditated by social and environmental performance. Social practices exert positive, direct effects on economic and social, but not environmental, performance. Such real-world findings offer three managerial implications: (1) social and environmental practices benefit the TBL; (2) environmental practices are best for improving environmental performance, but both environmental and social practices can contribute to social performance; and (3) environmental practices have positive effects on the economic dimension of the TBL only if they also improve environmental or social performance.

Nils Niehues and Andreas Dutzi then seek to explain voluntary carbon dioxide disclosures in "Disclosing the invisible: measurement and disclosure pitfalls of carbon dioxide emissions". That is, carbon accounting is a popular and advanced measurement tool, but significant problems remain and enable managers to make fragmentary disclosures of their actual carbon dioxide emissions. Theoretical hypotheses offer some insights, but no general model of voluntary carbon disclosure exists. Therefore, this chapter applies legitimacy, institutional, and agency theories to explain various, voluntary reporting strategies. Only agency and, to some extent, institutional theory account for the need to convince stakeholders that the company is environmentally responsible. A carbon dioxide inventory demands sound understanding of various disciplines, as well as detailed information about relevant trends, due to the complexity involved along the value chain and the dynamic nature of carbon dioxide emissions.

Next, in "social entrepreneurship and social impact assessment: the case of euforia", Florian Hoos proposes a fundamental difference between social and traditional entrepreneurship: social entrepreneurs pursue social instead of profit maximization goals. They thus need social impact measurement systems to measure their goal achievement. No generally accepted principles exist to inform the development of a social impact measurement system, so each social entrepreneur currently adopts its own, individual system. The case of the Swiss social enterprise euforia offers an illustration of one promising approach for designing and implementing such a system; the chapter reveals both advantages and drawbacks of different designs for internal and external use, as well as lessons gathered from the actual three-year project.

In the chapter "Mechanisms and tools for measuring and reporting sustainability in the hotel industry: a practical dimension", Piotr Zientara and Paulina Bohdanowicz-Godfrey discuss measurement and sustainability reporting issues for the hotel industry. Not only is measuring and reporting sustainability challenging in general, due to the need for corporate communicators and stakeholder engagement, but in the hotel sector in particular, it suffers from the difficulties of identifying standardized, industry-wide initiatives. This chapter focuses on environmental performance assessment systems maintained by international hotel chains, with an in-depth review of Hilton's LightStay. The insights gained prompt key questions about the role of smart feedback and the distinction between outputs and outcomes.

Another specific sector with the potential to offer compelling insights is social banks, that is, credit institutions that integrate social and environmental issues into their core business model and provide financial services in ways that establish positive social or environmental impacts. However, as Nikolas Höhnke and Susanne Homölle explain in "The growth of social banks: a new measurement approach", measuring their growth remains difficult, and no generally accepted, theoretically sound method has been established. This chapter suggests an approach based on the intermediation paradigm, which considers both financing and investment arms of the bank but excludes components that do not support social objectives. In addition to revealing reported growth, this new measure provides a differentiated assessment of social banks' contributions to the sustainable economy and identifies inherent drivers of and obstacles to their growth. When applied to data from GLS Bank, this measure shows that existing growth assessments tend to be too optimistic.

Choices, incentives, guidance, and ethics

The final section contains four articles. First, Matthias Sohn, Dominik Fischer, and Werner Sohn offer "An experimental study on corporate social responsibility in junior managers' project choice in an energy-producing company", with the belief that human workforces constitute key contributors to sustainable competitive advantages, and attracting good workers requires corporate social responsibility (CSR). To specify these effects, this chapter examines in particular whether junior managers regard projects that benefit their company's CSR performance as valuable or important. An experiment involving junior managers from a German subsidiary of an energy company reveals that CSR topics are relevant, but financial data and their consequences for managers (e.g., bonuses) dominate their decision-making. Notably, female managers consider the impacts of their project choices on CSR more important than do male managers.

Second, noting recent accounting and business scandals, Robert Huber, Bernhard Hirsch, and Matthias Sohn assert that the incorporation of responsible, sustainable business practices has gained momentum, as evidenced by revised incentive schemes that seek to align managers' incentives with sustainability targets. Yet few studies address ways to integrate sustainability concepts with incentive systems; those that do tend to be vague and without concrete, practical recommendations. Therefore, this chapter offers "Design options for sustainability-oriented incentive systems", covering different systematic options and providing a framework that organizations can use to implement their sustainability strategies in accordance with their business practices.

Third, by asking about "Sustainability reporting: do the Global Reporting Initiative Guidelines provide clear guidance?", Rudiger Waldkirch and Bernhard Hirsch take a contrarian approach to voluntary corporate reporting frameworks. That is, they address the conditions in which competing companies likely disclose information truthfully by analysing the Global Reporting Initiative's G4 Sustainability Reporting Guidelines. Do these guidelines offer clear suggestions for corporate management about disclosing sustainability performance information, in ways that match stakeholders' legitimate interests? Can stakeholders form reasonable expectations about which corporations in a competitive environment are likely to report voluntarily? Ultimately, this chapter suggests revising the guidelines, both to strengthen the internal consistency of their principles and to enhance their ability to provide practical guidance.

Fourth and finally, Peter Kirchschläger and Michaela Schaffhauser-Linzatti recognize that external accounting reports cannot be limited to financial or commercial information but instead must address broader stakeholder groups, interested in sustainability and ethical behaviour, if they want to address governance gaps. In their chapter, "Sustainability and ethics in financial reporting: an empirical study of German, Austrian, and Swiss groups", they use qualitative text analysis to review both legally mandated and voluntary publications of management reports by listed groups in Austria, Germany, and Switzerland. The results reveal virtually no regional differences, despite the three nations' distinct laws. Thus, the authors argue for legal regulations that oblige economic entities to detail their approaches to and efforts in support of corporate social responsibility, justice, and human rights.

Closing remarks

We extend a special thanks to Routledge and its staff, who have been most helpful throughout this entire process. Equally, we warmly thank all of the authors who submitted their manuscripts for consideration for this book. They have exhibited the desire to share their knowledge and experience with the book's readers – and a willingness to put forward their views for possible challenge by their peers. We also thank the reviewers, who provided excellent, independent, and incisive consideration of the anonymous submissions.

We hope that this compendium of chapters and themes stimulates and contributes to the ongoing debate surrounding the measurement and control of sustainability. The chapters in this book can help fill some knowledge gaps, while also stimulating further thought and action pertaining to the multiple aspects surrounding the measurement and control of sustainability.

Adam Lindgreen, PhD, Copenhagen, Denmark and Pretoria, South Africa
Christine Vallaster, PhD, Salzburg, Austria
Shumaila Yousafzai, PhD, Cardiff, Wales
Bernhard Hirsch, PhD, Munich, Germany
31 May 2018

References

Husted, B. W., and Allen, D. B. (2007). Corporate social strategy in multinational enterprises: antecedents and values creation. *Journal of Business Ethics*, 74, 345–361.

Jönsson, J. (2013). Social return on investment: room for improvement and research: a background study on SROI to identify research gaps. http://socialinnovation.se/wp-content/uploads/2013/10/Rooms-for-improvement-and-research_A4_lowres_131024.pdf

Kanter, R. M. (1999). From spare change to real change: the social sector as a beta site for business innovation. *Harvard Business Review*, 77(3), 123–132.

McElhaney, K. (2009). A strategic approach to corporate social responsibility. *Leader to Leader*, 52, 30–36.

Pfitzer, M., Bockstette, V., and Stamp, M. (2013). Innovating for shared value. *Harvard Business Review*, 91(9), 100–107.

Porter, M. E., and Kramer, M. R. (2011). The big idea: creating shared value. *Harvard Business Review*, 89(1/2), 62–77.

SROI Network (2012). https://www.bond.org.uk/data/files/Cabinet_office_A_guide_to_Social_Return_on_Investment.pdf.

Part 1

Organizations and social value creation

Concepts, responsibilities, and barriers

1.1 The Responsible Care initiative as an enabler of implementing corporate social responsibility concepts in the chemical industry

Peter Letmathe and Ilja Rabinovitch

Introduction

Different approaches to corporate social responsibility (CSR) have been developed and implemented by numerous firms. Although a whole range of concepts exists, not all of them are seen as successfully promoting the environmental and social performance of organizations, as the broad strand of literature on greenwashing has illustrated (Bazillier & Vauday 2009; Gamper-Rabindran & Finger 2013; Laufer 2003).

There have already been studies covering the influences of voluntary reporting guidelines such as the Global Reporting Initiative (Nikolaeva & Bicho 2011), which found that firms not only tend to adopt CSR standards if the direct competitors apply them, but also when standards are implemented ubiquitously.

Prakash (2000) defines Responsible Care (RC) as a voluntary self-obligation that reaches beyond compliance with legal regulations. RC was officially launched by the Canadian Chemical Producers' Association in 1985. In the years that followed, the programme was established in more than half of the world by the national chemical associations, for example in Germany by the German Chemical Industry Association in 1991 (ICCA 2015; VCI 2016). Hence, RC can nowadays be regarded as an established system to specifically foster safety in the use of chemicals, to prevent disasters, to protect health, and to promote more sustainable production practices (ICCA 2015). However, RC is also criticized for allowing greenwashing of firm practices (Howard et al. 1999).

Research question

The question as to how a well-defined and restricted initiative, such as RC, can promote the implementation of much wider concepts, such as CSR, is barely considered in the research literature. More specifically, it would be interesting to analyse whether RC can be seen as a capacity-builder for CSR implementation. Such capacities can potentially relate to timing (When did firms implement CSR concepts?), speed (How long did it take to implement CSR concepts?), implemented CSR methodologies (How do firms implement CSR concepts?), and CSR performance (Does RC lead to a higher environmental and/or social performance?).

The research questions that need to be answered are:

- How did the RC initiative develop, and how was it implemented by firms in the chemical industry?
- How has the development and implementation of RC influenced the adoption of CSR concepts in these firms?

In this chapter, we focus on environmental aspects of RC and CSR, and the CSR performance.

Theoretical framework

When analysing the interplay between RC and CSR concepts, we adopt three different frameworks. The first framework of weak and strong sustainability according to Rennings and Wiggering (1997) and Daly (1990) is applied to identify the degree to which firms contribute to a sustainable development. The second framework uses Dillard, Brown, and Marshall's (2005) differentiation between a legal-driven, a market-driven, and an ethics-driven strategy of CSR. In this vein, King and Lenox (2000) argue that (in spite of their positive effects) self-regulative codes of conduct such as RC protect firms against strict legal regulation but do not lead to sanctions if the promises included in the code are not fulfilled. Third, the initiative will be valued according to Prakash's (2000) club good assessment. Overall, we assume that firms who implemented RC early on and who have invested substantially in this concept tend more towards strong sustainability and an ethics-driven CSR approach. The underlying argument is that they not only understand market rationale and requirements better, but that the RC implementation was used as an existing platform for the introduction of CSR concepts. There are two reasons for this hypothesis. First, firms that have implemented RC earlier on develop a higher degree of awareness for the environmental and social impacts of their business practices. Second, having adopted RC early on increases knowledge about the identification and assessment of environmental and social aspects and lowers the cost of CSR adoption, as firms establishing RC have to develop infrastructure, competences, and reporting standards that can be used in implementing CSR approaches. An overview of the relevant theoretical frameworks is presented in Table 1.1.1.

For our analysis, we consider previous studies to investigate the motivations behind adopting RC. We analyse relationships between RC and CSR to understand the mechanisms of their parallel developments. Our research design looks at the antecedents of RC adoption, the degree of RC implementation, the motivation and timing of the introduction of CSR concepts, the underlying motivation (legal, market, ethical), and the CSR performance. This is a suitable, and usable, but not exclusive classification of CSR (Rahman 2011).

Table 1.1.1 Frameworks used for the analysis of the interplay between responsible care and corporate social responsibility concepts

Framework	Influence on the research subject
Weak and strong sustainability (Daly 1990; Turner 1993; Rennings & Wiggering 1997)	An early-on adoption of RC influences firms to adopt a strong sustainability perception.
Legal-, market- and ethical-driven strategy of CSR (Dillard, Brown, & Marshall 2005)	Firms with an early adoption of RC tend to have an ethical-driven concept of CSR.
Club goods (Prakash 2000), combined with the resource-based view on firms (Pfeffer & Salancik 1978)	As part of the RC initiative, firms acquire an advantage over non-members. Once able to reap RC benefits, firms anticipate the value of CSR more than non-appliers.

Table 1.1.2 Extract of chemical industry disasters from the 1970s to the 1990s

Year	Place	Cause	Casualties (deaths/injured)	Source
1973	Staten Island (USA)	LNG explosion	40 / ?	Foss (2012)
1974	Flixborough (UK)	Cyclohexane	28 / 36	Venart (2014)
1974	Decatur (USA)	Isobutene explosion	7 / 107	Khan and Abassi (1999)
1975	Beek (NL)	Propylene explosion	14 / 107	Pekalski (1997)
1976	Seveso (IT)	Dioxin leakage	Indirect casualties > 1,000 (Bertazzi 1991)	De Marchi, Funtowicz and Ravetz (1996)
1984	Bhopal (IN)	Methyl isocyanate leakage	7,000 / 20,000	Broughton (2005)
1986	Basel/Schweizerhalle (CH)	Multiple chemical leakages to the Rhine	Massive environmental damage	Giger (2009)

The development of RC

Before RC was established in the 1980s, some severe chemical disasters happened that changed the public opinion about the chemical industry. An extract of these disasters is provided in Table 1.1.2.

RC was first developed between 1985 and 1988 by the members of the former Canadian Chemical Producers' Association, now known as the Chemistry Industry Association of Canada. Since 1992, a voluntary publication of environmental data was enforced by member companies and an external auditing process was established in 1993. Furthermore, a new code of ethics and other principles as well as a relaunch of the common RC code were introduced (CIAC 2016; Druckrey 1998). Since 2000, these codes, codified in the Responsible Care Global Charter, have been updated and relaunched (CIAC 2016).

Motivation for RC and CSR adoption

According to Conzelmann (2012), the origin of the RC initiative is not only a response to the Bhopal disaster in 1984, but can be dated back to the Seveso disaster in 1976. In fact, public pressure that increased with each disaster forced the chemical industry to become more pro-active (Delmas & Toffel 2004; Givel 2007; Gössling & Vocht 2007; Reinhardt et al. 2008). In a qualitative, explorative study, Givel (2007) stated that one of the main motivations for establishing RC was to prevent harsh legal regulations. Due to the political discussion and press coverage at the time, such regulations were discussed in public. At the same time, the public reputation of many chemical companies was harmed, potentially resulting in lower financial performance. Therefore, the concept of RC can be regarded as a legal- and market-driven approach. As a front-runner in terms of setting standards, the chemical industry tried to re-create a more favourable reputation and to avoid negative legal and market consequences.

As for the interplay between RC and CSR, it is worth taking a look at the development of CSR in firms, especially between the 1980s and 2000s. Pinkston and Carrol

(1996) investigated the motivation behind establishing CSR within the chemical industry. In a survey study, they asked decision-makers from the chemical industry in Western European countries, the United States, and Japan to assess their motivation for investing in CSR on a scale from 1 to 10. The motivation they used for introducing CSR was divided into four categories: market-, legal-, ethical-, and philanthropy-driven CSR. Their analysis showed that most firms implement CSR with the following order of priorities: market-, legal-, ethical-, and philanthropy-driven. By far, market- and legal-driven motivation were the most prominent. Pinkston and Carrol (1996) also found a lower importance of philanthropic-driven and a higher importance of ethical-driven CSR compared with previous and later studies (see also Aupperle 1982; Bansal & Roth 2006). These findings are consistent with those from Givel (2007), as firms try to avoid regulations that cause reductions to their income. As market-driven CSR refers to the motivation of increasing competitive advantage, legal-driven CSR can be considered as expenses that guarantee a continuation of the business, or in other terms, avoid competitive disadvantages.

In summary, the literature shows that pro-active engagement reduces the risk of harsher regulatory regimes. This is in line with Prakash's (2000) interpretations of RC as a club that offers advantages to its members compared to non-members. The commitment of participating firms to meet environmental requirements lowers the risk of losing one's reputation. However, if only one participant violates the rules of RC, resulting in an accident or disaster, the entire RC initiative is at stake. Hence, the established RC system might also be considered as a private regulation (Sethi & Schepers 2014; Sethi 2016). Similar motivations play a role for other non-governmental standards such as ISO 14001 (ISO 2004; King, Lenox, & Terlaak 2005; Prakash 1999; Prakash 2000; Potoski & Prakash 2005). In terms of CSR, we find that legal- and market-driven approaches were more important reasons to implement the respective CSR instruments and methodologies.

Interdependencies between RC and CSR

RC was established with an initial focus on preventing environmental accidents and the reduction of hazardous emissions in the chemical industry. Over time, several indicator categories measuring emissions, resource consumption, as well as health and safety aspects were introduced. Environmental indicators measure, among other aspects, nitrogen oxide, sulphur dioxide, and carbon dioxide emissions and their equivalents. The resource indicators monitor water, energy, and fossil fuel consumption. In the section on health and safety, aspects such as days lost due to accidents are documented (ICCA 2015). In particular, the safety of employees of member firms has been enforced since 1994 (Bélanger et al. 2013).

These aspects already cover domains commonly attributed to CSR. Moffet, Bregha, and Middelkoop (2004) state that RC is more of a firm's or an industry's philosophy and culture rather than an adopted code. Even though many firms adopt RC for market and legal reasons, internal reflection processes and learning about environmental aspects often lead to a more ethical-driven approach according to Dillard, Brown, and Marshall (2005). The more firms become aware of their environmental and social responsibilities, the more their management practices will develop towards a broader CSR implementation.

In general, RC includes a set of defined rules, and CSR is a much broader concept that can be and is complemented by more concrete guidelines such as the guidelines of the Global Reporting Initiative (GRI). Differences between RC and CSR are specifically relevant with regard to firm size. The implementation of CSR within smaller companies is often motivated by ethical reasons (Kechiche & Soparnot 2012), whereas the implementation of RC in smaller firms was initially driven by economic considerations, that is, the external pressure to adopt RC with the objective not to lose partners, suppliers, and customers within and outside the chemical industry. According to Prakash's club good model, small and medium-sized firms adopt RC because they do not wish to forfeit their acceptance by other participating business partners or stakeholders. The reason for such behaviour is the fear of a negative reputation after possible accidents due to low safety standards (Bélanger et al. 2013, Prakash 2000).

As the integration of RC, on the one hand, and the reporting requirements, on the other, are both requested, Baumann-Pauly et al. (2013) examined how companies of different sizes face this challenge. They found that smaller companies are able to align CSR better with the organizational structure of the firm, whereas bigger companies have to make less effort to meet the reporting specifications. Consistent with previous findings, there has always been a tendency to imitate environmental reporting standards within an industry (Aerts, Cormier, & Magnan 2006). This also applies to industry sectors (Delmas & Montiel 2008).

Similar to RC in the chemical industry, in the pharmaceutical industry that can be regarded as a sub-category, a very sophisticated system of CSR beyond RC has been established through stakeholder pressure (O'Riordan & Fairbrass 2008). As firms strive to align both RC and CSR, RC is now often embedded in CSR as the more general approach. Furthermore, both RC and CSR have faced common challenges for worldwide (or at least industry-wide) standardization. For RC, the Responsible Care Global Charter was adopted in 2005 and an update followed in 2015. The Responsible Care Global Charter is comprised of the following aspects:

- promoting the safe use of chemicals through corporate culture;
- caring for people and the environment through an ongoing improvement to the safety of the facilities in firms and complete supply chains;
- turning towards a lifecycle approach in the use of chemicals;
- actively promoting safety awareness among business partners;
- actively reaching out to stakeholders and addressing their concerns about the safety and environmental issues of each plant;
- committing to use economic opportunities to improve overall efforts towards more sustainable business practices (CEFIC 2005; VCI 2016).

Similar standards can be found for CSR in ISO 26000. According to this norm, the seven core topics of CSR are:

- leadership of the corporation,
- human rights,
- working conditions,
- environmental issues,
- 'fair' business models and practices,
- customer care,
- embedding and development of societal issues (ISO 26000: 2010).

It is hard to overlook the similarities between the two mentioned standards of RC and CSR in terms of working conditions, the leadership and business culture approach, and a stronger involvement of stakeholders overall.

Influence of RC on CSR performance

As stated above, RC and CSR were both developed with a joint framework in mind. Nevertheless, from the beginning, RC has been a highly standardized club good (Prakash 2000), a code of conduct that provides equal implementation guides to each of the participating chemical industry associations, for example, the German VCI with its RC management systems (VCI 2017). Furthermore, it was established in a relatively short time and much earlier than most CSR initiatives. According to its aims to prevent disasters and minimize hazards, the initiative can be considered to be associated with the strong sustainability concept (Turner 1993), because the focus of RC is not to compensate negative environmental effects through other goods but to stop the depletion of the environment (ICCA 2015).

One important objective of CSR is that firms have to face the expectations of the society around them and not only their shareholders (Bowen 1953). Originating from this very general definition to CSR, different approaches exist and occur even within one firm. Bayer's CSR activities, for example, range from classical philanthropy such as the sponsoring of an orchestra to bring social benefit to the inhabitants of Leverkusen (the city where Bayer's headquarters is located), to the support of globally recognized initiatives organized by the United Nations (UN Global Charter, United Nations Population Fund), and in-house programmes that improve product safety (Bayer 2017). Therefore, CSR is much broader and differently motivated (Dillard, Brown, & Marshall 2005). We therefore consider RC as an enabler and catalyst for deeper CSR activities, because we assume that a well-defined and structured initiative will decrease the marginal effort for CSR implementation. Returning to our research question, as to how an early adoption of RC can influence how CSR is adopted, we also want to examine the time factor.

If an early adoption of RC leads to an overall better CSR outcome, it is an indicator of how lower implementation costs and cognitive processes (knowledge transfer) are associated with the experience gained from embedding RC into corporate reporting systems, environmental management approaches, and decision-making processes.

Therefore, we examine publicly available firm data extracted from the ESG (environment, social, governance) Database of ASSET4, owned by Thomson Reuters. The focus lies on indicators providing information on CSR outputs with a particular focus on the environment ('E' pillar).

The CSR data available consist of indicators providing information about the following categories:

- the firms' activities to prevent hazardous emissions,
- the firms' products' innovative potential,
- the firms' use of resources.

We focused on finding the link between the duration of the application of RC with the CSR performance in those three categories.

The number of firms analysed was limited by the number of member companies of the American Chemical Council (ACC), as the application of RC is obligatory for a firm's membership within the ACC. The data for the year of establishing RC within the respective firm was taken from annual reports, sustainability reports, as well as from email and telephone requests.

Methodology

Firms were chosen according to the following criteria:

- publicly traded companies – to ensure a standardized reporting system and data from publicly available sources;
- membership in the American Chemical Council, which requires its members to apply RC.

Note that not only firms with their headquarters in the United States can be members of the ACC, but basically every chemical company worldwide that has implemented RC. The firms that are included in our sample have their headquarters in the following countries (alphabetical order): Brazil, Canada, China, France, Germany, Japan, South Korea, Sweden, Switzerland, the United Kingdom, and the United States. All of these companies can be considered as big companies according to the definition of the European Commission (2009). As ACC members, all firms have a relation to the chemical industry, although some of them overlap with other industries, such as the pharmaceutical and energy industries.

The request for information about the year when RC was adopted by each firm was provided by 35 out of 158 ACC members. Thomson Reuters delivered data for 20 more companies, leading to a sample size of 55 out of 158 companies. To test whether an early adoption of RC has a positive effect on CSR activities, we used the year that RC was adopted and the future CSR performance of the respective companies.

The variable *rc* stands for the year that RC was joined or the first time that RC principles were adopted within the firm. However, this variable does not reflect whether a firm started to apply RC at a distinct point because of a strategic decision or whether the firm was founded after responsible care had been initiated in 1985. As all the sample firms are big, we assume the ability to implement RC, regardless of whether RC was supported by the particular national chemical industry associations. Moreover, it is reasonable to presume that the sample companies have a powerful influence on policy recommendations of these associations. Hence, we introduce the variable (*rc_delay*) to measure the time between the starting point of RC and the time of joining it; and in the second case, the time span between the foundation of the respective firm and the year of adopting RC:

$$rc\_delay = \begin{cases} rc - 1985 & (\textit{for year of foundation} < 1985) \\ rc - \textit{year of foundation} & (\textit{for year of foundation} > 1985) \end{cases}$$

To distinguish between an early and late adoption of RC, we clustered the sample by the median of *rc*, that is, the year when each firm adopted RC. The same applies to *rc_delay*. The resulting clustered, binary variables (*rc_clusmed* and *rc_delay_clusmed*) therefore distinguish between an early or late adoption of RC.

The descriptive statistics of *rc* and *rc_delay* are shown in Table 1.1.3. We see that the median grouping *rc* and *rc_delay* is 1995 resp. 9.

Table 1.1.3 Descriptive statistics of *rc* and *rc_delay*

Variable	Obs	Mean	Std. Dev.	Median	Min	Max
rc	35	1999	8	1995	1985	2014
rc_delay	35	11	9	9	0	29

The CSR ratings consider the use of resources and a reduction thereof, the emissions of hazardous substances and their reduction, the activities and actions related to an improved environmental impact, as well as process and product innovations. Examples of questions that are included in the ratings are:

- How much coal energy, measured in Gigajoules, does a company purchase? (example for rating a firm's use of resources)
- Does the company have an environmental product innovation policy (i.e., eco-design, lifecycle assessment, dematerialization)? (example for a firm's product innovation potential)
- How much is the total carbon dioxide output and its equivalent emissions in tonnes? (example for a firm's emission output and activities undertaken to reduce it)

The specific raw data of companies, coded in the model as 'x' for the constructed indicators are taken by ASSET4 from company reports, company filings, company websites, NGO websites, CSR reports, and other media outlets (Blank 2013). ASSET4 was acquired by Thomson Reuters in 2009 and provides ESG data. These data come from publicly accessible sources. ASSET4 delivers data to organizations such as UNEP-FI, Eurosif, UKSIF, USSIF, 'Nachhaltiges Investment', and the 'Ceres Coalition' (Ribando & Bonne 2010).

According to Escrig-Olmedo, Muñoz-Torres, and Fernández-Izquierdo (2010), who have examined several common sustainability indicator databases, ASSET4, along with other databases, has the strength of being able to deliver plenty of information but the weakness of little comparability.

This means that it is hardly possible to compare data from different databases as the calculation procedure of the indices and key performance indicators (KPI) contain, for example, the subjective weight of the respective experts. In the case of the ASSET4 indicators, Thomson Reuters states this in its publications (Blank 2013). This subjective component can lead to a bias, as human decisions are rarely perfect. In our case, the missing comparability of different databases is less relevant, as we only use data from one database, namely ASSET4.

The subject element mentioned is compensated by the wide range of partial indicators used for our study (more than 300). For simplicity, we assume that possible biases due to subjectivity are averaged out over all indicators.

The key performance indicators used for the environmental indicators can be either metric or Boolean. The Boolean, binary KPI are derived from each of two yes or no questions derived from the respective KPI. Hence, the expressions of the KPI are subdivided into an ordinal scale using the following steps and value codes: 1 for a two yes/yes answer, 0.5 for a yes/no, no/yes, and 'not relevant question' answer, and 0 for a no/no and not available answer (Blank 2013).

The metric scores are calculated as follows. Here, the variable x represents the specific company data:

$$KPI_{positive\ impact} = 0.6 + 0,4 \left(\frac{x - x_{min}}{x_{max} - x_{min}} \right) - Specific\ to\ industry$$

$$KPI_{negative\ impact} = 0.6 + 0,4 \left(1 - \frac{x - x_{min}}{x_{max} - x_{min}} \right) - Specific\ to\ industry$$

The indices *min* and *max* stand for 'lowest/highest number reported among industry peers' (Blank 2013).

In case of the answer 'not relevant', ASSET4 defines the value as 0.5 and in case of the answer 'not available' as 0.4. For all KPI, it applies that if an affirmation to a question results in a negative impact on the environment, the expressions are coded in an inverted fashion, so that the scale is vice versa: for example, a high emission of nitric oxide leads to a low value of the corresponding KPI. This ensures the comparability of all KPI, regardless of their sign (Blank 2013).

The value for the variable 'Specific to industry' is calculated by ASSET4 using the following algorithm: the sum of all (environmental) KPI shall be 1, weights are applied to numeric data, and each firm's environmental raw score is the sum of the products of each KPI's score and weight. The weights themselves depend on the following criteria according to ASSET4:

- the relevance of the KPI to the industry – in our case, the chemical industry;
- the share of firms from the industry in question, reporting information that is needed to calculate the specific KPI;
- the statistical characteristics of the specific KPI: range, skewness, and standard deviation;
- the content of independent information of the specific KPI;
- the objective measurability of the KPI;
- the possibility of validating the statistical results with published scientific data (Blank 2013).

ASSET4 transforms the scores into z-scores and then into ratings, multiplied by 100, leading to values between 0 and 100 (Blank 2013).

As the ratings are standardized as well as transformed into a range from 0 to 100, we employ the means of environmental ratings of the following subgroups for the two years 2007 and 2014:

- Emission: *csr_emission_abs_2007, csr_emission_abs_2014*
- Product innovation: *csr_innovation_abs_2007, csr_innovation_abs_2014*
- Resource use: *csr_resource_abs_2007, csr_resource_abs_2014*

The variables *csr_emission_abs_2007, csr_innovation_abs_2007, csr_resources_abs_2007, csr_emission_abs_2014, csr_innovation_abs_2014* and *csr_resource_abs_2014* are the absolute values of every subgroup in the stated year.

We picked the year 2007 as many companies only started to implement CSR approaches in the early 2000 years. As it usually takes some years for significant (positive) results to materialize, we chose a year for which we can assume that CSR was well established and companies had already reaped some of the potential gains of their CSR efforts. The year 2007 is also the year before the financial crisis began after a relatively stable economic development in the prior years. Hence, we assume that possible interactions between RC and CSR activities can be measured for this year. We also consider the years 2007 and 2014 as pre- and post-crisis years and compare the ratings of 2014 with those of the year 2007 to ensure that our findings have not been biased by the effects of the financial crisis. Souto (2009) states that the crisis has demanded a lot of the firm's capacity. In particular, the ability to create innovations, the understanding of stakeholders and a deep internal reflection are crucial for effective CSR activities and to successfully master the crisis. The author concludes a positive long-term effect of CSR to master the crisis but states a negative short-term effect as the crisis binds the above-mentioned firms' capacities (Souto 2009).

In another study, Karaibrahimoglu (2010) revealed that firms all over the world reduced their activities during the crisis. As CSR is considered over a long-term time scale, we cannot conclude that this fall in activities has a direct short-term effect on CSR outcomes. As our reference years are 2007 and 2014 and the annual world GDP growth rate reached pre-crisis levels in 2010 (The World Bank 2017), we expect that firms' efforts to master the consequences of the financial crisis should be completed. Hence, the influence of an RC on CSR activities should not be biased by the effects of the financial crisis. Nevertheless, we test the data of the sample years 2007 and 2014 separately.

The set of variables and the descriptive statistics are shown below (Figure 1.1.1 and Table 1.1.4).

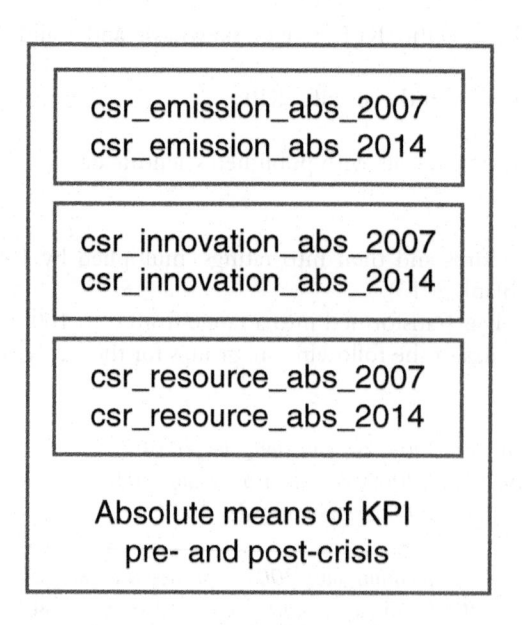

Figure 1.1.1 Framework of the CSR outcome variables

Table 1.1.4 Descriptive statistics of the CSR outcome variables

CSR outcome variable	Obs.	Mean	Std. Dev.	Median	Min.	Max.
csr_ emission_abs_2007	43	57,60787	10,72276	56,66042	32,34571	78,93250
csr_ emission_abs_2014	55	62,25521	12,71049	67,40385	30,38190	81,02280
csr_innovation_abs_2007	43	56,78183	14,40286	56,36733	32,73750	82,22750
csr_innovation_abs_2014	55	65,84987	16,01325	69,21643	31,67214	96,53250
csr_resource_abs_2007	43	57,63380	11,09150	58,66778	28,87273	83,02728
csr_resource_abs_2014	55	63,69089	13,58812	67,43182	24,26727	82,66273

Results

Due to a rather small number of companies, we used non-parametric methods. We test whether an early adoption of RC had a significant effect on CSR activities, using the two-sample Wilcoxon rank sum test for the assumed non-normal distributions of the variables delineated in Figure 1.1.1, grouped by the binary variables rc_delay_clusmed and rc_clusmed distinguishing between early and late RC adopters by the median.

Considering the two binary grouping variables rc_delay_clusmed and rc_clusmed, we expect a higher validity for tests with rc_delay_clusmed. This is due to the fact that a firm founded after the first official introduction of RC has a lower or no delay of RC introduction, relative to 1985.

An overview of the entire results is provided in Table 1.1.5.

We found significant results for csr_innovation_abs_2007 (p = 0.0105) and high significance for csr_emission_abs_2007 (p = 0.0062) and csr_resource_abs_2007 (p = 0.0074), grouped by rc_delay_clusmed. This result coincides with the theoretical considerations about the effect of an early adoption of RC on CSR.

Table 1.1.5 Overview of the Wilcoxon rank sum tests significances

Bold print = low significance (Prob > |z|) < 0.1);
* = significance (< 0.05);
** = high significance (< 0.01).

CSR outcome variable	Grouping variable	Significance (Prob > |z|)
csr_emission_abs_2007	rc_delay_clusmed	0.0062**
csr_innovation_abs_2007	rc_delay_clusmed	0.0105*
csr_resource_abs_2007	rc_delay_clusmed	0.0074**
csr_emission_abs_2007	rc_clusmed	0.7875
csr_innovation_abs_2007	rc_clusmed	0.1243
csr_resource_abs_2007	rc_clusmed	0.0798
csr_emission_abs_2014	rc_delay_clusmed	0.5580
csr_innovation_abs_2014	rc_delay_clusmed	0.4013
csr_resource_abs_2014	rc_delay_clusmed	0.0444*
csr_emission_abs_2014	rc_clusmed	0.0586
csr_innovation_abs_2014	rc_clusmed	0.2055
csr_resource_abs_2014	rc_clusmed	0.1653

In terms of the CSR outcomes grouped by the year, when RC was introduced within each firm (*rc_clusmed*), we only found a weak significance for the use of resources (*csr resource_abs_2007*; p = 0.0798). As for emissions (*csr_emission_abs_2007*) and innovation potential, we were not able to find any significance, which is surprising, because the reduction of hazardous emissions is one of the core targets of RC. One explanation might be the grouping variable *rc_clusmed*. This variable contains the years that each firm adopted RC. In contrast, *rc_delay* is adjusted for companies founded after 1985 – a fact that is not considered in *rc_clusmed*, although it could contribute to a lack of significant results regarding the latter variable.

When regarding the CSR outcome for the post-crisis year 2014, grouped by *rc_delay_ clusmed*, the Wilcoxon rank sum test was only significant for CSR activities involving the reduction of hazardous emissions (*csr_emission_abs_2014*; p = 0.0444). The most obvious interpretation of this result could well be the fall in CSR expenses caused by the efforts of mastering the crisis. As a result, the crisis effect needs to be examined in more detail. Additionally, the results for the CSR outcome for the post-crisis year 2014, grouped by *rc_clusmed* are only slightly significant for sustainability-relevant innovation outcomes (*csr_innovation_abs_2014*; p = 0.0586). To summarize, the significances occur within different CSR sectors (emissions vs. innovation) and should therefore be treated with caution.

Overall, the results point to a relation between an early adoption of RC and the CSR outcome, (at least for pre-crisis variables). We conclude that RC might act as an enabler for CSR. We see two reasons for this. First, firms introducing RC commit themselves to standards, for example, by banning certain hazardous chemicals. As the banned chemicals have to be substituted through less hazardous ones, firms have to invest in process innovations and find ways to produce their goods in a more eco-friendly way. Hence, the barrier to the introduction of sophisticated and efficient CSR systems should be considered lower than for firms without such capacities.

Second, the introduction of RC aims, as Givel (2007) stated, to prevent stricter regulation regimes by the legislators. The firms might have started to participate in RC for legal reasons and to prevent profit losses through official regulations. For CSR, the picture is similar to that painted by Pinkston and Carrol (1996) – firms from the chemical industry tend to introduce market- and legal-driven CSR approaches. As both RC and CSR are based on similar motivations, RC can be considered as an enabler or platform for further CSR activities.

This result can be used for considerations on regulations concerning the promotion of CSR. If a voluntary code of conduct, as Prakash (1999, 2000) regards RC, enables firms to foster their CSR efforts in the chemical industry, there might be other industries that are currently under-regulated, benefiting from this kind of self-introduced code of conduct, as voluntary codes of conduct often supplement state regulation rather satisfactorily (Vogel 2010).

Conclusions and outlook

We started the analysis with an overview of the development and interpretation of the Responsible Care initiative. As a voluntary code of conduct, RC gives participating firms the opportunity to gain competitive advantages as well as prevent stricter legal regulations (Givel 2007; Prakash 1999; Prakash 2000).

We examined how the environmental CSR performance is influenced by RC. Based on the data of 55 companies, we found a slightly positive impact of an early adoption of

RC on environmental CSR outcomes (to a higher extent where the outcomes of the use of resources and the prevention of hazardous emissions within the firms' boundaries were concerned and to a lower extent in terms of environmentally friendly product innovations). With regard to our research questions, we were able to show that the development and adoption of RC in the chemical industry was driven by environmental incidences and the resulting environmental pressures by different stakeholder groups. Moreover, the RC rule set was revised over time, and we find an interplay of the adopted methodologies and reporting standards with a variety of CSR guidelines. Although our evidence that early RC adopters yield a higher environmental performance concerning their resource consumption and emissions does not cover all CSR aspects, we conclude that RC and CSR approaches are positively related. Besides environmental awareness, intra-firm learning and established processes to protect the environment might be responsible for these results.

Future studies should concentrate on getting more detailed insights and enriching the data set. The focus should lie on presenting in detail when RC was adopted and how the initiative has been developed, that is, how successfully the firms have achieved set goals. Another relevant question is the influence of the financial crisis on CSR and the strength of this effect compared to the effect of RC on CSR. Another promising avenue might be to extend our methodological approach. Single case studies could be supplemented by expert interviews with RC managers from different chemical firms to gain more in-depth information in order to answer more in-depth research questions.

References

ACC. (2017). ACC Member Companies. Retrieved 10.12.2016, from https://www.americanchemistry.com/Membership/MemberCompanies/

Aerts, W., Cormier, D., & Magnan, M. (2006). Intra-industry imitation in corporate environmental reporting: an international perspective. *Journal of Accounting and Public Policy, 25*(3), 299–331.

Aupperle, K. E. (1982). *An Empirical Inquiry into the Social Responsibilities as Defined by Corporations: An Examination of Various Models and Relationships.* Athens, GA: University of Georgia.

Bansal, P., & Roth, K. (2000). Why companies go green: a model of ecological responsiveness. *Academy of Management Journal, 43*(4), 717–736.

Baumann-Pauly, D., Wickert, C., Spence, L. J., & Scherer, A. G. (2013). Organizing Corporate Social Responsibility in small and large firms: size matters. *Journal of Business Ethics, 115*(4), 693–705.

Bayer (2017). *Annual Report 2016: Augmented Version.* Leverkusen, Germany: Bayer AG.

Bazillier, R., & Vauday, J. (2009). The Greenwashing Machine: Is CSR More than Communication. DR LEO, 2009–2010.

Bélanger, J., Topalovic, M., West, J., Topalovic, P., & Krantzberg, G. (2013). *Responsible Care: A Case Study.* Boston, Berlin: De Gruyter.

Bertazzi, P. A. (1991). Long-term effects of chemical disasters: lessons and results from Seveso. *Science of the Total Environment, 106*(1), 5–20.

Blank, H. (2013). Thomson Reuters Corporate Responsibility Ratings (TRCRR). New York: Thomson Reuters.

Bowen, H. R. (1953). *Social Responsibilities of the Businessman.* New York: Harper.

Broughton, E. (2005). The Bhopal disaster and its aftermath: a review. *Environmental Health, 4*(1), 6.

CEFIC (2005). *Responsible Care Global Charter.* Brussels, Belgium: CEFIC.

CIAC (2016). Responsible Care®. Retrieved 08.11.2016, from http://www.canadianchemistry.ca/responsible_care/index.php/en/responsible-care-history.

Conzelmann, T. (2012). A procedural approach to the design of voluntary clubs: negotiating the Responsible Care Global Charter. *Socio-Economic Review, 10*(1), 193–214.

Daly, H. E. (1990). Sustainable development: from concept and theory to operational principles. *Population and Development Review, 16*, 25–43.

De Marchi, B., Funtowicz, S., & Ravetz, J. (1996). Seveso: a paradoxical classic disaster. In Mitchell, J. K., ed., *The Long Road to Recovery: Community Responses to Industrial Disaster,* 86–120. Tokyo: United Nations University Press.

Delmas, M., & Montiel, I. (2008). The diffusion of voluntary international management standards: Responsible Care, ISO 9000, and ISO 14001 in the chemical industry. *Policy Studies Journal, 36*(1), 65–93.

Delmas, M., & Toffel, M. W. (2004). Stakeholders and environmental management practices: an institutional framework. *Business Strategy and the Environment, 13*(4), 209–222.

Dillard, J., Brown, D., & Marshall, R. S. (2005). An environmentally enlightened accounting. *Accounting Forum, 29*(1), 77–101.

Druckrey, F. (1998). How to make business ethics operational: Responsible Care – an example of successful self-regulation? *Journal of Business Ethics, 17*(9), 979–985.

Escrig-Olmedo, E., Muñoz-Torres, M. J., & Fernández-Izquierdo, M. A. (2010). Socially responsible investing: sustainability indices, ESG rating and information provider agencies. *International Journal of Sustainable Economy, 2*(4), 442–461.

European Commission. (2009). Commission Staff Working Document on the Implementation of Commission Recommendation of 6 May 2003 Concerning the Definition of Micro, *Small and Medium-Sized Enterprises*. Brussels, Belgium: European Commission.

European Commission. (2011). *A Renewed EU Strategy 2011–14 for Corporate Social Responsibility*. Brussels, Belgium: European Commission.

Foss, M. M. (2007). Introduction to LNG. *Center for Energy Economics, Bureau of Economic Geology, Jackson School of Geosciences, University of Texas*. Austin, TX. Available: http://www/.beg.utexas.edu/energyecon/lng/documents/CEE_INTRODUCTION _TO_LNG_FINAL. pdf.

Gamper-Rabindran, S., & Finger, S. R. (2013). Does industry self-regulation reduce pollution? Responsible Care in the chemical industry. *Journal of Regulatory Economics, 43*(1), 1–30.

Giger, W. (2009). The Rhine red, the fish dead – the 1986 Schweizerhalle disaster, a retrospect and long-term impact assessment. *Environmental Science and Pollution Research, 16*(1), 98–111.

Givel, M. (2007). Motivation of chemical industry social responsibility through Responsible Care. *Health Policy, 81*(1), 85–92.

Gössling, T., & Vocht, C. (2007). Social role conceptions and CSR policy success. *Journal of Business Ethics, 74*(4), 363–372.

Howard, J., Nash, J., & Ehrenfeld, J. (1999). Industry codes as agents of change: responsible care adoption by US chemical companies. *Business Strategy and the Environment, 8*(5), 281.

ICCA (2015). *2015 Responsible Care Status Report*. Brussels, Belgium: ICCA.

ISO (2004). ISO 14001: 2004(E) Environmental Management Systems – Requirements with Guidance for Use. Geneva, Switzerland: ISO.

ISO (2010). ISO 26000:2010(E) Guidance on Social Responsibility. Geneva, Switzerland: ISO.

Karaibrahimoglu, Y. Z. (2010). Corporate social responsibility in times of financial crisis. *African Journal of Business Management, 4*(4), 382.

Kechiche, A., & Soparnot, R. (2012). CSR within SMEs: literature review. *International Business Research, 5*(7), 97.

Khan, F. I., & Abbasi, S. A. (1999). Major accidents in process industries and an analysis of causes and consequences. *Journal of Loss Prevention in the Process Industries, 12*(5), 361–378.

King, A. A., & Lenox, M. J. (2000). Industry self-regulation without sanctions: the chemical industry's responsible care program. *Academy of Management Journal, 43*(4), 698–716.

King, A. A., Lenox, M. J., & Terlaak, A. (2005). The strategic use of decentralized institutions: exploring certification with the ISO 14001 management standard. *Academy of Management Journal, 48*(6), 1091–1106.

Laufer, W. S. (2003). Social accountability and corporate greenwashing. *Journal of Business Ethics*, *43*(3), 253–261.

Moffet, J., Bregha, F., & Middelkoop, M. J. (2004). Responsible care: a case study of a voluntary environmental initiative. In Webb, K., ed., *Voluntary Codes: Private Governance, the Public Interest and Innovation*, 177–208. Carlton Research Unit for Innovation, Science and Environment, Ottawa.

Nikolaeva, R., & Bicho, M. (2011). The role of institutional and reputational factors in the voluntary adoption of corporate social responsibility reporting standards. *Journal of the Academy of Marketing Science*, *39*(1), 136–157.

O'Riordan, L., & Fairbrass, J. (2008). Corporate Social Responsibility (CSR): models and theories in stakeholder dialogue. *Journal of Business Ethics*, *83*(4), 745–758.

Pekalski, A. (1997). Review of Preventive and Protective Systems for Explosion Risk in the Process Industry. Delft, the Netherlands: TU Delft.

Pfeffer, J., & Salancik, G. R. (1978). *The External Control of Organizations: A Resource Dependence Approach*. New York: Harper and Row Publishers.

Pinkston, T. S., & Carroll, A. B. (1996). A retrospective examination of CSR orientations: have they changed? *Journal of Business Ethics*, *15*(2), 199–206.

Potoski, M., & Prakash, A. (2005). Green clubs and voluntary governance: ISO 14001 and firms' regulatory compliance. *American Journal of Political Science*, *49*(2), 235–248.

Prakash, A. (1999). A new-institutionalist perspective on ISO 14000 and Responsible Care. *Business Strategy and the Environment*, *8*(6), 322–335.

Prakash, A. (2000). Responsible Care: an assessment. *Business & Society*, *39*(2), 183–209.

Rahman, S. (2011). Evaluation of definitions: ten dimensions of corporate social responsibility. *World Review of Business Research*, *1*(1), 166–176.

Reinhardt, F. L., Stavins, R. N., & Vietor, R. H. K. (2008). Corporate Social Responsibility through an economic lens. *Review of Environmental Economics and Policy*, *2*(2), 219–239.

Rennings, K., & Wiggering, H. (1997). Steps towards indicators of sustainable development: linking economic and ecological concepts. *Ecological Economics*, *20*(1), 25–36.

Ribando, J. M., & Bonne, G. (2010). A new quality factor: finding alpha with ASSET4 ESG data. *Starmine Research Note, Thomson Reuters*.

Sethi, S. (2016). *Globalization and Self-Regulation: The Crucial Role that Corporate Codes of Conduct Play in Global Business*. Berlin: Springer.

Sethi, S. P., & Schepers, D. H. (2014). United Nations Global Compact: the promise–performance gap. *Journal of Business Ethics*, *122*(2), 193–208.

Souto, B. F.-F. (2009). Crisis and corporate social responsibility: threat or opportunity? *International Journal of Economic Sciences and Applied Research*, *2*(1), 36–50.

Turner, R. (1993). Sustainability principles and practice. *Sustainable Environmental Economics and Management*. London: Bellhaven Press, 3–36.

VCI (2016a). Die neue 'Responsible Care Global Charter' - ein Überblick - Verband der Chemischen Industrie e.V.'. Retrieved 28.03.2017, from: https://www.vci.de/nachhaltigkeit/responsible-care/rc-initiative/responsible-care-global-charter-ueberblick-weltchemieverband-icca.jsp.

VCI (2016b). The VCI Is Taking Stock: 25 Years Responsible Care Programme in the German Chemical Industry. Frankfurt am Main, Germany: VCI.

VCI (2017). RC-Managementsysteme. Retrieved 31.03.2017, *2017*, from https://www.vci.de/nachhaltigkeit/responsible-care/rc-managementsysteme/listenseite.jsp.

Venart, J. E. S. (2004). Flixborough: the explosion and its aftermath. *Process Safety and Environmental Protection*, *82*(2), 105–127.

Vogel, D. (2010). The private regulation of global corporate conduct. *Business & Society*, *49*(1), 68–87.

The World Bank (2017). GDP growth (annual %) | Data. Retrieved 17.04.2017, from: http://data.worldbank.org/indicator/NY.GDP.MKTP.KD.ZG?view=chart.

1.2 Mind the gap!

Existing barriers to standardizing the measurement of social value creation

Cecilia Grieco and Laura Michelini

Introduction

The measurement of social value creation is currently a prominent discourse. On the one hand, a growing number of academic publications attests to the efforts that scholars are making towards a better comprehension of the phenomenon (e.g., Epstein and Yuthas, 2014; Grieco, 2015). On the other hand, it is interesting to note that several voices beyond academia are actually pointing out the importance of the practice (OECD, 2010, 2015; GECES, 2014). Even though this topic is growing in popularity from a theoretical point of view, what is actually evidenced is that the practice of assessing the impact that organizations have on society is not always as widespread as it should be.

The evaluation of social value creation is a challenging endeavour (Ebrahim and Rangan, 2010). How is it possible, for example, to quantitatively measure a change in the life of a person? And how can this change be traced back to the development of a specific activity? (Bucaciuc, 2015). To provide answers to these questions, standardized guidelines and indicators have been developed to drive the implementation of the process. In the past decades, many metrics to demonstrate the generated impact have been developed, and numerous competing standardized measurement tools (SMTs) are currently available for both for-profit and non-profit organizations. This ongoing proliferation of models is due to the fact that organizations differ in size, capacity, activities, and focus, and consequently there is not a single model that is suitable for all of them (Grieco, 2015).

However, the methods of measurement in the existing approaches remain problematic. Despite their benefits in reducing the subjectivity of the process, SMTs have been harshly criticized for their intent to attribute a measurable value to something that cannot be expressed in quantitative terms alone. This could partially explain why the adoption of these models is quite limited among organizations. As Mulgan (2010) underlined, despite great enthusiasm for the development of metrics and measures for the assessment of social value, only a few organizations actually use them to guide decisions. This is particularly true in certain contexts. For example, a study of Italian social enterprises developed by Fondazione Sodalitas (2014) shows that despite the high value given to the practice of measuring social impact, only 32% of the sample actually carried out structured and regular measurement activities, and only 21.5% did so through the adoption of a specific model.

The idea of measurable social impacts is gaining importance; indeed, the very definition of third-sector organizations now includes it. At EU level, concerning the European fund for social entrepreneurship (EuSEF, EU Regulation n. 346/2013), social enterprises are defined as organizations whose primary objective is the achievement of a measurable positive social impact, and who use profits first and foremost for the achievement of that impact. In this paradigm shift, social impact becomes essential, posing the need for a shared knowledge about their measurement.

Examples such as the Anglo-Saxon experience of the Social Value Act can be seen as evidence for why a definition of measurement standards cannot be disregarded. The Social Value Act came into force on 31 January 2013. It requires people who commission public services to think about how they can also secure wider social, economic, and environmental benefits. After two years of testing, however, it was neither extended nor further developed because of unsolved problems such as a lack of proper knowledge, understanding, and practice of social impact assessment. Of course, social-purpose organizations such as social enterprises are explicitly designed to address social challenges and thus create social value. However, the actual measure of this value is of relevance for both non-profit and for-profit companies, as every business generates forms of societal and environmental impact. In recent decades, sustainability reporting has been of increasing interest to for-profit companies, leading to a growth in both the amount of non-financial disclosure and the different channels employed to do so (Montecchia et al., 2016).

Starting from these premises, the present work aims to gather evidence for the main obstacles that emerge concerning the adoption of SMTs to assess social impact. The focus is on the organizations that actually face the issue of implementing these processes, while the main point is that in the wide range of existing models, tools for almost every need are already in place. What is lacking, however, is a full comprehension of the limits that can hamper their use, which have to be overcome in order to strengthen the practice of measuring the social value generated by organizations. The analysis have been performed on social enterprises (SE), as representative of the overall categories of social-purpose organizations. SE are indeed organizations at the boundary of non-profit and for-profit sectors, which carry out an entrepreneurial activity as a mean for the achievement of a social mission (Mair et al., 2012). SE are defined as providing a response to societal issues, with a potential for innovation and sustainability (Bucaciuc, 2015), and this raises the issue to find the proper way to monitor and measure the (positive and negative) impact they are having on society. For this reason, the measurement of social impact is pivotal in these organizations (Grieco et al., 2015; OECD, 2015; Maas and Grieco, 2017). Nevertheless, while the analysed cases are SE, the insights, key questions, and observation are relevant for all the organizations and initiatives with a social mission that face the need to measure the generated social impact.

The contribution of this study lies in the focus on the entrepreneurs. Several articles have offered analyses of the barriers to social impact measurement; however, with the exception of Barraket and Yousefpour (2013), none of them is actually based on the direct experience of practitioners, while in the authors' view their perspective cannot be disregarded. Consistently with Barraket and Yousefpour (2013), the effort here is to drawn the barriers directly from practitioners' expertise, focusing on SMTs instead of on the overall measuring process.

The remainder of the chapter is as follows: the next section presents a review of the relevant literature in order to explain the topic of social impact measurement and the existing types of standardization in measurement tools. In the third section, the adopted methodology is described. The fourth section concerns the perspective of the entrepreneurs concerning existing barriers to SMTs, presenting and discussing the findings of the research. Concluding remarks close the chapter.

The measurement of social value creation

Defining what social impact is and how it can be assessed is a great challenge. An initial obstacle is the proper definition of the topic, as the existing literature shows a nebulously defined approach and terminology that is often confusing (Nicholls, 2007; Maas and Liket, 2011; OECD, 2015). Social impact is the societal and environmental change created by activities and investments (Epstein and Yuthas, 2014). As a result of externally induced actions, it encompasses their intended and unintended effects, their negative and positive effects, and their long- and short-term effects (Wainwright, 2002; Clark et al., 2004; Epstein and Yuthas, 2014). The process of assessing social impact allows organizations to clarify, measure, and gather evidence of the benefits they create for stakeholders in the environment and the local economy. This is extremely important as a way of knowing when an activity is actually revolutionizing an industry and changing the system (Ashoka, 2013). The development of specific models meets the need to find suitable ways through which performance can be assessed beyond economic results. This aspect is of great concern for social organizations that have a primary social mission. While economic performance can be summed up by quantitative data such as profits or returns on investment, social value creation is hard to capture, as it is descriptive in nature, mostly focused on programmes rather than being organization-wide, highly resource-consuming, and mostly subjective (Liket and Maas, 2015).

Measuring social impact has several benefits for organizations. It allows them to prove that what they are doing is actually making a difference, to help in refining and improving programmes, and to assure funders about the worthiness of their investments (Burdge, 2003; Nicholls, 2009; Hehenberger et al., 2013). The value of this information as a management tool has increased exponentially, as it enables a deep understanding of how best to allocate resources to maximize social outcomes (Olsen and Galimidi, 2009). Moreover, as it provides information related to the way in which the received investments are used in addressing social issues, this communication can be strategic (Porter et al., 2012; Ruttman, 2012).

However, this process also has some limits that scholars have largely underlined. Perplexities about the measurement of social impact are numerous, and concern both the underlining principles of the process and the specific SMTs developed. Bucaciuc (2015), for example, raises the issue of assessing subtle changes in the lives of people that can be hardly traced and even less linked to a specific action. Nicholls and Cho (2008) argue about the meaning of the word "social" in social impact, as it is itself an ambiguous and complex concept that implies an "unrealistic homogeneity of social interests" (p. 105). Epstein and Yuthas (2014) state that the first obstacle in measuring social impact is understanding the proper object of the process. Consistently, Maas and Liket (2011) identified four main obstacles to univocally define the concept of social impact: (a) the qualitative nature of impact, which makes it hard to link to an objective value and to summarize the various qualitative expressions it has; (b) organizations can have a positive or negative impact upon the society along several dimensions, and this can create confusion in adding up different kinds of impacts; (c) social impact includes short-term as well as long-term effects on society; (d) many components can contribute to social impact, and it is often hard to link activities and impact because of difficulties with attribution and causality questions.

Barraket and Yousefpour (2013) carry out a qualitative analysis with social entrepreneurs to grasp the main barriers to measuring and communicating social impact. What they came up with is the resource issue, the complexity of the process, the perception of outcomes as being immeasurable, the lack of support, and the difficulties of including the measurement process in the organizational practices.

Focusing on SMTs, Grieco (2015) pinpoints the scarce knowledge about existing tools within organizations. Arce-Gomez, Donovan, and Bedggood (2015) well explain one of the main critical points, that is, putting together the need for flexibility in SMTs with that of formalizing at least the core values and principles to guide this process.

Mulgan (2010) identifies two main obstacles to their adoption. A first one is the belief that value is somewhat objective and thus easily measurable while it depends on the interaction of several different actors. A second is that SMTs can play different roles such as accounting to external stakeholders, managing internal operations, and assessing the generated impact, thus it is essential that they are developed and adopted accordingly, while this aspect is often disregarded.

Arvidson, Lyon, McKay, and Moro (2010) provide a detailed analysis of the Social Return on Investment (SROI), one of the best known and diffused SMTs. In their work, the authors offer a critical view about this model, underlining its challenges and limitations, such as the potential for discretion, the practice of valuing the input, and the high cost of conducting an evaluation through it.

Given the growing importance of social impact measurement, the creation of a common language has become a pressing need (OECD, 2015). Consistently, several efforts have been made towards the development of SMTs, in order to ensure an approach to the assessment of social value creation that is as uniform as possible across organizations. SMTs meet a series of needs for information about social impact that must always be understandable, sometimes be comparable with other data, and of course must be collected and disclosed in a clear and consistent way, so that the recipients can be sure of its validity and reliability.

Standardization can happen at different levels. A first distinction is between using standardized indicators or models (GECES, 2014). When focusing on indicators, an organization can choose the most relevant among a set of different measures, be they forecast or historical, qualitative or quantitative, monetized or non-monetized (Clifford et al., 2013). Standardized indicators are quite easy to find, as several sources are available. In this way, each entrepreneur can pick the indicators that are best suited to the assessment of a specific project, and create his or her own combination of metrics. However, standardized indicators cannot be considered in the same light as an impact measurement programme, as the latter does not stop with the selection of metrics. To implement the overall process of tracking and managing progress towards the desired social and environmental objectives, the selection of metrics is only a small part, if a crucial one. In this regard, the standardized models describe the precise steps to take in order to ensure the comparability and reliability of the results. Both frameworks and methods fall within this category (Zappalà and Lyons, 2009). The former provides a structure through which an organization can think about, design, plan, implement, and embed performance measurements into a project, without prescribing particular methodologies or specific indicators to adopt. In contrast, such prescriptiveness does occur with methods, which are mostly quantitative and often based on monetization.

Regardless of this distinction, however, several difficulties emerge in defining a sort of "golden standard" for measuring social value (GECES, 2014; Grieco, 2015; Costa and Pesci, 2016), posing a strong need for further direction on how to approach this process (Hehemberger et al., 2013).

Method

In order to understand the main barriers to the use of SMTs for assessing social value creation, the choice was made to focus on the perceptions of entrepreneurs. Indeed, as they have to deal in practice with this issue in managing their organizations, their point of view cannot be disregarded. A case study analysis was conducted (Yin, 2003) on seven Italian social enterprises. The study has adopted a descriptive approach, and based on the multiple-case (holistic) model (Yin, 2003), where the single social enterprise has been considered as the unit of analysis.

To select the sample, we started from the database of Isnet (impresasociale.net), an association founded in 2007, whose aim is to foster the development of SEs and their relations with the stakeholder. The Isnet database was explored to identify the cases that could be suited with the purpose of the study.[1] In this sense, our goal was to identify those organizations that (i) carry out an entrepreneurial activity; (ii) have a clear and specific social mission; (iii) provide information about any activities aimed at the measurement of social impact (e.g., reports, data, certifications); (iii) provide valid and updated contact information. In a second step, a first contact via email led to the exclusion of those that felt they did not have the experience necessary to discuss the topic, those that were not interested in or available to participate in the research, and those that did not respond. This step ended up with 45 potential cases, within which we applied a criterion-based – or purposive – selection process (Patton, 2002; Mason, 2002), selecting those units that had particular features or characteristics which would enable detailed exploration and understanding of the central themes. This left us with a total of seven cases. This number was considered sufficient to fulfil the proposed purpose, and in line with previous analogous studies (Weerawardena and Mort, 2006; Short et al., 2009; Barraket and Yousefpour, 2013).

The information was gathered ensuring the triangulation of sources, thus collecting data from semi-structured interviews with managers of the selected organizations, both face to face and via Skype calls; text analysis of organizations' websites; reading of external and internal documents drafted by organizations in the sample (e.g., social reports, service charters, etc.).

The interviews were performed between June and September 2015, with the purpose of capturing the perspective of the respondents and gauging their interpretation of the analysed topic. To this end, the choice was to administer semi-structured interviews for which an outline had been defined concerning the topics to be discussed with respondents, but the order of questions and the way they could be expressed were within the discretion of the interviewer, allowing enough flexibility to explore other issues as they emerged (Kumar et al., 1997).

As shown in Table 1.2.1, the list of topics included: the organization profile (e.g., number of workers, year of foundation, industry); the description of the social impact the organization aims to achieve (e.g., social mission, sources of impact, planned outcomes); the attitude and behaviour towards the measurement process and the SMTs,[2] the perceived internal or external pressures (if any); the drivers of the measurement; and the emergent barriers.

Although the purpose of the chapter is to focus on the barriers, a comprehension of all of these other elements has been considered pivotal to an overall picture of the organizations and of their practices. Also, in many cases, it was easier for respondents to identify the barriers while answering other questions than when being directly asked about them.

Table 1.2.1 Topics and items included in the interviews

Topic	Item(s)
Organizational profile	Number of workers
	Year of foundation
	Industry
Social impact	Social mission
	Sources of impact
	Planned outcomes
Measurement process	Organization's culture concerning the measurement process
	Level of (regular) implementation
	Use of SMTs
Pressures (if any)	From which stakeholder, on which aspect, with which output
Drivers	Cultural, economic, managerial, strategic, other
Barriers	Cultural, economic, managerial, strategic, other

All the interviews were recorded and transcribed, with the permission of the people interviewed. Collected information was then content-analysed using the NVivo 11.0 software for qualitative data analysis (Pacifico and Coppola, 2010; Coppola, 2011), whereby all the materials were coded into cases and nodes. Specifically, each organization has been codified into a single NVivo case, so that all the related information was put together. As for the nodes, they were firstly defined in a top-down fashion, referring to the main barriers that emerged from the literature review. Further nodes were then added as they emerged during the coding process.

Emerging barriers to adopting SMTs: the perspective of the entrepreneurs

Findings

The analysed cases are all small organizations, with fewer than fifteen employees, and with a more or less wide network of volunteers working to support the developed activities. They have all been launched over the past fifteen years, with the oldest dating back to 2002 and the youngest to 2013.

The industries in which they carry out their activities differ among the sample, ranging from textiles to consulting, including cosmetics, social assistance, and education.

Nevertheless, despite this variety in terms of fields, the social missions these organizations strive for are quite close to each other. In four cases out of seven, the main aim of the organization is to increase job inclusion for a disadvantaged category of the population, whether they are former inmates, psychiatrically distressed people, or long-term unemployed workers. In the other three cases, the social mission fulfilled is the promotion of values and principles inspired by a specific culture (inclusivity in two cases and environmental protection in the other).

It is interesting to notice how the outcomes that these organizations want to reach go far beyond the specific activities they carry out. Indeed, the similarity in their social missions is also reflected in the way they argued the other topics of the interview, as the process of measuring social impact is totally oriented by the planned outcomes.

Asked about the measuring process, all the respondents showed a positive attitude. Indeed, the first point that emerged from the analysis was that measuring the generated social value seems to be an important practice for the respondents, chiefly for the opportunity to understand whether what they are doing is really contributing to the achievement of their social mission. In almost all the cases, respondents declared they were aware that monitoring and measuring their social value is essential to detect and correct any deviation from the planned goals. External accountability is a key driver for disclosing relevant information about the extent to which the organization is keeping the promises it has made to its stakeholders.

However, despite their acceptance of the value of the process, when asked about the adoption of SMTs, the respondents began to raise their first concerns. Standardized models are theoretically seen as a strength, as they could work as guides that provide organizations with the precise steps to take in assessing social impact. However, the guarantee of achieving objectives and comparable results contrasts with a deep bias toward the possibility of translating social change to "cold" quantitative or – even worse – monetized indications. What emerges from the respondents' perspectives is that the communicative power of translating the social value into an amount of money is closer to a social washing strategy, implemented to demonstrate at all costs that the organization is doing good.

> Assessing social impact is a contradiction in terms. We are a social-purpose organization; our very survival is proof of our social impact.
>
> (U.2)

> Explaining our social mission is enough to demonstrate that we will have an impact.
>
> (U.7)

Respondents all agree about the fact that the main purpose of an organization has to be the generation of outcomes, and thus all of its efforts must be directed towards this goal. Research activities aimed at calculating the exact value of these outcomes are a "distracting" element that focuses attention on demonstrating rather than creating a real impact.

> We omit this process because we have higher priorities.
>
> (U.1)

Our results reveal that the assessment of social value is mostly seen as a subjective evaluation; in particular, one where the case-specificity of each project has to be safeguarded.

> The best way to assess social value is to express it in a narrative style, instead of using quantitative indicators.
>
> (U.5)

> It would be preferable to conduct interviews with beneficiaries in order to understand whether they are actually feeling better.
>
> (U.4)

Social entrepreneurs perceive their organizations as greatly different among each other in terms of size, targets, social missions, and legal forms; and, within them, different projects and activities are carried out. In this sense, an issue they raise is that the adoption of

SMTs poses the risk of devaluing these specificities, providing "one-size-fits-all" types of measures in order to achieve uniformity of evaluation. This is perceived as a real threat, as the specificities of each organization have a strong influence in determining the creation of social value, and are thus valorized as much as possible.

> Models are too general. We need precise indicators that are tailored to the specificities of our organization.
>
> (U.1)

> It is impossible to find a model that meets everyone's needs.
>
> (U.3)

A further general belief about standardized models is that they have been mostly developed for traditional enterprises; thus, they cannot be easily applied to social organizations, as their business models are radically different. Closely linked to this, SMTs are perceived as being highly resource-consuming in terms of time, money, people, and skills. This is mostly felt by small non-profit organizations, where there is a strong voluntary component. Generally, standardized models are seen as something do-able only by big organizations that can afford the expenses linked to this process.

> We are too small to carry out social impact measurements. We are unable to devote time to this process, even if we know we should.
>
> (U.1)

This is an aspect that has been underlined by all of the organizations, and it emerges as being a common belief in respondents, regardless of their specificities.

> We do not have the resources that would enable us to afford the process.
>
> (U.2)

> To regularly implement an SMT, our budget would need to be quadrupled.
>
> (U.3)

Finally, what emerged as a strong barrier is the lack of any forms of support that would help organizations find the needed resources.

> We would be able to do more if we could have some form of support.
>
> (U.1)

> Public institutions do not consider this to be important.
>
> (U.6)

> Customers are not interested in the creation of social value.
>
> (U.4)

This aspect is particularly felt by those social enterprises that are more market oriented, and thus derive the most part of their revenues from the entrepreneurial activity, competing on the market along with traditional for-profit enterprises.

Discussion

Our findings shed light on a set of barriers that, in the practitioners' perspective, play a key role in hampering the adoption of SMTs, despite recognizing the potential value. What emerged from the case study analysis is a confirmation of the importance that measuring social value can have from a managerial point of view, to assess the effectiveness of the implemented activities and help to best allocate available resources. Also, it fosters the accountability of the organizations, and this is a topic of great relevance nowadays for both for-profit and non-profit organizations – especially for the latter, as they work to mitigate or solve social issues, thus making a real commitment to the wider society. In this way, organizations are required to enable their stakeholders to track the progress made toward planned goals.

However, in our view, the identified barriers pinpoint a significant gap between the attitude and the behaviour of entrepreneurs regarding the topic. The scarce motivation is, of course, one of the main obstacles. A partial explanation of this aversion can be found in the *warm glow theory* (Andreoni, 1990; Donegani et al., 2012) that has been largely applied to organizations with a social purpose (Baron, 2007; Hoogendoorn, 2011). According to this theory, the awareness of working for the fulfilment of a social mission makes any form of assessment process rather superfluous. As for the risk of being distracted by the measurement activity, which emerged from the interviews, this is an issue that has also been addressed in the literature. Bucacioc (2015) stated that if organizations are pressured to adopt SMTs to prove their impact, they may be tempted to shift their focus from their original goals and spend more time attempting to demonstrate evidence of their social performance. This aspect is even stronger where organizations have to produce some form of social impact report in order to mobilize support from external stakeholders such as funders, partners, or governments (André and Pache, 2014). In this sense, our findings show a cultural limit, where the practice of evaluation is mostly seen as a marketing tool rather than a management one. The fear of being judged is stronger than the interest in finding out what is not working in order to improve it.

Furthermore, the lack of interest towards the assessment of social impact for those organizations that are strongly market-oriented confirms an idea that has been recently raised in the academic literature. Indeed, the analysis of the reverse relation between market orientation and social impact measurement seems to show that, although social impact might be a piece of information that is important for funders, it does not necessarily have the same marketing appeal to influence customers' purchasing behaviours (Maas and Grieco, 2017).

There is a huge contradiction that comes out from our findings, expressing an aspect that is still vague in the academic literature, but that can be summed up in the trade-off between specificity and comparability in social impact measurement processes. On the one hand, the idiosyncrasies of organizations place a limit on generalizing what to measure, making standardized models greatly unsuitable. On the other hand, in order to carry out these processes, some forms of benchmarks and shared frameworks that can be referred to are essential. In the standardized models, the wide range of possible outcomes is reduced to a set of economic, social, and environmental indicators, which implies an oversimplification of reality. However, despite the need to safeguard the specificity of the project to assess, organizations look for shared guidelines that can work as landmarks.

Concerning the unsuitability of SMTs, despite respondents' observations that existing models are not well known, this perception expresses a severe barrier to their adoption. There is indeed a trend towards borrowing practices from business and economics and applying them to the measurement of social value, probably to make it more rigorous. For example, the SROI uses commercial discount rates to estimate how much good an action will achieve in future years. However, as Mulgan (2010) pointed out, the recent collapse of important profit companies is proof that even such seemingly objective metrics as profit are not always as reliable as they appear to be.

Perceiving the adoption of standardized models as being unaffordable from an economic point of view is also a great obstacle to motivating those entrepreneurs who would like to measure social impact. It is an objective limit that is hard to overcome.

One of the issues that have the most impact on the overall cost of evaluation is of course the data-collection process, for which organizations need strong support. SMTs such as the SROI do require a large amount of data, both internal and external (Arvidson et al., 2010; Costa and Pesci, 2016). For example, the generated outcome must be assessed and translated through financial proxies (requiring internal data), and then compared with a baseline to understand the differential change that occurs due to the organization's intervention (requiring external data). In countries such as Italy, there is a lack of intangible infrastructure, such as publicly available datasets, that would greatly reduce the cost of adopting SMTs.

Conclusions: how to bridge the gap?

The measurement of the creation of social value is a topic that is growing in popularity. Several voices are pointing out its importance, especially within those organizations that strive for the achievement of a social mission and thus require appropriate tools to detect the changes they are creating in the lives of their beneficiaries. However, despite the development of SMTs that could help organizations in implementing measurement processes, several barriers to their adoption are still perceived by entrepreneurs. The purpose of this chapter was to explore these barriers and shed light on a set of elements that are worth considering in order to encourage the adoption of SMTs.

This chapter is drawn from the experiences of seven Italian social enterprises, to offer an overview of what are perceived as the main barriers to the adoption of SMTs in measuring the social impact the enterprises generate with their activities. Specifically, the emergent barriers are mostly linked to the idea that the process itself is not necessary, the difficulty of quantifying the qualitative concept of social value, the risk of oversimplifying and generalizing the specificity of each project, the large amount of resources required, and the lack of support in carrying out the process.

These barriers appear to be closely linked to each other. If the practice itself is perceived as being useless and not strategic, it is not worthwhile for an organization to invest all the resources that would be required, especially when there are no external supports or pressures to do so. For those who would be more interested, the lack of shared practices and the perceived inappropriateness of existing tools also have a negative influence on the decision to invest resources.

There seems to be a general scepticism towards the possibility of measuring the social value created by an organization, regardless of the adoption of SMTs. In fact, despite an awareness of the value of the process expressed by the respondents, several limits are perceived as hindering the effective tracking of social value creation. However, this scepticism seems to be due most of all to a lack of an established culture on the topic and of concrete supports to its implementation. It is interesting to note the seeming contradiction between the usefulness and necessity of measuring social value creation. It is always considered to be a *useful* practice that could provide organizations with important benefits; yet it is not seen as a *necessary* practice, leaving room for a number of biases that hamper both its implementation and the search for solutions to overcome them. This reflects a noteworthy gap between theory and practice. Measuring social value is a much-talked-about topic whose benefits have been greatly extolled. The risk is that this interest will remain only theoretical, as the need for implementation – at least in some contexts – does not seem to be equally felt and widespread. This is an initial issue to deal with when investigating the topic of SMTs, as a precondition to their diffusion.

This chapter underlines some other gaps that need to be addressed. The knowledge of existing SMTs has to be promoted. There must also be a focus on the validation of the wide variety of tools that have been developed. For example, the TRASI database (trasi. foundationcenter.org) contains more than 150 models to assess impact and performance against economic, social, and environmental goals. Grieco (2015) collected and analysed 75 models and developed a self-assessment of model categories that could help entrepreneurs determine their needs in assessing social impact and proposing a set of models that actually fit the cases. A deeper knowledge of SMTs could allow an organization to underline their pros and cons as a whole. Paradoxically, the multitude of models from which to choose can be an obstacle to their implementation, as entrepreneurs may struggle to find the best one for their organization. Existing SMTs range from simple to complex, from general to specific. Enhancing knowledge of them also allows the trade-off between comparability and specificity to be overcome. A "one-size-fits-all" model can devalue an organization's specific features; yet the development of approaches that are tailored to each unique situation is unthinkable, and is directly related to barriers such as a lack of benchmarks and resources. However, the perception of SMTs as being resource-consuming might be mitigated as organizations can choose the model that best matches with their available resources. In particular, as pointed out by Costa and Pesci (2016), a participatory process should be promoted, inviting stakeholders to collaborate with the organization in the selection of the most suitable model to adopt and in the validation of the information included in the reports. This is mostly to overcome the risk that organizations may opportunistically select SMTs with the sole purpose of demonstrating higher levels of impact. Furthermore, promoting the culture about the topic goes along with supporting its implementation, as well as through the development and dissemination of guidelines and macro-indications that are often asked for by the organizations themselves.

This research has the purpose of identifying the barriers to the adoption of SMTs in practitioners' views. It has the potential to shed light on some gaps that need to be overcome to foster the practice. Nevertheless, it also presents limitations, most of all because the adopted methodology hampers by its nature the possibility of generalizing the achieved results. On the other hand, it opens interesting avenues for future research on the topic, whereby the identified barriers can be confirmed with quantitative analysis, and investigated in relation with the conditions of the specific contexts in which they emerge.

Notes

1 It is important to note that for the specificities of the law on social entrepreneurship, Italian SEs are a set of organizations that differ a great deal among each other in terms of legal form, size, industry, and mission. For this reason, it was necessary to apply some selection criteria, to ensure the uniformity among the cases and the consistency with the purpose of the research.

2 Even though, as aforementioned, SMTs can also include single indicators, in performing the analysis this term has been used to refer to frameworks and methods as these allow us to carry out a complete impact measurement programme.

References

André, K., and Pache, A.-C. (2014). From caring entrepreneur to caring enterprise: addressing the ethical challenges of scaling up social enterprises. *Journal of Business Ethics*. doi:10.1007/s10551-014-2445-8.

Andreoni, J. (1990). Impure altruism and donations to public goods: a theory of warm-glow giving. *The Economic Journal*, 100(401), 464–477.

Arce-Gomez, A., Donovan, J. D., and Bedggood, R. E. (2015). Social impact assessments: developing a consolidated conceptual framework. *Environmental Impact Assessment Review*, 50, 85–94.

Arvidson, M., Lyon, F., McKay, S., and Moro, D. (2010). *The ambitions and challenges of SROI*. Middlesex University, London.

Ashoka. (2013). How do you know when you've revolutionized an industry? *Ashoka's approach to assessing impact*. https://www.ashoka.org/files/2013-Impact-Study-FINAL-web.pdf.

Baron, R. A. (2007). Behavioral and cognitive factors in entrepreneurship: entrepreneurs as the active element in new venture creation. *Strategic Entrepreneurship Journal*, 1(1–2), 167–182.

Barraket, J., and Yousefpour, N. (2013). Evaluation and social impact measurement amongst small to medium social enterprises: process, purpose and value. *Australian Journal of Public Administration*, 72(4), 447–458.

Bucacioc, A. (2015). Social enterprises: from potential to impact. *The Annals of the University of Oradea. Economic Sciences*, XXIV(1), 408–412.

Burdge, R. J. (2003). The practice of social impact assessment – background. *Impact Assessment and Project Appraisal*, 21(2), 84–88.

Clark, C., Rosenzweig, W., Long D., and Olsen, S. (2004). Double bottom line project report: assessing social impact in double bottom line ventures. http://www.riseproject.org/DBL_Methods_Catalog.pdf.

Clifford, J., Markey, K., and N. Malpani (2013). *Measuring Social Impact in Social Enterprise: The State of Thought and Practice in the UK*. London: E3M.

Costa, E., and Pesci, C. (2016). Social impact measurement: why do stakeholders matter? *Sustainability Accounting, Management and Policy Journal*, 7(1), 99–124.

Donegani, C. P., McKay, S., and Moro, D. (2012). A dimming of the "warm glow"? Are nonprofit workers in the UK still more satisfied with their jobs than other workers? *Advances in the Economic Analysis of Participatory and Labor-Managed Firms*, 13, 313–342.

Ebrahim, A., and Rangan, V. K. (2010). The limits of non profit impact: a contingency framework for measuring social performance (No. 10-099). Harvard Business School.

Epstein, M., and Yuthas, K. (2014). *Measuring and Improving Social Impacts: A Guide for Nonprofits, Companies, and Impact Investors*. San Francisco, CA: Berrett-Koehler Publishers.

Fondazione Sodalitas (2014). Come le organizzazioni Nonprofit valutano l'impatto delle proprie attività. http://www.sodalitas.it/conoscere/ricerche/come-le-organizzazioni-nonprofit-valutano-l%E2%80%99impatto-delle-proprie-attivita

GECES Subgroup on Impact Measurement (2014). Proposed approaches to social impact measurement in European Commission legislation and in practice relating to: EuSEF and the EaSI, European Commission.

Grieco, C. (2015). *Assessing Social Impact of Social Enterprises: Does One Size Really Fit All?* Berlin: Springer International Publishing.

Grieco, C., Michelini, L., and Iasevoli, G. (2015). Measuring value creation in social enterprises: a cluster analysis of social impact assessment models. *Nonprofit and Voluntary Sector Quarterly*, 44(6), 1173–1193.

Hehenberger, L., Harling, A., and Scholten, P. (2013). *Practical Guide to Measuring and Managing Impact*. European Venture Philanthropy Association.

Hoogendoorn, B. (2011). *Social Entrepreneurship in the Modern Economy: Warm Glow, Cold Feet*. Rotterdam: Erasmus University Rotterdam.

Kumar, V., Aaker, A. D., and Day, G. S. (1997). *Essentials of Marketing Research*. New York: John Wiley.

Liket, K. C., and Maas, K. (2015) Non-profit organizational effectiveness: analysis of best practices. *Non-Profit and Voluntary Sector Quarterly*, 44(2), 268–296. Doi: 10.1177/0899764013510064.

Maas, K., and Grieco, C. (2017). Distinguishing game changers from boastful charlatans: which social enterprises measure their impact? *Journal of Social Entrepreneurship*, 8(1), 110–128.

Maas, K., and Liket, K. (2011). Social impact measurement: classification of methods. *Environmental Management Accounting and Supply Chain Management, Eco-Efficiency in Industry and Science*, 27, 171–202.

Mair, J., Battilana, J., and Cardenas, J. (2012). Organizing for society: a typology of social entrepreneuring models. *Journal of Business Ethics*, 111(3), 353–373.

Mason J. (2002). *Qualitative Researching*, 2nd edition. London: Sage.

Montecchia, A., Giordano, F., and Grieco, C. (2016). Communicating CSR: integrated approach or selfie? Evidence from the Milan stock exchange. *Journal of Cleaner Production*, 136, 42–52.

Mulgan, G. (2010). Measuring social value. *Stanford Social Innovation Review*, 8(3), 38–43.

Nicholls, A. (2009). We do good things, don't we? Blended value accounting in social entrepreneurship. *Accounting, Organizations and Society*, 34 (6–7), 755–769.

Nicholls, A., and Cho, A. H. (2008). Social entrepreneurship: the structuration of a field. *Social Entrepreneurship: New Models of Sustainable Social Change*, 99–118.

Nicholls, J. (2007). Why measuring and communicating social value can help social enterprise become more competitive, Cabine Office, Office of the Third Sector. http://evpa.eu.com/wp-content/uploads/2010/09/Why-measuring-and-communicating-social-value-can-help-social-enterprise-become-more-competitive1.pdf.

OECD (2010). SMEs, entrepreneurship and innovation. http://www.oecd.org/document/16/0,3746,en_2649_33956792_44938128_1_1_1_1,00.html.

OECD (2015). Policy Brief on social impact measurement for social enterprises http://www.oecd.org/industry/Policy-Brief-social-impact.pdf.

Olsen S., and Galimidi, B. (2009). Managing social and environmental impact: a new discipline for a new economy. *Brown Journal of World Affairs*, 15(2), 43–56.

Olsen, S., and Nicholls, J. (2005). *A Framework for Approaches to SROI*. University of California, Berkeley, 1–35.

Patton, M. Q. (2002). *Qualitative Research and Evaluation Methods*, 3rd edition, Thousand Oaks, CA: Sage.

Porter, M. E., Hills, G., Pfitzer, M., Patscheke, S., and Hawkins, E. (2012). Measuring shared value: how to unlock value by linking social and business results. *FSG*. http://www.fsg.org/Portals/0/Uploads/Documents/PDF/Measuring_Shared_Value.pdf.

Ruttman, R. (2012). New ways to invest for social and environmental impact. In R. Ruttman, P. Elmer, G. Fleming, and L. Hemrika (Eds.), *Investing for Impact: How Social Entrepreneurship Is Redefining the Meaning of Return* (pp. 4–9). Zurich, Switzerland: Credit Suisse Research. http://www.weforum.org/pdf/schwabfound/Investing_for_Impact.pdf.

Wainwright, S. (2002). *Measuring Impact: A Guide to Resources*. London: NCVO Publications.

Weerawardena, J., and Mort, G. S. (2006). Investigating social entrepreneurship: a multidimensional model. *Journal of World Business*, 41(1), 21–35.

Yin, R. (2003). *Case Study Research: Design and Methods*. London: Sage Publications, 5, 11.

Zappalà, G., and Lyons, M. (2009). Recent approaches to measuring social impact in the third sector: an overview, Centre for Social Impact, Background Paper, n. 5 http://www.csi.edu.au/assets/assetdoc/b20aada17ffad8f7/V2%20CSI%20Background%20Paper%20No%205%20%20Approaches%20to%20measuring%20social%20impact.pdf. Accessed October 2013.

Part 2

Accounting, measurement, performance, and diffusion of social value

2.1 The sustainability balanced scorecard

An introduction to the SBSC and its links to accounting and reporting

Florian Lüdeke-Freund and Stefan Schaltegger

The SBSC: a tool for integrated sustainability management

The balanced scorecard (BSC) was developed in the early 1990s as a reaction to one-sided, short-term, and past-oriented management practices that mainly relied on quantitative performance measurement and tended to overemphasize purely financial indicators (Cooper et al. 2017; Johnson & Kaplan 1987; Kaplan & Norton 1992). Measurement systems influence managers' and employees' behaviour and can even give misleading signals. Thus, management must rely not only on information like return-on-investment or earnings per share but also on more operational measures (e.g., cycle times, defect rates). Consequently, the BSC was introduced as an alternative concept of performance measurement and management that balances financial measures (results from past activities) and operational measures (drivers of future performance) and helps in controlling for corporate performance in several areas simultaneously. The crucial point is that these operational measures can have different characteristics: quantitative and qualitative, and financial and non-financial.

For this reason, scholars from the field of sustainability management identified the BSC as a promising starting point for the development of integrated sustainability performance measurement and management approaches. Concepts of so-called sustainability balanced scorecards (SBSC) were developed, aiming at the integration of non-monetary, qualitative, and sometimes 'soft' factors related to environmental and social issues (Hansen & Schaltegger 2016, 2017). The most challenging task of corporate sustainability management is to contribute to sustainable development by addressing the environmental, social, and economic dimensions of sustainability simultaneously (Baumgartner & Rauter 2017; Schaltegger & Burritt 2005). The scorecard's ability to integrate different perspectives on business and different kinds of information is seen as an opportunity to enable mainstream businesses to tackle the challenge of corporate sustainability (Hansen & Schaltegger 2016).

Therefore, this chapter summarizes the theoretical and conceptual foundations of SBSCs, which have been published and developed further over the past fifteen years. We are building on different theoretical, conceptual, and case study publications to provide a concise overview of the most important SBSC basics. This chapter also includes a summary of an early, yet comprehensive and insightful case study on Hamburg Airport (Diaz Guerrero et al. 2002), which has been extended and adapted for the purposes of this chapter. Finally, some general relationships between SBSCs and performance measurement and reporting are discussed, before concluding with a brief summary.

The BSC concept

The BSC concept is based on the assumption that competitive advantages are not only derived from quantifiable 'hard facts' referring primarily to the efficient use of fixed capital, but also rather 'soft' and intangible assets like intellectual property, employees' knowledge and abilities, or customer relationships have to be measured and managed. These factors are becoming increasingly important sources of competitive advantages and long-term economic success in the post-industrial information age (Cooper et al. 2017; Kaplan & Norton 1992, 1996a, 2000). When developing the BSC and related concepts like the 'strategy map', Kaplan and Norton were influenced by alternative topics, like the increasing relevance of digital data, information technologies, new challenges for organizational learning, and the re-organization of the industrial business model. Thus, to better cope with soft factors and intangible assets, the BSC performance measurement concept was developed to integrate financial and non-financial as well as quantitative and qualitative information – a feature that is crucial for developing sustainability balanced scorecards.

The basic BSC perspectives

In its default layout, the BSC is based on four perspectives, which are derived from the explicitly formulated strategy of a business unit (if a firm is rather small and no unit-level strategies exist, the BSC can also be derived from a firm-level strategy; cf. Figge et al. 2002b).

- *Financial perspective*: In the hierarchical BSC concept, all perspectives are directed towards finances. Objectives and measures refer to profitability (e.g., operating income, return-on-capital-employed, economic value-added), sales growth, shareholder value, or cash flow generation. The guiding question for the financial perspective is: 'To succeed financially, how should we appear to our shareholders?' (Kaplan & Norton, 1996a, 9).
- *Customer perspective*: This perspective helps to identify current and future market segments and customers. Customers are mainly concerned about time, quality, service, and cost of offerings. The task is to evaluate what they really value, today and in the future, and translate this into value propositions that lead to customer satisfaction and retention. This perspective asks: 'To achieve our vision, how should we appear to our customers?' (Kaplan & Norton 1996a, 9).
- *Internal business process perspective*: Here, the focus is on the internal value-chain. It defines what the company must do to provide attractive customer value propositions and realize an adequate financial performance for shareholders. Critical innovation and operations processes are identified, referring to product design and development, manufacturing, marketing, and post-sale service. The question is: 'To satisfy our shareholders and customers, what business processes must we excel at?' (Kaplan & Norton 1996a, 9).
- *Innovation and learning perspective*: Global competition and changing business environments require companies to innovate, improve, and learn continuously to offer compelling value propositions and better processes. The ability of organizational learning is based, for example, on employees, IT systems, and organizational quality. This infrastructure is crucial for moulding a company into a learning organization. It asks: 'To achieve our vision, how will we sustain our ability to change and improve?' (Kaplan & Norton 1996a, 9).

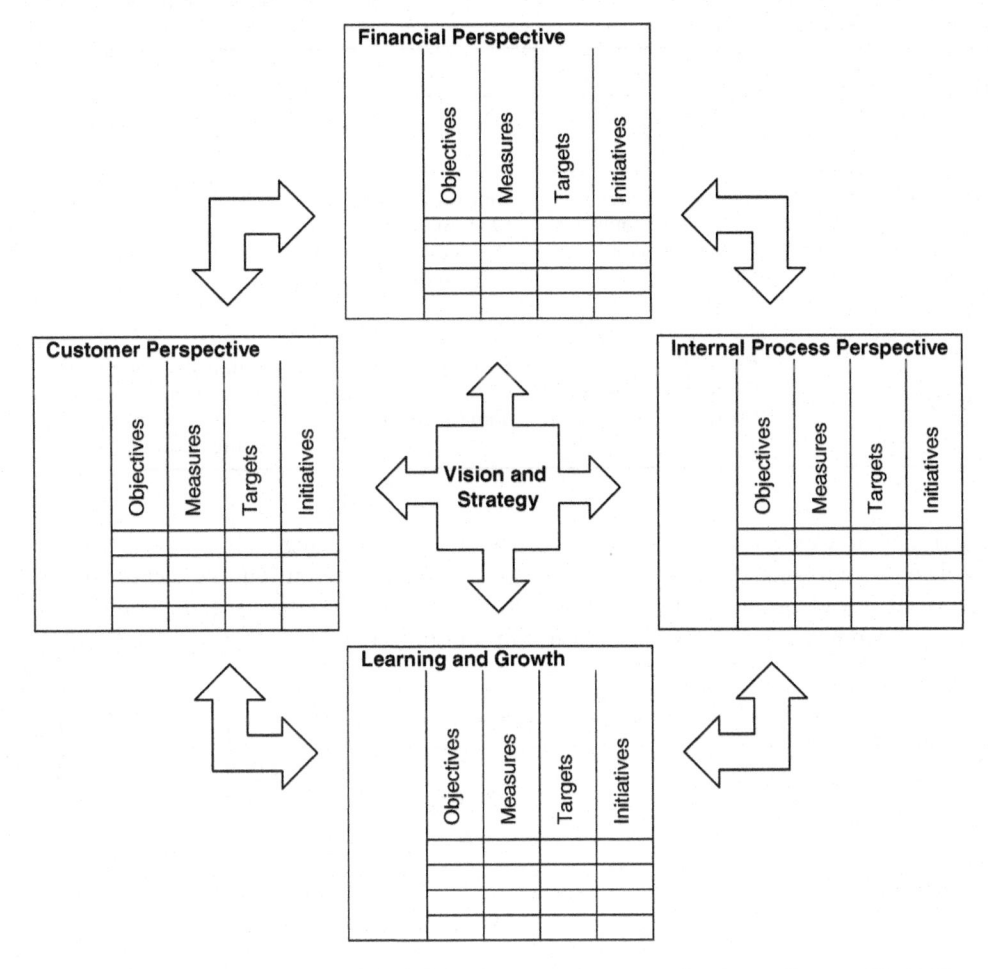

Figure 2.1.1 Basic perspectives of the balanced scorecard concept (Kaplan & Norton 1996a, 9)

Figure 2.1.1 displays the four basic perspectives. Their hierarchical relationships become obvious when the role of indicators and causal chains is described.

BSC indicators and causal chains

The BSC process starts from a company's vision and strategy, which are translated into objectives, measures, targets, and initiatives for every perspective. Here, objectives and measures are crucial as these are operationalized as lagging indicators (outcome measures) and leading indicators (performance drivers) (Kaplan & Norton 1996a). *Lagging indicators* refer to the long-term strategic objectives in every perspective and are formulated for every strategic core issue in the respective area. These indicators are used to define and control for the degree of objective achievement. Table 2.1.1 shows generic categories of lagging indicators, which are suitable for any strategic unit as proposed by Kaplan and Norton. *Leading indicators* define how the strategic objectives – as expressed by the

Table 2.1.1 Examples of generic categories of lagging and leading indicators (cf. Kaplan & Norton 1996a)

Lagging indicators

Financial perspective	*Customer perspective*	*Process perspective*	*Learning and growth perspective*
Revenue growth	Market share	Innovation process	Employee retention
Productivity growth	Customer acquisition	Operations process	Employee productivity
Asset utilization	Customer retention	Post-sale service	Employee satisfaction
	Customer satisfaction	process	
	Customer profitability		
Leading indicators			
–	Product attributes	Cost indicators	Employee potentials
	Customer relationship	Quality indicators	Technical
	Image and reputation	Time indicators	infrastructure
			Climate for action

lagging indicators – should be realized. In relation to the strategic objectives that were broken down to lagging indicators, the main performance drivers must be identified and managed as leading indicators. These are usually based on very firm specific competencies and competitive advantages, and can thus not be generalized. Nevertheless, Kaplan

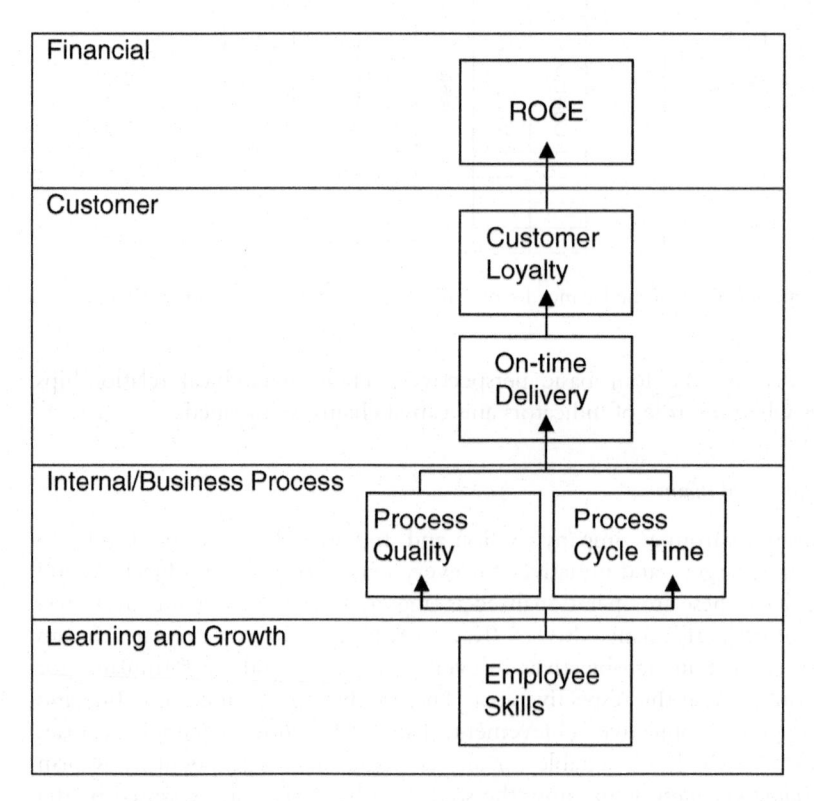

Figure 2.1.2 Example of a cause-and-effect chain in a simple strategy map (Kaplan & Norton 1996a, 31)

and Norton also propose some categories (Table 2.1.1). At least, based on the identification of strategic objectives and measures, concrete operative *targets* and *initiatives* are defined to guarantee for the operational realization of the broken-down strategy.

In addition to the four perspectives and their indicators, *cause-and-effect relationships* between perspectives, objectives, and measures are another conceptual element of the BSC (Kaplan & Norton 1996a, 2000, 2004). They make the BSC more than a loose collection of indicators. Figure 2.1.2 shows the four perspectives in their hierarchical order and some basic causal relationships. These relationships are hypotheses about cause and effect in accordance with the strategy. In turn, any strategy itself is a set of hypotheses (Kaplan & Norton 1996a). Often, these cause-and-effect chains are not directly 'visible' – and thus not manageable.

Given that return-on-capital-employed (ROCE) is a scorecard measure (lagging indicator) to be optimized in the financial perspective (Figure 2.1.2), one must identify causal relationships throughout the complete BSC that affect this measure. The standard example of Kaplan and Norton then identifies customer loyalty as a performance driver (leading indicator) for increased sales, which in turn are a lever for ROCE (Kaplan & Norton 1996a). The question here is, what leads to increased customer loyalty? On-time delivery may be one reason, that is, on-time delivery is identified as a leading indicator in the customer perspective that drives loyalty as a lagging indicator in this relationship. When working with the concept of lagging and leading indicators, this special feature must be acknowledged: a lagging indicator of a lower perspective is concurrently a leading indicator for a higher perspective. Therefore, the development of a BSC results in an interlinked, hierarchically structured system directed towards the financial perspective.

From BSC to SBSC

Twenty years after Kaplan and Norton identified reasons for the development of their concept, different types of significant changes and challenges confront entrepreneurs and managers. The greatest challenge of coming decades is to realize corporate sustainability as a necessary contribution to sustainable development of the economy and society (cf. Baumgartner & Rauter 2017; Burritt & Schaltegger 2010; Schaltegger & Burritt 2005; Schaltegger 2010). Companies are moving from challenges of disrupting information technologies to challenges of corporate sustainability. Accordingly, management research tries to support and guide entrepreneurs and managers through the development of more appropriate management instruments, concepts, and systems. As discussed above, the BSC can integrate soft, intangible, and qualitative aspects, but nevertheless it has to be developed further to become an integrated system of corporate sustainability management. In this context, research brought about different approaches to developing SBSCs to integrate sustainability aspects into corporate performance measurement and management systems (e.g., Bieker & Waxenberger 2002; Epstein & Wisner 2001; Figge et al. 2002a, 2002b; Maas et al. 2016; Schaltegger & Wagner 2006a).

From a methodical point of view, the main question is where and how to integrate environmental and social aspects of sustainability. Hansen identifies four basic approaches in the literature (Hansen 2010, 89f.):

- integrating environmental and social aspects into the four standard perspectives,
- adding further perspectives to the standard BSC layout to take up sustainability issues,
- changing the original hierarchy and replacing the financial perspective with a sustainability perspective,
- adding further perspectives to guide the financial perspective at the top.

Figge et al. (2002a, 2002b) and Schaltegger and Dyllick (2002) developed a comprehensive SBSC concept comprising different *methods of integrating sustainability aspects* and
a complete *process of formulating a SBSC*. These will be described in the following sections (the variety of potential resulting SBSC architectures has recently been reviewed in
Hansen & Schaltegger 2016).

Integrating sustainability aspects

SBSCs can be developed by either subsumption of environmental and social aspects to
the basic BSC perspectives and/or the introduction of an additional non-market perspective (Schaltegger & Dyllick 2002; Figge et al. 2002). Moreover, these two variants
can be complemented by the deduction of an extra environmental and social scorecard
from an existing BSC. This method is an optional step which can only complement
subsumption or an additional perspective. Table 2.1.2 summarizes these methods.

  Subsumption requires the identification of environmental and social aspects' relevance
for the business unit's strategy and the definition of according strategic objectives and
performance drivers. The resulting lagging and leading indicators, as well as targets and
initiatives, then must be integrated into the existing four perspectives. An advantage is the
direct integration into cause-and-effect chains and orientation towards superior financial
objectives. This method requires environmental and social aspects to be previously incorporated in the market system – the basic four perspectives do not go beyond the market
mechanism, that is, market prices and transactions (Figge et al. 2002b). However, most
sustainability aspects are treated as externalities, that is, they are not reflected in market
prices and transactions. Strategically relevant issues are often neglected as they appear
in the socio-cultural or legal sphere and are thus not realized as strategic objectives or

Table 2.1.2 Methods of developing an SBSC (see Figge et al. 2002a, 2002b; Schaltegger &
Dyllick 2002)

Method	Approach
Subsumption – integration into four basic perspectives (optional first step)	Environmental and social aspects are subsumed under the existing four perspectives, lagging and leading indicators, targets and measures. Captures strategically relevant environmental and social aspects that are already integrated in the market system.
Addition – formulation of a fifth, non-market perspective (optional first step)	Strategically relevant but not market-integrated environmental and social aspects are included in an additional non-market perspective. This refers to aspects that are of strategic relevance and influence a firm's success but are not reflected in the four basic perspectives. Therefore, lagging and leading indicators, and targets and initiatives, have to be formulated and linked towards the financial perspective.
Deduction – development of an extra sustainability scorecard (optional second step)	Deduction of a derived environmental and social scorecard. Optional second step that is only possible as an extension of subsumption or addition. Used to coordinate, organize, and further differentiate environmental and social aspects due to their strategic relevance and position in the cause-and-effect chains.

performance drivers (cf. Schaltegger & Burritt 2005). Therefore, Figge et al. propose the introduction of a fifth non-market perspective (*addition*). Non-financial, environmental, and/or social aspects with strategic influence on the business unit's performance – either directly via the financial perspective, or indirectly through the other perspectives – are included in the non-market perspective (Figure 2.1.3). The addition of an explicit non-market perspective must be justified through environmental and social aspects from outside the market system that influence the implementation and execution of the respective business unit's strategy. The task for sustainability management then is to identify formerly unrecognized influences from outside the market. The first two methods are not mutually exclusive; they can be combined. The third method, *deduction* of an environmental and/or social scorecard, is only possible as an extension of the first two methods. Subsumption

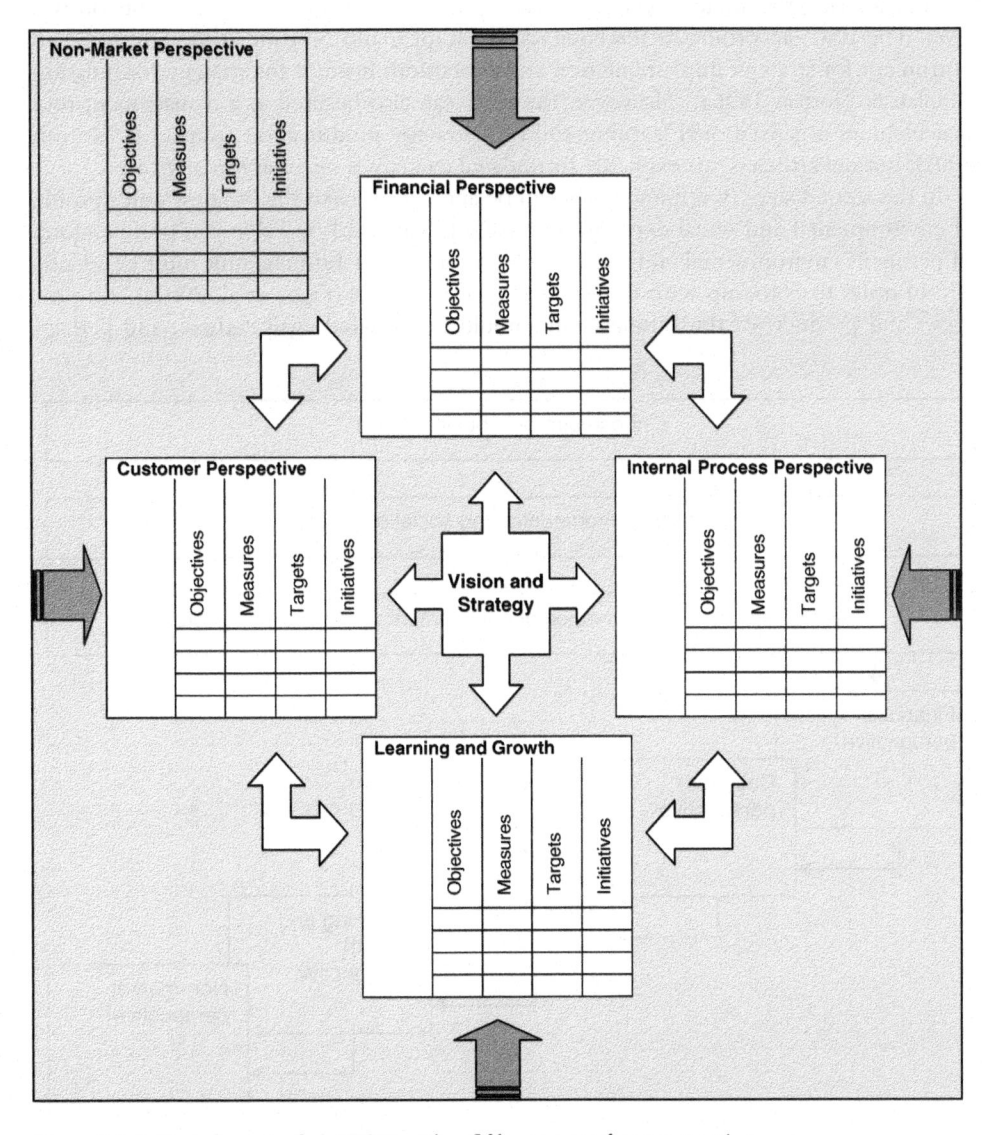

Figure 2.1.3 Basic layout of an SBSC with a fifth, non-market perspective

and addition are the basic methods to identify and formulate sustainability aspects and to enable their integration and management into the core BSC cause-and-effect chains. A deduced sustainability scorecard can then be used for more explicit and deepened management of the identified environmental and social issues regarding the objectives of economic performance as defined in the financial perspective.

Formulating the SBSC

The process of formulating a SBSC takes three steps: (1) choosing the strategic business unit for which the scorecard shall be developed; (2) identification of environmental and social aspects relevant to this unit; (3) determination of these aspects' relevance for the unit's strategy (Schaltegger & Dyllick 2002).

For choosing the strategic business unit, it is important that a strategy exists on this level. The BSC, according to the basic idea of Kaplan and Norton, is thought to be an instrument for strategy implementation and execution, but not for strategy formulation (Kaplan & Norton 1996a). However, the BSC can also be used as a management tool that includes organizational learning and thus strategy modification (Kaplan & Norton 2001); but nevertheless, an explicitly formulated strategy is necessary in any case.

In the second step, two frameworks can be applied to make the business unit's profile of environmental and social exposure transparent (Table 2.1.3, Table 2.1.4). Therefore, all pertinent environmental and social interventions of the business unit must be identified in order to come up with those of strategic relevance (Figge et al. 2002a). All processes and products of the business unit should be checked against these, and perhaps

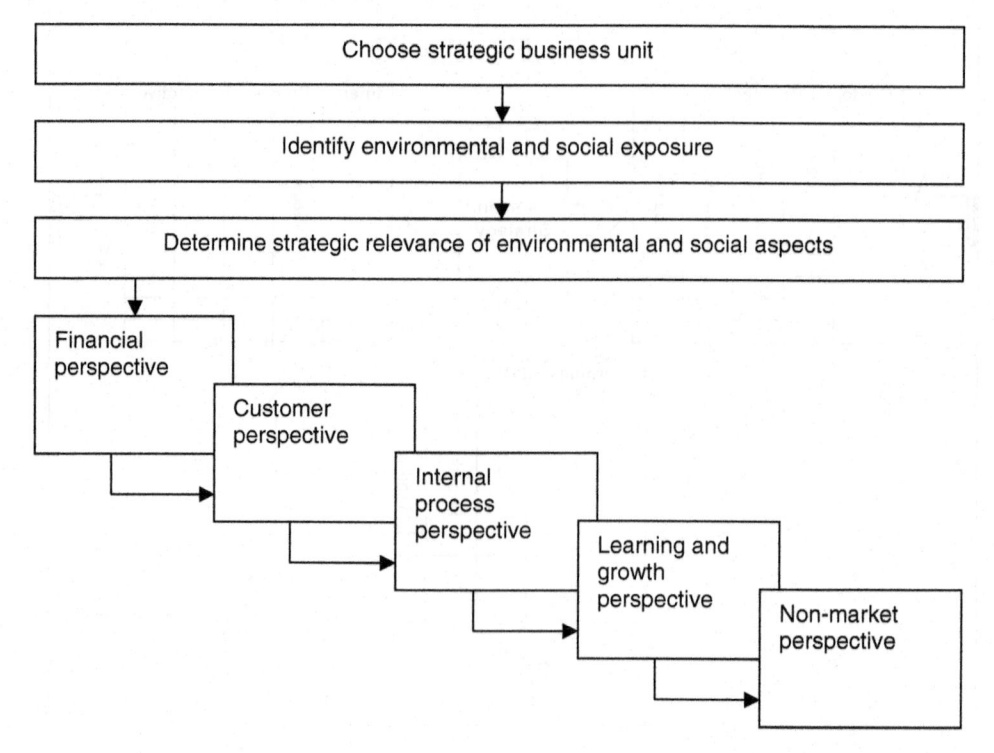

Figure 2.1.4 Process and steps of formulating an SBSC (Figge et al. 2002b; Schaltegger 2004)

further, environmental aspects to develop the profile of environmental exposure, which is a prerequisite for assessing its strategic relevance in step three. The template for the identification of the social exposure proposes to differentiate between direct and indirect stakeholders. The template in Table 2.1.4 follows a different approach than the one used for environmental interventions. The latter can be categorized according to objective scientific classifications, whereas social interventions are judged subjectively from the relevant actors' points of view. Thus, it seems appropriate not to pre-classify interventions and their effects, but to start from stakeholders' perspectives (e.g., Freeman et al. 2010), where direct and indirect stakeholders can be distinguished on the company and societal level, and then to define their individual claims and issues (Table 2.1.4). Direct stakeholders are connected to the business unit through direct material resource exchange flows; indirect stakeholders are not linked in this way, but have different interests that are communicated, for example by NGOs, the media, or neighbours (cf. Spitzeck & Hansen 2010).

The third step is the determination of the environmental and social aspects' relevance for strategy implementation and execution. As described above, the BSC process aims at identifying and causally linking strategic objectives and indicators. According to Figure 2.1.4, this is done in a cascade-like process from the financial perspective down to the non-market perspective. This process guarantees for aligning sustainability aspects, both from market and non-market spheres, towards long-term economic success. The strategic relevance of sustainability objectives and indicators can be differentiated into three qualities (Figge et al. 2002b; Schaltegger 2004):

- Environmental and social aspects are *strategic core issues* for which *lagging indicators* can be defined; the question to be answered is: 'Does the environmental or social aspect represent a strategic core issue for the business strategy of our business unit?'
- Sustainability aspects might also have the quality of *performance drivers* (Schaltegger et al. 2012); thus, *leading indicators* have to be developed: 'Does the environmental or social aspect contribute significantly to a strategic core issue and, therefore, represent a performance driver for the business unit?'
- If sustainability aspects cannot be identified as strategic core issues or performance drivers, they might be *hygienic factors*. That is, factors that must be managed to successfully execute a business strategy, but do not bring about any competitive advantage. Thus, hygienic factors and their *diagnostic indicators* are not included in the scorecard: 'Is the environmental or social aspect simply a hygienic factor, which necessarily has to be managed well, but leads to no particular strategic or competitive advantage?'

Table 2.1.3 Template for the identification of the environmental exposure (Hahn et al. 2002)

Environmental exposure of a business unit	
Type of environmental intervention	*Business unit specific occurrence*
Emissions (to air, water, and soil)	. . .
Waste	. . .
Materials input/materials intensity	. . .
Energy intensity	. . .
Noise and vibrations	. . .
Waste heat	. . .
Radiation	. . .
Direct interventions on nature and landscape	. . .

Table 2.1.4 Template for the identification of the social exposure (Hahn et al. 2002)

Social exposure of a business unit

Direct stakeholders				Indirect stakeholders			
Internal	*Along the value chain*	*In the local community*	*Societal*	*Internal*	*Along the value chain*	*In the local community*	*Societal*
particular stakeholder group	*particular stakeholder group*	*particular stakeholder group*	*particular stakeholder group*	*particular stakeholder group*	*particular stakeholder group*	*particular stakeholder group*	*particular stakeholder group*
. . .	. . .	. . .	. . .	. . .	. . .	. . .	. . .
claim/issue	*claim/issue*	*claim/issue*	*claim/issue*	*claim/issue*	*claim/issue*	*claim/issue*	*claim/issue*
. . .	. . .	. . .	. . .	. . .	. . .	. . .	. . .

Table 2.1.5 Template for the determination of environmental and social aspects' strategic relevance (Hahn et al. 2002; Figge et al. 2002a)

| | Environmental exposure | | | | | | | | Social exposure | | | | | | | |
| | | | | | | | | | Direct stakeholders | | | | Indirect stakeholders | | | |
	Emissions	Waste	Material input / intensity	Energy intensity	Noise and vibrations	Waste heat	Radiation	Land use	Internal	Along the value chain	In the local community	Societal	Internal	Along the value chain	In the local community	Societal
Strategic core issues #1																
#2																
#n																
Performance drivers #1																
#2																
#n																

The guiding questions from the above list can be used to determine the strategic relevance of sustainability issues. To bring order to the task of developing lagging and leading indicators for environmental and social issues and to align this task with the BSC process (Figure 2.1.4), Figge et al. (2002) propose another template that builds on the aforementioned templates. Table 2.1.5 suggests a concept of how to identify the environmental and social exposure (main columns), define classes of environmental interventions and stakeholders' issues and claims (sub-columns), and determines associated lagging and leading indicators (rows of strategic core issues and performance drivers).

After going through the four perspectives and related environmental and social strategic core issues and performance drivers, aspects that are not subject to the market mechanism but have a significant influence on the business unit's strategy implementation and execution must be considered. Therefore, non-market mechanisms must be identified and connected to the unit's strategic economic objectives. Finally, based on the template in Table 2.1.5, environmental and social strategic core issues and performance drivers can thus be integrated into conventional or additional non-market perspectives. As can be seen from Figure 2.1.3, Figge et al. (2002b) and Schaltegger and Dyllick (2002) consider the non-market perspective as a frame that embeds the other scorecard perspectives. Based on a thorough literature review, Hansen and Schaltegger (2016, 2017) discuss further sustainability-related perspectives and techniques of integrating these within the basic BSC concept in more detail.

Having described possible methods of integrating environmental and social aspects into the basic BSC layout (Table 2.1.2) and the complete SBSC process (Figure 2.1.4), the following section introduces the case of Hamburg Airport Corporation to illustrate how the strategic relevance of specific environmental and social aspects can be evaluated in practice, and how a non-market perspective can be derived from these insights. Therefore, the next section presents the results of a practical SBSC at Hamburg Airport Corporation. Additionally, another instrument developed by Kaplan and Norton will be applied in the following section: the strategy map (Kaplan & Norton 2000, 2004).

Case: SBSC development at Hamburg Airport Corporation

This section gives an overview of the results produced during a SBSC project with Hamburg Airport Corporation (see Diaz Guerrero 2002; Diaz Guerrero et al. 2002; Schaltegger & Wagner 2006a, for further details). This case is used to illustrate some of the aforementioned concepts. An overview of more recent research and cases can be found in the review by Hansen and Schaltegger (2016).

Profile of Hamburg Airport Corporation

Hamburg Airport Corporation is the operator of one of Germany's biggest airports and is responsible for both aviation and non-aviation businesses, from providing apron and runway services to managing shopping malls. One of the airport's special characteristics is its location: with only a nine-kilometre distance to Hamburg's city centre, it is located amidst the town's north-western residential areas, surrounded by various districts. Hamburg Airport formulated a detailed vision and strategy for its future development (cf. Diaz Guerrero et al. 2002): it strives for outstanding aviation and non-aviation businesses and superior customer-oriented air travel services. Their aspiration is to connect northern Germany with the world. Regarding their employees, the vision promotes motivation, team spirit, and cooperation, while being a fair and responsible partner in business and for the broader Hamburg region. Economic success and environmental protection must not exclude each other. Thus, Hamburg Airport has an environmental management system (EMS). With its explicitly formulated vision and strategy, and its environmental awareness Hamburg Airport and the project team could derive a SBSC. Table 2.1.6 shows the strategic core issues and performance drivers that were identified during this process. Therefore, the steps outlined in Figure 2.1.4 were taken; the strategic business unit was the corporate level of Hamburg Airport Corporation, where the business is managed from the top, down to the divisions and subsidiaries. Its environmental and social exposure was mainly identified through its certified EMS. The primary task of the SBSC thus was to determine and communicate specific strategic aspects of this exposure.

The non-market perspective: location-related aspects

In 2000, Hamburg Airport started its 'HAM 21' development programme. More than 350 million Euros were invested until 2008 to modernize and extend the existing infrastructure and offerings. Increased competitiveness as an international airport was the main objective – but also environmental and social challenges related to local interventions at the airport site and its neighbourhood such as noise pollution, increased local traffic, waste water treatment, and air pollution had to be managed. These and further aspects needed special attention from a strategic point of view, and thus gave cause for adding a non-market perspective to integrate these and further location-related aspects into the scorecard (Table 2.1.6). Hence, the SBSC of Hamburg Airport was built according to the addition method, and an additional 'location perspective' was added to the basic perspectives because many strategically relevant location aspects could not be taken into the conventional BSC layout (Table 2.1.2 above).

Of highest strategic relevance are the non-market objectives of legitimacy and autonomy of action (Diaz Guerrero et al. 2002). The former is based on good relationships with neighbours through proactive compliance with legal demands and voluntary proactive

Table 2.1.6 Strategic core aspects and performance drivers of Hamburg Airport (based on Diaz Guerrero et al. 2002; Schaltegger & Wagner 2006)

	Financial	Customer	Internal process	Learning and growth	Location
Strategic core aspects (lagging indicators)	High and long-term stable returns and profitability	Expansion of market share in German air travel	Development of new products and services	Entrepreneurial employees	Strengthened role as regional growth driver
			Commercializing of know-how and services		
			High service quality and safety standards	Strengthening the role as reliable and attractive employer	Good relationships with neighbours
			Noise and environmental protection		
	Development of non-aviation business fields (offerings of the airport that are not directly related to air travel)	Increase in customer satisfaction	Development of hub function	Support of employees' engagement and performance through trustful teamwork	Proactive compliance with legal environmental demands
		Competitive price/ performance ration	Development of direct connections		Voluntary definition of proactive standards
			Needs-based airport expansion		Settlement of further regional companies
Performance drivers (leading indicators)	Development of air travel offerings	Expansion of customer-specific service concept 'One-stop shop services'	Excellent environmental management	Active participation of employees in corporate success	Cooperation with other airports and the port of Hamburg
			Passenger-friendly facilities		Optimal air travel offerings for northern Germany and Hamburg
		Support of image and acceptance, establishing the brand 'Hamburg Airport'	Frictionless travel management	Securing and developing attractive jobs	
			Competitive ground services		Support of the regional infrastructure
			Lean and fast processes		

standards (e.g., through suspended aircraft movements at night), while the latter is based on the airport's role as a regional growth driver (which might partly contradict neighbours' needs). Managing these location-related lagging indicators and the associated leading indicators regarding the company's main strategic objectives is the key to maintaining legitimacy and autonomy of action while achieving the main objectives as formulated in the financial perspective.

Hamburg Airport's strategy map

By going through the steps of the SBSC process (Figure 2.1.4), lagging and leading indicators as shown in Table 2.1.6 and their causal relations can be identified. Figure 2.1.5 shows the resulting strategy map of Hamburg Airport. The strategy map concept serves the purpose of connecting the indicators in and across the scorecard's perspectives to make strategically relevant cause-and-effect chains visible and manageable. In this Figure, the location perspective is included as grey background which embeds the four conventional perspectives (see also Figure 2.1.3). According to the SBSC concept, this fifth perspective includes non-market aspects which influence the other perspectives, and thus the objectives of strategy implementation and execution, directly and indirectly (here, in the context of the 'HAM 21' programme) (see Diaz Guerrero 2002; Diaz Guerrero et al. 2002; Schaltegger & Wagner 2006a, for further details).

Going beyond strategy implementation and execution as described in the example of Hamburg Airport, the SBSC can also be used for further tasks of performance

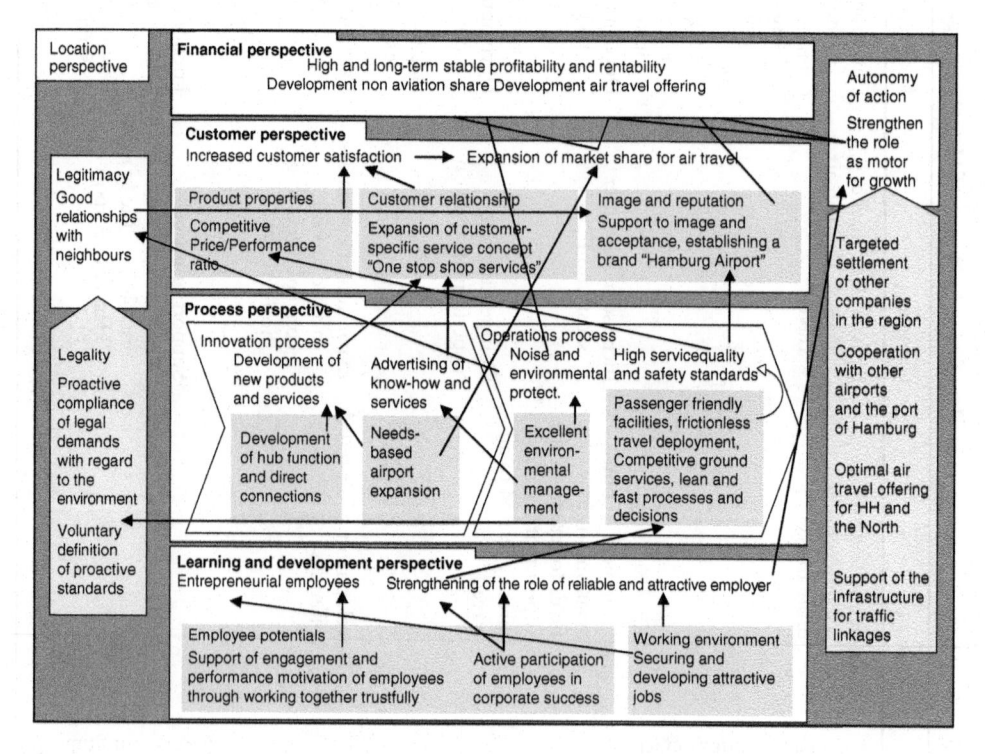

Figure 2.1.5 Strategy map of Hamburg Airport's SBSC (Diaz Guerrero et al. 2002; Schaltegger & Wagner 2006)

measurement, management, and reporting. The following section introduces a framework based on a combination of the SBSC and sustainability accounting and reporting.

Sustainability performance measurement and reporting with the SBSC

The case of Hamburg Airport includes several different interactions between business, the natural environment, and society. Dealing with these interactions is the purpose of sustainability performance measurement and management (Burritt & Schaltegger 2010; Maas et al. 2016). Here, Schaltegger and Wagner (2006a) differentiate three levels: individual sustainability performance indicators, the overall performance measurement system, and the relationships of this system with the external environment. They propose a framework for the measurement system level based on the SBSC, and sustainability

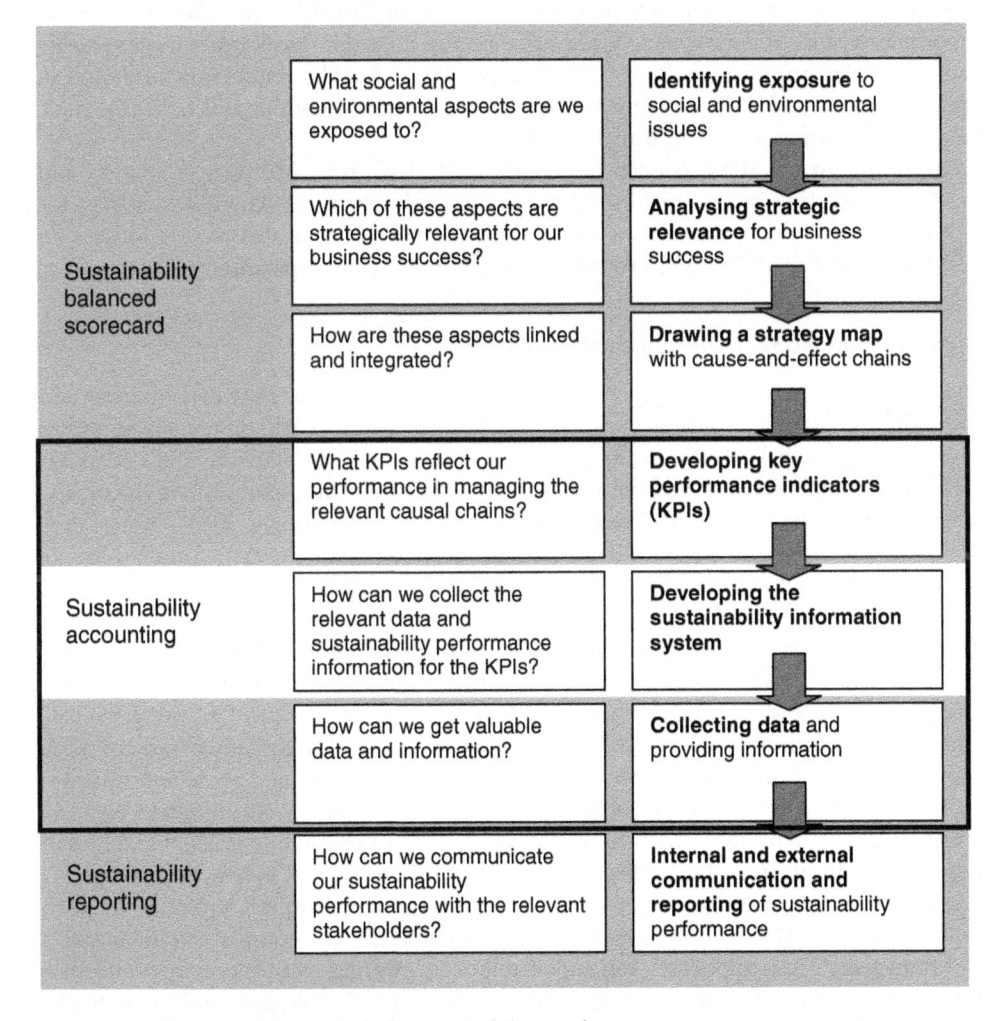

Figure 2.1.6 Integrated framework for sustainability performance measurement, management, and reporting (Schaltegger & Wagner 2006a) (top–down oriented arrows indicate the inside-out perspective of this framework)

accounting and reporting. The idea behind this integrative framework can be described as follows:

> By providing information for strategic management and for reporting purposes, sustainability accounting serves as an important link between the SBSC and reporting. The information requirements are deducted from the Sustainability Balanced Scorecard, collected and analysed with sustainability accounting and communicated externally with sustainability reporting.
>
> (Schaltegger & Wagner 2006a, 10)

The SBSC (to identify strategically relevant information needs), accounting (to generate and process data), and reporting (for internal and external communication) are combined. These three approaches share common tasks and questions. For example, the SBSC and accounting share the question: 'What KPIs [key performance indicators] reflect our performance in managing the relevant causal chains?' Accounting and reporting need to find answers to another common question: 'How can we get valuable data and information?' (Schaltegger & Wagner 2006a, 4). The framework proposed in Figure 2.1.6 identifies those overlaps and provides further questions and tasks that must be addressed by integrative information management.

According to the SBSC concept, the framework starts from a company's strategy and the factors affecting its successful implementation and execution. The relevant steps for developing a SBSC are described above. Thus, the remainder of this section focuses on how to connect the SBSC with sustainability accounting and reporting.

Connecting the SBSC to sustainability accounting

Sustainability accounting deals with three types of relationships between business and sustainability aspects: economic impacts that are environmentally or socially induced, ecological and social impacts from business activities, and simultaneous links between social, environmental, and economic issues that constitute the three dimensions of sustainability (e.g., Baumgartner & Rauter 2017; Schaltegger & Burritt 2005). Whereas in the SBSC process lagging and leading indicators are developed, the function of accounting is to gather and provide the necessary information to properly calculate KPIs. Here, the SBSC process serves not only to determine strategically relevant impacts of environmental and social aspects, but also to support the accounting function of developing and calculating KPIs that reflect the SBSCs causal chains. Consequently, strategic issues interfere with the design of the accounting system (Figure 2.1.6). The greatest challenge at this intersection of the SBSC and accounting is to develop existing accounting approaches further to record, analyse, and report environmental and social information. However, even simple measures of eco-efficiency, such as energy consumption per passenger (e.g., kWh/person) or waste volume in relation to revenue (e.g., kg/€), are often not reported in practice. Regardless whether this is a problem of accounting or reporting, internal information systems need to be adapted to such information requirements to avoid informational satellite systems that are hardly linked to the company's core business and strategies. Using the SBSC and sustainability accounting in an integrative information management system helps strengthen those links. But Schaltegger and Wagner also point to conceptual limitations of this approach: 'Sustainability accounting based on the SBSC is focused on the provision of those strategic and operational indicators which have been identified as key to business success and the creation of shareholder value' (cf. Schaltegger & Wagner 2006a, 9f.). That is, this approach differs from measuring and reporting the overall sustainability performance of a company.

The SBSC and sustainability reporting

Sustainability reporting refers to internal and external communication on corporate sustainability issues. An increasing number of companies use different formats and channels going beyond printed reports to communicate on environmental, social, and occasionally financial issues which are often not included in conventional performance reports. This kind of communication evolved from environmental reporting practices and is now increasingly used to signal transparency and accountability to the public (e.g., Burritt & Schaltegger 2010; Maas et al. 2016). According to the latest KPMG survey of corporate responsibility reporting, climate change, corporate governance, and responsibility in the supply chain are amongst the top issues (KPMG 2015). Sustainability reporting aims to satisfy the information needs of diverse stakeholders such as NGOs, the media, legislative bodies, shareholders, and employees: 'Among the main reasons for companies to publish a sustainability report are to communicate with stakeholders about non-market issues, to secure or increase legitimacy, credibility and corporate reputation and to motivate employees to deal with sustainability issues and benchmarking' (Schaltegger & Wagner 2006a). The major challenge lies in the multitude of addressees, information needs, and potential topics to report on. Sustainability reporting has become a delicate strategic issue since research shows that readers use this information to support risk evaluations and investment decisions, for example (Maas et al. 2016). To cope with this challenge, performance measurement and reporting can be built on widely accepted reporting standards, as proposed by the Global Reporting Initiative, for example. However, even if comprehensive standards are available, sustainability reporting challenges accounting to gather and deliver adequate information.

Here, the SBSC can be used to structure the indicators to be measured and reported. The inside-out perspective of the integrated framework in Figure 2.1.6 suggests focusing on strategically relevant information corresponding to the findings from the SBSC process. The KPIs and accounting information can be structured by standards such as the GRI guidelines, followed by individual 'customizing' through the SBSC. Consequently, the scorecard helps to systematically choose sustainability indicators from external guidelines and to structure the information needed for sustainability accounting, which then provides the main content for sustainability reporting (cf. Schaltegger & Wagner 2006a).

The case of Hamburg Airport is prototypical regarding the practical implementation of an integrated measurement and reporting system. The company has overseen environmental issues since 1989 and introduced an EMS around 1998. The SBSC project was faced with existing structures and routines on all levels from measurement to reporting, which required the SBSC team to deal with these structures and routines and their effect on daily business (cf. Diaz Guerrero et al. 2002; Schaltegger & Wagner 2006a). It can be assumed that most companies that try to implement either a SBSC or a comprehensive framework of sustainability performance measurement and reporting are confronted with similar situations, as this is merely a blueprint process. Hamburg Airport was motivated to develop its SBSC to better understand potential links between its vision, strategy, and environmental management. Such links were identified and made transparent in the SBSC process. Consequences and approaches to further develop corporate accounting and reporting were also formulated (see Diaz Guerrero 2002; Diaz Guerrero et al. 2002; Schaltegger & Wagner 2006a).

Summary and conclusions

This chapter provided a theoretical and conceptual overview of the sustainability balanced scorecard (SBSC) approach according to Figge et al. (2002b) and Schaltegger and Dyllick (2002; see also Hansen & Schaltegger 2016). The balanced scorecard (BSC), as developed in the 1990s by Kaplan and Norton (1992, 1996a), was introduced with an emphasis on conceptual elements such as the four basic perspectives, the role of indicators, as well as strategy maps based on cause-and-effect chains in and across the BSC perspectives. Due to its openness first to modifications in terms of perspectives and indicators, and second in terms of the type of information that can be handled with this concept, the BSC was further developed as a tool for integrated corporate sustainability management. The SBSC addresses environmental and social aspects regarding their relevance for a business unit's (or company's) strategy. Therefore, different methods of integrating sustainability aspects into the conventional BSC were introduced and a process of formulating a SBSC was described.

The SBSC is part of the wider field of strategic management. It is not used to develop strategies but to identify sustainability-related aspects that may be crucial when it comes to strategy implementation and execution. For this reason, the SBSC is also well suited for mainstream companies that wish to integrate environmental and social aspects into their performance measurement and management. Here, it proves to be a valuable concept for the development of comprehensive approaches to sustainability performance measurement, management, and reporting. Some authors propose a framework that consists of the SBSC, sustainability accounting and reporting (Schaltegger & Wagner 2006a, 2006b). The idea is to start from the strategic issues of the SBSC, consider external standards such as the GRI Guidelines, and then develop corporate accounting and reporting according to the information needed for calculating the identified key performance indicators from the SBSC process. Besides the discussed integrated measurement and reporting framework, the SBSC is also proposed as a tool for other purposes such as eco-efficiency analyses or environmental and social management control (Figge et al. 2002b; Möller & Schaltegger 2005; Schaltegger 2004, 2010).

Regarding possible conceptual shortcomings, the explicit focus on financial objectives might be critical. The SBSC is formulated from the top down, beginning with the financial perspective. This method might in some cases tend to ignore relevant sustainability aspects which cannot (obviously) be related to financial objectives because of too complex cause-and-effect chains. Here, the problem might not be strategic insignificance, but barriers to communicating such relationships. Moreover, when cause-and-effect chains are identified, situations can be imagined where plausible causal chains are formulated with broad consensus amongst managers. But are plausible, convincing, and easy to communicate cause-and-effect relationships always the most important ones? Therefore, approaches to formulating and validating causal chains by means of quantitative measures might be discussed to identify not only the strategic relevance of environmental and social aspects *per se*, but also to assess the effectiveness of cause-and-effect chains. The Analytic Network Process (ANP) could serve as reference method for such approaches, as it measures the strength of relationships between variables in decision-making contexts (e.g., Saaty 2015).

In this chapter, the classic case of Hamburg Airport Corporation was used to illustrate theoretical and practical features of the SBSC concept. Diaz Guerrero et al. (2002), who were directly involved in the SBSC process at Hamburg Airport, drew the following conclusions. In the case of Hamburg Airport, the focus was primarily laid on environmental aspects and problems of noise pollution. These environmental aspects were centrally managed by an executive department, while social aspects were spread across different departments. In part, practitioners perceived the BSC as a management trend and were sceptical of its value. Benefits were observed as the SBSC process helped to identify already existing environmental and social activities which were merely recognized before. The result was increased transparency and the identification of valuable causal chains between non-market aspects and economic targets. The causal hypotheses also helped to define value-oriented environmental and social measures, support communication, and better integrate with general management and strategic objectives. The location perspective addresses crucial non-market issues which are significant for the legitimacy and autonomy of action of Hamburg's airport and thus support value-oriented stakeholder management.

The case of Hamburg Airport shows that the SBSC process described in the theory section works in practice and helps with the formulation of strategic core issues and performance drivers in the context of concrete practical strategy programmes. Conducting the three steps of the SBSC process and going through the perspectives helps to identify company and situation-specific environmental and social aspects, and contributes to a clarification of whether these aspects are already integrated and managed in existing management systems. Notably, the SBSC offers different approaches to integrating these aspects into existing performance measurement, management, and reporting systems.

References

Baumgartner, R. J., & Rauter, R. (2017). Strategic perspectives of corporate sustainability management to develop a sustainable organization. *Journal of Cleaner Production, 140,* 81–92.

Bieker, T., & Waxenberger, B. (2002). Sustainability balanced scorecard and business ethics: developing a balanced scorecard for integrity management. *Tenth Conference of the 'Greening of Industry Network'.* Retrieved from http://www.alexandria.unisg.ch/publications/person/W/Bernhard_Waxenberger/17766.

Burritt, R., & Schaltegger, S. (2010). Sustainability accounting and reporting: fad or trend? *Accounting, Auditing and Accountability Journal, 23*(7), 829–846.

Cooper, D. J., Ezzamel, M., & Qu, S. (2017). Popularizing a management accounting idea: the case of the balanced scorecard. *Contemporary Accounting Research, 34*(2), 991–1025.

Diaz Guerrero, A. (2002). *Analysis of the Implementation of a Sustainability Balanced Scorecard at Hamburg Airport: Application of Performance Indicators to Selected Causal Chains.* Hamburg: Northern Institute of Technology.

Diaz Guerrero, A., Möller, D., & Wagner, M. (2002). Sustainability Balanced Scorecard in der Flughafen Hamburg GmbH [Sustainability Balanced Scorecard at the Hamburg Airport GmbH], in: Schaltegger, S. & Dyllick, T. (Eds.), *Nachhaltig managen mit der Balanced Scorecard. Konzept und Fallstudien [Sustainability Management with the Balanced Scorecard – Concept and Cases;* in German]. Wiesbaden: Gabler, 229–257.

Epstein, M., & Wisner, P. (2001). Using a Balanced Scorecard to implement sustainability. *Environmental Quality Management, 11*(2), 1–10.

Figge, F., Hahn, T., Schaltegger, S., & Wagner, M. (2002a). Development of a sustainability balanced scorecard: translating strategy into value-based sustainability management. *Journal of the Asia Pacific Centre for Environmental Accountability, 8*(1), 3–16.

Figge, F., Hahn, T., Schaltegger, S., & Wagner, M. (2002b). The Sustainability Balanced Scorecard: linking sustainability management to business strategy. *Business Strategy and the Environment, 11*(5), 269–284.

Freeman, R. E., Harrison, J. S., Wicks, A. C., Parmar, B. L., & De Colle, S. (2010). *Stakeholder Theory: The State of the Art.* Cambridge: Cambridge University Press.

Hansen, E. G. (2010). *Responsible Leadership Systems: An Empirical Analysis of Integrating Corporate Responsibility into Leadership Systems.* Berlin: Springer Science & Business Media.

Hansen, E. G., & Schaltegger, S. (2016). The sustainability balanced scorecard: a systematic review of architectures. *Journal of Business Ethics, 133*(2), 193–221.

Hansen, E., & Schaltegger, S. (2017). Sustainability Balanced Scorecards and their architectures: irrelevant or misunderstood? *Journal of Business Ethics.* doi:10.1007/s10551-017-3531-5.

Hansen, E. G., Sextl, M., & Reichwald, R. (2010). Managing strategic alliances through a community-enabled balanced scorecard: the case of Merck Ltd, Thailand. *Business Strategy and the Environment, 19*(6), 387–399.

Kaplan, R., & Johnson, H. (1987). *Relevance Lost: The Rise and Fall of Management Accounting.* Boston, MA: Harvard Business School Press.

Kaplan, R., & Norton, D. (1992). The Balanced Scorecard: measures that drive performance. *Harvard Business Review, 70*(1), 71–79.

Kaplan, R., & Norton, D. (1993). Putting the Balanced Scorecard to work. *Harvard Business Review, 71*(5), 134–147.

Kaplan, R., & Norton, D. (1996a). *The Balanced Scorecard: Translating Strategy into Action.* Boston, MA: Harvard Business Press.

Kaplan, R., & Norton, D. (1996b). Using the Balanced Scorecard as a strategic management system. *Harvard Business Review, 74*(1), 75–85.

Kaplan, R., & Norton, D. (2000). Having trouble with your strategy? Then map it. *Harvard Business Review, 78*(5), 167–176.

Kaplan, R., & Norton, D. (2001). Transforming the Balanced Scorecard from performance measurement to strategic management: part I. *Accounting Horizons, 15*(1), 87–104.

Kaplan, R., & Norton, D. (2004). *Strategy Maps: Converting Intangible Assets into Tangible Outcomes.* Boston, MA: Harvard Business Press.

KPMG (2015). *The KPMG Survey of Corporate Responsibility Reporting 2015.* Amstelveen, the Netherlands: KPMG Sustainability Services.

Maas, K., Schaltegger, S., & Crutzen, N. (2016). Integrating corporate sustainability assessment, management accounting, control, and reporting. *Journal of Cleaner Production, 136,* 237–248.

Möller, A., & Schaltegger, S. (2005). The Sustainability Balanced Scorecard as a framework for eco-efficiency analysis. *Journal of Industrial Ecology, 9*(4), 73–83.

Saaty, T., & Vargas, L. (2015). *Decision Making with the Analytic Network Process.* New York: Springer.

Schaltegger, S. (2004). Unternehmerische Steuerung von Nachhaltigkeitsaspekten mit der Sustainability Balanced Scorecard. *Controlling (Sonderheft Strategische Steuerung), (8/9),* 511–516.

Schaltegger, S. (2010). Nachhaltigkeit als Treiber des Unternehmenserfolgs. Folgerungen für die Entwicklung eines Nachhaltigkeitscontrollings. *Controlling, 22*(4/5), 238–243.

Schaltegger, S., & Burritt, R. (2005). Corporate sustainability, in: Folmer, H., & Tietenberg, T. (Eds.), *The International Yearbook of Environmental and Resource Economics.* Cheltenham: Edward Elgar, 185–232.

Schaltegger, S., & Dyllick, T. (Eds.) (2002). *Nachhaltig managen mit der Balanced Scorecard. Konzept und Fallstudien [Sustainability Management with the Balanced Scorecard – Concept and Cases; in German].* Wiesbaden: Gabler.

Schaltegger, S., & Wagner, M. (2006a). Integrative management of sustainability performance, measurement and reporting. *International Journal of Accounting, Auditing and Performance Evaluation, 3*(1), 1–19.

Schaltegger, S., & Wagner, M. (2006b). Managing sustainability performance measurement and reporting in an integrated manner: sustainability accounting as the link between the sustainability balanced scorecard and sustainability reporting, in: Schaltegger, S., Bennett, M., & Burritt, R. (Eds.), *Sustainability Accounting and Reporting*. Berlin: Springer, 681–697.

Schaltegger, S., Lüdeke-Freund, F., & Hansen, E. (2012). Business cases for sustainability: the role of business model innovation for corporate sustainability. *International Journal of Innovation and Sustainable Development*, *6*(2), 95–119.

Spitzeck, H., & Hansen, E. G. (2010). Stakeholder governance: how stakeholders influence corporate decision making. *Corporate Governance: The International Journal of Business in Society*, *10*(4), 378–391.

Wagner, M., & Schaltegger, S. (2006). Mapping the links of corporate sustainability: Sustainability Balanced Scorecards as a tool for sustainability performance measurement and management, in: Schaltegger, S., & Wagner, M. (Eds.), *Managing the Business Case for Sustainability: The Integration of Social, Environmental and Economic Performance*. Sheffield: Greenleaf.

2.2 Sustainability accounting standards in the USA – procedural legitimacy

Governance, participation, and decision-making processes

Delphine Gibassier

Introduction

A growing number of 'regulatory innovators', that mostly take the form of global environmental and social non-governmental organizations (NGOs), have carved out a space in the making of standards for a more responsible global business (Boström and Hallström 2010). These innovators, or 'entrepreneurial private authorities' (Green 2010), often take the form of multi-stakeholder initiatives (MSIs). They are defined as 'global institutions involving mainly corporations and civil society organizations, [as] one type of regulatory mechanism that tries to fill this gap by issuing soft law regulation' (Mena et al. 2012).

MSIs focusing on corporate social responsibility (CSR) topics are multiple (e.g., the Marine Stewardship Council, Social Accountability International, the Forest Stewardship Council, or the Fairtrade Labelling Organizations International). Recently, MSIs specialized in sustainability reporting have mushroomed in the wake of the pioneering 'Global Reporting Initiative' in the early 2000s (Tschopp and Nastanski 2014). Today, the arena comprises the Global Reporting Initiative (GRI), the Climate Disclosure Standards Board (CDSB), the International Integrated Reporting Committee (IIRC), and the most recent initiative, the Sustainability Accounting Standards Board (SASB).

There are few studies of MSI due processes in sustainability accounting and reporting (the IIRC is an exception; see Reuter and Messner 2015). The due process is defined as the different steps and methods used to attain standardization (Jorissen et al. 2012). Little is known about how MSIs construct their procedural legitimacy in the field to ensure that their standards are disseminated and adopted in practice. In accounting standardization, Cooper and Robson (2006) had called for further research into constituents' participation in the IASB's due process in terms of representation (constituents' diversity and characteristics) and drivers to participation, stating the importance of public participation (Jorissen et al. 2012). Since standards tend to shape both the economic and societal relationships of organizations with their stakeholders once they are applied, organizations have a strong interest in shaping nascent sustainability accounting standards (Jorissen et al. 2012). Therefore, understanding the different elements of the procedural legitimacy of the SASB's due process is of key importance because it will influence how sustainability accounting will be defined for US-based organizations, and subsequently for the subsidiaries of US multi-national enterprises throughout the world. This could impact global industries that would have to use similar standards so that their investors could compare their sustainability performance, for example.

The world has changed: nowadays, non-state actors contribute not only to the implementation but also directly to the formulation of public policy (Mele and Schepers 2013).

Therefore, it is crucial to understand the formulation process of these new privately made policies to understand how they become legitimate. We need to understand whose voices are heard or silenced in any particular standardization process. This is even more important in the context of sustainability, where the rules of measurement and calculability could be defined by dominant stakeholder groups such as worldwide industry unions, the elite (Gibassier 2017), or a group of experts (Jorissen et al. 2012), thereby silencing dissident voices from marginalized actors such as SMEs, NGOs, civil society, or academia. The procedural legitimacy of sustainability accounting MSIs is a policy issue (how to ensure that each voice is heard – including critical ones), a practical issue (how can SMEs, for instance, participate in a standardization process?), and a theoretical issue, since the literature has only just begun to conceptualize what it could be – and to investigate its application to actual MSIs.

This research is based on a single case study, that is, the SASB standardization process. The SASB's goal is 'to create industry-based standards that will allow investors and other stakeholders to compare firms' environmental and social impacts' (Eccles and Serafeim 2013; Pfitzer et al. 2013; Tschopp and Nastanski 2014). The first step entailed collecting all the documents available on the SASB website pertaining to how the standards are created, and in particular the 'Consumption I' sector standard, to be able to reflect on participation. Data was analysed through an analytical framework designed to study procedural legitimacy. While the discussion compares the procedural legitimacy of the SASB with that of the GRI, the sole purpose of this comparison is to bring more depth to the analysis of the SASB case study.

Contributions to the literature on procedural legitimacy are twofold: first, there is an empirical contribution to the study of MSIs, procedural legitimacy literature being mainly conceptual, with very few empirical case studies. The second contribution entails analysing a rare case of expert-based procedural legitimacy – which is a unique and extreme case study (Yin 2009) in the field of sustainability. There are also two main contributions to the literature on sustainability accounting: the first is another empirical contribution through the first empirical study of the SASB, a standard-setter that is shaping the future of sustainability measures in one of the world's major economies, the USA. The second contribution is the investigation into the way that stakeholders' voices are included or silenced in the drafting of sustainability accounting standards (Reutner and Messner 2015; Gibassier 2017; Berquier et al. 2017), a topic that is relevant to policy-making and a contribution to critical accounting research.

This chapter is divided into several sections. The next section introduces the framework developed to assess procedural legitimacy and its consequences. That is followed by a review of the literature on the procedural legitimacy of two major multi-stakeholder initiatives in the realm of CSR. Then I describe the research design, and present the case study findings. Finally, I discuss case study findings, before drawing conclusions.

Analytical framework

The procedural legitimacy of MSIs is defined in terms of inclusiveness, transparency, and deliberativeness (Beisheim and Dingwerth 2008). Procedural legitimacy includes several principles such as representation, participation, neutrality, and procedural regularity (Koppell 2008). Representation means that those governed need to have a voice in the decision-making process. Participation is related to the opportunity to observe and comment on the initiative. Neutrality means that all should be treated equally.

Regularity means that decisions must be transparent, open to public scrutiny, and have a right of appeal (Koppell 2008).

Two different frameworks related to procedural legitimacy are combined in this research. The first framework was developed by Fransen and Kolk in 2007 to study the procedural legitimacy of this sustainability accounting MSI. Fransen and Kolk use three categories to analyse the development of MSIs: governance, participation, and implementation. It focuses on two major elements of an MSI: its governance, and its standard-making process through participation. Implementation is not discussed in this study because it does not explore the implementation of SASB standards within companies. The second framework used has additional key values that represent procedural legitimacy: transparency and accountability (Schaller 2007; Beisheim and Dingwerth 2008). Governance and participation are necessary to gain legitimacy, while transparency and accountability are necessary to maintain that legitimacy (Beisheim and Dingwerth 2008).

Governance

Public governance involves a set of rules and standards, monitoring and enforcement, as well as judicial review (O'Rourke 2006). However, non-governmental MSIs involve 'multiple actors in new roles and relationships, experimenting with new processes of standard setting, monitoring, benchmarking, and enforcement' (O'Rourke 2006). Therefore, governance in MSIs is defined differently: it includes open membership and the possibility for any interested stakeholder to participate (Fransen and Kolk 2007). Moreover, expert groups usually take governance positions in the rule-making process. There is little research about the optimal governance processes of MSIs and how they are linked to the development of standards and principles such as inclusiveness, consensus building, or knowledge sharing. Governance of multi-stakeholder standardization processes can be evaluated by looking at the membership and the representation of those involved, and the decision-making processes that are open to the participation of each and every stakeholder.

Participation

Participation can be judged through two elements: the quality and nature of stakeholders, and the nature of interactions (decision-making processes). This is called 'input legitimacy'. Multi-stakeholder standardizers build on the idea of 'assembling actors from diverse societal spheres into one policy-making or rule-setting process, to make use of their resources, competences, and experiences' (Boström and Hallström 2013). For example, the Forest Stewardship Council attempted to balance the voting power between their different members through a tripartite structure made up of social, environmental, and economic membership chambers (Black 2008).

Including all the stakeholders relevant to a specific topic increases the authority of the decision-making process, and is considered a good governance practice of MSIs (Fransen and Kolk 2007). This increases the legitimacy and credibility of the standard. NGOs can play the role of watchdogs, and business organizations can engage with their particular expertise and create synergies in the learning process. The quality of the rules is consequently heightened. Furthermore, the inclusion of governmental bodies lends greater credibility and authority, and can facilitate the implementation and dissemination of the standard. The representativeness of stakeholder groups therefore needs to be assessed to understand how participation has or has not been promoted as an axis of procedural legitimacy for a particular MSI. It is legitimate to ask whether a particular MSI has promoted the representativeness and involvement of vulnerable groups (Fransen and Kolk 2007).

Fransen and Kolk (2007) note that, in relation to the nature of interactions, participation in an MSI can be defined together with an involvement–consultation continuum, so there is a need to further investigate what leads an MSI to be more open to consultation or foster less involvement.

Transparency and accountability

Transparency and accountability values are complementary to governance and participation in procedural legitimacy. Indeed, this legitimacy is granted by society as a whole; there is no need to participate in the standard-making process to assess its transparency. The accountability of an MSI grants a wider audience the ability to remotely control the process's transparency – or the lack of it. This ability to control and assess will 'likely increase the willingness of addressees to adhere to the outcome' (Beisheim and Dingwerth 2008). For those not involved directly in the standardization process, transparency is used as a proxy for procedural legitimacy (Beisheim and Dingwerth 2008).

Two case studies have been the subject of a thorough analysis of procedural legitimacies in sustainability MSIs. Using the analytical framework described above, this chapter will review what these case studies have taught us about the three elements of procedural legitimacy.

Case studies of the procedural legitimacy of multi-stakeholder initiatives in CSR

The literature on the procedural legitimacy of MSIs has been mainly conceptual (Black 2008) and rarely applied to the analysis of existing standard-setters. To be able to understand how the case of the SASB will enhance our understanding of standard-setting procedures, and how these procedures bring legitimacy to the standards themselves and influence their adoption, two examples of procedural legitimacy analysis will be explored: the Roundtable on Sustainable Palm Oil and the Global Reporting Initiative.

Schouten and Glasbergen (2011) studied the broad legitimacy of the Roundtable on Sustainable Palm Oil (RSPO) by splitting it into procedural legitimacy, moral legitimacy, and social acceptance. They focused on the representational issue, stating that procedures for consultation and decision-making should overcome any imbalances in representation – as the RSPO recognized that Indonesian producers lacked representation. Inclusiveness was to be managed through the development of seven groups representing key interest groups relating to palm oil. In the end, board-level representation was not balanced because negotiations turned in favour of producers (who were given double the seats of the other groups), while the NGOs battled to equal the producers' number of votes. The general assembly voting process (one vote per member) emphasized the imbalance of representation. Indeed, processors and traders were seven times more numerous than NGOs in the assembly. To counter this issue, consensus working groups were set up. Moreover, the RSPO had a grievance procedure to guarantee accountability for any complaints made against RSPO members.

The Global Reporting Initiative's procedural legitimacy has been analysed through three lenses by Beisheim and Dingwerth (2008). These three lenses are inclusion, deliberative procedures, and social control based on transparency and accountability. The GRI considered its credibility through a balanced input of private sectors, NGOs, and labour sectors. This was considered key for the future acceptance of the standards. The GRI fostered numerous entry points to participation such as the GRI governing bodies, stakeholder council, working groups, and the possibility of responding to structured feedback processes. According to Beisheim and Dingwerth (2008), the GRI's commitment to inclusiveness was massive and sincere, having a direct impact on its uptake in non-financial reporting by business organizations. Secondly, the GRI emphasized the consensual decision-making processes it fosters within its different bodies. This again, according to Beisheim and Dingwerth (2008), is a key aspect for fostering compliance with the standards. Finally, Beisheim and Dingwerth (2008, p. 24) conclude by saying that 'while inclusiveness and deliberation serve as a trigger for adherence, transparency and accountability therefore seem relevant primarily as safeguards for progress made as a result of inclusive and deliberative decision-making'.

Both empirical cases demonstrate that the keys to output legitimacy are a clear commitment to inclusiveness, sound deliberation processes, and governance, combined with adherence to transparency and accountability principles. Despite demonstrating that both cases tend to show similar results in terms of procedural legitimacy, one could ask whether a different type of standard-setting procedure might lead to a different outcome. Studying the particular case of the SASB will refine our understanding of both the procedural legitimacy of MSIs and its boundaries. There will also be a discussion on the risks of the model developed by the SASB versus the optimal MSI procedural legitimacy described by Fransen and Kolk (2007).

Research design

Research setting

This research focuses on a multi-stakeholder initiative in sustainability reporting, namely the Sustainability Accounting Standards Board, based in the USA. An MSI can be defined as self-regulatory governing arenas often operating on a transnational scale and based on the voluntary contributions of participants (Utting 2002; Rasche 2010). To be able to study the procedural legitimacy of MSIs, this research focused on a recent multi-stakeholder initiative, for which the documents related to the standard-making process were available online.[1] The SASB is an MSI addressing sustainability reporting standards. It 'defines indicators and guidelines for corporations to use to standardise non-financial reporting practices and to communicate their social and environmental impact to interested stakeholders' (Rasche 2010). It considers and therefore positions itself as following on from the financial standards in the 'natural evolution of corporate reporting' (SASB website) in extending the accounting infrastructure to material sustainability factors.

The Sustainability Accounting Standards Board is an NGO founded in 2011 by Jean Rogers. It was developed after Steve Lydenberg, Jean Rogers, and David Wood published their Harvard research paper entitled 'From transparency to performance' in 2010. This research developed the backbone of future sustainability standards, as the authors unfolded at that time the methodology for determining industry-specific material issues and their associated performance indicators, which they were able to test on six industries.

The SASB develops industry-specific sustainability accounting standards for publically traded US companies with a focus on investors. Its mission is 'to develop and disseminate sustainability accounting standards that help public corporations disclose material, decision-useful information to investors' (SASB 2016c). Consequently, it wants sustainability performance to be evaluated alongside financial performance (SASB 2014b). It is the latest of a series of MSIs developed around non-financial reporting. It aims to support non-financial performance through the development of key performance indicators, thus competing with the Global Reporting Initiative (see Figure 2.2.1: the non-financial reporting arena). Sustainability measurements reported through guidelines issued by organizations such as the GRI or SASB are often part of a larger set of key performance indicators that a company follows internally to monitor their non-financial performance.

In the past five years, the SASB has developed provisional industry-specific sustainability accounting standards for 79 industries in 10 sectors. It is currently in the process of codifying these standards. The SASB is an interesting case study as it claims that its development process is 'evidence-based, facilitates broad participation, and objectively considers all stakeholder views' (SASB 2016a).

Data collection and analysis

The data needed to analyse procedural legitimacy are documents related to due process, comment letters, or meeting minutes (when available) that demonstrate deliberation, and a participants' list that attests to inclusiveness.

The SASB website was the source of information regarding both the SASB's standardization due process and its application to one of the industry-specific standards

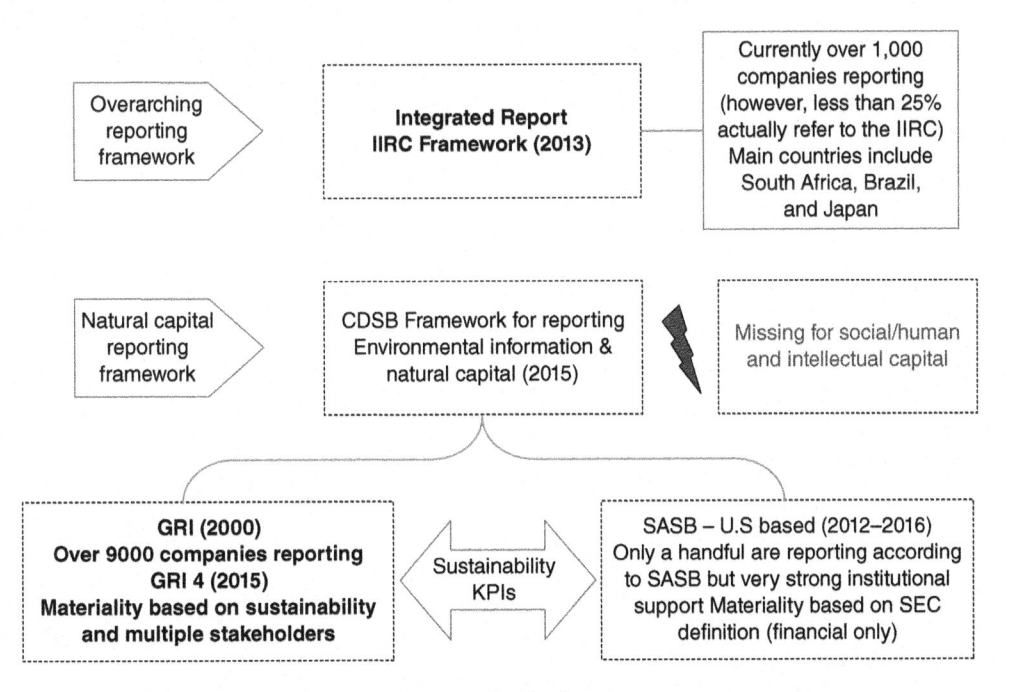

Figure 2.2.1 The non-financial corporate reporting landscape

on consumption. Data collected on participation include comment letters, names of participants in working groups, and the SASB's answers to the comment letters. The outcomes of the working group meetings, for example, were not available. The SASB's due process is explained in several areas such as the brochure, the Conceptual Framework, and the Rules of Procedure. All of these documents were therefore collected for analysis. The outcome of the process review was also available from the Standards Council. The data made available online gave a complete overview of the standardization procedures and their implementation, making it possible to assess procedural legitimacy.

All the documents were read and coded according to the analytical framework explained in the next section: the analysis covered topics such as governance, participation, and decision-making processes, in addition to key values such as transparency and accountability.

Findings: the rules of an expert-based procedural legitimacy

To establish whether the due process established by the SASB lends legitimacy to its standards through the procedures implemented to develop and publish sustainability accounting standards, the analysis focuses on three different topics: governance, participation, and decision-making processes; and two values: transparency and accountability.

Table 2.2.1 Data collected to analyse the SASB's procedural legitimacy

On the standardization due process	On participation
Implementation Guide	List of SASB CONSUMPTION I working group members
One mock 10K	Compiled public comments
Seven industry briefs	Standards Outcome Review
Standards Council Meeting Report	SASB Responses to Public Comments on Consumption I Standards
SASB Industry Working Groups Due Process Report	
Consumption I Issues Table	
Seven industry standards	
AGRICULTURAL PRODUCTS Sustainability Accounting Standard (for public review 2015)	
SASB Brochure 2016	
SASB Rules of Procedure: 2016 draft for public comment	
SASB Conceptual Framework 2013	
SASB Conceptual Framework: 2016 draft for comment	
Public comments on governance documents 2016	
Public comments and SASB response to the 2013 Conceptual Framework	

Table 2.2.2 The SASB standard-making process

Phase	Date	Activities	Responsibility	Approval	Participation
Provisional	**2012–2016**	Establish Priorities	Technical Advisory	Board	Closed
		In-depth industry research	Committee	75% approval benchmark	Closed
		Valuation analysis	Analysis		Closed
		Vetting	Analysis		Semi-open
		Survey	Industry working group		Semi-open
		Development of standards	Industry working group		Closed
		Comment letters	Analysis		Open
		Ventilation with current	Public		Closed
		disclosure	Analysts		Closed
		Validation	SASH Standards Council		Closed
		Provisional standards release	SASH Standards Council		Open
		Road testing	Companies		
Codification	**2016–2017**	Consultation phase	With issuers and investors		Semi-open
		Review	Analysts		Closed
		Cost–benefit analysis	Analysis		Closed
		Comment letters	Public		Open
		Basis for conclusion	Analysts		Closed
		Approval	Standards Council		Closed
		Codification	Analysis		Closed

Governance

Internal governance

Three different bodies oversee the standard-making process: the SASB Foundation Board of Directors, the Standards Oversight Committee, and the Standards Council. The SASB's Conceptual Framework and Rules of Procedure govern the way standards are written.

The SASB Foundation Board of Directors governs the SASB and is responsible for fiduciary oversight of the SASB as a standard-setting organization. The Board of Directors is composed of members such as the former chair of the US Securities and Exchange Commission, Mary Schapiro, or the former chairman of the Financial Accounting Standards Board, Robert H. Herz, thus lending political legitimacy to their quest to establish a position in the field of corporate reporting.

An independent Standards Council oversees the standard-making process. It is composed of 'experts in standards development, securities law, environmental law, metrics and accounting' (SASB 2016a). It also has a metrics sub-committee working specifically on the key performance indicators proposed within the standards. In the Consumption I sector, for instance, the Council raised the issue of which data are available to management to be able to apply the standards, and whether it would be appropriate to include a company perspective when determining the metrics in order to progress from provisional to final versions of the standards (SASB 2015b).

The SASB has developed an enhanced standard-making governance process, including a Standards Oversight Committee to oversee the due process. Committee members are also members of the SASB Foundation Board of Directors. This committee receives and reviews appeals and complaints on the adequacy of the due process application. It also evaluates the adequacy, comprehensiveness, effectiveness, and adherence to due process procedures throughout the standard-setting process (SASB 2016d). However, it refrains from engaging in technical standard-setting.

From 2016 on, the Standards Council has focused on setting the agenda, reviewing both the process and the content of standards, and approving standards. It is composed of 'nine members appointed by the SASB Board of Directors, including a Chair, with equal representation of corporate issuers, investors, and a third category of other stakeholders such as accountants, lawyers, public servants, non-governmental organisations' (SASB 2016d). A majority vote is necessary to approve updates to the standards.

The SASB is completely transparent on the rules applied to standard-setting, the standard-making process itself, and its oversight: 1) the Conceptual Framework guiding the standard-making process and the Rules of Procedure can be found online; 2) both were the subject in 2016 of a public comment period; 3) the SASB aims to respond to each and every comment letter received, all of which (letters and answers) are published online. It must therefore be concluded that the SASB has developed a high level of transparency in its due process.

External governance

The SASB was accredited by the American National Standards Institute (ANSI) as a national developer of standards in December 2012. Despite this external guidance on how a standardization process should be conducted, some stakeholders have voiced their concern about the SASB not fully applying the due process safeguards:

> despite continuing to cite ANSI accreditation, the Proposal fails to meet ANSI's due process requirements. In the spirit of public disclosure and transparency, it would be appropriate for SASB to publicly provide its ANSI-accredited procedures and an explanation of why it decided not to incorporate them in the Proposal.
>
> (SASB 2016b)

Actual participation

Participation restricted to 'experts'

There are openings for participation in the standard-making process at several levels. Firstly, one can be involved through the SASB Foundation Board and the Oversight Committee. Secondly, one can be involved in the Standards Council, which is composed of members of interest groups. Thirdly, one can participate through the Industry Working Groups (IWG) or through public comments during the consultation and road-testing periods. Additionally, SASB analysts can contact 'industry experts' when the standards are being drafted, modified, or codified. There are therefore numerous possibilities for participating in the standard-making process from 2012 to today. However, it should be noted that the vast majority of these possibilities for interaction are restricted to 'experts' from a small number of interest groups, thereby excluding NGOs, governmental bodies, or non-listed companies, for example.

Inclusiveness: restricted and expert-based

The working groups are restricted to three types of stakeholder: 1) members of interest groups identified by the SASB (issuers, such as corporations); 2) market participants (investors and analysts); 3) public interest organizations and intermediaries. The SASB has put an emphasis on reaching the right expertise to develop its standards, and restricts IWG participation to 'industry experts with at least five years of experience in the industry for which they are reviewing SASB standards' (SASB 2014b). Therefore, there is a dual barrier to inclusiveness in their standardization process: firstly, it limits stakeholders to groups that it has itself identified as relevant, and secondly, it describes a membership profile required for participation.

Despite these restrictions, the SASB has maintained at least one public comment period for each of its industry standards as well as for its own standard-setting procedures and framework. It has also vowed that, in the future, any updates to the standards will be subject to a public comment period. The issue with public comment periods is the widespread dissemination of the information to all stakeholders. In the Consumption I sector, one stakeholder voiced discomfort in regard to the circulation of a draft saying that he had polled 'more than a dozen national and international industry leaders (. . .) none were aware of the draft or opportunity to comment' (SASB 2015). There is no optimal way of checking that the dissemination process for the draft to be commented on is the 'right' one. However, the SASB should be able to prove that the draft has been distributed to the industry leaders and associations concerned, as well as to the NGOs and government agencies in the targeted sector.

Moreover, during the public comment period, stakeholders have voiced their concern about the standards not being applicable to everyone, for example 'it is important that the metrics, which must be meaningful to investors, are also practical and relevant to agricultural producers. We believe some of the Draft Standard metrics are not material to agricultural sustainability' (SASB 2015). Despite these concerns, the SASB was unable to achieve their desired representation, and switched to a different evaluation of the representation they had finally implemented.

From equal representation to financial prevalence

It is not always easy to achieve the equal representation of stakeholders (Schouten and Glasbergen 2011). In the case of the SASB's industry working groups, the target was to achieve 36 participants with a balance of 12 from each of the three interest groups. In this situation, there would be a perfect balance between the different stakeholder groups. However, in reality, it was not possible to obtain 36 participants or a balance between the different interest groups. The SASB then switched its evaluation of representation to an effort-based approach, with metrics such as the number of 'top companies' registered per industry and the outreach efforts to industry associations (SASB 2015). These metrics clearly demonstrate the move from equal representation to an acknowledgement that certain stakeholders were more important than others (top companies). This is re-emphasized in the SASB brochure when it states that 'More than 2,800 individuals – affiliated with companies with $11T market capital and investors representing $23.4T assets under management – participated in provisional-phase industry working groups' (SASB 2016a). The legitimacy of the process is thus clearly not acquired from equal representation any longer, but through the financial weight of the participant stakeholders in their working groups.

Throughput legitimacy: decision-making process

Throughput legitimacy refers to how decisions are made about the original drafting of a particular standard and later changes to its content. How, for example, is the content of comment letters taken into account? Are decisions consensus-based?

On the basis of this study of the Consumption I sector, the SASB has responded exhaustively to each and every comment voiced on the standards. Moreover, all the comment letters and answers have been made public in a readable manner, so that it is clear to the reader whether or not a particular comment has influenced the revised version, and why (or why not).

Although public comment periods have been included in the SASB's standard-making process, this does not guarantee that all the comments will be incorporated into the updated version of each standard. It does, however, ensure that everybody can express an opinion.

The arguments developed by the SASB to respond negatively to a requested change are consistent with its approach to the standard-making process (see Conceptual Framework): the SASB develops standards that are material, evidence-based, and targeted at investors. In one of its answers, it insisted that SASB standards have been developed 'to assist investors' (SASB 2015) in their decision-making processes, notably when one item might have a financial impact (such as a fluctuation in the price of a raw material). Other responses mention 'further research' conducted to exclude, for example, scope

1 GHG emissions from the Alcohol Beverages industry standard. Responses also often refer to what would likely constitute material information. Non-material information is systematically excluded – often based on what is called 'SASB research'.

Discussion

SASB versus GRI multi-stakeholder processes

The goals of both multi-stakeholder processes appear to be very much aligned. As an analogy to financial reporting, both seek to provide business organizations with a set of non-financial performance metrics to include in corporate reporting. However, the two organizations differ substantially when it comes to how they are seeking to achieve this goal. They differ in their inclusiveness and in their definitions of sustainability and materiality.

The GRI has developed metrics based on achieving sustainability. Allen White, one of its co-founders, said about sustainability that 'it means that the company is positioned to prosper for the long-term and in a way that respects limits, thresholds and norms that are externally defined' (SASB 2015). GRI 2 called for companies to discuss 'the performance of the organisation in the context of the limits and demands placed on environmental or social resources at the sector, local, regional or global level'.

In contrast, one comment on the SASB Consumption I sector standards indicated that the term 'sustainability standards' as used by the SASB was misleading, because 'absolute and intensity metrics have been shown to be unfit for' the purpose of demonstrating the sustainability of an organisation (SASB 2015). This first difference between the two standard-setters in their definition of sustainability is one explanation as to how they have built their standard-making procedures. The GRI is very inclusive, while the SASB has developed an expert-based approach.

Indeed, the SASB develops standards that are geared to publicly traded companies and developed to suit participants in the US capital markets' needs. The SASB's definition of sustainability is linked to a corporation's financial risks:

> sustainability includes both the management of a corporation's environmental and social impacts, as well as the management of environmental and social capitals necessary to create long-term value. It also includes the impact of environmental and social factors on innovation, business models, and corporate governance.
>
> (SASB 2013)

This definition is restrictive in terms of what can be included in reporting: for example, in its Consumption I sector standard, the SASB has not included scope 3 emissions[2] in its metrics because organizations have no control over them (and therefore the financial risks are not borne by the issuer). While discussing animal welfare measures, the SASB refers to materiality and market concerns to refute a commenter's desire to include a more inclusive definition of animal welfare sustainability. When asked to include metrics related to water, sanitation, and hygiene in the supply chain (an item linked to one of the Sustainable Development Goals), the SASB again refers to its own research and materiality to justify the absence of such metrics.

The second difference between the two standardizers is their vision of inclusiveness. The GRI has clearly sought to include all stakeholders within its board, council, and

Table 2.2.3 SASB versus GRI multi-stakeholder processes

Definitions	Process	Output
Sustainable performance is defined by the GRI 'in the context of the limits and demands placed on environmental or social resources at the sector, local, regional or global level' and a comment to the SASB about its standards said that 'absolute and intensity metrics have been shown to be unfit for' the purpose of demonstrating the sustainability of an organization. Materiality is based on investors taking financial risk (SASB) and is based on all stakeholders (GRI).	The GRI has clearly sought to include all stakeholders within its board, council, and working groups, whereas the SASB's conception of inclusiveness embraces only the group of stakeholders concerned and, within it, the 'most important' and 'most relevant' experts.	The GRI has established an exhaustive list of key performance indicators and has evaluated companies' achievements mainly on completeness, while the SASB has developed key performance indicators regarding only material elements according to its evidence-based research and the experts in its IWGs.

working groups, whereas the SASB's conception of inclusiveness embraces only the group of stakeholders concerned by the industry-specific standards and, within it, the 'most important' and 'most relevant' experts.

Finally, the output of both standardization processes is radically different, embodying their vision of the world. The GRI has established an exhaustive list of key performance indicators and has evaluated companies' achievements mainly on completeness, while the SASB has developed key performance indicators regarding only material elements according to its evidence-based research and the experts in its IWGs. The concept of sustainability defended by the GRI is reflected in its vision of what non-financial reporting metrics should be, while the output of the SASB reflects its initial commitment to focus on materiality and investors' needs.

An expert-based due process

The SASB has developed an expert-based due process to develop its standards. Firstly, it does not apply the principles of inclusiveness, as it does not allow all the stakeholders to be represented in IWGs that were convened before the provisional standards were drafted. The SASB has defined interest groups that they prioritize in many of their interaction processes, including IWGs, road testing, and the current consultation phase prior to codification. They have restricted broad inclusiveness to certain periods open to feedback through public comments.

Secondly, the SASB has developed what is termed 'evidence-based' and 'market-based' standards. These two principles are reflected in the 'in-depth research' phases during which the standard-making process is exclusively handled inside the SASB. The latter also acknowledges referring to 'expert consultation' during the standard-making processes, reinforcing the prevalence of research over participation in key phases of the standard-making process. Indeed, it has often referred to market-based or in-depth research when refuting stakeholders' positions during the public comment period.

Finally, the SASB often refers to authoritative sources as a basis for its standards and arguments while responding to public comments, such as ISO 14021 for packaging, or the World Health Organization. On the other hand, it refutes the possibility of referring to or accepting smaller groups' proposals, such as Field to Market, the Stewardship Index for Speciality Crops, or the Potato Sustainability Initiative (for the Consumption I sector). By focusing on a restricted group of stakeholders and developing an expert-based approach, the SASB might have avoided what Koppell (2005) named the 'multiple accountability disorder'. At the same time, the SASB should be careful to remain accountable to the right group of stakeholders, because its audience might evolve over time (Black 2008).

Driving an expert-based standard-setting procedure does not imply that the principles of MSI procedural legitimacy could not be applied. One comment made during the public comment period with respect to the SASB's 2013 Conceptual Framework stated that:

> the standard-setting process described in the Conceptual Framework relies heavily on the opinions of experts. We recommend the SASB consider how to structure the process so that it (a) solicits opinions from the right experts, (b) ensures those participants have sufficient expertise and information, and (c) incorporates diverse evidence beyond just expert opinions.
>
> (SASB 2014a)

Indeed, representation, quality, and further evidence could balance out the over-reliance on expertise as it is described in the current SASB standardization process.

Moreover, the selection of key expert stakeholder groups must also remain consistent over time and between the different steps of the standardization process. One comment letter rightly mentioned how the new Standards Council format in the 2016 revision of the SASB Rules of Procedure would include a fourth stakeholder group (NGOs, accountants, lawyers, etc.) which would consequently lead to the increased 'likelihood of companies reporting immaterial and less decision-useful information'.

Conclusions

The first conclusion following an assessment of the SASB's procedural legitimacy is that it is 'expert-based'. Although in 2015 fewer than 5% of companies declared that they were applying SASB standards, the number of users tripled in the three years following their first issue in 2013 (Greenbiz 2016). The SASB has acquired an 'expert-based' legitimacy thanks to the inclusion of renowned board members and the quality of its standard-setting process. However, the impact of an expert-based due process on implementation by US and global companies remains to be seen, although uptake has risen in 2017 (e.g., Arcelor Mittal and JetBlue have advertised their use of SASB standards). By studying the procedural legitimacy of the SASB's due process, it was possible to assess the potential impact on the dissemination of these new sustainability reporting guidelines. The theoretical understanding of procedural legitimacy based on inclusiveness, participation, and consensus-building leads to increased legitimacy, and therefore the dissemination of a new standard is contrary to the SASB's decision to structure its procedural legitimacy on expert input, closed membership, and restricted participation.

Secondly, this study sheds light on the 'market for virtue' concept (Gibassier 2015), and on how the different NGOs involved in sustainability reporting co-exist and work towards the convergence of rules. The SASB due process is diametrically opposed to that developed by the Global Reporting Initiative fifteen years ago. Although they both provide key performance indicators for sustainability reporting, their vision of a legitimate and effective due process is quite different. Whereas the GRI standards have been widely adopted across the globe, the restrictive vision of inclusiveness developed by the SASB and its preference for an expert-based approach could help explain today's very low uptake by US-based firms. Although due process legitimacy is not the only factor to take into account when evaluating the success of an MSI-based standard, it is widely considered to be a key to successful adoption. Some of the criticisms voiced by stakeholders directly target the SASB's standard-making process, and notably its handling of concerns raised and appeals. The shadow of doubt that can easily shroud a standardization process's legitimacy can very quickly bring its adoption to a standstill and negatively affect earlier adopters. The transparency and accountability of standardization in its governance, participation, and decision-making processes are critical for achieving procedural legitimacy and influencing output legitimacy.

Finally, to acknowledge the full legitimacy of MSIs, one must also further explore the perspective of consent and acceptance by the market and the social arena (NGOs and civil society) (Schouten and Glasbergen 2011). The legitimacy of SASB could be enhanced if it were acknowledged or even supported by government bodies. It would also benefit from endorsement by investors' professional bodies. On the other hand, its restrictive expert-based procedural legitimacy limits the SASB's opportunities for working with NGOs and other professionals (in accounting or law, for instance), as it would undermine the consistency with which the SASB has developed its Rules of Procedure and the values that guide the development of their standards.

The analysis discussed above took into consideration only one of the SASB's standards (Consumption I sector). The results might be slightly different were the whole process to be studied. Moreover, this research is based only on publically available documents describing the SASB due process. These results could be refined in the future by interviewing SASB members or the staff of participating organizations.

Future research on procedural legitimacy could include interviews of different stakeholders as well as the standard-setter to understand the choices made and their consequences on adoption. Moreover, researchers should carefully monitor the dissemination of SASB standards to understand how procedural legitimacy based on expertise and financial sustainability leads to a different adoption pattern than the widespread adoption of GRI measures observed in the last fifteen years.

Notes

1 Despite their claim to transparency, many MSIs do not share the documents pertaining to their standard-making procedure, or they withdraw the documents after a certain period of time (the GHG Protocol 2001 and 2004 comment letters, for example, are no longer available online).

2 Scope 3 emissions include

> Other indirect emissions, such as the extraction and production of purchased materials and fuels, transport-related activities in vehicles not owned or controlled by the reporting entity, electricity-related activities (e.g. T&D losses) not covered in Scope 2, outsourced activities, waste disposal, etc.
>
> (GHG Protocol, accessed on 25 September 2017, http://www.ghgprotocol.org/calculationg-tools-faq)

References

Beisheim, M., and Dingwerth, K. (2008). Procedural legitimacy and private transnational governance: are the good ones doing better? *SFB-Governance Working Paper Series.*

Berquier, R., Martinez, I., and Gibassier, D. (2017). Marginalized actors' institutional work in standardization processes: an environmental accounting case study. *Working Paper.*

Black, J. (2008). Constructing and contesting legitimacy and accountability in polycentric regulatory regimes. *Regulation and Governance*, 2(2), 137–164.

Boström, M., and Hallström, K. T. (2010). NGO power in global social and environmental standard-setting. *Global Environmental Politics*, 10(4), 36–59.

Boström, M., and Hallström, K. T. (2013). Global multi-stakeholder standard setters: how fragile are they? *Journal of Global Ethics*, 9(1), 93–110.

Cooper, D. J., and Robson, K. (2006). Accounting, professions and regulation: locating the sites of professionalization. *Accounting, Organizations and Society*, 31(4), 415–444.

Eccles, R., and Serafeim, G. (2013). The performance frontier: innovating for a sustainable strategy. *Harvard Business Review*, 50–60.

Fransen, L. W., and Kolk, A. (2007). Global rule-setting for business: a critical analysis of multi-stakeholder standards. *Organization*, 14(5), 667–684.

Gibassier, D. (2015). The corporate reporting landscape: a market for virtue or the virtue of marketization? *Sustainability Accounting, Management and Policy Journal*, 6(4), 527–536.

Gibassier, D. (2017). From écobilan to LCA: the elite's institutional work in the creation of an environmental management accounting tool. *Critical Perspectives on Accounting*, 42, 36–58.

Green, J. F. (2010). Private standards in the climate regime: the Greenhouse Gas Protocol. *Business and Politics*, 12(3), 1–39.

Greenbiz (2016). Battle of Giants: GRI versus SASB. Available at: https://www.greenbiz.com/article/battle-giants-gri-vs-sasb-vs-ir [Accessed January 2017].

Jorissen, A., Lybaert, N., Orens, R., and van der Tas, L. (2012). Formal participation in the IASB's due process of standard setting: a multi-issue/multi-period analysis. *European Accounting Review*, 21(4), 693–729.

Koppell, J. G. S. (2005). Pathologies of accountability: ICANN and the challenge of 'Multiple Accountabilities Disorder'. *Public Administration Review*, 65(1), 94–108.

Koppell, J. G. S. (2008). Global governance organizations: legitimacy and authority in conflict. *Journal of Public Administration Research and Theory*, 18(2), 177–203.

Mele, V., and Schepers, D. H. (2013). E Pluribus Unum? Legitimacy issues and multi-stakeholder codes of conduct. *Journal of Business Ethics*, 118(3), 561–576.

Mena, S., Palazzo, G., and Arnold, D. G. (2012). Input and output legitimacy of multi-stakeholder initiatives. *Business Ethics Quarterly*, 22(3), 527–556.

O'Rourke, D. (2006). Multi-stakeholder regulation: privatizing or socializing global labor standards? *World Development*, 34(5), 899–918.

Pfitzer, M., Bockstette, V., and Stamp, M. (2013). Innovating for shared value. *Harvard Business Review*.

Rasche, A. (2010). Collaborative Governance 2.0. *Corporate Governance*, 10(4), 500–511.

Reuter, M., and Messner, M. (2015). Lobbying on the integrated reporting framework. *Accounting, Auditing and Accountability Journal*, 28(3), 365–402.

SASB (2013). Conceptual Framework.

SASB (2014a). Conceptual Framework: Record of Public Comment.

SASB (2014b). SASB Industry Working Groups Due Process Report: Consumption I Sector.

SASB (2015a). Consumption I Sector Standards: Record of Public Comment.

SASB (2015b). SASB Standards Council. Standards Council Meeting Report.

SASB (2016a). Brochure.

SASB (2016b). Compilation of all comments received: governance documents.

SASB (2016c). Conceptual Framework: draft for comments.

SASB (2016d). Rules of Procedure: draft for comments.

Schaller, S. (2007). *The Democratic Legitimacy of Private Governance: An Analysis of the Ethical Trading Initiative*. Institute for Development and Peace (INEF), University of Duisburg-Essen.

Schouten, G., and Glasbergen, P. (2011). Creating legitimacy in global private governance: the case of the Roundtable on Sustainable Palm Oil. *Ecological Economics*, 70(11), 1891–1899.

Tschopp, D., and Nastanski, M. (2014). The harmonization and convergence of corporate social responsibility reporting standards. *Journal of Business Ethics*, 125(1), 147–162.

Utting, P. (2002). *Regulating Business via Multistakeholder Initiatives: A Preliminary Assessment*. Geneva: NGLS Development Dossier.

Yin, R. K. (2009). *Case Study Research: Design and Methods*. Applied social research methods series, 4th edn. Los Angeles, CA: Sage Publications.

2.3 Adapting the measuring rod for social returns in advanced welfare states

A critique of SROI

Konstantin Kehl, Gorgi Krlev, Volker Then, and
Georg Mildenberger

Introduction

The social return on investment (SROI) has gained momentum all over the world. It attempts to measure socio-economic returns by linking positive value created for society to costs avoided as a consequence of a specific intervention. What differentiates it from standard (social-)cost–benefit analysis, is its embrace of new ways of capturing fuzzy and indistinct social effects in addition to those that are easily measured. To date, this ambition is only partially realized at best.

In principle, SROI is an appropriate and distinguished instrument of performance and sustainability measurement for social purpose organizations (Nicholls 2009), such that work to create social value (Zahra et al. 2009), for instance foundations, non-profits, non-governmental and civil society organizations, but also firms' corporate social responsibility activities, government-funded programmes and public–private partnerships. Its suitability for assessing social purpose activity lies in its focus on impact, instead of inputs, outputs, efficiency, or other measures of performance. Impact can be defined as gross effects minus 'dead-weight' (i.e., effects that would have occurred anyway) (Krlev et al. 2013; Then et al. 2017). Therefore, SROI is particularly useful in cases where a good or service is not provided as an end in itself but for generating positive effects for society or the environment in the long run. A major challenge, though, comes with the considerable emphasis that has been put on the so-called 'SROI coefficient', a ratio relating (monetized) impact to (financial) input.[1]

Emphasizing the SROI coefficient produces substantial legitimacy problems in corporatist Bismarck-style welfare 'regimes' like the Continental-European ones with universal social insurance schemes (Esping-Anderson 1990; Hinrichs 2000), where social-purpose activity needs to show that it acts as a 'good partner' of the state (Salamon 1995), which provides a general level of welfare. In such contexts, with comprehensive legal entitlements to health and social services, social purpose activity should not be assessed by its ability to deliver welfare services on (quasi-)markets only, but by its capacity to deliver additional value – for example, by stimulating innovation, empowering people (e.g., by giving voice to marginalized clients and issues), or shaping cultural norms and values. If organizational performance is rated by a monetized social return here, the analysis misses out on a large part of relevant information. A related but distinct problem occurs when SROI is applied to environmental sustainability: environmental damage or returns can be expressed in financial categories (Costanza et al. 1997), but it is much easier to report in categories of biodiversity, air quality, or the availability of potable water. SROI therefore needs to embrace and report on multidimensional conceptions of impact, which can be looked at in different ways, depending on the concrete goals of the assessment or the impact levels and stakeholders included.

Our contribution provides the following. First, we outline how SROI and the sustainability discourse are related as well as the basics of impact measurement (why, what for, and how?). We then present an updated version of SROI, originally developed by the Roberts Enterprise Development Fund in the 1990s, consisting of qualitative and quantitative impact dimensions capturing social and environmental returns. We discuss the applicability of the updated SROI version within strong and corporatist welfare regimes, with regard to how it meets three typical problems of an oversimplified interpretation of impact (in terms of methodology, organizational development, and advocacy). Finally, we illustrate how the problems can be dealt with in practice by drawing on a short case discussion of measuring the impact of the 'Free Welfare Associations' in Germany to provide pathways for the durable improvement of SROI.

Sustainability and SROI

As mentioned above and will further be outlined below, the strengths of SROI lie in that it puts significant weight on 'social' benefits or returns, such as empowerment, social cohesion, political participation, and so on. In the desire to turn to these aspects, which are much less tangible than socio-economic returns such as savings for the state, it relates to welfare (economic) approaches that have the development of 'human capabilities and well-being' at their centre (Sen 1993). The latter are core to sustainable development goals globally (United Nations 2015), which relate to education, health, and combating poverty just as to energy use and environmental preservation. SROI is a tool to assess contributions to these goals in both developing and industrialized country contexts.

We focus on the latter for a particular reason: although they are typically at lower needs levels, due to a relatively lower severity of social and environmental problems, it may be more challenging to apply SROI in the context of established welfare structures, where organizations and institutional structures intertwine and effects are hard to isolate and measure reliably.

As for the measurement of effects, SROI stands in the tradition of the triple bottom line concept (Elkington 1998). Although the stress of the concept is on social and environmental issues alike – alongside the generation of profits – the sustainability discourse has always focused somewhat more on environmental aspects (Foxon et al. 2013; Markman et al. 2016; Loorbach 2010) than on social ones. The same applies to tools developed for measuring sustainability (Möller and Schaltegger 2005; Ny et al. 2006; Schmidt et al. 2004). Although most of them incorporate social aspects in some way, they primarily relate to ecological ones, not least due to the settings in which they have originated, namely that of industrial firms.

The 'Social Return on Investment' takes the alternative stance, not least visible in the applied terminology. It has also emerged in a non-profit rather than a for-profit context (Emerson et al. 2000). It is to be remarked, though, that SROI has since evolved to be applied across a variety of contexts and extended to include ecological aspects too (see Krlev et al. 2013). It is therefore clearly relevant to the practice and research of sustainability in both of its primary facets.

Impact measurement: why, what for, and how?

Measuring impact can be a prospective effort, an analysis complementary to other assessments of organizational performance, or a retrospective reflection. To conduct an impact analysis of a specific project, initiative, or organization, a systematic impact model with causal interrelations between actions and effects needs to be developed. Impact on specific stakeholders can then be identified, measured, and, if desired, expressed in monetary values. As a next step, the identified impacts can be aggregated in order to examine the relation between overall impact and input (investment). Sophisticated measurement focuses on impact instead of output performance or other 'key performance indicators' found, for instance, in the balanced score card (Kaplan 2001).

The development of monetary indicators is not the principal objective of impact measurement. Instead, its goal is to understand the wider causal effects of social or environmental investments (actions creating value for society) (Then and Kehl 2012; Kehl and Then 2012), and only where reasonable to monetize them. Thus, impact measurement is not just about assessing possible future savings or positive monetary benefits. Of course, clear and simple figures have a fascination in the context of accounting, and they are particularly attractive with regard to reporting and fund-raising issues, but generally there is much more impact measurement can and should do (Then et al. 2017).

There are several reasons why organizations are interested in social impact analyses. An important reason is to improve their communication. They might want to respond to the current trend of 'evidence-based practice' (Allan 2016), which spans to greater demands and external pressures on social purpose organizations by funders and regulators through evidence-based policy (Fox and Albertson 2011). Furthermore, organizations are interested in better information for their strategic decision-making (Whittington 2012). Impact measurement can also help organizations mobilize resources, and may be most important of all to gain and maintain legitimacy towards stakeholders and the general public (Dart 2004).

Gaining a pioneering position in carrying out well-grounded impact analyses holds great potential for organizations – not least to distinguish themselves from competitors. Dealing with impact, or phenomena that feed into it such as social innovation, may also trigger a revision of expectations and goal sets within social purpose organizations. Some of them approach the topic proactively, while others meet it with general scepticism (compare to our sketching of conflicting images of innovation in major German non-profit organizations; Nock et al. 2013). Measurement enthusiasts believe that every social or environmental impact can easily be measured. This view entails that principles and logics used to assess firms' commercial success can simply be transferred to organizations and initiatives in the social and environmental sector. Measurement sceptics by contrast regard impact measurement as a tool of over-rationalization and marketization.

Both perspectives have in common that they generally underestimate the potential that impact analyses may have on organizational learning, organizational development, and decision-making (Arvidson and Lyon 2014; Maier et al. 2014). Impact analyses lay the foundations for decision-making that is directed by proofs of concept, and they help understand the 'theory of change' or logic model (Weiss 1998) of an organization or initiative. To enable the latter, impact modelling is crucial. An impact model is a logical sketch of how an organization, project, or initiative works under certain circumstances. Each model consists of individual chains which are varied by the stakeholder group taken into focus as the main beneficiary of the activities performed. The sum of impact chains then yields the comprehensive impact model comprising a sequence of inputs, activities, outputs, outcomes, and impacts (Clark et al. 2004).

Input refers to (financial and non-monetary) resources and in-kind benefits. Activities implemented and carried out generate an output. The directly measurable goods or services of a project, initiative, or organization, such as course lessons and consultancy sessions, are referred to as output. It produces effects which can be called outcome. The social and environmental reality is complex, and it is likely that some of the effects would have happened anyway, that is, without the intervention. These effects are called 'dead weight' and must be deducted from the outcome. The result is the generated impact. Highly elaborated impact analyses aim at identifying measures that are capable of grasping and gauging this 'net impact' (Then et al. 2017).

We observe a recent trend towards more differentiated instruments and a growing consideration for the particularities of public benefit activities as different from measuring economic success of for-profit activities performed in commercial markets (Social Impact Investment Taskforce 2014). However, we still lack sophisticated instruments, ways, and strategies of giving credit to the distinct roles social purpose organizations can take apart from their service-providing function. Those entail acting as 'advocates or value guardians' (Anheier 2014), as 'brokers' in policy networks (Weible et al. 2009), or in the stimulation of societal advancement and renewal through innovation (Anheier et al. 2014).

Until now, it has been common practice in the world of impact measurement to assess what is easy to measure instead of measuring what matters in the context of an organization, a project, or initiative, its goals, and stakeholders. A large-scale systematic review of 112 SROI studies performed internationally between 2000 and 2012 (Krlev et al. 2013) has shown that the field of work integration – where the approach has also originally been developed – is still the dominant field of application, because here it is rather easy to apply and calculate a monetary value. Along with other positive effects work integration efforts might have, ranging from increased self-worth to individual pro-activeness to wider positive dynamics in the individual's peer group, their main impact lies in moving a person from a state of financial dependence to financial independence, or from state benefits to earned income. Since there are reliable and comprehensive data on state benefits for unemployed people, or on the income earned in a new job and the tax payments that ensue, SROI analyses in the field almost exclusively focus on the latter.

While targeting economic and direct socio-economic benefits (reduced state benefits) may be justified in a field like work integration, this is much less so in fields where effects are harder to assess. Among the latter, we find life coaching, education, social integration, housing, development assistance, and so on. Effectiveness in those fields lies in the promotion of social cohesion, individual empowerment, participation, or awareness-raising. Although about 45 per cent of the investigated SROI studies were located in the listed fields, the respective effects made up only about 25 per cent of applied indicators against 75 per cent focusing on the aforementioned (socio-) economic measures, skill levels (knowledge and expertise) that can be tested by standardized tests, or accessible satisfaction measures (mostly related to health or general well-being). What is more, the measurement quality of the more 'fuzzy' indicators was particularly poor. They drew mostly on single questionnaire items or episodic interview statements, and focused more on forcefully finding monetary proxies rather than making sure that suggested individual-level effects were robust. This underscores that the application of SROI needs to be improved and in which areas such improvement would need to take place.

SROI revisited: measuring what matters instead of focusing on what is easy to measure

Before sketching roads to improvement, let us first reconsider how SROI works in its original outfit. SROI tracks the social benefits of a social investment and translates certain aspects of the social value created into a coefficient expressing the return in relation to the input. It also encourages alternative quantitative and qualitative capturing of returns. Thus, three dimensions of impact are considered, which we summarize in relation to the classical work integration example:

- *Economic returns*, i.e., financial returns that a project or organization creates (e.g., the revenues a work-integration project, initiative, or organization produces through selling products on the market);
- *Socio-economic returns*, i.e., savings for the state (the government or social insurance systems) through the avoidance of public transfers (e.g., to jobless people) as well as the increase in personal income and tax revenues;
- *Social returns*, i.e., non-tangible effects such as increased self-esteem or individual pro-activeness.

In addition to the systemization of returns, SROI embraces three key rationales (Krlev et al. 2013):

- *Monetizable value creation: 'economic' and 'socio-economic value'*
  In parallel to a standard return on investment calculation, some aspects of social value can be translated into financial value. This pertains to all economic returns and some socio-economic returns.
- *Non-monetizable value creation: 'social value'*
  Other aspects of social value cannot be monetized. SROI accounts for it by encouraging both quantitative and qualitative methods from different social sciences. This usually relates to the social returns and also to some socio-economic returns.
- *Value is primarily created for society, not for the investor*
  A third important insight is that a social investment creates value for different stakeholders. The investor might be among them but usually she is not the main beneficiary. Instead of focussing on the investor, SROI tries to identify and capture returns generated for other stakeholder groups, including society as a whole.

Based on the above, SROI is marked by two main attractions: (1) a logic that is familiar to decision-makers and accountants, namely that of returns; (2) the embrace of alternative methods of impact assessment and a stress on 'social' effects, whereby social translates into hard to assess. As outlined above considerably more attention has been given to the first aspect, leading to the challenges and deficiencies we sketched (and will be specified below).

Therefore, an integrated version of SROI is needed (see for the distinction Then et al. 2017). In this version, social effects are not interpreted as a residual category but central to the instrument – and therefore identified by a set of qualitative and quantitative impact dimensions, most of which are fundamentally non-monetary. They include social capital and network density, social trust, or political advocacy. These components need to be assessed as rigorously as the monetizable parts of impact. And this is needed in view of the organizational population SROI mainly relates to.

What makes social purpose organizations different from economic organizations is that they are typically oriented toward public welfare in a wider sense and characterized by a mix of activities. They serve a multitude of functions or roles at the same time. Of course, they are often service providers in a rather economic sense (e.g., church-based welfare organizations). A classical argument in institutional theory assumes that demand heterogeneity exists in the provision of public goods and that social organizations fill niches left by the state's inability to provide adequate supply (Kingma 2003; Weisbrod 1975). By transferring service provision to external organizations, the state focuses on what it is 'specialized' in (i.e., decision-making and legal guarantees), whereas non-profits offer services on the basis of governments' commitments to pay (Salamon 1995). This is exactly what the 'Free Welfare Associations' in Germany (see our case discussion) do and how they are seen by many observers first and foremost – as the 'longer arm' of the state.

But most non-profit organizations are much more than that. In terms of their inclusive role, they help in coping with the transformation of society by building social cohesion and creating trust relationships on a local or regional level. They generate spheres in which particularistic demands can be disseminated and protected beyond the secure space of the family, and enhance the proclamation and practice of religious and cultural values within and across communities. Finally, they are key actors when it comes to safeguarding the political function of interest intermediation and advocacy (Anheier 2014; Putnam and Goss 2002). The functioning of democratic societies can be attributed to social and political capital, which enable collective action through the creation of basic conditions for cooperation – trust, reciprocity, and networks. They are indispensable for vital democracies (Putnam et al. 1993; Almond and Verba 1989; Verba et al. 1995). Similar arguments can be made with relation to the preservation of natural capital that affects human life in even more fundamental ways (or to the debate on sustainable production and consumption) and should therefore be accounted for in impact measurements just as in sustainability reporting systems.

The effects achieved and thus to be analysed span a variety of levels, from individuals, more specifically beneficiaries but also employees (micro level), single organizations or entire organizational fields (meso level), and society as a whole (macro level). Further differentiations can be made in a geographical dimension where impacts refer to the municipal, regional, or state level, or even the national or international level. Taking several perspectives into account becomes necessary when a social investment draws on (and potentially affects) a variety of resources such as the budgets of federal agencies (located in various federal units), social insurance funds (usually located at the national level), municipal subsidies, and resources from civil society (financial, but also time contributed by volunteers). The different levels help identify all relevant stakeholders in order to precisely present all impact aspects of a social intervention. Stakeholder analysis helps determine which groups are affected by the impact model or those that may have an influence on it. Impact analysts should be prepared to find 'unexpected' stakeholders.

To keep complexity manageable, they should however also focus on the most important stakeholder groups.

In addition to the level of actors, impact analysts have to be aware of the dimensions of time (short-, medium-, long-term) and how they relate to the specific intervention. It makes a difference whether an intervention is assumed to have a short (sheltered workshop for training unemployed people) versus a long-term impact (integration into the first labour market and job retention). Some analysts tend to calculate effects over decades thereby levering SROI ratios and other social effects. They do so, although it is rather obvious that projecting life trajectories within complex social realities with precision is almost impossible to do – threatening the reputation of the instrument and the community surrounding it, whose ambition it was and is to make the assessment of impact more sound and clear.

It is becoming evident that integrated SROI has to strike a delicate balance between comprehensiveness and precision, and across several dimensions of impact. In order to accomplish a high-quality SROI analysis, impact should be ordered by the main measurement components (economic, social, political, ecological, cultural, psychological, and physiological), affected levels (micro, meso, and macro level), and projected time frames (short-, medium-, long-term).

Once this is done, the conceptualization of impact has to be connected to a measurement design. The goal is to back up one's claim that effects are causally attributed to the intervention under study. There are several ways to achieve this, most of which stem from evidence-based medicine (Glasziou and Heneghan 2009):

- Experimental designs: two random groups to be examined for effects in comparison with each other, one being subject to the intervention, the other not (randomized controlled trials).
- Quasi-experimental/observational designs: cross-sectional or cohort observations of two existing groups – again, one consisting of people affected by the intervention and the other of people who are not affected, but groups being otherwise as similar as possible.
- Non-experimental designs: before-and-after comparisons (a longitudinal analysis with measurement at several points in time of one group without a comparator).

Before starting the impact analysis process, it has to be checked which of the designs and methods would prove useful with regard to the study focus and the resources available. The mentioned approaches help achieving the overall objective of matching of impacts with the respective activity, but all of them have specific properties influencing the time horizon and the costs and competencies required for the measurement. Some designs might not be feasible for practical or ethical reasons (randomization). Other difficulties might occur. For example, in the observation of two groups (control-group comparison), the difficulty lies in finding two groups of people who live in circumstances as similar as possible. It is usually impossible to arrive 'naturally' at perfect comparability so that 'statistical twins' have to be built using statistical matching methods (i.e., requiring statistical expertise). Generally, there is lots of need for promoting the issue of designs further. In the systematic SROI review only 3 per cent used a controlled design and another 18 per cent some before-and-after comparison (Krlev et al. 2013). Most assessed effects without a baseline.

SROI as a governance tool in the Continental European context

In the following, we discuss the applicability of the integrated SROI approach based on our experience with European social purpose organizations. We argue from a Continental European perspective and put the integrated version to a test in terms of comparability and the appropriateness of SROI becoming a governance tool in the context of strong and corporatist welfare regimes (with large non-profits providing social services and expertise on behalf of governments and social insurance systems).

We address three open questions raised by an oversimplified interpretation of impact and the widespread focus on the SROI coefficient/ratio in particular: how much comparability of SROI analyses do we need, and to what degree do analyses need to be tailor-made? How can we use the potential of impact analyses on learning, development, and decision-making? And how can we better integrate the specific complementary or primary roles social purpose organizations take in corporatist welfare regimes into the measurement approach?

- *Comparability, transparency, and comprehensiveness*

    SROI ratios of different social interventions are far from being comparable. Some observers of the debate on impact measurement therefore argue that we should try to obtain a higher level of methodological comparability in order to base decisions regarding the usefulness of a certain approach on the comparison of the coefficients of different interventions (Ogain et al. 2013). This is an important issue for many European non-profits which are active in diverse fields of social services and sometimes have very different answers to social or environmental problems in their portfolio.

    Even if there were standards on which methods to use and how to apply them, final coefficients will always depend on model assumptions and social contexts. A job integration programme is and always will be an educational effort different from environmental education. The challenge is to find a systematic and shared way of reporting impacts and the respective analysis. This is far more important than standardizing the process of measurement, and thereby stymieing its context adaptability. In this, we need to trust that informed impact analysts and those reading the analysis will be able to make sense of the results, based on the assumptions formulated, just as we (try to) do (though to a lesser extent) with commercial accounts and accountants (Ruff and Olsen 2016).

    Transparency and detail will undoubtedly be assets in this; two features that SROI has lacked in the past, for instance through the publication of summaries without access to the full impact study (Krlev et al. 2013). An integrated SROI approach is better suited for achieving this because it is not limited to a single monetary figure but presents a range of variables and indexes (and their causal relations) for different scenarios (modelling assumptions) and time frames.

    Comprehensive information also informs us on how economic and social returns interact, and how it is possible that a non-profit organization – in a situation of 'market failure' – creates any value at all. According to traditional non-profit theories (Weisbrod 1975), there is no reason for non-profits to exist as long as there are business models which generate constant returns through customers' buying decision. Thus, non-profits mainly exist where customers are not able to pay for services or satisfy their needs in any other fashion. In other words, they operate in contexts of relative deprivation. Some areas of non-profit activity are marked by their persistent character, meaning that non-profits can only mitigate the deprivation and partly (or temporarily) satisfy social needs, but might not be able to solve the problem which produces the deprivation. Most of such activities in turn would produce low SROI ratios. If we were only to look at the latter, they would suggest non-profits do not create any value at all for those affected and society. This might of course be true occasionally, but is likely to change if we systematically assess the social effects that otherwise remain disregarded.

- *Organizational development and compliance*

   In impact measurement it is important not to focus only on reporting and potential communication effects, but to use the measurement process for organizational learning. This would include defining and testing how common goals can be achieved and procedures implemented that enable these goals. Impact measurement could for instance help (dis-)prove whether a vision of blended or shared values, that is commercial, environmental and social ones can be achieved (Emerson 2003; Porter and Kramer 2011). It can also help safeguard comprehensive compliance and support in complex organizational structures, in the sense of defining and implementing bottom-up rather than top-down approaches of governance (see Power et al. 2010 on international NGOs). This is particularly relevant where conflicting institutional logics occur, for example against processes of organizational hybridization (Battilana and Lee 2014). The potential that impact analyses may have on learning effects and organizational development is generally under-estimated, and decision-makers may have to internally solicit support of their measurement initiatives (Paton 2003).

- *Advocacy*

   In developed welfare states, social purpose organizations do not only provide services but are key actors in democratic policy routines and the definition of the 'public good'. It will be important to investigate how impact measurement approaches such as the SROI method can account for that by including the political dimension into a comprehensive measurement approach. The same holds for the field of environmental sustainability on an international level where NGOs, think tanks, and green technology firms are crucial for arbitrating between dichotomous positions (Geels et al. 2015).

   Mechanisms of achieving the goals of an organization through political advocacy on different levels (local, regional, national, etc.) can be empirically analysed with tools from discourse and network analysis; e.g., 'Political Claims Analysis' (PCA) and 'Discourse Network Analysis' (DNA); relating back to advocacy coalitions (Weible et al. 2009). Recent methodological developments allow us to quantitatively track contributions of an organization or a coalition of actors to the discourse about a political conflict, reform debates, and institutional policy negotiations. The content of such discursive contributions can be indexed and positively or negatively related to claims. The material can be translated into a graph and then be analysed statistically by means of social network analysis. From the result, it can be measured how actors or coalitions positioned themselves in a situation of conflict or who was able to successfully fight for a certain position.

   Without such improvements of the impact measurement methodologies, it we will be unlikely that SROI or other approaches will become broadly acceptable at the European level. This is because economic value creation and the orientation toward clients both, in terms of the quality of services but also, and often more importantly, in relation to advocacy work performed are conceptualized and embedded as common practice and strongly interdependent. In particular, large welfare organizations, such as the German 'Free Welfare Associations', do put at least as much weight on service provision as on advocacy, since the latter is crucial for shaping legal standards that govern (quasi-)markets or the entitlement of fundamental rights to target groups, for instance in relation to people with disabilities.

In consequence, SROI in the Continental European context, and in countries similar to it, needs to embrace a variety of dimensions and come with a rather large repertoire of defining, operationalizing, and measuring different facets of impact. This includes quantitative variables (ratios) for social cohesion, networks, trust, advocacy, etc., and qualitative accounts thereof. We have tested how far the integrated version of SROI would be practically capable of assessing some of the impacts produced by major players in the German non-profit landscape. To do this, we have screened the relative performance or capacity of SROI to capture impacts relative to alternative approaches. The insights gained are presented in the following brief case discussion.

SROI as an instrument to measure the impact of multi-faceted organizations

Here, we discuss methods appropriate to capture the impact of the 'Free Welfare Associations' in Germany. The 'Free Welfare Associations' (Freie Wohlfahrtspflege) include six major entities: Caritas and Diakonie (church-related), Arbeiterwohlfahrt (AWO; workers' welfare), Paritätischer (free association of otherwise independent providers), Deutsches Rotes Kreuz (DRK; Red Cross) and Zentralwohlfahrtsstelle der Juden in Deutschland (ZWST; Jewish providers). Together, they account for about two-thirds of the German non-profit sector in terms of employees (1.7 million) and 2.6 per cent of the German GDP. Professional social services provided by the associations in fields like health, eldercare, and social work for children, families, or the unemployed are complemented by approximately three million volunteers in different contexts of local communities and informal networks.

Different approaches of impact measurement can (partly) capture and represent impacts in the sense of the production of goods and services, increased social capital, values expressed and represented, and effective advocacy for political claims. Impact approaches, however, should also be capable of integrating these perspectives, include in their framework a range of relevant stakeholders, and (at least potentially) support an assessment of overall impact on society. Candidates that could be considered along these dimensions are very rare, though.

A state-of-the-art list of approaches placed in this realm and identified in the current literature has been recently rated according to the following criteria (Kehl et al. 2016): (1) methodological quality; (2) quantitative and monetized measurement of impact; (3) variety of impact dimensions and levels of impact; (4) degree of standardization and resource requirements; (5) fields of application and target audiences. The analysis looked in depth at five approaches for the purpose of illustrating strengths and weaknesses: Conventional Cost–Benefit Analysis (CBA)[2] (Drèze and Stern 1985), Impact Reporting and Investment Standard (IRIS) (Global Impact Investing Network (GIIN) 2010),

SROI, Quality of Life (QoL) (Kahneman and Krueger 2006), and Political Discourse Network Analysis (DNA) (Leifeld and Haunss 2010). The latter two are frameworks of analysis which are usually not considered when people think about impact measurement, since they are broad umbrella concepts (QoL) or used for specific analyses in an academic niche (DNA). However, they can contribute to filling substantial gaps left by the 'conventional' candidates (Tuan 2008): for example, none of them has ever focused explicitly on political impact while there are many approaches in policy research to address and measure how actors frame and influence public policy.

Table 2.3.1 summarizes the results of the comparison. It covers the following aspects: (1) the main impact levels of the approaches (ranging from micro: individual clients – macro: society), (2) the impact dimensions captured (covering economic goods/services, social integration effects, cultural value-added, political influence and power), (3) the application of a causal impact model ('theory of change') as a core part of the analysis, (4) the scope of quantification, and (5) monetization procedures (on an ideal-type continuum from purely qualitative approaches to mere monetization), (6) the methodological sophistication (on a continuum between 'no (variety of) social science methods applied' at one end and 'transparent and extensive use of social science methodology' on the other), (7) range of target groups, (8) standardization (ease of reproduction), and (9) resources/competencies required to perform the analysis.

The table illustrates the different foci, strengths, and weaknesses of existing methodologies. We can see that all approaches, except for the integrated SROI, cover impact levels and dimensions only partly, and some have a very strong focus on the economic dimension (CBA, and also, but to a somewhat lesser degree, IRIS). It is also becoming apparent, though all have predefined methodologies, only SROI incorporates explicitly the identification of the impact model of the analysed intervention. SROI is furthermore capable of quantifying and monetizing effects, while it encourages the application of qualitative research. The other approaches either focus on the former exclusively (CBA) or are not or only partly able to perform these steps (IRIS, DNA). Only QoL can in principle also cater to both, but does not embrace qualitative assessments of effects in the same way as SROI. In terms of methodological sophistication, we can say that SROI is in principle capable of integrating a rather diverse set of methods, while the other approaches rely mostly on one logic and method of assessing impact. Sophistication in DNA is rated high, since it is rather new and tries to translate discourse constellations and trajectories into statistical data. There is also some variation as regards the addressees of the different measurement tools. Only SROI, as outlined initially, explicitly takes account of funders, the organization, and society as a whole alike. A potential downside of the integrated SROI against the other approaches comes from its multi-facetedness, which demands a high degree of resources, both at single or first use and when repeated, and also a high and diverse level of skills or competencies throughout.

How are these traits relevant against our organizational population of the 'Free Welfare Associations' in Germany? Some of the observations made above are crucial for them:

- *Impact model*: The variety of activities performed by the 'Free Welfare Associations' necessitates a systematic account of which activities, or elements therein, are supposed to have which kinds of impact. An approach incapable of providing such information would likely lead to a short-sighted or ambiguous analysis. What is more, in particular in view of advocacy effects, it is not sufficient to look at activities

Table 2.3.1 Five approaches to measuring the impact of multi-faceted organizations

		CBA	QoL	IRIS	DNA	Integrated SROI
(1)	Impact level	Micro	Micro	Micro/Meso	Macro	Micro/Meso/Macro
(2)	Impact dimensions	Economic Social	Cultural Social	Economic Social	Political	Economic Social Cultural
(3)	Impact model	↓	↓	↓	↓	↑
(4)	Quantification	Yes	Partly	Partly	Possible	Partly
(5)	Monetization	Yes	Partly	No	No	Partly
(6)	Methodological sophistication	↔	↔	↔	↗ to ↑	↗ to ↑
(7)	Target groups	Donors/funders, internal decision-makers	Decision-makers, wider public	Investors, donors/ funders	Decision-makers, wider public	Donors/funders, decision-makers, wider public
(8)	Necessary resources (first time)	↔	↔	↓	↑	↑
(8.1)	Necessary resources (regular assessment)	↘	↘	↓	↗	↗
(9)	Necessary skills/ competencies	↔	↔	↓	↑	↗ to ↑

performed or outputs, which some of the alternative methodologies do. The explicit formulation of an impact model as contained in SROI is vital in our case.

- *Levels of impact*: Pertaining to the above issue but from another angle, namely that of legitimacy and accountability towards the state, but also other societal stakeholders, the measurement model applied to the 'Free Welfare Associations' needs to take into account the micro level (beneficiaries), meso level (organizations and fields of activity), and the macro level (society). Besides, the measurement approach would need to uncover interconnections between the three.

- *Dimensions of impact*: As discussed previously, the economic dimension is not the most important for the 'Free Welfare Associations'. They exist under conditions where economic principles can insufficiently explain the value they create. Measuring their impact thus has to take into account their other functions and effects, in particular cultural and political dimensions, which are hardly covered by (single) approaches other than SROI.

The above suggests that SROI in its integrated outfit is a promising methodology for assessing the impact in contexts marked by developed welfare structures. The beauty of SROI lies in its methodological richness and openness. Some of its drawbacks or imperfections in its original outfit can, however, benefit from drawing on other, long-existing (CBA) or new approaches, some of which have been developed in parallel (IRIS) or independent of impact measurement focusing on organizational activities (QoL and DNA). In addition to this, there is more potential in developing SROI further by enriching it with insights from various academic disciplines, such as education, medicine, social care, cultural sociology, or public policy.

At a generic level, SROI is already very useful as a methodological and conceptual base from which we can determine the level of rigour and abstraction needed in an impact analysis as well as the concrete instruments to be applied. In order to draft a comprehensive measurement for the 'Free Welfare Associations', a coordinated, large-scale effort would be necessary to clarify the relevant impact models in the different fields of activity and the strategic relevance of their measurement. This would best happen at the level of the 'General Assembly' (BAGFW) in which all six 'Free Welfare Associations' are represented. A combination of integrated approaches based on the conceptual background of an integrated SROI could then yield different modules of a comprehensive impact measurement concept and help establish continued monitoring efforts.

Where is the beef? Insights on applying the integrated SROI

What would be SROI building blocks in the context of the 'Free Welfare Associations'? There is no doubt about the economic dimension that should capture the contribution to social welfare by taking into account the sum of services provided and exchanged on markets.

The Free Welfare Associations create impact in many other ways, though: in local networks, for instance, welfare organizations perform a substantial accelerator function by bringing people together, initiating exchange, and spurring mutual support. Of course, such aspects are anything but easy to measure. However, we can ask the people involved about their attitudes and beliefs, social relations, and time dedicated to a range of activities they perform. Reliable instruments such as those applied in the *European Values Study* or the *World Values Survey* are helpful in this endeavour.

Another important aspect of the Associations' daily business refers to the political dimension of issue framing, advocacy, and influencing the political discourse. In relation to a variety of themes, and in order to pin down the Association's impact in these areas, we would need to outline why certain policy initiatives succeeded (or failed) and how the 'Free Welfare Associations' defined their role in the process of iterative argumentation and coalition-building. Although causal attribution is hardly ever possible in real socio-political contexts, we can generate strong evidence to suggest that (coalitions of) actors were central to a discourse and decisions (or not) and the policy would have gone in another direction without their intervention (counterfactual reasoning). Mixed-method designs, combining approaches from discourse (Foucault 1972; Habermas and MacCarthy 1984), network (Newman 2015; Wasserman and Faust 1994), and power resources theory (Esping-Anderson 1985; Korpi 1983) can help understand processes, outcomes, and actor contributions in a targeted fashion.

An exercise of this kind has been performed by Kehl (2016) in the field of eldercare policy and the role of the 'Free Welfare Associations' therein. He studied the development and implementation of a strategy that was to more strongly focus on prevention, ease tensions produced by reconciling job requirements and care for individuals who cared for one of their family members, and promote informal and civic structures of support.

Kehl applied DNA and used communicative structures at given phases of the discourse to identify coalitions, that is, groups of actors that argue for or against political ideas and programmes in a similar way. He transformed qualitative date generated in a content analysis of relevant documents (official records, media articles, press releases) to a standardized network graph by categorizing claims and frames, identifying actors, and connecting them systematically to dominant discourse networks. In a second step, he computed clusters and centrality measures as predictors of the actors' roles.

He found that the 'Free Welfare Associations' were strongly involved in the process, but not the most passionate advocates of innovative eldercare policies due to an endogenous conflict between their service providing rationales and civil society identities. Yet, they provided prompts towards reaching the formulated goals that would likely not have been achieved if not for their presence.

Since the study employs quantitative (social network) metrics, it is possible – in an integrated SROI framework – to replicate it with respect to other discourses and decisions, and to compare organizations' roles in other policy domains. Based on strategic goals, the intended use of the measurement, or the (lower) complexity of individual fields of application, less rigorous instruments could also be helpful and sufficient to assess the impact of organizations' actions. For cursory estimates of impact and performance the mere development of an impact model – that is, a formulation of expected causal links between activities and effects – might suffice to derive some simple indicators that can be used in everyday management.

When it comes to far-reaching and potentially conflict-ridden decision-making, though, we would need evidence that emerges from a measurement model that is more demanding in terms of methodology, resources, skills, scope of analysis, and rigour of results. This applies in particular when results are to be used for political advocacy and in public communication. The integrated SROI allows us to do both.

Conclusions

In our chapter, we discussed the applicability of the social return on investment (SROI) approach from a Continental European perspective. We have shown the capabilities as well as the current deficiencies of SROI and how they could be addressed by promoting an integrated SROI, characterized by a number of traits: (1) a more balanced view on evidence, in particular a shift from focusing on the SROI ratio to developing and embracing other sorts of evidence, including qualitative data; (2) the acknowledgement and explicit assessment of social, political, and cultural aspects next to economic and socio-economic ones; (3) the enrichment of tools, methods, approaches, and principles of analysis by incorporating elements of other impact approaches and a variety of academic disciplines; (4) the appreciation of complexity and multi-facetedness over the urge for simplification as a presumed road to standardization. In this outfit, integrated SROI can not only help assess individual initiatives, but also conceptualize and fathom the impact of large providers (networks) located in developed welfare contexts, such as the 'Free Welfare Associations' in Germany, and similar organizations and contexts.

Notes

1 An SROI ratio of 1:2 implies a social return of 100 per cent. In other words, every invested Euro (or Dollar) creates effects worth two Euros (or Dollars).
2 Please note that SROI is essentially a variation of (social) cost–benefit analysis (Krlev et al. 2013).

References

Allan, W. L., 2016. Factors that impact how civil society intermediaries perceive evidence. *Evidence & Policy: A Journal of Research, Debate and Practice.*

Almond, G. A., and Verba, S., 1989. *The Civic Culture Revisited: Political Attitudes and Democracy in Five Nations.* Newbury Park, CA: Sage Publications.

Anheier, H. K., 2014. *Nonprofit Organizations: Theory, Management, Policy.* 2nd edn. London: Routledge.

Anheier, H. K., et al., 2014. *Social Innovation as Impact of the Third Sector.* Deliverable 1.1 of the project: 'Impact of the Third Sector as Social Innovation' (ITSSOIN), European Commission – 7th Framework Programme, Brussels: European Commission, DG Research.

Arvidson, M., and Lyon, F., 2014. Social impact measurement and non-profit organisations: compliance, resistance, and promotion. *VOLUNTAS: International Journal of Voluntary and Nonprofit Organizations,* 25(4), 869–886.

Battilana, J., and Lee, M., 2014. Advancing research on hybrid organizing: insights from the study of social enterprises. *The Academy of Management Annals,* 8(1), 397–441.

Clark, C., et al., 2004. *Double Bottom Line Project: Assessing Social Impact in Double Bottom Line Ventures.* Working Paper 13. Center for Responsible Business, University of California Berkeley.

Costanza, R., et al., 1997. The value of the world's ecosystem services and natural capital. *Nature,* 387(6630), 253–260.

Dart, R., 2004. The legitimacy of social enterprise. *Nonprofit Management and Leadership,* 14(4), 411–424.

Drèze, J., and Stern, N., 1985. The theory of cost–benefit analysis. In: A. J. Auerbach and M. S. Feldstein, eds., *Handbook of Public Economics.* Amsterdam: North-Holland, 909–990.

Elkington, J., 1998. Partnerships from cannibals with forks: the triple bottom line of 21st-century business. *Environmental Quality Management,* 8(1), 37–51.

Emerson, J., 2003. The Blended Value Proposition: integrating social and financial returns. *California Management Review*, 45(4), 35–51.

Emerson, J., Wachowicz, J., and Chun, S., 2000. Social return on investment: exploring aspects of value creation in the nonprofit sector. In: Roberts Enterprise Development Fund, ed. *REDF Box Set.* Vol. 2, 132–173.

Esping-Anderson, G., 1985. *Politics against Markets: The Social Democratic Road to Power.* Princeton: Princeton University Press.

Esping-Anderson, G., 1990. *The Three Worlds of Welfare Capitalism.* Princeton: Princeton University Press.

Foucault, M., 1972. *The Archaeology of Knowledge and the Discourse on Language.* New York: Pantheon Books.

Fox, C., and Albertson, K., 2011. Payment by results and social impact bonds in the criminal justice sector: new challenges for the concept of evidence-based policy? *Criminology and Criminal Justice*, 11(5), 395–413.

Foxon, T. J., et al., 2013. Towards a new complexity economics for sustainability. *Cambridge Journal of Economics*, 37(1), 187–208.

Geels, F., McMeekin, A., Mylan, J., and Southerton, D., 2015. A critical appraisal of sustainable consumption and production research: the reformist, revolutionary and reconfiguration positions. *Global Environmental Change*, 34(1), 1–12.

Glasziou, P., and Heneghan, C., 2009. A spotter's guide to study designs. *Evidence-Based Medicine*, 14(2), 37–38.

Global Impact Investing Network (GIIN), 2010. *Impact Reporting and Investment Standards (IRIS).*

Habermas, J., and MacCarthy, T. A., 1984. *The Theory of Communicative Action.* Boston: Beacon.

Hinrichs, K., 2000. Elephants on the move: patterns of public pension reform in OECD countries. *European Review*, 8(3), 353–378.

Kahneman, D., and Krueger, A. B., 2006. Developments in the measurement of subjective well-being. *The Journal of Economic Perspectives*, 20(1), 3–24.

Kaplan, R. S., 2001. Strategic performance measurement and management in nonprofit organizations. *Nonprofit Management and Leadership*, 11(3), 353–370.

Kehl, K., 2016. *Sozialinvestive Pflegepolitik in Deutschland. Familiäre und zivilgesellschaftliche Potenziale im Abseits wohlfahrtsstaatlichen Handelns.* Wiesbaden: Springer VS.

Kehl, K., and Then, V., 2012. *Social Investment: A Sociological Outline.* Paper presented at ISTR's 10th International Conference on Democratization, Marketization, and the Third Sector 2012 in Siena, Italy: Centre for Social Investment Heidelberg.

Kehl, K., et al., 2016. *Möglichkeiten, Wirkungen (in) der Freien Wohlfahrtspflege zu messen:* Centre for Social Investment Heidelberg.

Kingma, B., 2003. Public good theories of the nonprofit sector. In: H. K. Anheier and A. Ben-Ner, eds., *The Study of the Nonprofit Enterprise: Theories and Approaches.* New York: Kluwer Academic / Plenum Publishers, 53–66.

Korpi, W., 1983. *The Democratic Class Struggle.* London: Routledge.

Krlev, G., Münscher, R., and Mülbert, K., 2013. *Social Return on Investment (SROI): State-of-the-Art and Perspectives. A Meta-Analysis of Practice in Social Return on Investment (SROI) Studies Published 2000–2012.*

Leifeld, P., and Haunss, S., 2010. *A Comparison between Political Claims Analysis and Discourse Network Analysis: The Case of Software Patents in the European Union.* Max Planck Institute for Research on Collective Goods.

Loorbach, D., 2010. Transition management for sustainable development: a prescriptive, complexity-based governance framework. *Governance*, 23(1), 161–183.

Maier, F., Schober, C., Simsa, R., and Millner, R., 2014. SROI as a method for evaluation research: understanding merits and limitations. *VOLUNTAS: International Journal of Voluntary and Nonprofit Organizations*, 26(5), 1805–1830.

Markman, G. D., et al., 2016. Entrepreneurship as a platform for pursuing multiple goals: a special issue on sustainability, ethics, and entrepreneurship. *Journal of Management Studies*, 53(5), 673–694.

Möller, A., and Schaltegger, S., 2005. The sustainability balanced scorecard as a framework for eco-efficiency analysis. *Journal of Industrial Ecology*, 9(4), 73–83.

Newman, M. E. J., 2015. *Networks: An Introduction*. Oxford: Oxford University Press.

Nicholls, A., 2009. 'We do good things, don't we?': 'Blended Value Accounting' in social entrepreneurship. *Accounting, Organizations and Society*, 34(6–7), 755–769.

Nock, L., Krlev, G., and Mildenberger, G., 2013. *Soziale Innovationen in den Spitzenverbänden der Freien Wohlfahrtspflege. Strukturen, Prozesse und Zukunftsperspektiven.*

Ny, H., et al., 2006. Sustainability constraints as system boundaries: an approach to making life-cycle management strategic. *Journal of Industrial Ecology*, 10(1–2), 61–77.

Ogain, E. N., Las Casas, L. de, and Svistak, M., 2013. *Blueprint for Shared Measurement: Developing, Designing and Implementing Shared Approaches to Impact Measurement*. New Philanthropy Capital.

Paton, R., 2003. *Managing and Measuring Social Enterprises*. London, Thousand Oaks: Sage Publications.

Porter, M. E., and Kramer, M. R., 2011. Creating shared value: how to reinvent capitalism – and unleash a wave of innovation and growth. *Harvard Business Review* (January–February), 2–17.

Power, G., Maury, M., and Maury, S., 2010. Operationalising bottom-up learning in international NGOs: barriers and alternatives. *Development in Practice*, 12 (3–4), 272–284.

Putnam, R. D., and Goss, K. A., 2002. Introduction. In: R. D. Putnam, ed., *Democracies in Flux: The Evolution of Social Capital in Contemporary Society*. Oxford, New York: Oxford University Press, 1–19.

Putnam, R. D., Leonardi, R., and Nanetti, R. Y., 1993. *Making Democracy Work: Civic Traditions in Modern Italy*. Princeton, NJ: Princeton University Press.

Ruff, K., and Olsen, S., 2016. *The Next Frontier in Social Impact Measurement Isn't Measurement at All.* Available from: https://ssir.org/articles/entry/the_next_frontier_in_social_impact_measurement_isnt_measurement_at_all.

Salamon, L. M., 1995. *Partners in Public Service: Government Nonprofit Relations in the Modern Welfare State*. Baltimore: Johns Hopkins University Press.

Schmidt, I., et al., 2004. SEEbalance: managing sustainability of products and processes with the socio-eco-efficiency analysis by BASF. *Greener Management International*, 45(Spring), 80–94.

Sen, A. K., 1993. Capability and well-being. In: M. Nussbaum and A. Sen, eds., *The Quality of Life*. Oxford: Oxford University Press, 30–53.

Social Impact Investment Taskforce, 2014. *Measuring Impact.*

Then, V., and Kehl, K., 2012. Soziale Investitionen. Ein konzeptioneller Entwurf. In: H. K. Anheier, A. Schröer, and V. Then, eds., *Soziale Investitionen. Interdisziplinäre Perspektiven*. Wiesbaden: VS Verlag für Sozialwissenschaften, 39–86.

Then, V., Schober, C., Kehl, K., and Rauscher, O., 2017. *Social Return on Investment: Measuring the Impact of Social Investment*. Basingstoke: Palgrave Macmillan.

Tuan, M. T., 2008. *Measuring and/or Estimating Social Value Creation: Insights into Eight Integrated Cost Approaches*. Bill & Melinda Gates Foundation.

United Nations, 2015. Sustainable development goals [online]. Available from: http://www.un.org/sustainabledevelopment/sustainable-development-goals/ [Accessed 8 June 2017].

Verba, S., Schlozman, K. L., and Brady, H. E., 1995. *Voice and Equality: Civic Voluntarism in American Politics*. Cambridge, MA: Harvard University Press.

Wasserman, S., and Faust, K., 1994. *Social Network Analysis*. Cambridge: Cambridge University Press.

Weible, C. M., Sabatier, P. A., and McQueen, K., 2009. Themes and variations: taking stock of the Advocacy Coalition Framework. *The Policy Studies Journal*, 37(1), 121–140.

Weisbrod, B. A., 1975. Toward a theory of the voluntary nonprofit sector in a three-sector economy. In: E. S. Phelps, ed., *Altruism, Morality and Economic Theory*. New York: Russell Sage Foundation.

Weiss, C. H., 1998. *Evaluation: Methods for Studying Programs and Policies*, 2nd edn. Upper Saddle River, NJ: Prentice Hall.

Whittington, R., 2012. Big strategy/small strategy. *Strategic Organization*, 10(3), 263–268.

Zahra, S. A., et al., 2009. A typology of social entrepreneurs: motives, search processes and ethical challenges. *Journal of Business Venturing*, 24, 519–532.

2.4 Measuring the impact of strategic corporate social responsibility (S-CSR)

Finding the right approach

Fabian Herkenrath and Christine Vallaster

Introduction

With advancing globalization, the restructuring of the welfare state, corporate and environmental scandals (Müller-Christ and Rehm, 2010), as well as the incremental loss of control of national states (Ankele and Schank, 2016), the adoption of responsibility is increasingly being demanded by politicians, consumers, non-governmental organizations (NGOs), and other stakeholders that are affected directly or indirectly.

Companies are expected to adopt social and ecological responsibility in addition to their economic activities. In this way, companies have to increasingly deal with the negative consequences of their actions, such as environmental pollution, employee exploitation, or wage inequality (Müller-Christ and Rehm, 2010). They are expected to contribute towards finding solutions to help solve these issues. This principle is not new; it has a long tradition in Central Europe as well as in the USA. Nevertheless, today's understanding goes beyond pure charity (Müller-Christ and Rehm, 2010) and philanthropy. The debate evolving around corporate social responsibility has become increasingly public and has spread to numerous levels (Hansen and Schrader, 2005), increasingly affecting the legitimacy of an organization.

In this chapter, we discuss first the conceptual nuances that exist when talking about corporate social responsibility. We then introduce four approaches that are frequently used in practice to measure the social and ecological impact of organizational activities. These are finally evaluated on the basis of their thematic focus, target group, level of detail, transparency, legal status, and addressee.

Setting the stage

We start by defining the term corporate social responsibility (CSR) and delineate the concept from terms such as corporate citizenship (CC), including corporate giving (CG), corporate foundations (CF), and corporate volunteering (CV), as well as sustainability.

Corporate citizenship is referred to as civic engagement and goes beyond economic activity (Curbach, 2009). CC includes corporate donations and sponsorships, for example to sports clubs or cultural events on the company's premises. Such an engagement is also referred to as Corporate giving (Curbach, 2009). Corporate citizenship also encompasses corporate volunteering, that is, various forms of employee engagement, mostly on a voluntary basis. Some organizations also set up charitable foundations, which are referred to as corporate foundations. Corporate citizenship is thus made up of various forms of commitment. The organization's perspective is to represent a sustainable development of the company and its social engagement, that is, to present the company as a "good citizen" (Müller-Christ and Rehm, 2010).

Amongst practitioners, the concept of sustainability is often equated with CSR (Curbach, 2009). Sustainability has its origins in the forestry industry and describes a lasting balance between social, ecological, and economic aspects (Curbach, 2009). The 1987 Brundtland Report of the United Nations defines sustainability as "development that satisfies the needs of the present without risking that future generations will not be able to meet their own needs" (World Commission on Environment and Development, 2015).

Building on this definition, the European Commission has defined CSR as a concept that goes beyond legal and contractual obligations, which includes social responsibility, raising social and environmental standards, open corporate policy, and sustainability. By committing themselves to their social responsibility and voluntarily accepting commitments that go beyond the legal and contractual obligations that are already to be met, companies are striving to raise social and environmental protection standards and to ensure that fundamental rights are more consistently respected. In doing so, they practise an open corporate policy that seeks to reconcile conflicting interests in a global view of quality and sustainability.

In 2011, this definition was extended to include the strategic component of CSR, which combines all the above-mentioned aspects and is linked to the core business of the companies and thus goes far beyond the voluntary basis of the terms (European Commission, 2011). At this point, the concept of strategic CSR is intentionally addressed, since social and ecological commitment associated with the core business can actually be described as a responsibility towards society. Companies that adopt such an inclusive approach exist (e.g., Patagonia www.patagonia.com), yet typically engage in a long transition period.

Approaches to measure strategic CSR

In the following, we present the Global Reporting Initiative (GRI), ISO 26000, Social Return on Investment (SROI), as well as *Gemeinwohlökonomie* (GWÖ).

The Global Reporting Initiative (GRI)

The Global Reporting Initiative was founded in 1997 and developed in cooperation with the United Nations Environment Programme (UNEP). GRI has set itself the task of standardizing and evaluating sustainability reports in a joint effort with international stakeholders from business, employers' and employees' representatives, government authorities, the financial markets, and auditors (Global Reporting Initiative, 2015). A catalogue of indicators in the fields of social welfare, ecology, and economy has been developed with the intention to create globally standardized framework conditions (Köppl and Neureiter, 2004).

The first part of the GRI guidelines provides reporting principles and standard disclosures for reporting, regardless of the size, industry, or location of the organization. The second part provides guidelines for sustainability reporting that supports companies in implementing their CSR commitment.

The reporting principles are divided into the "Principles for determining the content of reports" and the "Principles for determining the quality of reports". They serve to increase the transparency of sustainability reporting and should therefore be observed by all companies.

The *principles for determining the content* of the report are intended to prescribe the procedure and content of the report, taking into account the activities, impacts, and significant expectations and interests of the stakeholders of a company. The principles include the aspects of stakeholder involvement, sustainability context, materiality, and completeness.

The *principle of stakeholder engagement* states that each company should identify its stakeholders and report on the extent to which their expectations and interests have been addressed. The sustainability context is the presentation of a company's performance in the broader context of sustainable development. It should not only focus on individual (partial) services, but also on all improvements and deteriorations at a local, regional, and global level. Only essential aspects are to be included in the report. This applies to issues relating to the ecological, economic, and social impact of the company as well as to issues that could have an impact on the decision of stakeholders.

The principles for determining the quality of reporting include the aspects of balance, comparability, accuracy, timeliness, clarity, and reliability. They are intended to ensure the quality of the information and to provide an appropriate presentation in order to enable an appropriate assessment by stakeholders. The report should contain both positive and negative achievements. It should also be written in a non-judgemental way, without selective representations and presentation formats. This could influence decisions or judgements. The information is to be presented in a comparable way. Services are to be made easily comparable for the stakeholders, both with previous services, the targets, and, as far as possible, with those of other companies. The accuracy requirements depend on the type of information. These should be as precise as possible in order to enable stakeholders to make an assessment. In order to make sound decisions, stakeholders need regular updates. Their value for stakeholders is linked to the time of publication. The information contained in the report must be presented in a way that is understandable to each of the stakeholders. The report should also stand up to review in terms of information retrieval and analysis. This is the only way to ensure that it is reliable for stakeholders (Global Reporting Initiative, 2015).

The standard specifications are divided into *general* and *specific* standard specifications. The general standard disclosures include strategy and analysis, organizational profile, identified key aspects and limits, stakeholder engagement, reporting profile, governance, ethics, and integrity. They apply to all companies that prepare sustainability reports. Information on strategy and analysis provides a strategic overview of a company's sustainability. The organizational profile represents the characteristics of the company or organization. When determining the essential aspects and limits, the process by which they are determined is described. During the period under review, stakeholder engagement may extend beyond the stakeholders mentioned in the preparation process. The report profile contains information about the report itself. It describes basic information, the GRI content index, and the concept of external review. The corporate governance section describes the structure and composition of the company as well as the role of the highest governance body in the areas of risk management, sustainability reporting, and setting objectives. Ethical and integrity information ultimately provides an overview of the organization's values, norms, and standards (Global Reporting Initiative, 2015).

The specific standard information is divided into the categories economic, ecological, and social, with the last category additionally subdivided into working conditions and decent procurement, human rights, society, and product responsibility.

The economic dimension includes the impact of the organization on the local, national, and international economic system as well as on stakeholders. The ecological dimension covers the impact of activities on nature, including soil, air, water, biodiversity and ecosystem, inbound and outbound products, transport and services, as well as expenditure on environmental protection and compliance. The sub-category of labour practices and humane employment, grouped together in the societal dimension, is made up of different international standards, such as the UN's "International Covenant on Civil and Political Rights". The subcategory of human rights is also based on such standards as the "Universal Declaration of Human Rights". However, this is supplemented by aspects of voluntary guidelines. They concern, *inter alia*, equal treatment and gender equality. The company sub-category describes the impact of the organization or enterprise on the local community. The rights of both population groups and individuals must be respected. The last sub-category, product stewardship, refers to products and services that have an impact on stakeholders and customers (Global Reporting Initiative, 2015).

The aspects of the three dimensions are summarized in Table 2.4.1.

With its comprehensive guidelines, the GRI sets global standards for sustainability reporting on a voluntary basis. As a result, it offers companies and stakeholders alike a similarly good and transparent comparability to financial reports. Furthermore, it helps companies to continuously improve their CSR commitment (Fischbach, 2007).

ISO 26000 (www.iso.org/store.html)

After six years of work by more than 400 experts from 99 countries, and under the direction of the "International Organisation for Standardization" (ISO), the "Guidance on Social Responsibility" (ISO 26000) was published in 2010.

In response to growing consumer concerns about corporate social responsibility and its activities, the ISO Consumer Policy Committee, the Committee on Consumer Policy (COPOLCO), launched an initiative to develop a standard for corporate social responsibility. Since ISO 26000 has been designed for each type of organization, CSR is not explicitly referred to as CSR, but only as social responsibility (Curbach, 2009). This is due to the authors'[3] view that global challenges cannot be met by individual stakeholders, but only by all relevant actors (Schmiedeknecht and Wieland, 2012). It offers companies of all sizes a guide to achieving, evaluating, and comparing their CSR objectives, particularly due to the involvement of all stakeholders and the associated global acceptance, and aims to promote an understanding of corporate social responsibility worldwide (Schmiedeknecht and Wieland, 2012). Stakeholders include consumers, the public sector, business, trade unions, NGOs, service providers, consultants, and scientists. ISO 26000 is intended to ensure a balanced distribution of the continents, as well as the industrialized and emerging countries (Schmiedeknecht and Wieland, 2012). ISO 26000 is comprised of the scope of application, the definition of the term, the understanding of social responsibility, the seven principles that are seen as prerequisite for the implementation of social responsibility, the seven core issues that include various fields of action, and recommendations for action with regard to the integration of social responsibility (Schmiedeknecht and Wieland, 2012). By definition, each organization should recognize that its decisions and activities have an impact on society and the environment. In accordance with the understanding of social responsibility, every organization must behave transparently and ethically with respect to the impact of its decisions and activities. They should contribute to sustainable development, take into account the expectations of stakeholders, comply with applicable law and international standards of conduct, and integrate this behaviour throughout the organization and in its relationships.

Tabl. 2.1.1 Categories and aspects of the Global Reporting Initiative

Categories	Economic	Ecological	social			
			Working conditions and humane procurement	Human rights	Society	Product responsibility
	Economic performance	Material	Employment	Investments	Local communities	Customer health and safety
	Market presence	Energy	Employer–employee relationship	Equal treatment	Fight against corruption	Labelling of products and services
	Indirect economic impact	Water	Occupational safety and health protection	Freedom of association and the right to collective bargaining	Policy	Marketing
	Procurement	Biodiversity	Education and training	Child labour	Anti-competitive behaviour	Protection of customer privacy
		Emissions	Diversity and equal opportunities	Forced or compulsory labour	Compliance	Compliance
		Wastewater and waste	Diversity and equal opportunities	Security practices	Evaluation of suppliers with regard to social impacts	
		Products and services	Evaluation of suppliers with regard to labour practices	Rights of the indigenous population	Complaint proceedings regarding social consequences	
		Compliance	Complaint procedures concerning labour practices	Evaluation of suppliers with regard to human rights		
		Shipment	Complaint procedures concerning labour practice	Complaint proceedings concerning human rights violations		
		Summary	Evaluation of suppliers with regard to environmental aspects			
			Complaint procedure regarding environmental aspects			

This understanding is reflected in the seven principles of accountability, transparency, ethical conduct, respect for the interests of stakeholders, respect for the rule of law, respect for international standards of conduct, and human rights. Compliance with these principles is seen as the basis and prerequisite for credible social responsibility. The seven core themes comprise governance, human rights, labour practices, the environment, fair operating and business practices, consumer concerns, community involvement and development (Bundesministerium für Arbeit und Soziales, 2011). Recommendations for action suggest that organizations should first narrow down their key issues and areas of action and then introduce procedures for the integration of social responsibility into leadership, systems and practices, as well as internal and external policies. Finally, the guide contains examples of cross-industry and cross-industry initiatives and tools for integrating social responsibility (Schmiedeknecht and Wieland, 2012). For the analysis and operationalization of the recommendations contained in the guide, indicators from existing indicator systems such as the GRI, the IÖW/future ranking of sustainability reports, the Product Sustainability Assessment or the Eco-Management and Audit Scheme (EMAS) were selected (Hardtke et al., 2014).

In its own right, ISO 26000 therefore does not represent an independent measurement model, but offers companies the possibility of developing metrics and key figures as well as setting standards (Bundesminesterium für Arbeit und Soziales, 2011) for the operationalization of their CSR objectives.

Social Return on Investment (SROI)

The Social Return on Investment (SROI) was developed in 1996 by the US–American foundation "Roberts Enterprise Development Fund", and in 2003 was decisively supplemented by the stakeholder perspective approach by the British "New Economics Foundation". SROI can be used to measure the social or ecological impact, the attributable effect of an activity, in monetary terms. This is then set in relation to the input, the investment (Simsa et al., 2013). By supplementing the classical cost–benefit analysis with socio-economic and environmental values, the work of organizations contributing to the common good is to be measured and financially assessed (Reichelt, 2009). This allows an analysis to be made of whether the goals set have been achieved or whether there is room for improvement (Münscher and Eggersglüß, 2011).

The SROI is divided into two types of analyses. Firstly, as a retrospective evaluation that measures and evaluates the impact generated, and secondly, as a forecast that can be used to plan and continuously compare the values actually achieved. The SORI is based on seven principles. First, all stakeholders should be involved. This means that they must first be identified and then continuously involved in the analysis. Second, all changes, both positive and negative, must be recorded. Third, for all relevant effects, financial approximate values must be found in order to be able to evaluate them. Fourth, only important information and documents should be included. Fifth, the aim is to avoid overvaluations of one's own effects by recording only that part of the changes which is attributable to one's own actions. Sixth, the analysis must be transparent and, finally, all results must be verified by an external audit (Tria, 2013). The analysis is divided into six steps. First of all, the scope of the analysis is to be delimited and the stakeholders defined. In a second step, the relations between input, output, and outcome are illustrated with the help of the so–called impact map and in cooperation with the stakeholders. In the following step, each outcome is assigned an indicator to evaluate it. In the fourth step,

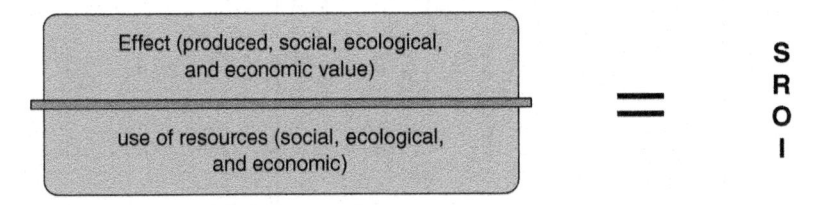

Figure 2.4.1 The calculation of the Social Return on Investment (Tria, 2013)

it is important to distinguish one's own effect from that of others, that is, from those that would have resulted without the company's action. This is followed by the actual calculation of the SROI (shown graphically in Figure 2.4.1). Costs are weighed against their usefulness and compared with the resources used. In the final step, the results must be made available and verified in a report to all parties involved (Nicholls et al., 2012). However, the key figures can only be compared if the same indicators have been selected for analysis (Franssen and Scholten, 2008).

The SROI is an instrument that makes it possible to record and evaluate the impact of an organization's CSR commitment (Tria, 2013).

Die Gemeinwohlökonomie (common good economy)

The common-good economy, which was first developed in Vienna in 2010, is a movement that sees itself as an alternative to the current economic system by aiming to resolve the contradiction between business and society. Rewards for behaviour and values in the economy are to be aligned with those in society for confidence-building, appreciation, cooperation, solidarity, and sharing. The values and objectives of the constitution should be enforced more strongly. The measurement of success should be seen as a benefit value indicator and not as an exchange value indicator. The gross domestic product and the financial profit are to be replaced by the general interest product and the public interest balance sheet. However, the aim is not to prohibit companies from making profits or from carrying out financial statements. GWÖ wants to change the actual goal of entrepreneurial aspiration, to which the financial gain is to contribute, into a maximum contribution to the common good (Felber, 2012).

In order to measure this newly defined economic success, namely the increase in the general interest, it is necessary to have other indicators than those for the financial balance sheet. The common good balance sheet was developed for this purpose. As a new main balance sheet, it is intended to replace the financial balance sheet, which will henceforth be seen as a secondary and medium balance sheet (Felber, 2012). The indicators are recorded in the common good matrix, the activities of a company with regard to the indicators in the common good report are evaluated and documented by awarding points. The report is then checked in what is known as the "attestation" (Gemeinwohl-Ökonomie, 2013).

The matrix consists of seventeen indicators. The X-axis includes: human dignity, solidarity, ecological sustainability, social justice, democratic co-determination, and transparency; and the Y-axis: suppliers, donors, employees and owners, customers, products, services and co-entrepreneurs, social environment. Additional negative criteria are also evaluated. These consisted of legal behaviour, some of which was not in the public

Table 2.4.2 Common good matrix (Gemeinwohl-Ökonomie)

Value Target group	Human dignity	Solidarity	Ecological sustainability	Social justice	Democratic co-determination and transparency
Suppliers	A1: Ethical procurement management				
Investors	B1: Ethical financial management				
Employees and owners	C1: Workplace quality and equality	C2: Equitable distribution of gainful employment	C3: Promotion of ecological behaviour of female employees	C4: Fair distribution of income	C5: Internal company democracy and transparency
Customers, products, services, partnership organizations	D1: Ethical client relationship	D2: Solidarity with companies	D3: Ecological design of products and services	D4: Social design of products and services	D5: Increase in social and ecological industry standards
Social environment	E1: Sense and social impact of products/services	E2: Contribution to the community	E3: Reduction of environmental impact	E4: Distribution of profits in the public interest	E5: Social transparency and co-determination

interest, such as hostile takeovers or escaping into tax havens. Points are awarded for each indicator, up to a maximum of 90 points per indicator and 1000 points in total, with the companies deciding independently which ones to use. Points are only awarded for services that go beyond the legal requirements.

In the same way as the audit of the financial statements is checked by auditors, the public interest balance sheets are audited by public interest auditors.

The matrix can be applied to companies of all sizes and industries (Geimeinwohl-Ökonomie, 2013). The common good balance sheet can thus be used to measure strategic social responsibility within the framework of a points system and to compare participating companies with each other (Gemeinwohl-Ökonomie, 2013). It creates CSR standards for every type of organization and encourages improvements in social commitment.

Comparison of the introduced approaches in measuring strategic CSR

We now compare the introduced models based on the following criteria: origin, thematic focus, target group, support for CSR attainment of objectives, type, comparability, level of detail, transparency, legal status, certification and addressee (Table 2.4.3).

The individual models thus have different origins and objectives. However, the GRI and ISO 26000 are particularly noteworthy, as these models have emerged from a broad-based initiative and thus cover the interests of a large number of stakeholders. What all models have in common is that they want to make CSR increasingly public and can be applied to companies of all sizes and industries. Furthermore, almost all models provide good support for companies to achieve their CSR objectives.

The models achieve their goal in a variety of ways. The GRI, ISO 26000, and the Public Welfare Economy set standards for measuring CSR. The GWÖ goes one step further and evaluates these with a points system. The SROI, on the other hand, uses (monetary) key figures to calculate the community added value of an activity. All models meet the aspect of comparability. It should be noted that only companies within the same model can be compared with each other. However, comparability is still considered to be high for GRI, ISO 26000 and GWÖ because they are based on international standards and can therefore represent a wider spectrum of companies. The most important differences in the level of detail between the models are the following: while the CSR price consists of only one stakeholder survey and the SROI identifies its key figures on the basis of seven basic principles, the GRI and ISO 26000 are composed of numerous categories and indicators. This enables them to cover a much wider range of CSR commitments. GWÖ is also based on a variety of aspects. However, the allocation of points within the public interest balance sheet is considered to be too subjective. The transparency aspect, which is particularly important for stakeholders, is fully met by all models as it is one of the basic principles. The only exception is the CSR price. The evaluations of the individual companies are only made available to them. None of the models are legally binding. Companies are free to apply them. None of the models therefore meets this requirement. However, CSR measurements are still at the beginning, as there is a lack of a uniform definition and international standards. They cannot therefore be enshrined in the law at this time. The GRI and GWÖ therefore issue certificates. However, their significance is questionable due to the large number of CSR certificates (155). Each model is addressed to both the companies themselves and their stakeholders, thus fulfilling the last criterion.

Table 2.4.3 Comparison of GRI, ISO 26000, SROI, and GWÖ (common good model)

Criteria	GRI	ISO 26000	SROI	GWÖ
Origin	In cooperation with the UN and numerous stakeholders from the economy, employers, employees, NGOs, states, and the private sector.	Under the leadership of ISO and involving numerous stakeholders.[1]	Developed by the Roberts Enterprise Development Fund.[2]	Movement from Austria.[3]
Thematic focus	Comparability of sustainability reports, int. standard-setting.[4]	Setting standards, understanding.	Calculation of social added value.	Alternative to the current economic system.[5]
Target group	All organizations.[6]	All organizations.[7]	All organizations, political decision-makers.[8]	All companies.[9]
Support in achieving CSR goals	High, standard-setting enables measurement and gives recommendations for implementation.[10]	High, sets standards and gives recommendations for action.[11]	High, proves the success of a target as a key figure according to[12]	Up, scoring helps support comp. to measure your general interest.[13]
Type	Standards for reporting.[14]	Standards and guidelines for implementation.[15]	(monetary) key figure.[16]	Balance, measurement by awarding points.[17]
Comparability	Up, through int. standard-setting.[18]	High, offers uniform frame of reference.[19]	Average, only comparable if assumptions are identical.[20]	High, universal balance sheet for all companies.
Degree of detail	High, 96 indicators and recommendations for implementation.[21]	High, around 500 concrete requirements.[22]	Low, seven basic principles.[23]	Means, many indicators, points but no precise unit of measurement.[24]
Transparency	High, trial must be disclosed.[25]	High, transparency is one of the principles.[26]	High, transparency is one of the basic principles.[27]	High, transparency is one of the basic values.[28]
Legal status	Voluntary[29]	Voluntary[30]	Voluntary	Voluntary[31]
Certification	Yes[32]	No[33]	No	Yes[34]
Receiver	Stakeholder, comp.[35]	Stakeholder, comp.[36]	Stakeholder, comp.[37]	Stakeholder, comp.[38]

All models are suitable for contributing towards CSR measurement. However, they are only a step in the right direction. Building on the GRI and ISO 26000, the international standards can be optimized, which could then serve as the basis for CSR measurement. Independent agencies, similar to the GWÖ, could then evaluate companies, similar to the rating agency, with the creditworthiness of companies and governments.

Conclusions

The aim of this chapter is to outline frequently applied approaches in measuring strategic CSR. However, as previous measurements are usually not based on uniform definitions or international standards, they are not suitable for measuring or comparing CSR uniformly. Therefore, models should be presented that enable CSR to be measured or compared by setting standards and which already do so in the first steps.

There is also a lack of international standards. Responsible management depends on a whole range of framework conditions. In addition to the economic and social context, the size of the company, the industry, and the expectations of stakeholders also play a role. In order to measure CSR, the individual situation must always be taken into account. For example, companies can engage and act responsibly in areas that do not play a role for other companies. Despite these problems, CSR is continuously measured. According to the University of Stuttgart, there are up to 70 rating agencies in 2006, which award companies with their own rating systems. The problems become clear when you look at the counter-award of the NGO "Berne Declaration", which has been awarded since 2000. Companies with a particularly poor CSR record are nominated for this award. Some of the companies on this list are rated as excellent by other rating agencies (Müller-Christ and Rehm, 2010).

If CSR is to be measured or made comparable, it must be clearly defined and international standards set. The models must be transparent and comprehensible to everyone, including the end consumer. They must be applicable to companies of all sizes across all industries and provide a basis for decision-making for both stakeholders and the companies themselves.

Notes

1 Cf. Schmiedeknecht/Wieland (2012), S. 260.
2 Cf. Münscher/Eggersglüß (2011), S. 1.
3 Cf. Felber (2012), S. 9.
4 Cf. Global Reporting Initiative (2015), S. 5.
5 Cf. Felber (2012), S. 10.
6 Cf. Global Reporting Initiative (2015), S. 5.
7 Cf. Schmiedeknecht/Wieland (2012), S. 260.
8 Cf. Münscher/Eggersglüß (2011), S. 2.
9 Cf. Gemeinwohl-Ökonomie (2013), S. 12.
10 Cf. Global Reporting Initiative (2015), S. 3.
11 Cf. Hardtke et al. (2014), S. 6.
12 Cf. Münscher/Eggersglüß (2011), S. 2.
13 Cf. Gemeinwohl-Ökonomie (2013), S. 8.
14 Cf. Global Reporting Initiative (2015), S. 5.
15 Cf. Hardtke et al. (2014), S. 6.
16 Cf. Tria (2013), S. 1.
17 Cf. Gemeinwohl-Ökonomie (2013), S. 7.

18 Cf. Global Reporting Initiative (2015), S. 3.
19 Cf. Bundesministerium für Arbeit und Soziales (2011), S. 7.
20 Cf. Franssen/Scholten (2008), S. 150.
21 Cf. Hardtke et al. (2014), S. 28.
22 Cf. Hardtke et al. (2014), S. 28.
23 Cf. Tria (2013), S. 1.
24 Cf. Gemeinwohl-Ökonomie (2013), S. 8.
25 Cf. Global Reporting Initiative (2015), S. 13.
26 Cf. Bundesministerium für Arbeit und Soziales (2011), S. 12.
27 Cf. Nicholls et al. (2012), S. 9.
28 Cf. Gemeinwohl-Ökonomie (2013), S. 19.
29 Cf. Industrie- und Handelskammer Nürnberg für Mittelfranken (2013), S. 1.
30 Cf. Bundesministerium für Arbeit und Soziales (2011), S. 7.
31 Cf. Gemeinwohl-Ökonomie (2013), S. 15.
32 Cf. Hardtke et al. (2014), S. 28.
33 Cf. Bundesministerium für Arbeit und Soziales (2011), S. 7.
34 Cf. Verein zur Förderung der Gemeinwohl-Ökonomie , S. 1.
35 Cf. Global Reporting Initiative (2015), S. 3.
36 Cf. Bundesministerium für Arbeit und Soziales (2011), S. 26.
37 Cf. Nicholls et al. (2012), S. 10.
38 Cf. Gemeinwohl-Ökonomie (2013), S. 10.

References

Ankele, K. and Schank, C. (2016). *Zur Legitimität standardisierter Bewertungsverfahren, in: Bewertung unternehmerischer Nachhaltigkeit*, Ed. by Grothe, A., Schmidt, Erich Verlag Berlin, pp. 15–26.
Bundesministerium für Arbeit und Soziales (2011). Leitfaden zur gesellschaftlichen Verantwortung von Organisationen, http://www.bmas.de/DE/Service/Medien/Publikationen/a395-csr-din-26000.html [accessed: 17.05.2018].
Curbach, J. (2009). *Die Corporate-Social-Responsibility-Bewegung*, first edition, Springer Fachmedien Wiesbaden.
Europäische Kommission (2011). Mitteilung der Kommission an das europäische Parlament, den Rat, den europäischen Wirtschafts- und Sozialausschuss und den Ausschuss der Regionen. Eine neue EU-Strategie (2011-14) für die soziale Verantwortung der Unternehmen (CSR), http://eur-lex.europa.eu/legal-content/DE/TXT/?uri=CELEX%3A52011DC0681 [accessed: 29.11.2016].
Felber, C. (2012). *Die Gemeinwohl-Ökonomie. Eine demokratische Alternative wächst*, Vienna: Büchergilde Gutenberg.
Fischbach, K. (2007). *Nachhaltigkeitsberichterstattung von Unternehmen. Analyse der Global Reporting Initiative* (GRI), diplom. De, Hamburg.
Franssen, B. C., and Scholten, P. G. (2008). *Handbuch für Sozialunternehmertum*, Assen.
Gemeinwohl-Ökonomie: Gemeinwohl-Matrix, https://www.ecogood.org/de/gemeinwohl-bilanz/gemeinwohl-matrix/ [accessed: 12.12.2016].
Gemeinwohl-Ökonomie (2013). *Handbuch zur Gemeinwohl-Bilanz*, fourth edition, Carl Hanser Verlag GmbH &Co KG.
Global Reporting Initiative (2015). *G4 Leitlinien zur Nachhaltigkeitsberichterstattung*,second edition, Amsterdam.
Hansen, U., & Schrader, U. (2005). Corporate social responsibility als aktuelles Thema der Betriebswirtschaftslehre. Hannover, *Die Betriebswirtschaft*, 65(4), 373.
Hardtke, A., Weiß, D., and Irmler, I. (2014). *Gesellschaftliche Verantwortung von Unternehmen. Eine Orientierungshilfe für Kernthemen und Handlungsfelder des Leitfadens DIN ISO 26000*, Bundesministerium für Umwelt, Naturschutz, Bau und Reaktorsicherheit (BMUB) Wiesbaden.
Industrie- und Handelskammer Nürnberg für Mittelfranken (2013). *Lexikon der Nachhaltigkeit | Archiv | Global Reporting Initiative (GRI): Indikatoren für Nachhaltigkeitsberichterstattung, GRI-Indikatoren (Archiv)*, https://www.nachhaltigkeit.info/artikel/gri_indikatoren_948.htm [accessed: 17.12.2016].

Köppl, P., and Neureiter, M. (2004). Gesellschaftliche Verantwortung als Business-Motor. Was ist Corporate Social Responsibility? Ein globaler Rundgang. *Corporate Social Responsibility*. Editors von Köppl, P. and Neureiter, M., Linde Verlag, Vienna, pp. 13–42.

Müller-Christ, G., and Rehm, A. (2010). *Corporate Social Responsibility as Giving Back to Society? Der Gabentausch als Ausweg aus der Verantwortungsfalle?* Band 7 der Schriftenreihe Management und Nachhaltigkeit, Georg Müller Christ & Michael Hülsmann, Hamburg.

Münscher, R., and Eggersglüß, C. (2011). *Erfolg messen und belegen. Transparenz schaffen mit der "Social Return on Investment"-Methode.* Wiesbaden.

Neureiter, M. (2004). Die europäische Dimension von CSR. Das Grünbuch der EU-Kommission und die Stellungnahme des Europäischen Parlaments. *Corporate Social Responsibility*, editors Köppl, P. and Neureiter, M., Vienna, pp. 43–62.

Nicholls, J. et al. (2012). *A Guide to Social Return on Investment*, second edition. London: Sage.

Reichelt, D. (2009). *SROI: Social Return on Investment. Modellversuch zur Berechnung des gesellschaftlichen Mehrwertes*, Diplomica Verlag, Hamburg.

Schmiedeknecht, M. H., and Wieland, J. (2012). ISO 26000, 7 Grundsätze, 6 Kernthemen. *Corporate Social Responsibility*, editors Schneider, A. and Schmidpeter, R., Berlin, Heidelberg, pp. 259–270.

Schrader, U., Halbes, S., and Hansen, U. (2005). *Konsumentenorientierte Kommunikation über Corporate Social Responsibility (CSR). Erkenntnisse aus Experteninterviews in Deutschland, Universität Hannover , Institut für Betriebsforschung*, Hannover.

Simsa, R. et al. (2013). Das Konzept des Social Return on Investment: Grenzen und Perspektiven. *Performance Management in Nonprofit-Organisationen*, edited by Gmür, M., Haupt Verlag, Bern, pp. 198–248.

Tria, B. (2013). Social Return on Investment – ein Ansatz zur Messung der erzeugten Eigenwirkung. http://www.kompass-sozialmanagement.de/social-return-on-investment-ein-ansatz-zur-messung-der-erzeugten-eigenwirkung.html?src=1 [accessed: 13.12.2016].

Verein zur Förderung der Gemeinwohl-Ökonomie: Externe Prüfung, https://www.ecogood.org/de/gemeinwohl-bilanz/unternehmen/externe-prufung/ [accessed: 19.12.2016].

World Commission on Environment and Development (2015). Our Common Future, Chapter 2: Towards Sustainable Development – A/42/427 Annex, Chapter 2 – UN Documents: *Gathering a Body of Global Agreements*. http://www.un-documents.net/ocf-02.htm#I [accessed: 29.11.2016].

2.5 A performance tool for policy-makers to monitor the dual objective of social enterprises

A data envelopment analysis approach

Matthias Staessens, Pieter Jan Kerstens, Johan Bruneel, and Laurens Cherchye

Introduction

The importance of performance measurement for social enterprises has been widely acknowledged in recent years, leading to a significant increase in related studies (see, e.g., Maas & Liket, 2011; Millar & Hall, 2012). Social enterprises pursue social and economic missions simultaneously, and hence need to achieve goal duality, combining social and economic performance. Performance benchmarking should therefore also reflect this goal duality. Although current measurement methods are useful management tools for individual organizations, they do not offer the standardized numerical outputs necessary to undertake consistent comparative analyses across organizations (Rotheroe & Richards, 2007; Kroeger & Weber, 2014), and lack applicability in practice to enable policy-makers to compare the performance of supported organizations. Importantly, performance measurement plays a key role not only at the organizational level, but also at the level of policy-makers. These stakeholders widely acknowledge the importance of standardized performance tools to measure the accountability of social enterprises. After all, it is at this level that it is possible to oversee and compare the performance of organizations receiving support (Ebrahim & Rangan, 2014).

To do this, policy-makers need a more advanced performance measurement tool. In this chapter, we propose an innovative tool that allows policy-makers to measure the dual objectives of social enterprises, as well as to identify sources of performance change. We suggest adopting the data envelopment analysis (DEA) methodology to measure the performance of social enterprises over time. DEA is a promising technique that offers several important advantages highly relevant to the comparative performance analysis of social enterprises. Interestingly, DEA can also be used as a dynamic performance evaluation tool to assess performance over time (Cherchye et al., 2007b). A commonly proposed approach to quantifying and explaining changes in efficiency over time is the Malmquist productivity index (Caves et al., 1982; Färe et al., 1994). This index represents the productivity change between two consecutive periods. An important feature is that it can be decomposed to show how much of a firm's productivity change is due to efficiency changes in the firm itself, and how much to technical changes in the sector as a whole. By monitoring this decomposition in terms of efficiency and technical changes, policy-makers can analyse endogenous effects, such as changes in their policies toward social enterprises (Cherchye et al., 2007b). Note that this chapter does not provide a detailed review of DEA, but functions as an introduction to the DEA methodology for the performance measurement of social enterprises. We focus on how DEA can be used to monitor the performance of social enterprises by discussing the basics and advantages of the DEA methodology and how policy-makers can use it as a tool to guide policy-making for social enterprises.

In this chapter, we first elaborate on the importance of having a performance tool to enable policy-makers to monitor the performance of social enterprises. Second, we discuss the various performance measurement challenges facing policy-makers in monitoring the performance of social enterprises. Third, we introduce the DEA methodology and discuss its advantages for policy-makers. The fourth section describes, for a non-specialist audience, DEA and the Malmquist index, which is used to monitor performance over time, with an illustration showing its applicability. This approach allows for a straightforward presentation of the possibilities of DEA and Malmquist index outputs for policy-makers. Finally, we highlight how this chapter contributes to the practical and research fields of social entrepreneurship.

Literature review

Importance of performance measurement for policy-makers

Performance measurement of social enterprises plays a critical and highly politicized role in policy decisions such as subsidy mechanisms. As shown in a case study by Bruneel et al. (2016), governments must take account of the ethics of their subsidizing mechanisms by paying attention to both social and economic performance. Governments and other institutions must determine which organizations to support and how they should allocate available funding. They want to know whether their funds are making a difference, or whether it might be better to reallocate the funding (Sud et al., 2009). Hence, measurement of both the social and economic performance of social enterprises can help governments to allocate their resources as efficiently as possible.

Furthermore, the importance of performance tools to governments goes beyond simply measuring the performance of funded organizations. Performance measurement is an important evaluation tool for assessing the impact of policy measures. Policy decisions can have a radical impact on the social sector. As argued by DiMaggio and Powell (1991), radical institutional changes erode the normative institutional context and the legitimacy of norms that have formerly been taken for granted. In the context of social enterprises, in particular, this changing institutional environment is important, as these firms depend heavily on government subsidies. However, governments appear to be unable to measure their impact on the social sector systematically. Since policy-makers face pressure from taxpayers to demonstrate the results of their social policies, performance tools may help justify these. Ultimately, performance instruments can be used for public legitimization of their allocation decisions (Ebrahim & Rangan, 2014).

Stimulated by recent financial crises, governments are increasingly seeking to allocate their resources more effectively and strategically (Ebrahim & Rangan, 2014). According to Hart and Haughton (2007), governments share a vision of a more effective social sector, and are increasingly implementing institutional changes and demanding that social enterprises become more businesslike (Wellens & Jegers, 2014). This strategic transformation can be understood in terms of goals, service delivery models, and management (Dart, 2004). Commercialization captures the adoption of businesslike goals, generating internal demand to professionalize management and service models. Nevertheless, several researchers warn that this governmentally desired businesslike approach may have side-effects (Wellens & Jegers, 2014). In emphasizing the economic at the cost of the social, social enterprises may suffer from mission drift (Ramus & Vaccaro, 2014). As demand for accountability in the use of received funds increases, social enterprises will pay increasing attention to the economic logic, which may reduce commitment to their social mission. Governmental agencies should therefore be conscious of their indirect influence on the objectives set by social enterprises (Defourny & Nyssens, 2010; Tuckman, 1998). Hence, they must consider the impact of their policies and subsidy mechanisms more carefully. In addition, since the institutional environment exerts an important influence on the performance of organizations in society, governments need to be aware of their impact on the performance of social enterprises. Performance instruments may provide governments with guidance on evaluating the impact of their policies. Nevertheless, operationalizing the performance of social enterprises remains a daunting task for policy-makers.

The complication of measuring the performance of social enterprises for policy-makers

As previously mentioned, current methods do not yield comparable numerical outputs that allow policy-makers to measure performance across social enterprises and over time (Rotheroe & Richards, 2007; Kroeger & Weber, 2014). The difficulty of systematically measuring the performance of social enterprises is caused especially by their distinctive hybrid nature. Social enterprises pursue both social and economic missions, and thus need to achieve social and economic performance simultaneously (Battilana et al., 2012; Zahra et al., 2009). Therefore, this dual objective must be captured in a single criterion. As highlighted by Ebrahim et al. (2014), monitoring social and economic performance separately may harm the overall purpose of organizations.

Unfortunately, owing to the difficulty of aggregating social and economic performance, five key practical and methodological issues arise when systematically measuring the dual performance of social enterprises. First, while metrics for assessing economic performance are relatively well established, there is no commonly accepted method for social performance (Ebrahim & Rangan, 2014; Paton, 2003). Second, social and economic performance are expressed in different measurement units, in terms of monetary and non-monetary indicators (Kaplan, 2001).

Third, there is significant heterogeneity in the extent to which social enterprises adhere to their social and economic missions (e.g., Stevens et al., 2015a, 2015b; Peredo & McLean, 2006; Zahra et al., 2009). As discussed by Dees (1998), social enterprises appear in an idiosyncratic position on the social enterprise spectrum, between two ends of a continuum between economic and social missions (see Figure 2.5.1). These varying mission orientations further exacerbate the difficulty of measuring the performance of social enterprises (Ebrahim & Rangan, 2014). Unfortunately, only limited information is available on their strategic orientation.

Fourth, there is no established standard to determine whether the performance of certain social enterprises is high or low. Benchmark mechanisms allow strong and weak

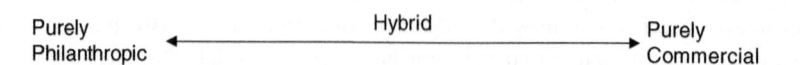

Figure 2.5.1 The social enterprise spectrum

social performance to be identified within the sample group. Last, a fifth issue of current performance tools is that they do not allow for dynamic performance evaluation of social enterprises over time. A dynamic feature allows policy-makers to estimate the impact of endogenous shock, such as radical institutional changes. In the absence of this feature, policy-makers cannot determine whether changes in their policies toward social enterprises have achieved desirable objectives such as improving their efficiency.

In conclusion, policy-makers face several issues in measuring the performance of social enterprises, making it difficult for governments to track the performance of funded organizations. To measure the performance of social enterprises, this chapter proposes a straightforward benchmark instrument that allows for meaningful aggregation of social and economic performance into a single criterion. This chapter builds on a conviction that the performance measurement of social enterprises should reflect both social and economic objectives, as well as the relative importance of each. Therefore, we propose using the performance benchmark technique known as data envelopment analysis (DEA).

Performance benchmark technique

Data envelopment analysis

Although DEA was originally introduced in the literature on organizational efficiency (Charnes et al., 1978; Banker et al., 1984), it also provides an opportunity for policy-makers to analyse organizations' competitive advantage. Attractively for policy-makers in the social sector, DEA is a production frontier methodology specifically tailored to deal with multiple outputs simultaneously, and allows for enterprise-specific weighting of various performance objectives. Moreover, DEA does not require these outputs to be expressed in a common measurement unit. Another important advantage of DEA in the context of social enterprises is that it has proved to be especially useful when there is no clear profit-maximization objective (Belu, 2009), and when the strategic orientation of objectives is heterogeneous (Cherchye, 2001; Kuosmanen & Kortelainen, 2005; Chen & Delmas, 2011). In this section, we discuss the advantages of DEA as a monitoring tool for policy-makers in the field of social entrepreneurship.

Advantages of DEA for policy-makers

First, DEA allows social and economic performance to be aggregated into a standardized and meaningful criterion. As a benchmark technique, it is able to pinpoint good performance based on the organizations being evaluated. Specifically, DEA will calculate the *industry best practice frontier*, which is a function that indicates the maximum attainable level of outputs corresponding to a given quantity of inputs using all observations in the sample (Chen et al., 2015). Some firms use their inputs as efficiently as possible in the current environment, and thus define the frontier itself. Others use their inputs less efficiently and are at some distance from the frontier. In fact, the industry best practice frontier represents the benchmark potential (Anokhin et al., 2011). A firm's performance is thus measured in terms of the relative efficiency of organizations in transforming resources into value creation. This relative efficiency is thus the ratio between the organization's present performance and what would be technically feasible if the organization were to operate fully efficiently. Graphically, each firm's efficiency can be defined as its distance from the industry best practice frontier (Chen et al., 2015). The distance from the frontier represents the

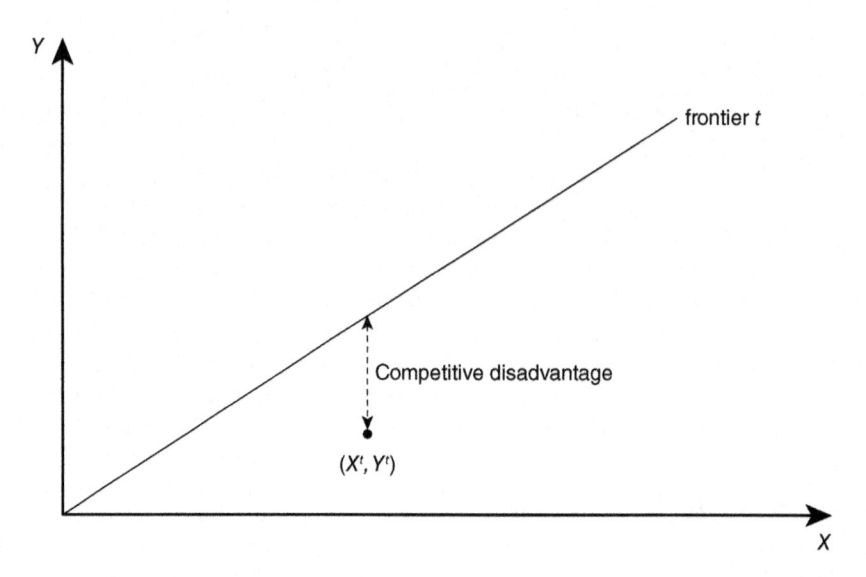

Figure 2.5.2 Industry best practice frontier

competitive disadvantage of the firm being evaluated (see Figure 2.5.2). Some firms with the same inputs achieve higher outputs and thus outperform the firm under evaluation. Clearly, no prior thresholds are required to decide whether a social enterprise is operating efficiently, as DEA calculates benchmarks endogenously.

Second, DEA is unit invariant, and thus social and economic outputs can be expressed in different measurement units. In social entrepreneurship, this property is extremely useful because it facilitates comparisons of performance across social and economic indicators such as the number of people helped, the number of employees from disadvantaged groups, or the amount of green energy produced for social output, alongside revenues or return on investment.

Third, additional insights can be gained by computing social and economic performance separately. Hence, policy-makers can also benchmark the economic and social performance of social enterprises. DEA thus provides a deeper understanding than a mere comparison of overall social and economic performance.

A last key advantage for policy-makers is that DEA allows assessment of performance over time (Cherchye et al., 2007a). An important feature is that this performance change can be decomposed into efficiency and technical change components. Efficiency change represents the catching up of individual organizations and indicates changes in performance due to technological advancements at the organizational level. Technical change represents shifts in the industry best practice frontier itself, and indicates overall progress (or regress) at the level of the sector as a whole. As this efficiency frontier also represents the boundary condition that a firm can achieve under the current technology or policy (Chen & Delmas, 2011), policy-makers can analyse endogenous effects by monitoring movements in the frontier (see, for example, Cherchye et al., 2007a). Policy-makers can thus measure the impact of changes in their policy-making on the sector, for example increasing or reducing subsidies to social enterprises, by calculating the technical change. Hence, by monitoring efficiency and technical change, policy-makers can determine the performance of individual organizations, as well as the impact of their policies on the sector. In the remainder of this chapter, we first discuss the logic behind performance benchmarking and explain how DEA calculates the performance. We then discuss the decomposition into efficiency and technical change components. Finally, we demonstrate the methodology using an empirical illustration.

DEA methodology and benefits for policy-makers

Performance benchmarking computes efficiency scores by assessing how efficiently firms transform inputs into outputs. For example, consider a setting in which governments credit social enterprises with subsidies to support their social output objectives. In this setting, governments can easily calculate which social enterprises are using the subsidies most efficiently. In this one-input-one-output case, the performance (i.e., efficiency score D_0^t) of social enterprises can be expressed as follows:

$$D_0^t = \frac{Y_0^t}{X_0^t} = \frac{Social\ output}{Subsidies} ,$$

(1)

with subsidy input $X_0^t \in \mathbb{R}_+$ and social output $Y_0^t \in \mathbb{R}_+$. The higher this ratio, the better the organization translates its subsidies into social output. Intuitively, this ratio can be improved by (i) lower subsidies for the same social output, (ii) higher social output with the same level of subsidies, or (iii) higher social output with lower subsidies. Hence, higher scores represent better social efficiency. One can then rank all available firms in the dataset according to these efficiency scores (Cherchye et al., 2007b) in order to identify good relative performance. Clearly, identifying organizations with an advantage over competitors is a straightforward exercise if performance can easily be captured by a single measure (Chen et al., 2015).

However, performance benchmarking of social enterprises is complicated by their distinctive hybrid nature. Owing to the issues of aggregating social and economic performance in a meaningful and systematic way, it is inconvenient to retain a single number representing the overall performance of social enterprises. Borrowing from conventional benefit/cost theory, one might express efficiency as the ratio of weighted outputs over weighted inputs (Cook & Seiford, 2009). In the multiple input-multiple output case with m inputs $X_0^t \in \mathbb{R}_+^m$ and s outputs $Y_0^t \in \mathbb{R}_+^s$ at time t, it is convenient to retain a single number representing performance. Therefore, in the case of a multiple input/output, we need to aggregate them in a meaningful manner by taking the weighted sum. This gives the following formula:

$$D_0^t = \frac{u_{01}^t Y_{01}^t + \cdots + u_{0s}^t Y_{0s}^t}{v_{01}^t X_{01}^t + \cdots + v_{0m}^t X_{0m}^t} = \frac{\sum_{r=1}^s u_{0r}^t Y_{0r}^t}{\sum_{i=1}^m v_{0i}^t X_{0i}^t} = \frac{u_0^t Y_0^{t\,\prime}}{v_0^t X_0^{t\,\prime}}$$

(2)

The weights $v_0^t \in \mathbb{R}_+^m$, $u_0^t \in \mathbb{R}_+^s$ allow the relative importance of the outputs and inputs to be emphasized. Unless all inputs and outputs have a monetary value (e.g., in US dollars), the choice of appropriate weights is debatable and depends on the viewpoint of different stakeholders (within and outside the firm) or among different firms. Since social and economic outputs are expressed in different measurement units, organizations, the government, and other stakeholders may debate the choice of weights. For instance, organizations may claim that they are inefficient because the government uses unfavourable weighting schemes. This is in the context of a key assumption that social enterprises occupy an idiosyncratic position on the social enterprise spectrum (see Figure 2.5.1). As argued above, social enterprises pursue social and economic objectives to varying degrees. To avoid debates about the choice of weights, the "benefit-of-the-doubt" weighting of DEA can be applied (Cherchye et al, 2007b). High relative weights are allocated to those dimensions on which an organization performs well, whereas low relative weights are allocated to dimensions on which the firm performs badly. Hence, the calculated weights act as proxies for organizations' mission orientation (Cherchye, 2001), and thus for their idiosyncratic place on the continuum.

This approach is not unreasonable, as scholars have considered that strategic orientation affects organizational performance. This is exactly the approach that DEA implements in order to calculate meaningful weights. DEA evaluates firms in "the best possible way" by giving every firm the most favourable weight, thus giving them the "benefit of the doubt". Policy-makers may therefore argue that firms with greater efficiencies exhibit performance superior to the firm under evaluation.

DEA formulation and efficiency scores

DEA generates efficiency scores through a mathematical optimization problem, without the need for explicit weight specifications for inputs and outputs. Two DEA approaches may be taken to calculate these efficiency scores, depending on whether the goal is output expansion or input reduction: input-oriented DEA models determine the minimal amount of inputs necessary while holding all outputs fixed, whereas output-oriented DEA models keep all inputs fixed and determine the maximal amount of outputs that can be achieved (Belu, 2009). Since governments aim to maximize value creation (i.e., social and economic value) from a given policy, we opt for an output-oriented DEA model. In this approach, the literature on DEA proposes the following nonlinear programming problem to evaluate firm 0 against all other n firms at time t:[1]

$$\frac{1}{D_0^t} \equiv \min_{v,u} \frac{v_0^t X_0^{t\prime}}{u_0^t Y_0^{t\prime}} \tag{3.1}$$

$$s.t.: \frac{v_0^t X_j^{t\prime}}{u_0^t Y_j^{t\prime}} \geq 1, \quad j = 1,..,n \tag{3.2}$$

$$u_0^t, v_0^t \geq 0 \tag{3.3}$$

This delivers an efficiency score D_0^t that is situated between 0 and 1 (i.e., $0 \leq D_0^t \leq 1$). These efficiency scores can be expressed as the ratio of the firm's observed output to the fully efficient output (Chen et al., 2015). Firms with an efficiency score D_0^t equal to one are the most efficient firms, and thus determine the efficient frontier. Next, inefficiencies are measured by the organization's distance from the efficient frontier (Chen et al., 2015). For instance, if a firm is not on this frontier, the distance from the best practice frontier (i.e., $\frac{1}{D_0^t}$) represents its competitive disadvantage with respect to efficient firms (Chen & Delmas, 2011; see Figure 2.5.3). Hence, the higher the efficiency score, the better the organization's performance, and thus the closer it is to the efficient frontier.

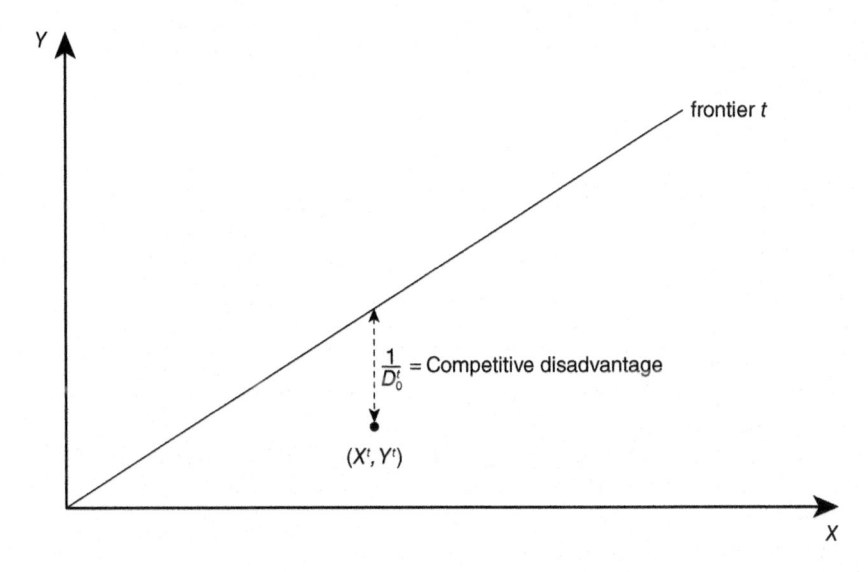

Figure 2.5.3 Graphical representation of efficiency score

This nonlinear programme can equivalently be transformed into a linear programme that is solvable by widely available software (e.g., Excel). Refer to Cook and Seiford (2009) for further details.

Except for non–negativity, the DEA mathematical programme has complete flexibility in assigning weights. This flexibility may lead to a situation that contrasts with prior knowledge of the industry. For example, in the context of social entrepreneurship, it would be against the hybrid assumption of social enterprises to have a zero-weight for one of the outputs. To avoid such situations, prior knowledge of the relative importance of inputs and outputs can be included by adding weight restrictions to the model (for discussion, see Cherchye et al., 2007b). In particular, we can add K restrictions of the form:

$$uQ_k' - vP_k' \leq 0, k = 1, \ldots, K, \text{ with } P_k \in \mathbb{R}^m \text{ and } Q_k \in \mathbb{R}^s \tag{3.4}$$

With these restrictions, it is possible to constrain the weight of the social output relative to economic output, or vice versa, in the DEA model, such that no weight will be zero. Furthermore, by enforcing a zero-weight on the social or economic output for every social enterprise, it is possible to calculate social and economic efficiency, respectively. This may provide additional insights into the total efficiency of the firms.[2]

Malmquist index and decomposition

Malmquist index

Governments can also use DEA as a dynamic performance evaluation tool to assess how the performance of each firm changes over time (Cherchye et al., 2007b). Intuitively, change in the performance of a social enterprise between periods t and $t+1$ in the one-input-one-output case can be expressed as:

$$\frac{Y_0^{t+1} \big/ X_0^{t+1}}{Y_0^{t} \big/ X_0^{t}} \tag{4}$$

This formulation satisfies some common-sense properties. For example: if $(X_0^{t+1}, Y_0^{t+1}) = (2X_0^t, 2Y_0^t)$, then intuitively there is no change in productivity, because both output and input have expanded by a factor of 2. This is indicated by a value of 1. However, if $(X_0^{t+1}, Y_0^{t+1}) = (X_0^t, 2Y_0^t)$, then the firm has become more productive because it is able to produce twice the amount of social output while holding the input constant. Indeed, the product of the above formula is 2, indicating improvement in productivity by a factor of 2. Conversely, if $(X_0^{t+1}, Y_0^{t+1}) = (2X_0^t, 1.5Y_0^t)$, then productivity equals three quarters and has declined, because by doubling the level of inputs, the firm has less than doubled its social output (i.e., by only 1.5).

This is the basic idea behind the Malmquist index introduced by Caves et al. (1982) and popularized by Färe et al. (1994). It can be applied as a nonparametric pro-gramming method to measure performance change over time in the multiple-input– multiple-output case (Chen et al., 2015), where the index represents productivity change between two periods. We can compute the Malmquist index by calculating distance functions $D_0^s(X^t, Y^t)$ with respect to two different time periods t and $t+1$. These distance functions calculate "how far" an organization in year t is from a given efficient frontier of year s. As previously discussed, in the multiple-input-multiple-output case, we have aggregate outputs and inputs using weights (v^t, u^t) for period t and (v^{t+1}, u^{t+1}) for period $t+1$. Using period t weights, the Malmquist output-oriented index is defined by:

$$M_o^t\left(X^{t+1}, Y^{t+1}, X^t, Y^t\right) = \frac{D_o^t(X^{t+1}, Y^{t+1})}{D_o^t(X^t, Y^t)} \tag{5.1}$$

Analogously, the period $t+1$ Malmquist output-oriented index is defined by:

$$M_o^{t+1}\left(X^{t+1}, Y^{t+1}, X^t, Y^t\right) = \frac{D_o^{t+1}\left(X^{t+1}, Y^{t+1}\right)}{D_o^{t+1}\left(X^t, Y^t\right)} \tag{5.2}$$

Both $M_o^t\left(X^{t+1}, Y^{t+1}, X^t, Y^t\right)$ and $M_o^{t+1}\left(X^{t+1}, Y^{t+1}, X^t, Y^t\right)$ measure productivity change, but use a different base period for the weights. Note that the two measures do not need to give the same results; in fact, they may give conflicting results because of the different weights. Therefore, to avoid an arbitrary choice of base period, it is common to use a geometric average of the two:

$$M_o\left(X^{t+1}, Y^{t+1}, X^t, Y^t\right) = \left[M_o^t\left(X^{t+1}, Y^{t+1}, X^t, Y^t\right) \times M_o^{t+1}\left(X^{t+1}, Y^{t+1}, X^t, Y^t\right)\right]^{\frac{1}{2}}$$

$$= \left[\left(\frac{D_o^t(X^{t+1}, Y^{t+1})}{D_o^t\left(X^t, Y^t\right)}\right) \times \left(\frac{D_o^{t+1}\left(X^{t+1}, Y^{t+1}\right)}{D_o^{t+1}\left(X^t, Y^t\right)}\right)\right]^{\frac{1}{2}} \tag{5.3}$$

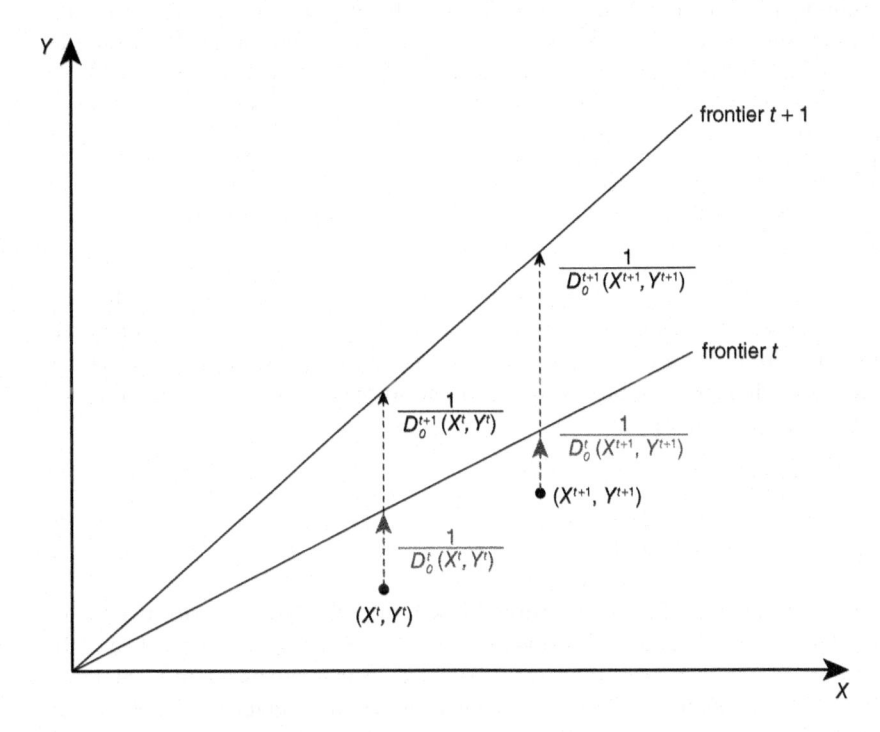

Figure 2.5.4 Malmquist index

Policy-makers can use the Malmquist index to evaluate whether the total performance of social enterprises has changed over time. Figure 2.5.4 depicts the distance functions required to calculate the Malmquist index between two successive periods (t and $t+1$). A ratio larger than one indicates progress in the performance of the organization, while equal to or smaller than one indicates the *status quo* or deterioration in organizational performance, respectively.

However, the Malmquist index itself does not demonstrate whether a performance change is due to an idiosyncratic organizational improvement or to a change in the environment. Therefore, policy-makers may decompose the Malmquist index into two components: (i) an "efficiency change" component that indicates the degree to which a firm improves or worsens its efficiency between the two periods; and (ii) a "technical change" component that reflects the change in the efficient frontier between the two time periods (Cooper et al., 2007). The Malmquist index exactly equals the product of both components; thus, formula (5.3) can be written as:

$$\text{Malmquist index} = (\text{efficiency index}) \times (\text{technical change}) \tag{5.4}$$

Note that these components may move in opposite directions: progress may be observed because of a strong idiosyncratic organizational performance (efficiency change > 1), even if the environment became less favourable (technical change < 1), and vice versa. The largest of both components determines the direction of the Malmquist index itself. Interestingly, DEA calculates for each organization its idiosyncratic Malmquist index and its decomposition into efficiency and technical changes. It is thus possible to distinguish between the sources of performance change of social enterprises. For example, some firms may improve their own internal performance, while others benefit only from a more favourable environment. Hence, the Malmquist decomposition yields policy-relevant information to identify the source of possible performance changes in each firm. We now discuss both sources in more detail.

Efficiency change or catch-up

As previously mentioned, the efficiency change represents the catch-up of individual firms over two successive periods: it measures whether the same enterprise has become more efficient in transforming inputs into outputs between two periods, given what it is technically feasible. Hence, it can be defined by the ratio of the efficiency score of period $t+1$ to the efficiency score for period t:

$$efficiency\ change = \frac{D_0^{t+1}\left(X^{t+1}, Y^{t+1}\right)}{D_0^{t}\left(X^{t}, Y^{t}\right)} \tag{6}$$

In other words, efficiency change measures how much the firm's performance has changed compared to the benchmark firms in both years (see Figure 2.5.5). If the efficiency change is greater than one, then we can speak of progress in relative efficiency or "catching up" with benchmark firms. Conversely, if the efficiency change is less than one, the efficiency of the organization has deteriorated between the two periods

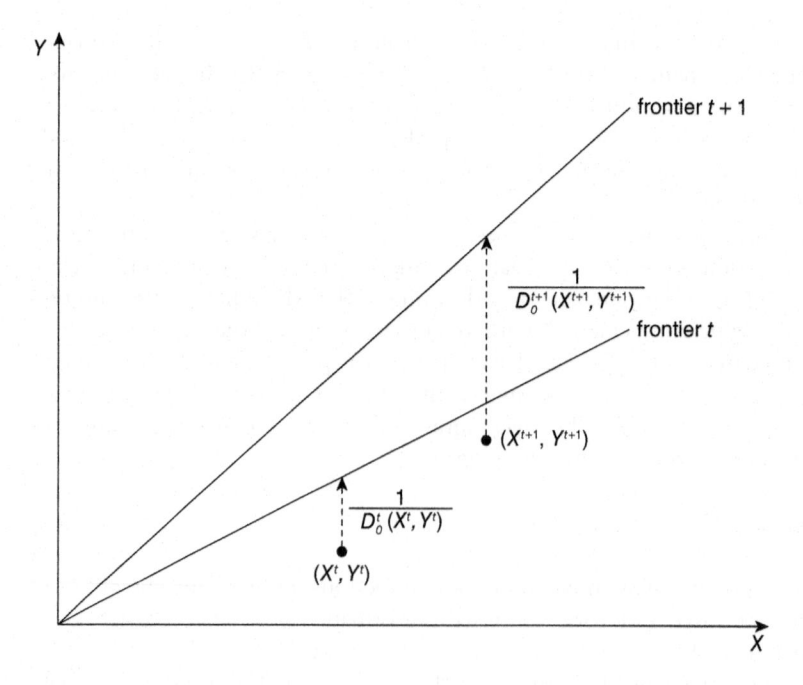

Figure 2.5.5 Efficiency change

or the firm is "lagging behind" benchmark firms. An efficiency change value of one implies a *status quo*. Put differently: "catching up" ("lagging behind") signals that a firm has moved closer to (farther from) the technology frontier between periods t and $t+1$. Hence, based on this ratio, governments can identify which firms are translating their subsidies more efficiently into social and economic output under a given policy (Cooper et al., 2007).

Note that the efficiency change component does not take into account that the frontier itself may have moved between periods. Thus, an individual firm may be trying to catch up by becoming more efficient, but the technology frontier itself may have moved faster. The second component, technical change, precisely measures this frontier shift.

Technical change or frontier shift

Policy-makers can measure how the environment has changed by evaluating technical change in the sector (i.e., sector best practice frontier). This change can be measured by the technical change, which indicates how much the frontier has changed over two successive periods. Based on Figure 2.5.4, this gives the following formula:

$$\text{technical change} = \left[\left(\frac{D_0^t(X^{t+1}, Y^{t+1})}{D_0^{t+1}(X^{t+1}, Y^{t+1})} \right) \times \left(\frac{D_0^t(X^t, Y^t)}{D_0^{t+1}(X^t, Y^t)} \right) \right]^{1/2} \tag{7}$$

As the efficiency frontier also represents the maximum efficiency that a firm can achieve under the current policy (Chen & Delmas, 2011), policy-makers can measure their impact on the sector by monitoring movements in this frontier. The magnitude of technical change may thus reflect the impact of institutional changes introduced into the sector in any given year. Technical change larger than one for a given social enterprise indicates that the environment has become more favourable for that organization (i.e., there is technical progress), whereas the environment has deteriorated if the technical change is smaller than one (i.e., technical regress). In other words, technical progress (regress) signals that the technology frontier in Figure 2.5.4 has shifted upwards (downwards) between periods t and $t+1$. Note that the technical change may differ between organizations, as the impact of institutional change may not have the same impact on the performance of every organization. This is an interesting feature, because policy-makers can measure on which firms their changes in policy have made the biggest impact.

Empirical illustration

To understand the interpretation of DEA and its applicability in allowing policy-makers to analyse the performance of social enterprises over time, consider the following simple illustration. Assume a context in which a government grants accreditation to 12 organizations to operate as social enterprises, and that these 12 social enterprises receive structural financial support through governmental subsidies. By definition, these social enterprises need to achieve both social and economic performance. In line with the literature, the government wants to improve the efficiency of these social enterprises

Table 2.5.1 Input and outputs of social enterprises

ID (j)	Time t0			Time t1			Time t2		
	Subsidy input	Economic output	Social output	Subsidy input	Economic output	Social output	Subsidy input	Economic output	Social output
1	1	100	1	1	300	2	1	300	4
2	1	100	3	1	200	4	1	200	8
3	1	100	5	1	130	6	1	130	12
4	1	140	2	1	420	2	1	420	4
5	1	150	1	1	450	2	1	450	4
6	1	750	7	1	750	7	1	750	14
7	1	1000	5	1	1000	5	1	1000	10
8	1	1000	10	1	1000	10	1	1000	20
9	1	1300	7	1	1300	7	1	1300	14
10	1	1200	10	1	1200	10	1	1200	20
11	1	1350	8	1	1350	8	1	1350	16
12	1	1500	6	1	1500	6	1	1500	12
Sector average	1	723.16	5.41	1	800	5.75	1	8	11.5

over time. Therefore, it has introduced two successive policy decisions to support these organizations: (1) individual management assistance for weak performers during $t1$; and (2) sector reform to stimulate the social impact at the end of $t1$.

In order to assess the impact of these two policy decisions, information about the subsidies, and the economic and social outputs of these 12 social enterprises has been collected. Table 2.5.1 shows this information for three successive periods $t0$, $t1$, and $t2$. Note that, although all social enterprises receive the same amount of input (subsidy = 1) during the periods $t0$ to $t2$, they achieve varying amounts of social and economic outputs. For illustration purposes, we simulate that 5 of the 12 social enterprises are operating inefficiently. From Table 2.5.1, one can derive from the level of social and economic outputs that the first five social enterprises (ID(j) 1 to 5) are underperforming because they have lower social and economic outputs than the sector average (at $t0$). This observation is further underlined by the DEA calculations. To illustrate how DEA can be used to measure the efficiency of social enterprises and may act as an important evaluation tool to assess the impact of policy decisions, we discuss the DEA calculations of this illustrative example in detail.

Efficiency scores

For a one-input-two-output setting of 12 social enterprises over three successive periods, $t = \{0,1,2\}$, the following DEA formulation is used to compute the efficiency of social enterprises ID(j) 1 to 12:

$$\frac{1}{D_j^t} \equiv \min_{v,u} \frac{v_{j1}^t \text{Subsidies}_j^t}{u_{j1}^t \text{Social output}_j^t + u_{j2}^t \text{Economic output}_j^t} \tag{8.1}$$

$$s.t. : \frac{v^t_{j1}\text{Subsidies}^t_k}{u^t_{j1}\text{Social output}^t_k + u^t_{j2}\text{Economic output}^t_k} \geq 1, \quad k = 1,..,12 \tag{8.2}$$

$$u^t_{j1}, u^t_{j2}, v^t_{j1} \geq 0 \tag{8.3}$$

This optimization problem delivers efficiency scores (D^t_j) for each social enterprise at $t0$, $t1$, and $t2$. From Table 2.5.2, one can derive that the average total efficiency at time $t0$ (D^0_j) amounts to 63 per cent. Since DEA is a benchmark technique, and thus efficiency scores are calculated based on what is technically feasible, it is correct to state that these social enterprises are operating at suboptimal efficiency. Moreover, given the feasibility in the sector, this could be improved by 37 per cent, on average. Remember that the efficiency scores are the ratio of the organization's present performance to what would be technically feasible if the organization were to operate fully efficiently. Hence, thanks to the benchmark characteristic of DEA, policy-makers can pinpoint good performance based on the evaluated organizations. In other words, no prior thresholds are needed to decide whether a social enterprise is operating at an efficient level, as DEA will calculate a benchmark endogenously. Specifically, the benchmark is defined in terms of firms that are using their inputs as efficiently as possible under the current environment. Policy-makers can easily classify these firms based on their efficiency scores. Benchmark firms are those with an efficiency score of one, and thus they define the industry best practice frontier.

Policy-makers can thus use DEA as a tool to analyse the comparative performance of social enterprises. Based on the efficiency scores, they can also rank the firms to identify

Table 2.5.2 Efficiency scores over time

ID (j)	D^0_j	D^1_j	D^2_j
1	0.10	0.23	0.23
2	0.30	0.40	0.40
3	0.50	0.60	0.60
4	0.20	0.29	0.29
5	0.12	0.30	0.31
6	0.70	0.70	0.70
7	0.71	0.71	0.71
8	1.00	1.00	1.00
9	0.94	0.94	0.94
10	1.00	1.00	1.00
11	1.00	1.00	1.00
12	1.00	1.00	1.00
Sector average	0.63	0.68	0.68

Table 2.5.3 Efficiency scores and ranking at $t0$

ID(j)	D_j^0	rank at t0
1	0.10	9
2	0.30	6
3	0.50	5
4	0.20	7
5	0.12	8
6	0.70	4
7	0.71	3
8	1.00	1
9	0.94	2
10	1.00	1
11	1.00	1
12	1.00	1
Sector average	0.63	/

strong and weak performers more easily (see, for example, Table 2.5.3). As expected, the first five social enterprises (ID(j) 1 to 5) are being outperformed by the other seven enterprises (ID(j) 7 to 12), as they only achieve efficiencies of between 10 and 50 per cent. This indicates that they have a large competitive disadvantage with respect to the other firms. Nevertheless, less efficient organizations have more room to improve their performance. Based on these observations, the government can focus on these poorly performing firms by giving them extra support to stimulate a catch-up movement, thus reducing their competitive disadvantage with respect to the top performers.

Policy decision 1: individual support package for weak performers during t1

The first support package aims to help the five weak performers (ID(j) 1 to 5) by offering them extra management assistance between years $t0$ and $t1$. This type of policy decision does not influence the external environment, but rather the internal operations of an organization under a given environment. From Table 2.5.1, one can derive that the supported firms have indeed enhanced their social and economic outputs between time periods $t0$ and $t1$.

The objective of this policy decision is to reduce the competitive disadvantage of these weak performers by improving their efficiency. To check whether the policy-makers have succeeded in their mission to stimulate the weak performers to "catch up", we calculate the efficiency scores at $t1$ (i.e., D_j^1), as well as the Malmquist index (MQ01), efficiency change (EC01), and technical change (TC01) between times $t0$ and $t1$. From Table 2.5.4, we see that the weak performers (ID(j) 1 to 5) have improved their performance with respect to $t0$. For instance, firm 1 has improved its total efficiency from 10 per cent at $t0$ to 23 per cent at $t1$.

Furthermore, the observed performance change is underscored by the observation that the Malmquist index (MQ01) of these firms is greater than one, whereas for the

Table 2.5.4 Efficiency change between *t*0 and *t*1

ID(j)	D_j^0	D_j^1	MQ01	EC01	TC01
1	0.10	0.23	2.30	2.30	1.00
2	0.30	0.40	1.33	1.33	1.00
3	0.50	0.60	1.20	1.20	1.00
4	0.20	0.29	1.46	1.46	1.00
5	0.12	0.30	2.60	2.60	1.00
6	0.70	0.70	1.00	1.00	1.00
7	0.71	0.71	1.00	1.00	1.00
8	1.00	1.00	1.00	1.00	1.00
9	0.94	0.94	1.00	1.00	1.00
10	1.00	1.00	1.00	1.00	1.00
11	1.00	1.00	1.00	1.00	1.00
12	1.00	1.00	1.00	1.00	1.00
Average	0.63	0.68	1.33	1.33	1.00

other seven firms, the Malmquist index (MQ01) equals one, indicating a *status quo* in performance. To gain a deeper understanding of the source of the performance improvement, policy-makers can refer to the efficiency and technical changes. As expected, while the environment has remained constant (i.e., technical change = 1 for every social enterprise), we can see that the weak performers have realized a catch-up by using their resources more efficiently due to extra internal assistance (i.e., efficiency change > 1). For example, firm 5 is using its subsidies 2.6 times more efficiently than at time *t*0. Since the top performers did not receive any internal management support, their technical efficiency equals one.

Policy decision 2: sector reform to stimulate social impact at end of t1

Next, we illustrate how a policy decision to reform the whole social sector may influence the external environment conditions of social enterprises. This is demonstrated for the period between times *t*1 and *t*2. Between these successive periods, the policy-makers established a more favourable environment to enable all organizations to achieve higher social outputs. Table 2.5.1 already depicts this favourable change in the environment in the growth in social output between periods *t*1 and *t*2: the average social output increased from 5.75 at *t*1 to 11.5 at *t*2. Note that efficiency scores remain unchanged for all social enterprises between these periods (see Table 2.5.5) because all organizations realized the same favourable change, and all benefited from this institutional change. The social output improved for all organizations by a factor of two (see Table 2.5.1). Although the efficiency score remains unchanged for all social enterprises between these periods, this does not indicate that there is no performance change.

In order to analyse whether the social sector has become more productive, policy-makers can refer to the Malmquist index and its decomposition (see Table 2.5.5). Clearly, the

Table 2.5.5 Technical change between *t*1 and *t*2

ID (n)	D_j^1	D_j^1	MQ12	EC12	TC12
1	0.23	0.23	1.41	1.00	1.41
2	0.40	0.40	2.00	1.00	2.00
3	0.60	0.60	2.00	1.00	2.00
4	0.29	0.29	1.20	1.00	1.20
5	0.31	0.31	1.15	1.00	1.15
6	0.70	0.70	1.78	1.00	1.64
7	0.71	0.71	1.22	1.00	1.22
8	1.00	1.00	1.68	1.00	1.68
9	0.94	0.94	1.27	1.00	1.27
10	1.00	1.00	1.57	1.00	1.57
11	1.00	1.00	1.33	1.00	1.33
12	1.00	1.00	1.11	1.00	1.11
Average	0.68	0.68	1.50	1.00	1.46

Malmquist index (MQ12) between *t*1 and *t*2 indicates progress in the performance of all organizations (Malmquist index > 1).

Since a policy reform influences the maximum efficiency that a firm can achieve (Chen & Delmas, 2011), and not necessarily its idiosyncratic catch-up, only the industry best practice frontier is expected to shift. In line with this expectation, one can derive from Table 2.5.5 that the technical change is greater than one for every firm, while the efficiency change equals one. This suggests that the improved overall performance is exclusively due to a more favourable environment (Cherchye et al., 2007b). An interpretation of this finding is that the policy-makers have succeeded in creating an environment that stimulates social enterprises to improve their impact. For instance, firms 2 and 3, especially, have fully benefited from the institutional change, as their technical change has the highest value. Hence, this illustration already gives insights into how DEA calculations can be used to analyse endogenous effects (such as institutional changes) by monitoring movement in the industry best practice frontier.

Based on these insights, the government might question whether it is still desirable to grant accreditation (and thus provide subsidies) to the 5 poorly performing social enterprises. Although they have improved their efficiency as a result of the policy-makers' additional support, they are still outperformed by the other 7 organizations. Firms 1, 4, and 5, especially, underperform as their efficiency amounts to only 23, 29, and 31 per cent at *t*2, respectively. Based on the results of the DEA analysis, policy-makers might consider whether their funds might be better spent elsewhere by reallocating the subsidies of firms 1, 4, and 5.

As previously mentioned, this application is provided simply for illustration. Nevertheless, it does demonstrate the potential of DEA to allow policy-makers to monitor the performance of social enterprises, to measure the impact of policy decisions, and to adjust policy measures if needed. It thus addresses the crucial question of whether performance progress is due mainly to favourable sector-specific policy changes, or rather to idiosyncratic organizational catching-up effects (Cherchye et al., 2007b). In our application, we have explained how policy decisions may impact on both environmental conditions and firm-specific internal operations. As a result, policy-makers can assess whether their changes in policy toward social enterprises have achieved their desired objectives.

Conclusions

Performance measurement of social enterprises plays a prominent role in allowing policy-makers to assess the impact of changes in their policies toward social enterprises. While various attempts have been made to measure the performance of social entrepreneurship, they lack applicability in practice for policy-makers to assess not only the performance of social enterprises, but also the impact of their policy decisions. Moreover, since policy-makers are better positioned than individual organizations to oversee the performance of these organizations, they should put more effort into monitoring their performance over time.

To this extent, this chapter has laid out the methodological basis for a new performance approach to social enterprises by proposing the adoption of data envelopment analysis (DEA). This approach offers a rich ground for policy-makers in the social sector. DEA is a straightforward and easy methodology of calculating the performance of social enterprises, as it allows for meaningful aggregation of social and economic performance into a single criterion. Based on efficiency scores, policy-makers can pinpoint good performance and identify strong and weak performers. Hence, DEA can help policy-makers to allocate their resources as efficiently as possible in the future.

The DEA approach also allows performance change over time to be measured by calculating the Malmquist index. Attractively, this index can be further decomposed into an "efficiency change" component that indicates the degree to which a firm improves or worsens its efficiency, and a "technical change" component that reflects changes in the environment of social enterprises. This decomposition allows policy-makers to identify the source of performance progress or regress for each social enterprise. It is thus possible to monitor the impact of policy decisions on idiosyncratic organizational catch-up effects and environmental conditions, as illustrated in the example above. These insights may help governments to assess the impact of their policy decisions.

Notes

1 Note that minimizing $\frac{v_0^t X_0^{t'}}{u_0^t Y_0^{t'}}$ is equivalent to maximizing $\frac{u_0^t Y_0^{t'}}{v_0^t X_0^{t'}}$ as discussed earlier.

2 Notably, while this particular formulation is for Charnes et al.'s (1978) output-oriented CCR model, one can also apply Banker et al.'s (1984) BCC model and/or an input-oriented approach. To focus our discussion, we present no details here, but refer interested readers to Charnes et al. (1978), Banker et al. (1984) for details, and Cook and Seiford (2009) for an overview of DEA.

References

Anokhin, S., Wincent, J., & Autio, E. (2011). Operationalizing opportunities in entrepreneurship research: Use of data envelopment analysis. *Small Business Economics*, 37(1), 39–57.

Banker, R.D., Charnes, A., & Cooper, W. (1984). Some models for estimating technical and scale inefficiencies in data envelopment analysis. *Management Science*, 30(9), 1078–1092.

Battilana, J., Lee, M., Walker, J., & Dorsey, C. (2012). In search of the hybrid ideal. *Stanford Social Innovation Review*, 10(3), 51–55.

Belu, C. (2009). Ranking corporations based on sustainable and socially responsible practices: A data envelopment analysis (DEA) approach. *Sustainable Development*, 17(4), 257–268.

Bruneel, J., Moray, N., Stevens, R., & Fassin, Y. (2016). Balancing competing logics in for-profit social enterprises: A need for hybrid governance. *Journal of Social Entrepreneurship*, 676(April), 1–26.

Caves, D.W., Christensen, L.R., & Diewert, W.E. (1982). Multilateral comparisons of output, input and productivity using superlative index numbers. *The Economic Journal*, 92, 73–86.

Charnes, A., Cooper, W.W., & Rhodes, E.L. (1978). Measuring the efficiency of decision making units. *European Journal of Operational Research*, 2, 429–444.

Chen, C., & Delmas, M.A. (2011). Measuring eco-inefficiency: A new frontier approach. *Operations Research*, 60(5), 1064–1079.

Chen, C., Delmas, M.A., & Lieberman, M.B. (2015). Production frontier methodologies and efficiency as a performance measure in strategic management research. *Strategic Management Journal*, 36(1), 19–36.

Cherchye, L. (2001). Using data envelopment analysis to assess macroeconomic policy performance. *Applied Economics*, 33(3), 407–416.

Cherchye, L., Lovell, C.A.K., Moesen, W., & Van Puyenbroeck, T. (2007a). One market, one number ? A composite indicator assessment of EU internal market dynamics. *European Economic Review*, 51, 749–779.

Cherchye, L., Moesen, W., Rogge, N., & Van Puyenbroeck, T. (2007b). An introduction to "benefit of the doubt" composite indicators. *Social Indicators Research*, 82(1), 111–145.

Cook, W.D., & Seiford, L.M. (2009). Data envelopment analysis (DEA): Thirty years on. *European Journal of Operational Research*, 192(1), 1–17.

Cooper, W.W., Seiford, L.M., & Tone, K. (2007). *Data Envelopment Analysis: A Comprehensive Text with Models, Applications, References and DEA-Solver Software*. New York, NY: Springer.

Dart, R. (2004). Being "business-like" in a nonprofit organization: A grounded and inductive typology. *Nonprofit and Voluntary Sector Quarterly*, 33(2), 290–310.

Dees, G.J. (1998). Enterprising nonprofits: What do you do when traditional sources of funding fall short? *Harvard Business Review*, 76, 55–67.

Defourny, J., & Nyssens, M. (2010). Conceptions of social enterprise and social entrepreneurship in Europe and the United States: Convergences and divergences. *Journal of Social Entrepreneurship*, 1(920117410), 32–53.

DiMaggio, P., & Powell, W. (1991). Introduction. In W. Powell & P. DiMaggio (Eds.), *The New Institutionalism in Organizational Analysis*: 1–38. Chicago: University of Chicago Press.

Ebrahim, A., Battilana, J., & Mair, J. (2014). The governance of social enterprises: Mission drift and accountability challenges in hybrid organizations. *Research in Organizational Behavior*, 34, 81–100.

Ebrahim, A., & Rangan, V.K. (2014). What Impact? A framework for measuring the scale and scope of social performance. *California Management Review*, 56(3), 118–141.

Färe, B.R., Grosskopf, S., & Norris, M. (1994). Productivity growth, technical progress, and efficiency change in industrialized countries. *The American Economic Review*, 84(1), 66–83.

Hart, T., & Haughton, G. (2007). Assessing the economic and social impacts of social enterprise. *Centre for City and Regional Studies, University of Hull*. Available at: https://www.escholar.man chester.ac.uk/ (accessed 15 June 2012).

Kaplan, R.S. (2001). Strategic performance measurement and management in nonprofit organizations. *Nonprofit Management and Leadership*, 11(3), 353–370.

Kroeger, A., & Weber, C. (2014). Developing a conceptual framework for comparing social value creation. *Academy of Management Review*, 39(4), 513–540.

Kuosmanen, T., & Kortelainen, M. (2005). Measuring eco-efficiency of production with data envelopment analysis. *Journal of Industrial Ecology*, 9(4), 59–72.

Maas, K., & Liket, K. (2011). Social impact measurement: Classification of methods. In R. Burritt, S. Schaltegger, M. Bennett, T. Pohjola, & M. Csutora (Eds.), *Environmental Management Accounting and Supply Chain Management: Eco-Efficiency in Industry and Science*, Vol. 27: 171–202. Delft, the Netherlands: Springer.

Mair, J., Battilana, J., & Cardenas, J. (2012). Organizing for society: A typology of social entrepreneuring models. *Journal of Business Ethics*, 111(3), 353–373.

Millar, R., & Hall, K. (2012). Social return on investment (SROI) and performance measurement: The opportunities and barriers for social enterprises in health and social care. *Public Management Review*, 15(6), 923–941.

Paton, R. (2003). *Managing and Measuring Social Enterprises*. London: Sage.

Peredo, A.M., & McLean, M. (2006). Social entrepreneurship: A critical review of the concept. *Journal of World Business*, 41(1), 56–65.

Ramus, T., & Vaccaro, A. (2014). Stakeholders matter: How social enterprises address mission drift. *Journal of Business Ethics*, 143(2), 1–16.

Rotheroe, N., & Richards, A. (2007). Social return on investment and social enterprise: Transparent accountability for sustainable development. *Social Enterprise Journal*, 3(1), 31–48.

Stevens, R., Moray, N., & Bruneel, J. (2015a). The social and economic mission of social enterprises: dimensions, measurement, validation, and relation. *Entrepreneurship: Theory and Practice*, 39(5), 1051–1082.

Stevens, R., Moray, N., Bruneel, J., & Clarysse, B. (2015b). Attention allocation to multiple goals: The case of for-profit social enterprises. *Academy of Management Journal*, 36, 1006–1016.

Sud, M., Vansandt, C.V., & Baugous, A.M. (2009). Social entrepreneurship: The role of institutions. *Journal of Business Ethics*, 85(Suppl. 1), 201–216.

Tuckman, H.P. (1998). Competition, commercialization, and the evolution of nonprofit organizational structures. *Journal of Policy Analysis and Management*, 17(2), 175–194.

Wellens, L., & Jegers, M. (2014). Effective governance in nonprofit organizations: A literature-based multiple stakeholder approach. *European Management Journal*, 32(2), 223–243.

Zahra, S.A., Gedajlovic, E., Neubaum, D.O., & Shulman, J.M. (2009). A typology of social entrepreneurs: Motives, search processes and ethical challenges. *Journal of Business Venturing*, 24(5), 519–532.

2.6 Diffusion of sustainability

A road map for developing corporate compliance programmes with high diffusion potential

Duygu Türker and Ceren Altuntaş Vural

Introduction

Responding to the rising customer demands of decreasing costs imposes high pressures upon firms to develop new strategies, structures, and technologies. In the face of global competition, many companies have expanded their operations into developing countries by marketing their products as well as transferring their production units. Starting from the 1980s and, particularly, after the globalization wave of the 1990s, many developing countries become the production hub of global firms. For instance, the textile and clothing industry was among the early-adopters of this trend, and many leading brands of this industry have off-shored their labour-intensive operations by spreading its supply chains to less-developed parts of the world (Los et al., 2014; Mair et al., 2016). The same goes for the automotive and electronic industries where 'intangibles' like brand development, design, and innovation are led by the focal companies and the 'tangibles' like transformation of physical goods are transferred to the world-class manufacturers located in developing countries (Gereffi and Kaplinsky, 2001). Actually, the main pressure comes from the big buyers, which are the large retailers, brand-named merchandisers, and trading companies located in the United States of America (USA) and Europe (Gereffi, 1994). These organizations manage long and decentralized production networks in developing countries for labour-intensive industries such as apparels, houseware, footwear, toys, ornaments, and electronics in order to decrease costs, focus on core competencies, and quickly respond to changing customer demands. However, the high-risk accidents or abusive labour practices (e.g., Ek and Kane, 2013; Thomson Reuters Foundation, 2016) cast doubt on the practices of global brands in those countries. Companies are increasingly held responsible from the actions and practices of their suppliers.

Although the existing standards (e.g., United Nations/UN Global Compact, Universal Declaration of Human Rights, International Labour Organization/ILO Convention) or new initiatives (e.g., The Organisation for Economic Co-operation and Development/ OECD's Responsible Supply Chains in the Garment and Footwear Sector, 2016) promote economic, social, and environmental sustainability among companies, the current level of progress is rather slow and inefficient. In most cases, companies develop their own management/compliance programmes to set principles in the form of codes of conduct, to monitor the process of implementation and to measure the level of progress among their suppliers deriving from these existing standards. However, these programmes are characterized by their voluntary and non-standardized nature. Each industry, or sometimes each large corporation, tries to develop its own code and assesses its suppliers based on this code, which creates confusion and repeating work processes for suppliers working for more than one buyer organization. In addition, these codes might have important components that can be used as benchmarks for other industry codes, but they rather stay within individual supply chains and are not diffused well across industries.

Considering these practical gaps, this study mainly aims to review the existing literature to identify the important factors for codes of conduct that have high compliance and diffusion characteristics throughout the supply chain. After discovering these factors, the study attempts to develop a road map for corporate compliance programmes with a high implication and diffusion potential. Such a framework is expected to provide a useful benchmark tool for various industries thinking about standardizing compliance programmes, and it can also present a helpful insight to understand the spill-over of sustainable practices among diverse organizations in different industries.

In order to achieve these aims, the study starts with the review of the relevant literature on corporate compliance programmes and codes on sustainability in the supply chain. The next section continues with the analysis of important factors that should be prevalent in effective compliance programmes. The chapter concludes with the introduction of a road map on corporate compliance programmes that are expected to be adopted and diffused to many suppliers in diverse industries. Implications for scholars and practitioners are summarized at the end of the chapter.

Corporate compliance programmes for sustainability in the supply chain

In line with the spread of corporate operations from developed countries to the developing or underdeveloped ones, companies obtain a global supplier network; but they also face new challenges (Oehmen et al., 2010). Despite the cost advantage of operating in those countries, managing supply chains have become more complex and involved many unforeseen risks due to the low working and environmental standards in such countries. Depending on the increasing pressures of global society and non-governmental organizations (NGOs), multinational companies (MNCs) have taken some responsibilities in the operations of their suppliers around the world. Although they accept the internationally recognized standards when operating in those countries, they also follow tailored-made approaches to ensure sustainability on their factory floors (Turker and Altuntas, 2014). Voluntary self-regulations emerged since the 1990s in line with the declining efforts of national and international organizations (Jenkins, 2001; Kolk et al., 1999) in various ways such as codes of conduct, social labelling programmes, or investor initiatives (Diller, 1999).

During the last decades, most companies have adopted their own guidelines, principles, or standards in the form of codes of conduct. As 'a set of written principles, guidelines or standards, which are intended to improve the company's social and environmental performance' (Pedersen and Andersen, 2006: 229), companies' codes of conduct are intended to deliver corporate messages to the general public, employees, suppliers (Oehmen et al., 2010), investors, managers, consumers, local community, government, NGOs, or the media (Diller, 1999), as the stakeholders who have different levels of power and interest over firms (Ozturkoglu and Turker, 2013). By providing a guideline, companies try to transfer their own philosophies and practices on the working, environmental, or ethical conditions to their suppliers. An example of a code of conduct for suppliers is presented in Table 2.6.1.

Table 2.6.1 The shortened version of Whirlpool Corporation's supplier code of conduct

Categories	*Explanations*
Laws and Regulations	Suppliers must operate in full compliance with all applicable laws and regulations of the countries in which they operate and also in full compliance with this Code.
Corruption	Bribery, extortion and kickbacks are prohibited. Suppliers must comply with all applicable anti-bribery and anticorruption laws
Child Labour	Suppliers must comply with local laws regarding the minimum age of employees.
Forced Labour	Suppliers must not use any type of involuntary or forced labour, including indentured, bonded, prison, slave or human trafficked labour.
Harassment	Suppliers must treat all workers with respect and dignity. No work shall be subject to corporal punishment, physical, sexual, psychological or verbal harassment or abuse. In addition, Suppliers will not use monetary fines as a disciplinary practice.
Wage and Benefits	Suppliers must pay workers at least the minimum compensation required by local law and provide all legally mandated benefits, accident insurances. In addition to payment for regular hours of work, workers must be paid for overtime hours.
Hours of Work	Suppliers must ensure that on a regularly scheduled basis, except in extraordinary business circumstances, workers are not required to work more than (a) 60 hours a week, including overtime, or (b) the limits on regular and overtime hours allowed by the law of the country of manufacture.
Health and Safety	Suppliers must provide workers a clean, safe and healthy work environment in compliance with all legally mandated standards for workplace health and safety in the countries in which they operate. This includes any residential facilities a Supplier provides to its workers.
Non discrimination	Suppliers must ensure employment – including hiring, payment, benefits, advancement, termination and retirement – is based on ability and not on beliefs or any other personal characteristics such as color, race, caste, religion, disability etc. or any other status or characteristic that is not related to the individual's merit or the inherent requirements of the job.
Women's Rights	Suppliers will ensure women workers receive equal treatment in all aspects of employment. Pregnancy tests will not be a condition of employment and pregnancy testing – to the extent provided – will be voluntary and the option of the worker. In addition, workers will not be forced to use contraception.
Freedom of Association & Collective Bargaining	Suppliers must recognize and respect any rights of workers to exercise lawful rights of free association, including joining or not joining any association. Suppliers also must respect any legal right of workers to bargain collectively.
Environment	Suppliers must comply with all local environmental laws applicable to the workplace, the products produced, and the methods of manufacture. Additionally, Suppliers must not use materials that are considered harmful to the environment, but should encourage the use of processes and materials that support sustainability of the environment.
Subcontracting	Suppliers must not use subcontractors to manufacture Whirlpool products or product components that contain Whirlpool's trademarks or tradenames without prior approval from Whirlpool, and only after the subcontractor has agreed to comply with this Code.

| Communication | Suppliers should communicate, through their existing ethical operating standards/practices or through this Code, so that their workers, supervisors and permitted subcontractors are aware of the expectations / requirements detailed in this Code. |
| Monitoring and Compliance | Whirlpool will take affirmative measures, such as announced and unannounced inspections of production facilities, to ensure compliance with this Code. |

Source: Whirlpool (2016).

As a leading appliance manufacturer, having 97,000 employees in 70 manufacturing/ research centres and approximately $21 billion in annual sales as of 2015, Whirlpool established its Supplier Code of Conduct in 2006, reflecting its fundamental expectations in business practices (Whirlpool, 2016). The code is compulsory for all suppliers, and it determines the conditions to avoid abusive, exploitative, or illegal conditions. However, a code of conduct can be seen as a simple policy statement (Sethi, 2002) without any legal obligation (Klein, 2000), when it is not backed up with a sound monitoring and enforcement framework (Emmelhainz and Adams, 1999). Hong (2000, p. 51) states that 'a particular code's effectiveness depends, in large part, on effective, neutral monitoring for compliance. Otherwise, these codes that purportedly protect workers' right can potentially serve as a curtain to disguise labor abuses from the consuming public'. Therefore, developing a code of conduct is the starting point and must be supported by a viable and comprehensive compliance programme that spreads the sustainability across suppliers. By redressing the power of MNCs on particularly social and environmental problems in developing and underdeveloped countries (Jenkins, 2001), the codes and complementary programmes can enable the diffusion of sustainability around the world (Jiang, 2009).

The role of global supply chains in the proliferation of codes of conduct cannot be ignored, and that role is mainly attributed to the decentralization of production and distribution of branded goods. Together with the increasing public visibility of strong brands, their reputation sensitivity, and the outreach of the conditions at supplier bases due to the accelerated pace of developments in communications technology, MNCs had to self-regulate the operations at their suppliers by giving rise to codes of conduct (Jenkins, 2001). However, these codes of conduct and especially their monitoring activities are widely criticized for being highly MNC–driven and not being focused on working conditions or environmental impact in reality, but instead securing MNC reputations by building up a procedure that was undertaken by the states before (Bartley, 2005). The governance gap (MacDonald, 2011) that arises due to the inadequacy and incapability of governments in controlling MNCs in terms of their global actions is said to be facilitated with especially developing country governments' hesitations due to the risk of losing competitive positions in terms of foreign investment flows (Deva, 2012). This situation points out the urgent need to define an alternative method, not only state-driven and not only corporation-driven, but more multi-dimensional and more participative. Therefore, the proposals for how a better code of conduct and monitoring system should be established in order to strengthen the states that want to attract the foreign direct investment by encouraging MNCs and secure the working conditions at equal terms with their Western facilities are debated among scholars (Seidman, 2003; Locke et al., 2007).

Effectiveness of compliance programmes

Despite the popularity of compliance programmes among global companies, we have still little understanding on the impacts of such programmes. In the literature, there is an ongoing debate on their positive or negative impacts. For some scholars, these corporate initiatives are viewed as tools for increasing corporate legitimacy (Blowfield and Dolan, 2008) or even threatening public regulations (O'Rourke, 2006); for some others, these corporate attempts have significant potentials to achieve real improvements (Zadek, 2004). The best way of figuring out the role of codes and compliance programmes is to observe and measure their impacts over time. For instance, the longitudinal study of Egels-Zandén (2014) on four Chinese toy suppliers successfully accomplished such a hard-core task by interviewing the employees of those factories between 2004 and 2009 and comparatively analysing the results of the qualitative study; the findings of the study show that private regulations on workers' rights improve the conditions on the factory floor substantially.

In practice, companies also monitor the effectiveness of their compliance programmes by following the diffusion of sustainability across their supply chain. Some companies annually report the progress among their suppliers and share the number of suppliers that adopt the code and comply with its standards. Although these annual data are useful to show the diffusion of sustainability, we have to bear in mind that it might be unreliable or inaccurate, since companies mostly rely on the self-reported measurement.

The corporate examples given below are indicative of the diffusion among suppliers of corporate compliance programmes between 2011 and 2015:

Apple

Apple explains that the corporate responsible practices guide suppliers in the areas of labour and human rights, worker health and safety, environmental impact, ethics, and management systems (Apple, 2011). The data on the last category is not provided in the latest company report (Apple, 2016). The code of conduct is stated as a mandatory condition to work with Apple and draws its content on internationally recognized standards. It is stated that the company follows a risk-based approach to conduct audits on its suppliers (through the unannounced visits of independent experts, anonymous complaint system or follow-up interviews) and stops working with them whenever they notice that suppliers do not follow this code or fail to implement corrective action plans. The company periodically reports the percentage of practices in compliances on the given categories since 2010. A comparison on the diffusion of sustainability across the supplier base shows that two out of four measured categories have declined between 2011 and 2015, whereas one category remains the same in both years (Table 2.6.2). The audits in 2010 revealed that 106 children were working at several suppliers in Asia. The company is esteemed on its self-criticism in its own report and later on improvements (SCDigest, 2012). However, it was still criticized since the audits are not performed by an independent third party and do not provide accurate information on the practices; the report does not provide detailed, transparent, and comparable information, and it involves inaccurate and self-serving rhetorical claims, and so on (Nova and Shapiro, 2013).

Table 2.6.2 The diffusion of sustainability across the suppliers of Apple (2011–2015)

Category	Example Subcategories	2011	2015
Labour and Human Rights	Anti-discrimination, anti-harassment and abuse, prevention of involuntary labour, etc.	74%	84%
Health and Safety	Health and safety permits, occupational health safety and hazard prevention, working and living conditions, etc.	76%	73%
Environment	Environmental permits, wastewater management, air emissions management, boundary noise management, etc.	79%	76%
Ethics	Business integrity, disclosure of information, whistle-blower protection and anonymous complaints, etc.	95%	95%*
Management Systems	Company statement, management accountability and responsibility, documentation and records, etc.	68%	–

*Management systems in place

Source: Apple (2012, 2016)

H&M

Sustainability Commitment of H&M was replaced with the previous Code of Conduct on the 1st of February 2016, and the company started to implement a Sustainable Impact Partnership Program (SIPP) instead of its Full Audit Program (FAP) in 2015. As of 2015, the company measures the sustainability at eleven categories: child labour, young workers' requirements, workers' basic rights, workers' rights, health and safety, environment, housing conditions, home workers, chemical handlings, metal plating, and transparency and monitoring. The company states that it commits to a transparent reporting process and dedicates its resources to monitor and improve its suppliers' sustainability performance. It is indicated that the company conducts an in-depth analysis in the case of the detection of non-compliance among its suppliers; 'at the end of the reporting period a number of factories were subject to investigations or in a phase out transition' (H&M, 2016). Table 2.6.3 shows the level of diffusion among suppliers. Except two categories (young workers and metal plating), the company reports an increasing diffusion in all categories and in all regions. However, the company is still accused of working with suppliers, which are problematic in terms of social and environmental conditions. After the collapse of Rana Plaza in Bangladesh, H&M took some measures like being the first large-scale company that signed on the 2013 Accord on Fire and Building Safety in Bangladesh, but a recent report on H&M suppliers' factories revealed that many garment workers of H&M's suppliers still continue to work without any fire exit (Kasperkevic, 2016).

Although many companies develop their code of conduct, only some of them successfully enable the diffusion of sustainability across their suppliers. For instance, the study of Egels-Zandén (2007) on the Chinese suppliers of a Swedish toy retailer shows that more than two-thirds of the suppliers do not fully comply with the company codes by deceiving the retailers by decoupling the formal monitored part from the actual operations. In some cases, the existence of codes may improve outcome standards, but only slightly affect the process on labour rights, for example, the freedom of association and bargaining power (Egels-Zandén and Merk, 2014). The effectiveness of compliance programmes depends on many variables regarding the company, supplier, process, or context.

Table 2.6.3 The diffusion of sustainability across the suppliers of H&M (2011–2015)

Category	2011				2015			
	EMEA*	Far East	South Asia	Total	EMEA*	Far East	South Asia	Total
Child labour**	65%	84%	99%	84%	100%	100%	100%	100%
Young workers' requirements*	65%	84%	99%	84%	28%	82%	100%	65%
Workers' basic rights	70%	84%	76%	77%	80%	90%	77%	84%
Workers' rights	76%	62%	83%	75%	90%	73%	87%	81%
Health and safety	76%	73%	81%	78%	87%	82%	89%	86%
Environment	68%	59%	63%	62%	84%	75%	77%	77%
Housing conditions	68%	85%	80%	84%	N.A.	95%	94%	95%
Home workers	N.A.	32%	N.A.	32%	90%	51%	89%	63%
Chemicals***	52%	70%	75%	70%	74%	85%	86%	83%
Metal plating	N.A.	78%	100%	82%	100%	75%	86%	80%
Transparency and monitoring	95%	93%	98%	96%	99%	99%	99%	99%

*Europe, the Middle East, and Africa
**Child labour and young workers' requirements were evaluated under the same title in 2011 and then they were divided into two categories in 2015.
***The category is entitled as 'sandblasting and chemicals' in 2011, 'chemical handlings' in 2015.

Source: H&M (2011, 2016)

Factors of importance in compliance programmes for sustainability in the supply chain

In order to build up an effective compliance programme and monitor suppliers for sustainability, it is firstly essential to define sustainability for the supply chain and take a perspective in terms of supplier scope. Sustainability in the supply chain is not actually the effort of the supply chain members to decrease their negative impacts on the environment solely, although the environmental dimension seems to attract greater attention from scholars (Seuring and Müller, 2008). Instead of its current fragmented character in terms of philanthropy, corporate care in labour issues, environmental consciousness, and the like (Carter and Easton, 2011), sustainable supply chains need a holistic perspective that is dependent on the triple bottom line approach (Elkington, 1997) where the three facets of economy, society, and the environment should be integrated. A sustainable supply chain needs to have characteristics and practices from both business sustainability concepts and supply chain management concepts (Ahi and Searcy, 2013), and it can be defined as the alignment of goals, practices, and policies of individual supply chain members regarding the intersection points of the triple bottom line, with the former and latter members of the supply chain with whom they are in contact (Göçer et al., 2012; A. Vural, 2015).

Most companies think that choosing suppliers with some global management systems such as an environmental management system (EMS) or social accountability system (like SA8000) is adequate to build sustainability in the supply chain. However, there are certain doubts about this approach. These globally recognized management standards are criticized to be focused on sole creation and documentation of policies and procedures instead of improving an organization's environmental or social performance (Krut and Gleckman, 1998).

Therefore, it is essential to design the supply chain in the form of a cooperating network where initiating, implementing, and sustaining sustainability practices should be done in partnerships, under mentoring, and through both formal and informal relationships (Curkovic and Sroufe, 2011).

This dimension is also emphasized within the main critics of traditional compliance programmes that are dependent on the assumed power of MNCs on suppliers and the information stemming from these traditional programmes' factory audits. Locke, Amengual, and Mangla (2009) suggest the adoption of commitment-based approach to compliance programmes with a focus on joint problem-solving, information exchange, and the diffusion of best practices. Such an approach underlines the way of managing the compliance programme, especially at the monitoring and auditing phases.

In addition to an effective design, as suggested by Carter and Rogers (2008), sustainability should be incorporated as a part of the overall supply chain strategy. This requires an in-depth look into the sustainability-focused environmental analysis where the drivers for the company and for the suppliers towards sustainability are explored. The analysis of the member profiles in the supply chain, and the assessment of risky points, may contribute as inputs for a successful performance analysis.

Hu and Hsu (2010) identify four critical dimensions for the effective management of green supply chains in the electronics industry, which are supplier management, product recycling, organization involvement, and lifecycle management. Reuter et al. (2010) underline the importance of external stakeholder pressure. Labour equity, healthcare, philanthropy, and safety are the social sustainability indicators that are offered by Hutchins and Sutherland (2008) as measurable and important social criteria for supply chain decisions. These are exemplary studies trying to define the essential factors for sustainable supply chain management. However, many are industry-based and, therefore, related to the sectors that they act within. A generic road map, on the other hand, needs to have a broader perspective and should be valid for each and every supply chain in order to enable benchmarks.

The literature provides invaluable knowledge on how to increase the diffusion of sustainability among suppliers. For some authors, such corporate efforts go beyond a public relations exercise only if they can reflect a new form of stakeholder control over company (Jenkins, 2001) and through an effective monitoring and compliance (Hong, 2000; Liubicic, 1998). Schleper and Busse (2013) list the key success factors of a standardized supplier code of ethics within the areas of content coverage and specificity, inclusion and coordination of stakeholders, communication and trainings, global applicability, and enforcement system. The authors suggest several propositions on how these factors affect relative advantage, trialability, compatibility, simplicity, image, and observability. On the other hand, Lund-Thomsen (2008, pp. 1015–1016) addresses some myths about the impacts of codes in developing country contexts by five recommendations:

- One needs to find more meaningful ways of assessing the ultimate impact of codes of conduct as opposed to simply assessing compliance with their stated requirements;
- One needs to take the social, economic, environmental, and linguistic contexts in which codes are being implemented into consideration to avoid producing unintended, often negative, consequences;
- Governments and international organizations still have a role to play in ensuring responsible social and environmental behaviour on the part of companies in the developing world;

- Global sourcing companies that want to act in a socially responsible manner need to engage with suppliers over the longer term, or provide the necessary resources and expertise that will enable them to improve their social and environmental performance;
- There must be an emphasis on incorporating their concerns and voices in the design, implementation, monitoring, and impact assessment of the codes.

In line with the existing literature and with these recommendations, this study posits that it is essential to develop a road map that might provide guidance to plan and build up codes of conduct and compliance programmes for sustainability in the supply chain. The next section introduces such a map and discusses the steps to take in order to create a compliance programme that has a high diffusion potential among suppliers.

Developing an integrative code and programme to increase diffusion

Despite the existing literature that has multiple perspectives and recommendations for increasing the effectiveness of compliance programmes, they lack a systematic approach to take into account all dimensions of the phenomenon. The current study attempts to take a holistic view, which embraces the multifaceted and interrelated dimensions of codes and compliance programmes to ensure the diffusion of sustainability among suppliers. Figure 2.6.1 presents a road map that includes the dimensions and some exemplary questions of developing codes and programmes to increase sustainable supply chains. One needs to respond to these critical challenges about the emergence, drivers, processes, or outcomes of supplier compliance programmes.

Company

The first and foremost dimension on Figure 2.6.1 is the company that initiates a code and programme for its suppliers. The organizational factors that influence the adoption and diffusion of codes (Bia and Kalika, 2007) and the reasons for adoptions must be investigated. Particularly the latter dimension attracts the scholarly interests more and the drivers of adopting a code and programme become a critical issue in the literature. In their study, Bondy et al. (2008) try to investigate whether the codes are developed to manage corporate social responsibility (CSR) and they find that it is not about CSR engagement; except the codes that are a requirement for companies (mandatory: 27.2%), companies adopt codes due to more traditional reasons such as improving reputation, increasing consistency across the global network, ensuring employee compliance, and so on.

The sectoral characteristics and trends are also considered as the drivers for adopting codes and developing compliance programmes. For instance, the study of Kolk (2005) reveals how coffee producers follow the same trend of developing their own codes to address a sectoral crisis arising from societal pressures about supplier conditions. Jenkins (2001, p. 27) identifies the characteristics of the sectors in which companies increasingly adopt codes and programmes:

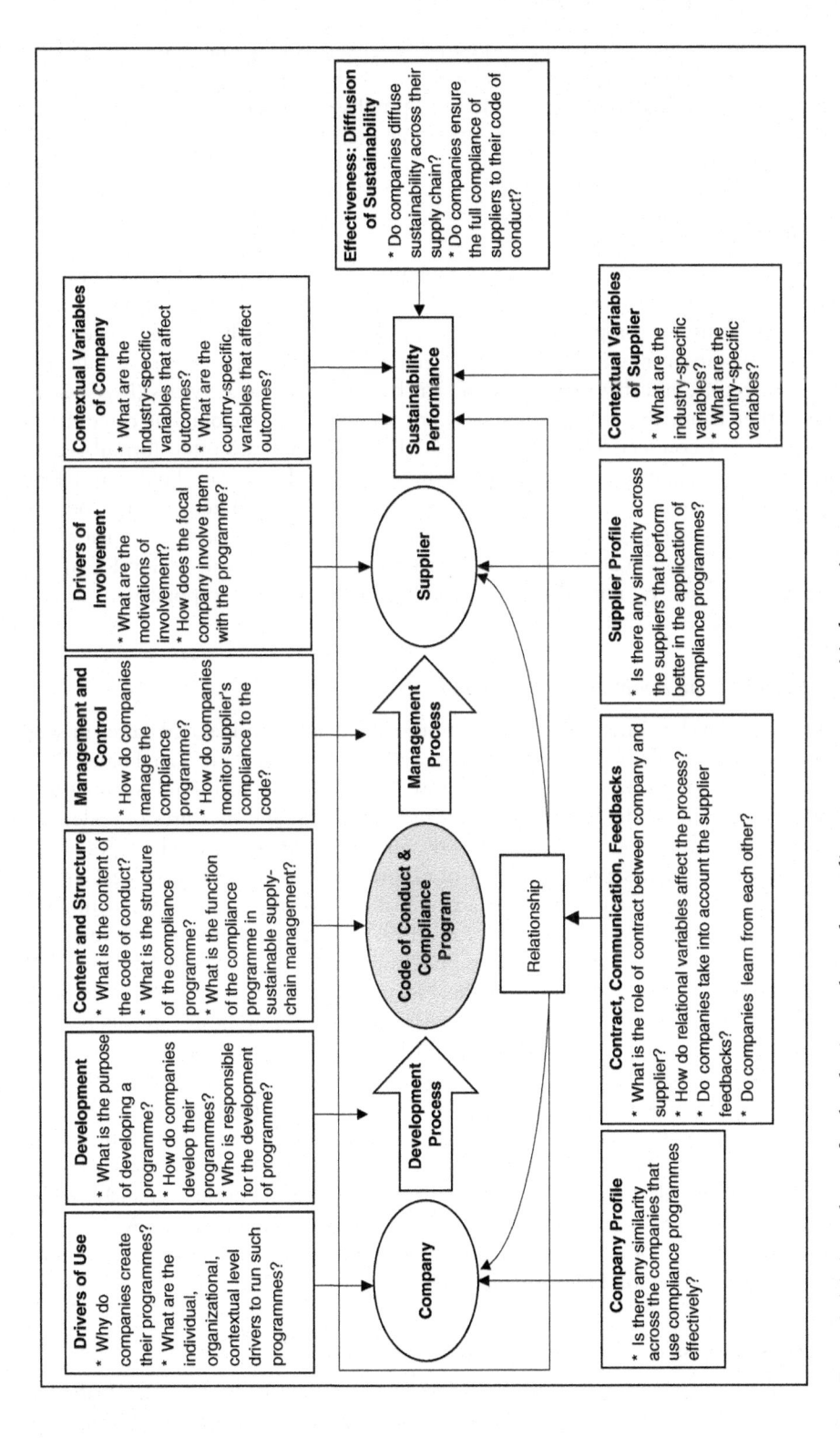

Figure 2.6.1 A road map for developing codes and compliance programmes: critical questions

- the sectors where brand names and corporate image is very important,
- the sectors where codes cover social issues,
- the sectors in which the cost of individual purchases is relatively low,
- the sectors where production costs often make up a relatively small part of the final product price.

Development process

The development process of codes and programmes is also important to increase their effectiveness. For instance, a survey on the state of compliance shows that most companies have an in-house compliance committee, a department, a chief compliance/ethics, and compliance officer who reports to the general counsel, chief executive officer, or board of directors, and they spare a significant budget for these activities (PwC, 2016). On the other hand, the industry practices are used in the development of company-specific codes of conduct (Oehmen et al., 2010). The codes are often formulated and implemented based on the interactions with the stakeholders (van Tulder and Kolk, 2001); 'the likelihood of compliance not only depends on the contents of the code, but is also heavily influenced by the interaction of various stakeholders in its formulation and implementation' (Kolk et al., 1999, p. 143). Moreover, the codes can be developed in an evolutionary manner by reflecting the variability in the factory, corporation, or nation over time (Locke et al., 2007, p. 35).

Code of conduct and compliance programmes

The literature on the content of codes demonstrates that it considerably varies in scope (Jenkins, 2001), specificity and strictness (Kolk et al., 1999; Kolk and Van Tulder, 2002) and shows limited uniformity without substantial details (Emmelhainz and Adams, 1999). There is a considerable diversity in the language, concepts, and measures of codes even on the same topic (Gordon and Miyake, 2001), and these differences on the types of code and monitoring activities affect the level of enforcement as well (Rodríguez-Garavito, 2005). Although some believe the importance of developing a cohesive and universal code of conduct for all MNCs (Payne et al., 1997), companies often follow their own industry-level standards to generate a code of conduct. For instance, both HP and IBM build their code of conducts based on the Electronic Industry Citizenship Coalition's (EICC) code of conduct, which includes the categories of labour, health and safety, environment, ethics and management (HP, 2015; IBM, 2004). A recent study also reveals that the issues like ethical and social responsibility in suppliers' codes are isomorphic across industry, geography, or organizational size (Dooley and Augustin-Behravesh, 2016).

The code of conducts and compliance programmes act as the backbone of the sustainable supply chains. Following the study of Seuring and Muller (2008), Türker and Altuntas (2014) reveals the function of compliance programmes in the sustainable supply chain management based on a qualitative study of the fast fashion industry. According to the authors, the code of conduct is at the heart of this system linking the sustainability criteria, perceived risks, and performance outcomes.

Management process

It is stated in the previous section that the performance at the supply chain largely depends on monitoring and management activities. However, these tasks can be very difficult due to the nature of global supply chain, which involves geographically dispersed suppliers from different economic, legal, cultural, and political contexts (Pedersen and Andersen, 2006). The frequency of monitoring activities is a factor that improves the conditions at factories (Lindholm et al., 2016); however, independence of those activities is also critical to ensure the effectiveness of systems. Although some companies can use third-party NGOs to monitor compliance to their codes, the soft law policy of NGO-centred approaches are not found to be effective (Wells, 2007). Caro et al. (2015) also discuss two new mechanisms, joint audit and shared audit mechanisms, based on the game theory framework. Therefore, companies can be more innovative in designing their management approach in compliance programmes.

Supplier

Suppliers' profiles and the drivers of their involvement into the programme must be addressed also to increase the effectiveness of the supplier compliance programme. For instance, in a recent study, Foerstl et al. (2015) indicate that first-tier suppliers follow either the strategies of cost- and risk-minimizing compliance or value maximization beyond compliance commitment and classify drivers as stakeholder-related, process-related, and product-related drivers. However, the supply side of compliance programmes is usually neglected both in literature and in practice.

Relationship

The relationship between company and supplier has a critical role in increasing the sustainability performance by ensuring the full compliance of suppliers to codes of conduct. This relationship is formalized through contracts, and its nature can be important to explain why some suppliers succeed but some others fail to integrate codes into their business. By analysing such contract characteristics (e.g., contract duration or production complexity), Jiang (2009) finds out that hierarchy/relational norms mediate the link between contract details and supplier commitment. Therefore, a formal link between company and supplier must be supported by informal relationship characteristics to enable the diffusion of sustainability. For instance, even if one party accepts to comply with a mandatory code of conduct, only a few of them are willing to report any code violation due to psychological and moral reasons (Nitsch et al., 2005). The study of Locke et al. (2007, p. 34) on Nike's two plants shows that more frequent visits and more open communication between Nike's regional staff and Plant A management led to the development of greater trust and a better working relationship between these two actors. This, in turn, contributed to the upgrading of Plant A's production system and its consequent positive impact on working conditions at the plant.

Additionally, comparing various sectors, Roberts (2003) proposes the network characteristics that increase the adoption of codes of conduct:

- number of links between supply network members demanding code of conduct and stage of supply network under scrutiny like first-tier, or second-tier, forward or backward;
- diffuseness of stage of supply network under scrutiny;
- reputational vulnerability of different network members;
- power of different members of supply network.

Sustainability performance

Improving ethical behaviour (Oehmen et al., 2010), reducing information asymmetry (Ciliberti et al., 2011), and increasing the sustainability performance throughout the supply chain by spreading the same principles and practices are among the overarching outputs of a code and compliance programme. However, the sustainability performance is also affected by contextual variables. The aforementioned study of Egels-Zandén (2014) provides evidence on the long-run positive impact of compliance programmes on workers' rights from the perspective of new institutional theories. Whereas Yu (2008) states that, although the labour-related codes of Reebok set the minimum working standards for suppliers, workers at suppliers worked harder and faster while earning less money without the protection of an autonomous workers' union. According to the author, this result is not only linked with the company's profit-maximization motive, but it is also related to the industrial, national, and local context (e.g., high competition, insufficient protection by government). Therefore, 'effective and empowering code monitoring systems requires sustained cross-border political pressures' of national or international bodies (Rodríguez-Garavito, 2005, p. 206).

Conclusions

This study has summarized the existing approaches to company codes of conduct towards increasing sustainability in the supply chain. Considering the criticisms directed to the nature and intentions of company-led compliance programmes, certain proposals are being recommended about the nature and structure of more effective programmes. The points that are highlighted by the critics also posit the reasons behind the lag of diffusion among suppliers. In order to be successful, a compliance programme should not stay within one or two highly visible supplier factory audits, but it should be diffused, possibly to the whole supply eco-system in various industries.

The road map proposed by this study has several implications for practitioners. Firstly, it might provide a useful tool to develop and manage a code of conduct that has a high diffusion potential over suppliers. The listed questions might enlighten the differences among industries, which is a very important barrier in front of the generalization possibility of sustainability programmes. Sustainability requirements and sensitivities vary significantly across industries; therefore, it is necessary to ask the right questions to delimit the scope and perspective of sustainability compliance programmes for different sectors.

As underlined by Reuter et al.'s (2010) study, sustainable management of global suppliers can be a resource, a specific asset that it is hard for competitors to imitate. Self-development of a highly diffused supplier compliance programme to sustainability may create a dynamic capability for companies that are in deep need of competitive advantage in the current intense state of global rivalry. The use of such a holistic road map can be an input for the creation of a company-specific dynamic capability and a first-mover advantage.

The proposed road map presents the multidimensional nature of developing a viable code and programme with the consideration that codes and compliance programmes must be carefully designed to increase the diffusion effectively. Rather than focusing on a single or a few dimensions in the framework, practitioners should recognize how the system works as a whole and how sub-systems are closely interrelated. Developing a system, maintaining its operations in the long run, and measuring and monitoring its progress in the end is obtained as a combination of all these efforts. However, it can be noticed that some questions in the proposed framework are partly addressed and some of them remain unanswered. For instance, we know very little about the supply-side interactions of models, such as their characteristics, motives, context, and so on. Therefore, these questions should be also addressed to obtain a complete picture and understanding on the role of each dimension on overall performance results.

The road map proposed by the study recommends several research avenues for scholars as well. In-depth case studies, comparing the existing successful codes of conduct with the proposed road map, can lead the way for potential gaps. Action research with new compliance programme development incentives, and the application of this map for the development process, might act as a validation tool for the proposed model. Delphi studies regarding the inadequate and malfunctioning parts of existing compliance programmes for sustainability might provide important insights for the industry. The impact of each dimension on the success of compliance programmes are suggested to be measured for different supply chains. Being a conceptual study based on some real-life cases, this study's proposition should be tested by other studies using various methods in order to be generalized.

Despite being criticized in terms of their scope and their governance, compliance programmes seem to have seized their role as the essential tools of monitoring global supply chains in terms of sustainability. Therefore, the discussion about them will be going on in academia. Good examples should be shared, analysed, and diffused among practitioners, and new methods to manage and control sustainable supply chains should be recommended by both practitioners and scholars for a more sustainable future.

References

Ahi, P., and Searcy, C. (2013). A comparative literature analysis of definitions for green and sustainable supply chain management. *Journal of Cleaner Production*, 52(1), 329–341.

Altuntaş Vural, C. (2015). Sustainable demand chain management: an alternative perspective for sustainability in the supply chain. *Procedia - Social and Behavioral Sciences*, 11th International Strategic Management Conference, Vienna/Austria [23-25.07.2015].

Apple (2012). *Apple Supplier Responsibility: 2012 Progress Report*. http://images.apple.com/supplier-responsibility/pdf/Apple_SR_2012_Progress_Report.pdf (Accessed on 10.12.2016).

Apple (2016). *Supplier Responsibility 2016 Progress Report*. http://images.apple.com/supplier-responsibility/pdf/Apple_SR_2016_Progress_Report.pdf (Accessed on 10.12.2016).

Bartley, T. (2005). Corporate accountability and the privatization of labor standards: Struggles over codes of conduct in the apparel industry. *Research in Political Sociology*, 14, 211–244.

Bia, M., and Kalika, M. (2007). Adopting an ICT code of conduct: An empirical study of organizational factors. *Journal of Enterprise Information Management*, 20(4), 432–446.

Blowfield, M. E., and Dolan, C. S. (2008). Stewards of virtue? The ethical dilemma of CSR in African agriculture. *Development and Change*, 39(1), 1–23.

Bondy, K., Matten, D., and Moon, J. (2008). Multinational corporation codes of conduct: Governance tools for corporate social responsibility? *Corporate Governance: An International Review*, 16(4), 294–311.

Caro, F., Chintapalli, P., Rajaram, K., and Tang, C. S. (2015). Improving supplier compliance through joint and shared audits. https://ssrn.com/abstract=2683515 or http://dx.doi.org/10.2139/ssrn.2683515 (Accessed on 22.12.2016)

Carter, C. R., and Easton, P. L. (2011). Sustainable supply chain management: Evolution and future directions. *International Journal of Physical Distribution & Logistics Management*, 41(1), 46–62.

Carter, C. R., and Rogers, D. S. (2008). A framework of sustainable supply chain management: Moving toward new theory. *International Journal of Physical Distribution and Logistics Management*, 38(5), 360–387.

Christopher, M., Lowson, R., and Peck, H. (2004). Creating agile supply chains in the fashion industry. *International Journal of Retail and Distribution Management*, 32(8), 367–376.

Ciliberti, F., De Haan, J., De Groot, G., and Pontrandolfo, P. (2011). CSR codes and the principal-agent problem in supply chains: Four case studies. *Journal of Cleaner Production*, 19(8), 885–894.

Deva, S. (2012). Guiding principles on business and human rights: Implications for companies. *European Company Law*, 9(2), 101–109.

Diller, J. (1999). A social conscience in the global marketplace? Labour dimensions of codes of conduct, social labelling and investor initiatives. *International Labour Review*, 138(2), 99–129.

Dooley, K., and Augustin-Behravesh, S. A. T. (2016). Social influence and similarities in supplier codes of conduct. *Academy of Management Proceedings*, 1, 11677 (DOI: 10.5465/AMBPP.2016.11677)

Egels-Zandén, N. (2007). Suppliers' compliance with MNCs' codes of conduct: Behind the scenes at Chinese toy suppliers. *Journal of Business Ethics*, 75(1), 45–62.

Egels-Zandén, N. (2014). Revisiting supplier compliance with MNC codes of conduct: Recoupling policy and practice at Chinese toy suppliers. *Journal of Business Ethics*, 119(1), 59–75.

Egels-Zandén, N., and Merk, J. (2014). Private regulation and trade union rights: Why codes of conduct have limited impact on trade union rights. *Journal of Business Ethics*, 123(3), 461–473.

Ek, V., and Kane, C. (2013). H&M, others back new Bangladesh factory safety accord. http://www.reuters.com/article/us-bangladesh-building-safety-hm-idUSBRE94C0GJ20130513 (Accessed on 10.07.2016).

Elkington, J. (1997). *Cannibals with Forks: The Triple Bottom Line of 21st-Century Business*. Oxford: Capstone Publishing.

Emmelhainz, M. A., and Adams, R. J. (1999). The apparel industry response to 'sweatshop' concerns: A review and analysis of codes of conduct. *Journal of Supply Chain Management*, 35(2), 51–57.

Foerstl, K., Azadegan, A., Leppelt, T., and Hartmann, E. (2015). Drivers of supplier sustainability: Moving beyond compliance to commitment. *Journal of Supply Chain Management*, 51(1), 67–92.

Gereffi, G. (1994). The organization of buyer-driven global commodity chains: How US retailers shape overseas production networks. In Gereffi, G. and Korzeniewicz, M. (Eds.), *Commodity Chains and Global Capitalism* (pp. 95–122). London: Praeger.

Gereffi, G., and Kaplinsky, R. (2001). Introduction: Globalisation, value chains and development. *IDS Bulletin*, 32(3), 1–8.

Gordon, K., and Miyake, M., 2001. Business approaches to combating bribery: A study of codes of conduct. *Journal of Business Ethics*, 34(3), 161–173.

Göçer, A., Altuntaş, C., and Şakar, G. D. (2012). Sustainable supply chains: An item generation study. *Proceedings of 10th International Logistics and Supply Chain Congress*, Kemerburgaz University, İstanbul, Turkey, 8/9 November, pp. 263–272.

H&M (2011). *Conscious Actions Sustainability Report 2011*. http://sustainability.hm.com/content/dam/hm/about/documents/en/CSR/reports/Conscious%20Actions%20Sustainability%20Report%202011_en.pdf (Accessed on 10.12.2016).

H&M (2016). *Supplier Compliance Level in Detail*. http://sustainability.hm.com/en/sustainability/downloads-resources/resources/supplier-compliance.html (Accessed on 10.12.2016).

HP (2015). *HP Supplier Code of Conduct*. http://www.hp.com/hpinfo/globalcitizenship/environment/pdf/supcode.pdf (Accessed on 10.12.2016).

Hong, J. C. (2000). Enforcement of corporate codes of conduct: Finding a private right of action for international laborers against MNCS for labor rights violations. *Winconsin International Law Journal*, 19(1), 41–69.

Hu, A. H., and Hsu, W. (2010). Critical factors for implementing green supply chain management practice: An empirical study of electrical and electronics industries in Taiwan. *Management Research Review*, 33(6), 586–608.

Hutchins, M. J., and Sutherland, J. W. (2008). An exploration of measures of social sustainability and their application to supply chain decisions. *Journal of Cleaner Production*, 16(15), 1688–1698.

IBM (2004). *IBM Supplier Conduct Principles*. http://www-03.ibm.com/procurement/proweb. nsf/objectdocswebview/fileibm+supplier+conduct+principles/$file/scp-v2.0.pdf (Accessed on 10.12.2016).

Jenkins, R. (2001). Corporate codes of conduct: Self-regulation in a global economy. *The United Nations Research Institute for Social Development (UNRISD) Programme Paper*. No. 2. Geneva: UNRISD.

Jiang, B. (2009). Implementing supplier codes of conduct in global supply chains: Process explanations from theoretic and empirical perspectives. *Journal of Business Ethics*, 85(1), 77–92.

Kasperkevic, J. (2016). Rana Plaza collapse: Workplace dangers persist three years later reports find. *The Guardian*, 31 May. https://www.theguardian.com/business/2016/may/31/rana-plaza-bangladesh-collapse-fashion-working-conditions (Accessed on 10.12.2016).

Klein, N. (2000). *No Logo*. London: Flamingo.

Kolk, A. (2005). Corporate social responsibility in the coffee sector: The dynamics of MNC responses and code development. *European Management Journal*, 23(2), 228–236.

Kolk, A., and Van Tulder, R. (2002). The effectiveness of self-regulation: Corporate codes of conduct and child labour. *European Management Journal*, 20(3), 260–271.

Kolk, A., Van Tulder, R., and Welters, C. (1999). International codes of conduct and corporate social responsibility: Can transnational corporations regulate themselves? *Transnational Corporations*, 8(1), 143–180.

Krut, R., and Gleckman, H. (1998). *ISO 14001: A Missed Opportunity for Sustainable Global Industrial Development*. London: Earthscan.

Lindholm, H., Egels-Zandén, N., and Rudén, C. (2016). Do code of conduct audits improve chemical safety in garment factories? Lessons on corporate social responsibility in the supply chain from Fair Wear Foundation. *International Journal of Occupational and Environmental Health*, 22(4), 283–291.

Liubicic, R. J. (1998). Corporate codes of conduct and product labelling schemes: The limits and possibilities of promoting international labor rights through private initiatives. *Law and Policy in International Business*, 11, 112–113.

Locke, R., Amengual, M., and Mangla, A. (2009). Virtue out of necessity? Compliance, commitment, and the improvement of labor conditions in global supply chains. *Politics and Society*, 37(3), 319–351.

Locke, R., Qin, F., and Brause, A. (2007). Does monitoring improve labor standards? Lessons from Nike. *Industrial and Labor Relations Review*, 61(1), 3–31.

Locke, R., Kochan, T., Romis, M., and Qin, F. (2007). Beyond corporate codes of conduct: Work organization and labour standards at Nike's suppliers. *International Labour Review*, 146(1–2), 21–40.

Los, B., Timmer, M. P., and de Vries, G. J. (2014). How global are global value chains? A new approach to measure international fragmentation. *Journal of Regional Science*, 1, 66–92.

Lund-Thomsen, P. (2008). The global sourcing and codes of conduct debate: Five myths and five recommendations. *Development and Change*, 39(6), 1005–1018.

Macdonald, K. (2011). Re-thinking 'spheres of responsibility': Business responsibility for indirect harm. *Journal of Business Ethics*, 99(4), 549–563.

Mair, S., Druckman, A., and Jackson, T. (2016). Global inequities and emissions in Western European textiles and clothing consumption. *Journal of Cleaner Production*, 132, 57–69.

Nitsch, D., Baetz, M., and Hughes, J. C. (2005). Why code of conduct violations go unreported: A conceptual framework to guide intervention and future research. *Journal of Business Ethics*, 57(4), 327–341.

Nova, S., and Shapiro, I. (2013). Apple's self-reporting on suppliers' labor practices shows violations remain common. *Economic Policy Institute*. http://www.epi.org/publication/apples-reporting-suppliers-labor-practices/ (Accessed on 10.12.2016).

OECD (2016). *Responsible Supply Chains in the Garment and Footwear Sector.* https://mneguidelines.oecd.org/responsible-supply-chains-textile-garment-sector.htm (Accessed on 10.07.2016).

Oehmen, J., De Nardo, M., Schönsleben, P., and Boutellier, R. (2010). Supplier code of conduct – state-of-the-art and customisation in the electronics industry. *Production Planning and Control,* 21(7), 664–679.

O'Rourke, D. (2006). Multi-stakeholder regulation: privatizing or socializing global labor standards? *World Development,* 34(5), 899–918.

Ozturkoglu, Y., and Turker, D. (2013). Application of TOPSIS to analyze stakeholder relations. *International Journal of Business and Social Research,* 3(5), 245–255.

Payne, D., Raiborn, C., and Askvik, J. (1997). A global code of business ethics. *Journal of Business Ethics,* 16(16), 1727–1735.

Pedersen, E. R., and Andersen, M. (2006). Safeguarding corporate social responsibility (CSR) in global supply chains: How codes of conduct are managed in buyer–supplier relationships. *Journal of Public Affairs,* 6(3–4), 228–240.

PwC (2016). *State of Compliance Study 2016.* http://www.pwc.com/us/en/risk-assurance/state-of-compliance-study.html (Accessed on 10.12.2016).

Reuter, C., Foerstl, K., Hartmann, E., and Blome, C. (2010). Sustainable global supplier management: The role of dynamic capabilities in achieving competitive advantage. *Journal of Supply Chain Management,* 46(2), 45–63.

Roberts, S. (2003). Supply chain specific? Understanding the patchy success of ethical sourcing initiatives. *Journal of Business Ethics,* 44(2–3), 159–170.

Rodríguez-Garavito, C. A. (2005). Global governance and labor rights: Codes of conduct and anti-sweatshop struggles in global apparel factories in Mexico and Guatemala. *Politics and Society,* 33(2), 203–333.

SCDigest (2012). *Supply Chain News: 2013 Apple Supplier Progress Report Does Indeed Show Improved Compliance to Its Standards.* http://www.scdigest.com/ontarget/13-01-29-2.php?cid=6671 (Accessed on 10.12.2016).

Schleper, M. C., and Dusse, C. (2013). Toward a standardized supplier code of ethics: Development of a design concept based on diffusion of innovation theory. *Logistics Research,* 6(4), 187–216.

Seidman, G. W. (2003). Monitoring multinationals: Lessons from the anti-apartheid era. *Politics and Society,* 31(3), 381–406.

Sethi, S. P. (2002). Standards for corporate conduct in the international arena: Challenges and opportunities for multinational corporations. *Business and Society Review,* 107(1), 20–40.

Seuring, S., and Müller, M. (2008). From a literature review to a conceptual framework for sustainable supply chain management. *Journal of Cleaner Production,* 16(15), 1699–1710.

Thomson Reuters Foundation (2016). Cambodia and big brands fail to tackle garment worker abuse: Researchers. http://www.reuters.com/article/us-rights-cambodia-textiles-idUSKBN0M808020150312 (Accessed on 10.07.2016).

Turker, D., and Altuntas, C. (2014). Sustainable supply chain management in the fast fashion industry: An analysis of corporate reports. *European Management Journal,* 32, 837–849.

van Tulder, R., and Kolk, A. (2001). Multinationality and corporate ethics: Codes of conduct in the sporting goods industry. *Journal of International Business Studies,* 32(2), 267–283.

Wells, D. (2007). Too weak for the job corporate codes of conduct, non-governmental organizations and the regulation of international labour standards. *Global Social Policy,* 7(1), 51–74.

Whirlpool (2016). *Supplier Code of Conduct.* http://www.whirlpoolcorp.com/supplier-code-of-conduct/ (Accessed on 10.12.2016).

Yu, X. (2008). Impacts of corporate code of conduct on labor standards: A case study of Reebok's athletic footwear supplier factory in China. *Journal of Business Ethics,* 81(3), 513–529.

Zadek, S. (2004). The path to corporate responsibility. *Harvard Business Review,* 82(12), 125–132.

Practical and managerial insights from real-life cases

Part 3

Practical and managerial insights
from real-life cases

3.1 The impact of environmental and social practices on the triple bottom line

A mediated model

Cristina Gimenez, Vicenta Sierra, Cristina Sancha,
Joan Rodón, and Stefan Markovic

Introduction

In recent years, the concept of sustainability has become a key concern for managers and researchers. On the one hand, more and more, firms report on their environmental and social performances (KPMG, 2008) and develop initiatives to become more sustainable. For instance, Wal-Mart has devoted high efforts to reduce its environmental burden. In 2012, the company was able to reduce by 20% the greenhouse gas emissions from its stores (Bloomberg, 2013). Despite these achievements on the environmental side, Wal-Mart has been largely criticized due to the poor working conditions in their facilities (The Huffington Post, 2012). This shows that companies should focus not only on the environmental side of sustainability but also on the social one. In that sense, the adoption of the triple bottom line (TBL) concept, which encompasses environmental, social, and economic dimensions, is key to acting sustainably. The same happens in the research field. While the concept of sustainability has begun to appear in the literature of disciplines such as operations or supply chain management (SCM), there is a lack of studies that have simultaneously considered environmental, social, and economic bottom lines (Seuring and Muller, 2008; Pagell and Gobeli, 2009) as a way to measure the impact of sustainability practices.

In fact, the sustainable supply chain management literature has mainly focused on studying the greening of supply chains, neglecting a holistic view of the concept of sustainability (Seuring and Muller, 2008). In that sense, the aim of this chapter is to analyse the impact of both environmental and social practices on the three dimensions of the TBL (i.e., environmental, social, and economic). In fact, the adoption of the TBL perspective is relevant and needed since considering only one dimension of sustainability does not provide a complete view on the impact that these practices have on performance. By considering both environmental and social practices and their impact on the three dimensions of sustainability, our study contributes to the literature on sustainable operations in the following aspects. First, it analyses the impact of sustainable practices on the three dimensions of the TBL. Second, it examines both environmental and social practices as suggested by Seuring and Muller's (2008) definition of sustainable operations. Third, by studying the concept of sustainability in the field of operations management, we respond to the call made by Pagell and Gobeli (2009) to conduct more research at the operational level, which is of crucial importance, because when firms try to become more sustainable, discrepancies between top management objectives and the decisions made at the operational level are likely to arise (Wheeler et al., 2002). For instance, while at the top management level the implementation of a cleaner production process is decided;

the reality at the operational level might be that the technical specificities required by the product are not met. Finally, the results of this research have also important implications for managers, as they show the impact of various sustainable practices on performance.

Literature review

Sustainable operations management

Sustainable operations management is defined as the set of skills and leverages that allow a company to structure its business processes so as to achieve a defined level of sustainability (Kleindorfer et al., 2005). As we have already mentioned, the sustainability concept is operationalized through the TBL (Elkington, 1998), which emphasizes that attention should be paid to all the three dimensions of sustainability (i.e., environmental, social, and economic). However, just a few empirical papers consider them simultaneously (Seuring and Muller, 2008), and most of them focus on the environmental and economic dimensions of sustainability, neglecting the social one (Gimenez et al., 2012; Hollos et al., 2012; Sancha et al., 2016). This chapter adopts the TBL perspective, considering its three dimensions, in order to measure improvements in sustainability performance. Environmental sustainability refers to the use of energy and other resources and the footprint companies leave behind as a result of their operations. Social sustainability has to do with ensuring the quality of life of both the firm's internal community (e.g., workforce) and its external community (e.g., local economies and civil society) by providing equitable opportunities, encouraging diversity, promoting connectedness, ensuring democratic processes and accountable governance structures (Elkington, 1994). Finally, economic sustainability means that by achieving sustainable operations, firms may obtain positive financial gains. In this chapter, instead of classical financial measures, we consider the firm's operational performance as a proxy of the economic dimension. The main reason for that is that our research aims to analyse the implementation of the concept of sustainability at the operational level (i.e., at the plant level). Accordingly, the economic impact of sustainability is measured at the plant level. In this sense, as operations managers are able to better perceive the firm's operational performance (quality, delivery times, costs, etc.) than its financial performance, we use operational performance for the purpose of this study. Operational performance is defined as the company's ability to achieve abnormal outcomes in the dimensions of quality, delivery, flexibility, and cost related to the performance achieved by its competitors (Schoenherr and Swink, 2012).

To achieve a sustainable supply chain, a firm can rely on internal and external practices. Internal practices are those implemented in a business function (Carter and Carter, 1998) (e.g., production) and aim to achieve a firm's specific internal target (Rao, 2002). In addition, sustainable practices can also be extended to other actors in the supply chain. For instance, in order to green products and processes, firms can develop sustainable programmes with their suppliers (Vachon and Klassen, 2008). De Giovanni (2012) claims that in order to green a supply chain, internal practices are required first, and external practices, such as collaboration with suppliers, come at a later stage. This means that once the concept of sustainability is internally adopted, it can then be extended to other members of the supply chain. In line with this reasoning, this study focuses on the first described step (i.e., implementation of internal practices) and analyses the impact of environmental and social internal practices on the TBL (economic, environmental, and social performance).

Environmental internal practices aim to reduce the negative environmental impact of the company's own activities (Bowen et al., 2001; Rao, 2002). Some of the practices examined in previous studies are: green product design (Azzone and Noci, 1996; Maxwell and van der Vorst, 2003), use of environmentally friendly materials (Carter and Carter, 1998) and processes (Rao and Holt, 2005), pollution prevention training (Theyel, 2000), and recycling programmes (Dobos and Floriska, 2007).

Internal social practices aim to provide economic development, while improving the quality of life of the workforce and their families as well as of the local community and society at large (WBCSD, 1999). Previous literature reports some examples of internal social practices: employees' health and safety, work environment, skill development, job satisfaction, fair compensation, and employment status (Awaysheh and Klassen, 2010; Klassen and Vereecke, 2012; Pullman et al., 2009). Although social sustainability has an influence on internal and external communities, this study focuses on the internal practices that aim to improve employees' working conditions, in line with the previous operations management literature (Pagell and Gobelli, 2009).

Internal sustainable practices and the TBL

In the operations management field, when studying internal sustainable practices, authors have adopted an environmental perspective (Cagliano et al., 2010), and there is little research expanding sustainable practices to also contemplate social issues (Sancha et al., 2016). This chapter aims to address this lack of research by incorporating the social dimension in the study of sustainability practices (e.g., de Giovanni, 2012; Gimenez et al., 2012; Sancha et al., 2016). Thus, this chapter differentiates from previous studies by analysing the impact of both environmental and social practices on each dimension of the TBL (i.e., economic, social, and environmental). To the best of our knowledge, only two papers have analysed the impact of sustainable practices on the TBL: De Giovanni (2012) and Gimenez et al. (2012). De Giovanni (2012) investigated the effect of both internal and external environmental management on environmental, social, and economic/operational performance. In this chapter, we take a step further and study not only the impact of environmental management on the TBL but also the impact of social practices on each dimension of sustainability. In this sense, our chapter follows a similar approach to Gimenez et al. (2012), who analysed the impact of environmental and social practices on the TBL, but with some key differences regarding the operationalization of constructs and the relationships between them. First, while Gimenez et al. (2012) used single items to measure each performance dimension (i.e., environmental, social, and economic), we use multiple items. Second, to shed light onto the existing debate regarding the impact of sustainable practices on the economic dimension of the TBL (Golicic and Smith, 2013), we hypothesize that the impact of sustainable practices on operational performance is mediated by the environmental and social performances. In other words, we suggest that as a result of the implementation of environmental and social practices better operational results will be achieved, if environmental and/or social performance has been previously improved. Although many papers in the sustainable SCM literature consider the analysis of external practices (e.g., Gualandris et al., 2014), in this chapter we focus on the analysis of internal practices, since to make a supply chain more sustainable, internal practices are required first (de Giovanni, 2012).

Furthermore, Gimenez et al. (2012) showed that internal practices had a greater impact on sustainable performance than external practices. In the following section, we develop our hypotheses and present the model we aim to test.

Hypotheses development

This study is grounded on the Resource-Base View (RBV). The RBV suggests that a firm may achieve economic sustainability by effectively employing its resources (Barney, 1991; Penrose, 1959). Valuable, rare, and difficult to copy resources and capabilities can provide critical sources of competitive advantage (Barney, 1991; Peteraf, 1993; Wernerfelt, 1984). Based on this idea, Pullman et al. (2009) suggested that achieving a sustainable supply chain could be a source of competitive advantage for a firm. In fact, sustainability practices are part of a firm's capabilities, which according to the RBV, may lead to competitive advantage. Hart (1995) and Aragon-Correa and Sharma (2003) extended the RBV to also include environmental issues: the Natural-Resource-Base View (NRBV). They suggested that firms can gain competitive advantage based on their relationship to the natural environment (Hart, 1995). Surroca et al. (2010) found that responsible firms are more capable than irresponsible firms of generating intangibles such as innovation, human capital, and culture, which in turn lead to better financial performance. In this chapter, we extend the RBV by also contemplating social practices undertaken in operations management.

As mentioned above, the NRBV (Aragon-Correa and Sharma, 2003; Hart, 1995) suggests that there is a link between environmental practices and environmental performance. Accordingly, several scholars have shown a positive impact of the implementation of internal environmental practices on environmental performance (Rao, 2002; Zhu and Sarkis, 2004; Zhu et al., 2005; Cagliano et al., 2010; de Giovanni, 2012; Gimenez et al., 2012). More specifically, these scholars found that the adoption of practices such as waste management or environmentally friendly product design lead to better environmental results. This improvement in environmental performance can be seen as a result of the reduction of waste and other pollutants that comes from the adoption of environmental practices such as the use of more energy-efficient resources, the use of more efficient raw materials, and the implementation of cleaner production or distributions processes. Therefore, we hypothesize that:

> H1a. Internal environmental practices have a positive impact on environmental performance.

Although the impact of sustainable practices on the social sustainability dimension is largely unexplored, the few empirical studies on this topic have found that environmental practices positively contribute to social performance (de Giovanni, 2012; Gimenez et al., 2012). De Giovanni (2012) showed that internal environmental management practices are a successful and effective driver of social performance. Gimenez et al. (2012) found that the implementation of internal environmental practices such as the use of cleaner production processes is expected to have a positive effect on employees' health and safety conditions. This positive effect can be explained as follows: the implementation of a production process and/or the use of handling systems that pollute less improve not only the firm's environmental performance but also the plant employees' working conditions, since these employees would be working in a healthier environment. Accordingly, we postulate that:

H1b. Internal environmental practices have a positive impact on social performance.

The literature shows mixed results regarding the impact of environmental practices on operational performance. On one hand, some authors claim that environmental initiatives may worsen operational performance due to the high costs of their implementation (e.g., Waley and Whitehead, 1994; Colby et al., 1995; Angell and Klassen, 1999). On the other hand, some scholars suggest that environmentally responsible firms are able to improve economic and/or operational performance by reducing costs (Hart, 1995; Hoffman and Ventresca, 1999). Given these mixed results, further research is needed to examine and clarify this relationship (de Giovanni, 2012). Various empirical studies have shown a positive relationship between internal environmental practices and operational performance at the plant level (Zhu and Sarkis, 2004; Zhu et al., 2005; Rao and Holt, 2005; Gimenez et al., 2012). In accordance with these results, it is reasonable to expect that the adoption of more energy-efficient processes will lead to a cost reduction, as less energy is to be bought. In the same line, the adoption of cleaner production processes is likely to contribute to reducing costs, as less end-of-pipe mechanisms to diminish pollution would be needed. Also, the implementation of production processes that generate less waste can reduce costs, because fewer activities would need to be performed to eliminate this waste. In accordance with this rationale, we hypothesize that:

H1c. Internal environmental practices have a positive impact on operational performance.

Regarding social practices, some studies have provided support for a positive link between internal social practices and environmental performance (i.e., Florida, 1996; Gimenez et al., 2012; Marshall et al., 2005). Florida (1996) found that worker participation and training lead to environmental improvements. Marshall et al. (2005) showed that concern for employee welfare leads to more desirable environmental behaviours (i.e., potentially damaging environmental actions are reduced). Gimenez et al. (2012) found that the implementation of social practices aimed at enhancing safety or improving working conditions lead to an improvement in environmental performance. However, Pullman et al. (2009) did not find any direct relationship between social initiatives and environmental performance. Thus, the objective of this study is to further examine the relationship between these two constructs. It is plausible to expect that the adoption of internal social practices (e.g., practices aimed at improving employees' health and safety, work–life balance, working conditions in the plant) leads to better environmental performance. For instance, implementing health and safety standards through training programmes may make workers aware of potentially damaging environmental practices, which may result in a reduction of their use. Furthermore, work–life balance policies and career development programmes motivate employees, and thus increase their participation in the search for ways to improve the firm's environmental performance. Therefore, based on these lines of argument and the previous findings (Florida, 1996; Gimenez et al., 2012; Marshall et al., 2005), we postulate that:

H2a. Internal social practices have a positive impact on environmental performance.

Gimenez et al. (2012) provided empirical evidence for a positive impact of social practices on social performance. This means that the adoption of social practices such as those aimed at enhancing employees' health, safety, social progress, and career development lead to better social results by achieving better working conditions or a decrease in the number of accidents. For example, programmes aimed at enhancing employees' health and safety are likely to improve working conditions and reduce the number of accidents. Furthermore, work–life balance and career development programmes can increase worker satisfaction and motivation, which in turn may have a positive impact on the workers' commitment to search for ways to improve working conditions and safety levels (Sancha et al., 2016). Accordingly, we hypothesize that:

H2b. Internal social practices have a positive impact on social performance.

As in the case of the relationship between environmental practices and operational perfor-mance, empirical studies analysing the impact of social initiatives on operational performance show contradictory results. On one hand, one stream of the literature claims that there is a positive relationship between social practices and operational and economic performance. For example, Orlitzky et al. (2003) and Margolis and Walsh (2003) provided empirical support for a modest but positive relationship between these dimensions. In addition, Brown (1996) and Brown et al. (2000) found that better worker safety programmes reduced costs, thereby improving operational performance. On the other hand, Gimenez et al. (2012) showed a negative effect of social practices on manufacturing costs. Although some social practices may increase manufacturing costs in the short term, the implementation of these practices may have a global positive effect on operational performance when considering not only manufac-turing costs but also additional performance dimensions such as quality or delivery times. For instance, the improvement of health and safety conditions as well as the adoption of work–life balance policies can lead to lower levels of absenteeism, which in turn may result in a decrease of both costs and delivery times. Besides, the adoption of practices such as providing career development programmes and promotion paths can enhance employees' motivation, which is likely to result in an increase in the quality of the products/services offered. Based on the previous arguments, and in line with the findings of Brown (1996) and Brown et al. (2000), we hypothesize that:

H2c. Internal social practices have a positive impact on operational performance.

It is important to highlight that various studies show that the different dimensions of the TBL are not mutually exclusive and that the improvements in one of them (i.e., environ-mental and/or social performance) can bring improvements to the other ones (i.e., eco-nomic or operational performance) (e.g., Pagell and Gobeli, 2009; Hutchins and Sutherland, 2008). Waddock and Graves (1997) found a positive association between corporate social performance and companies' financial performance. In the same line, Brown (1996) argued that improved safety conditions in companies can generate better operational results. For instance, fewer accidents in the firm's premises may lead to fewer disruptions in the process, improving delivery times. Based on these currents of thought, we postulate that:

H3. Environmental performance has a positive impact on operational performance.

H4. Social performance has a positive impact on operational performance.

In summary, we have hypothesized direct and positive effects between each type of practice (i.e., environmental and social internal practices) and each dimension of the TBL (H1a, H1b,

H1c, H2a, H2b, H2c). We have also hypothesized a direct and positive effect between environmental and operational performance and between social and operational performance (H3 and H4). In addition, we also aim to hypothesize the following indirect effects. Rao (2002) suggested that the impact of Green Supply Chain Management on operational performance is mediated by environmental performance. In a recent empirical study of the contribution of environmental management to the TBL, de Giovanni (2012) showed an indirect influence of environmental practices on operational performance. In the case of social practices, the literature shows contradictory results when studying the relationship between social practices and operational performance. These mixed results indicate that the relationship between internal social practices and operational performance may also be mediated. Thus, it is reasonable to expect that operational performance will increase as a result of the implementation of environmental and/or social practices once environmental and/or social performances have already improved. For instance, once the company has implemented better safety and labour conditions, the number of accidents will decrease, which in turn will contribute to the reduction of costs resulting from absenteeism. Accordingly, we hypothesize that:

H5. Environmental performance mediates the relationship between internal practices and operational performance.

H5a. Environmental performance mediates the relationship between internal environmental practices and operational performance.

H5b. Environmental performance mediates the relationship between internal social practices and operational performance.

H6. Social performance mediates the relationship between internal practices and operational performance.

H6a. Social performance mediates the relationship between internal environmental practices and operational performance.

H6b. Social performance mediates the relationship between internal social practices and operational performance.

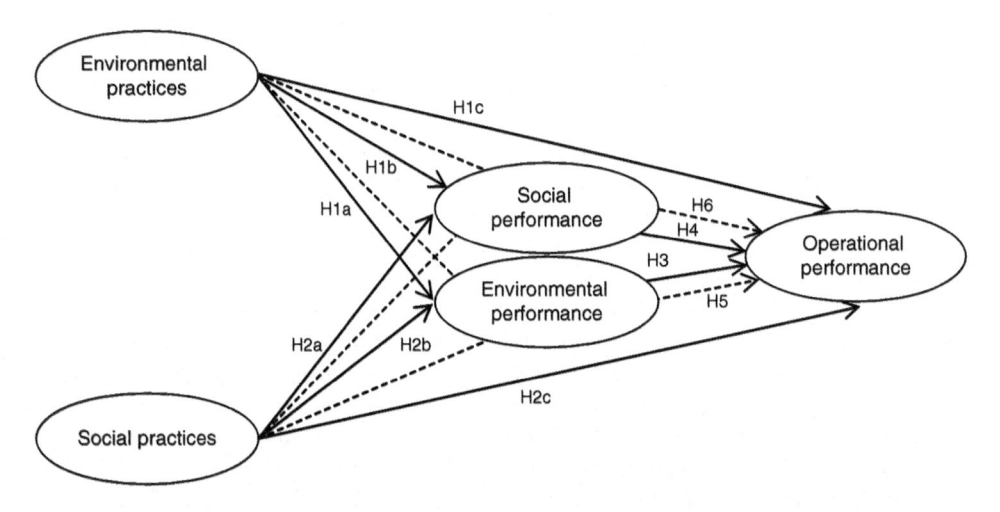

Figure 3.1.1 Hypothesized model of the impact of environmental and social practices

Methodology

Questionnaire design and measures

A questionnaire was drawn up based on previous literature. The list of items is provided in Appendix A. Three items were used to measure internal environmental practices, and four for internal social practices. The internal environmental practices items are in line with the indicators used by Carter and Carter (1998) and Rao and Holt (2005). These indicators include the use of green practices in the following dimensions: energy resources, waste and raw materials, and production processes. In the case of internal social practices, the items capture practices related to employees' health and safety conditions (see Pagell and Gobeli, 2009), social progress, and career development (see Pullman et al., 2009). A fourth item measuring the presence of work–life balance policies was also included (Longo et al., 2005). A review of several corporate social responsibility (CSR) reports of multinational firms revealed that this set of environmental and social practices is appropriate.

For environmental, social, and operational performance constructs, multiple items were considered. Environmental performance items include the reduction of pollution and waste, the fulfilment of environmental legislation, increased levels of recycling, and the improvement of the company's environmental reputation. Similar items have been used in the previous literature (e.g., Florida, 1996; Rao, 2002; Suhaiza et al., 2012; Zhu and Sarkis, 2004; Zhu et al., 2005). Regarding social performance, it is important to mention that due to a lack of literature focusing on the social dimension of the TBL, there is no agreement on how this construct should be measured (de Giovanni, 2012). Taking this into account, and in line with the work of Maxwell et al. (2006), de Giovanni (2012), and Golini et al. (2014), this study used the following three items to measure social performance: the improvement of the company's social reputation, the reduction of industrial accidents, and the improvement of safety and labour conditions. Finally, for economic performance, this study focused on the operational level (Rao and Holt, 2005; Cruz and Wakolbinger, 2008; de Giovanni, 2012; Gimenez et al., 2012) and included the following three indicators: improvement of product quality, reduction of delivery times, and decrease of costs. All indicators were measured using a seven-point Likert scale, where higher values indicated higher level of adoption or better performance.

Following Peng and Lai (2012) and Jarvis et al. (2003), this study considered operational performance as a formative construct. In this case, the construct is defined by the cost, quality, and flexibility dimensions and not the opposite way (Jarvis et al., 2003). In addition, the different dimensions that form the construct are not expected to change in the same direction and magnitude. An increase in quality does not necessarily imply an increase in flexibility. Finally, the items (i.e., quality, cost, and flexibility) are not interchangeable. This is not the case for the other two dimensions of sustainability performance (i.e., social and environmental). For instance, an improvement on the safety and labour conditions in the firm's premises can lead to a reduction in the number of industrial accidents. In the same line, a reduction of pollution and waste materials may result in a better environmental reputation of the firm. In that sense, we have considered the remaining four constructs (i.e., environmental practices, social practices, environmental performance, social performance) as reflective.

In this study, we controlled for company size since different authors have found that larger firms have higher implementation levels of sustainability practices (e.g., Min and Galle, 2001; Wilkinson et al., 2001). Because of this, the natural logarithm of the number of firm's employees was included as a control variable in the model.

Sampling and data collection

The starting population in this study was made up of Spanish companies in different NACE business codes (see Table 3.1.1). Firms had at least 50 employees in 2009. The original sample was composed of 580 firms and was extracted from SABI Database. A phone call was made requesting participation in this study, but 204 companies declined to participate. From the remaining companies (376), a total of 99 answered the questionnaire by phone, whereas the rest asked to have the survey e-mailed (from which, 21 responded). In total, we obtained 120 (99 + 21) questionnaires completed, representing an effective response rate of 20.69%.

Table 3.1.1 provides the description of the sample. Firm size was measured in terms of annual turnover and number of employees. Firms with an annual turnover lower than 10 million euros amounted to 5.8% of the total sample; 52.5% had an annual turnover between 10 and 50 million euros; and the remaining 41.7% had an annual turnover higher than 50 million euros. Regarding industry, 10% of the companies belong to the textile sector; around 22% to the wood and paper industries; chemical and pharmaceutical industries account for 33%; electronics 29%; and the remaining firms belong to the printing sector. In addition, Table 3.1.1 shows that there is a high diversity of respondents' positions. In that sense, non-parametric tests were performed to check for any possible difference in the response due to its position. Results showed that there are no significant differences.

The use of different data collection methods (telephone and e-mail) may be a threat to the study. Due to the big difference in size regarding the total number of responses obtained by telephone (99) and e-mail (21), a subsample of 20 responses was randomly selected from each group. Man-Whitney and T tests were performed and no significant differences between phone and e-mail responses were found.

Non-response bias could have also been a threat to this study. If respondents differ substantially from individuals who do not respond, then responses cannot be generalized to the population (Miller and Smith, 1983). In that sense, we performed non-response bias tests comparing the demographic data (number of employees and turnover) of respondents and non-respondents. Results showed that non-response bias is not a threat to this study.

Table 3.1.1 Descriptive statistics of the companies studied

Position	n	%	Number of employees	n	%
Health & Safety Director or Manager	7	5.83	Less than 50	1	0.80
Environmental Director or Manager	14	11.67	Between 50 and 249	75	62.50
Health, Safety & Environmental Director or Manager	13	10.83	Between 250 and 499	31	25.80
Quality and Environmental Director or Manager	23	19.17	More than 500	13	10.80
Quality, Health, Safety and Environmental Director or Manager	13	10.83	TOTAL	120	100.00
Managing Director	7	5.83			
Operations or Supply Chain Director or Manager	8	6.67			
Quality Director or Manager	8	6.67			
Human Resources Director or Manager	16	13.33			
Other	11	9.17			
TOTAL	120	100.00			

(continued)

Table 3.1.1 (continued)

Industry	n	%	Turnover	n	%
Textile (NACE codes 13, 14, and 15)	12	10.00	Less than €10 million	7	5.80
Wood and products of wood and cork, except furniture (NACE code 16)	11	9.20	Between €10 and €50 million	63	52.50
Paper and paper products (NACE code 17)	16	13.30	More than €50 million	50	41.70
Printing (NACE code 18)	6	5.00	TOTAL	120	100.00
Chemical (NACE code 20)	25	20.80			
Pharmaceutical (NACE code 21)	15	12.50			
Electronics (NACE codes 26 and 27)	35	29.20			
TOTAL	120	100.00			

Data analysis and results

We used PLS-SEM analysis to simultaneously assess the measurement model and determine the effects of environmental and social internal practices on each dimension of the TBL (see Figure 3.1.1). The impossibility to fulfil the set of assumptions of the parametric structural equation modelling technique (based on maximum likelihood estimators) including multivariate normality of data and minimum sample size suggests PLS procedure to be the best approach to the test the hypothesized model (Hair et al., 2017). PLS-SEM is a variance-based estimation procedure based on a set of multiple regressions. In that sense, we conducted the analysis as a hierarchical (sequential) multiple regression analysis. The estimated beta coefficients are the coefficients shown in the typical figures that are used to display the results of the path analysis. Given that the PLS-SEM is based on an iterative algorithm, the estimation of our model was performed following a two-step approach. First, we evaluated the adequacy and quality of the scales (measurement assessment). Second, we estimated the structural model, which entails the relationships between latent constructs. The specific details of both analyses can be found in Appendices B and C.

Results provide support for six out of the eight hypotheses related to direct effects. Regarding the impact of environmental internal practices on the TBL, we found support for both H1a and H1b, which predicted that environmental practices are positively related to both environmental and social performance. However, no support was found for the impact of environmental practices on operational performance (H1c). Regarding the impact of social practices on the TBL, we found support for the positive impact of social practices on social (H2b) and operational performance (H2c), but not on environmental performance (H2a). Furthermore, results provide support for H3, which posited a positive effect of environmental performance on operational performance, and for H4 that claimed a positive impact of social performance on operational performance.

Related to the mediating effects hypotheses, results show that H5a, H6a, and H6b are supported. In the case of the relationship between environmental practices and operational performance, both environmental (H5a) and social performance (H6a) are full mediators. In the case of H6b, the relationship between social practices and operational performance is partially mediated by social performance. Finally, the relationship between social practices and operational performance is not mediated by environmental performance, providing no support to H5b. To conclude, it is important to mention that we controlled for firm size in the model and no differences were found with respect to this control variable.

Table 3.1.2 Hypotheses: results

Hypotheses	Result
Direct effects	
H1a. Env Practices -> Env Performance	Supported
H1b. Env Practices -> Soc Performance	Supported
H1c. Env Practices -> Op Performance	Not supported
H2a. Soc Practices -> Env Performance	Not supported
H2b. Soc Practices -> Soc Performance	Supported
H2c. Soc Practices -> Op Performance	Supported
H3. Env Perf -> Op Performance	Supported
H4. Soc Perf -> Op Performance	Supported
Mediating effects	
H5a. Env Pract -> Env Perf -> Op Perf	Supported (full mediation)
H5b. Soc Pract -> Env Perf -> Op Perf	Not supported (no mediation)
H6a. Env Pract -> Soc Perf -> Op Perf	Supported (full mediation)
H6b. Soc Pract -> Soc Perf -> Op Perf	Supported (partial mediation)

The last step in data analysis was to check the coefficients of determination (R^2) for each dependent construct, which indicates whether the independent variables of the model exert substantial influence on this construct (Chin, 1998). In our model, the coefficients of determination are comparatively small but of considerable value. In particular, the variances explained for social, environmental, and operational performances are around 16%, 34%, and 40%, respectively. These results show that the model is suitable.

Discussion

The discussion is structured around the following three relationships: (1) the impact of environmental practices on the TBL, (2) the impact of social practices on the TBL, and (3) the direct versus the indirect effect of environmental and social practices on operational performance.

The impact of environmental practices on the TBL

Results regarding the positive impact of environmental practices on environmental performance are consistent with previous literature (e.g., Zhu and Sarkis, 2004; Zhu et al., 2005). These results imply that the implementation of practices such as the better usage of energetic resources, the implementation of environmentally friendly production processes, and/or the use of raw materials that are less harmful for the environment allow firms to reduce pollution levels, improve the fulfilment of environmental legislation, and have a better environmental reputation. In addition, in line with de Giovanni (2012) and Gimenez et al. (2012), results suggest that these practices not only improve the environmental performance of firms, but also the social one. In fact, by implementing environmentally friendly practices, employees' working conditions in a firm's facilities improve. This can be explained by the fact that employees work in a healthier environment.

Regarding the impact of environmental practices on the operational performance, our results shed some light on the existing academic debate. Contrary to what was expected, the implementation of environmental practices does not directly contribute to improve the operational performance of firms, which is in line with Zhu et al. (2007). However, from the results of this chapter, it can be observed that environmental practices will improve the firm's operational performance once they have enhanced the firm's environmental and/or social performance. Therefore, results provide support for the mediated impact proposed by Rao (2002): environmental practices will improve operational performance only if these practices have been effectively implemented and really contribute to improve the environmental and/or social performances of the firm. For instance, the implementation of an environmentally friendly production process will result in better-quality outcomes only if it has previously reduced the pollution level in the firm and/or resulted in a healthier and safer working environment for employees.

The impact of social practices on the TBL

Regarding the impact of social practices on social and operational performance, the results provide support for these relationships. This is an important contribution to the literature, as previous studies in the field of operations management have largely neglected social practices. Results show that those practices aimed at improving employees' health and safety, those programmes aimed at reconciling work and family, and those practices supporting employees' social progress and their development, positively influence operational and social performance.

The contribution of social practices to reducing the number of industrial accidents and improving the working conditions is in line with the results of Gimenez et al. (2012). If the firm provides employees with work and life balance policies and career development plans, the social reputation of such firm will be improved. In addition, implementing health and safety policies in the firm's premises reduces the number of accidents and improves the working conditions for employees. However, the positive effect of the implementation of social practices on operational performance seems to contradict the results of Gimenez et al. (2012), who found that the implementation of social practices lead to an increase in manufacturing costs in the short term. These apparently contradictory results in the social practices to operational performance relationship can be explained as follows: Whereas Gimenez et al. (2012) operationalized performance using one single item (manufacturing costs), this chapter considered multiple items. By considering not only costs but also dimensions such as quality and delivery times, this chapter provides a more complete conceptualization of performance. Results show that the implementation of social practices leads to direct improvements in quality, delivery times, and costs. This means that the implementation of employees' health and safety programmes, social progress, career development, and work–life balance policies results in higher productivity, which leads to a reduction in costs, delivery times, and quality problems in turn. In addition, as a result of the implementation of social practices, better operational results can be indirectly obtained through improvements in social performance. That is, not only the implementation of these practices but also their effective implementation (i.e., resulting in higher social performance) lead to improvements in quality, delivery, and costs outcomes.

Contrary to what was expected, results do not provide support for the relationship between social practices and environmental performance. These results are in line with those of Pullman et al. (2009), who did not find any relationship between social sustainability practices (a similar construct to the one used in this study) and environmental performance, in the case of food and beverage handlers in the US. However, results differ from those of Marshall et al. (2005) and Gimenez et al. (2012). Marshall et al. (2005) found that in vineyards, employee welfare is related with the reduction of toxic spray applications, which not only improves employee working conditions but also environmental performance. Gimenez et al. (2012) also found that the firm's direct contribution to safety and work conditions improves social and environmental performance. The main conclusion that can be derived from these results is that social practices aimed at improving health and safety may also improve the environmental performance if the improvement of the working conditions entails the elimination of hazardous and/or toxic materials. However, until now, no study has been successful in relating other social practices, such as career development plans and work–life balance policies, with environmental performance.

The direct versus the indirect effect of environmental and social practices on operational performance

To conclude the discussion, it is important to compare the impact of both sustainability practices (i.e., environmental and social) on operational performance. Social practices have a direct effect on operational performance, and also an indirect effect through social performance. However, environmental practices only have an indirect effect on operational performance. The impact of environmental practices on operational performance is mediated by the environmental and social performance achieved. One possible explanation for this difference is that social practices are actions that directly affect employees (their working conditions, health and safety, career development plants, work–life balance, etc.). The implementation of this type of practices lead to improvements in productivity, since employees will be more satisfied, which in turn may result in a better operational performance (reduced costs, better quality, and reduced lead times). However, environmental practices are usually actions over processes or materials, and not over people. The implementation of environmental practices will only lead to a better operational performance if these practices result in reduced waste, lower energy consumption, and more environmentally friendly processes. This means that environmental practices will lead to a better operational performance if a better environmental performance is achieved. Also, the implementation of these practices over processes or materials will not directly lead to a higher employee satisfaction and productivity, unless employees perceive that their working conditions have improved. This argument explains why environmental practices improve social performance and thereby operational performance.

Theoretical contributions

The aim of this chapter was to examine the impact of internal social and environmental practices on environmental, social, and operational performance. Our results contribute to the sustainable operations literature by extending the current understanding we have about the impact of both social and environmental practices on performance. In fact, they have shown that environmental practices have a positive and direct effect on the social and environmental dimension of the TBL, whereas their effect on operational performance is meditated by both the social and environmental performance. Regarding social practices, they have a positive direct effect on operational and social performance, but not on environmental performance. These mediating results help to shed light on the contradictory results found in the literature.

In addition, this study contributes to the existing body of research in the following aspects. First, by analysing both types of sustainability practices and the three dimensions of the TBL, it fills a gap in the sustainable operations literature. Second, it extends the RBV to include not only environmental issues but also social ones. As discussed above, the implementation of social practices leads also to improvements in performance. Third, it responds to the recent call by Pagell and Gobeli (2009) to develop more research at the operational level.

Managerial implications

This study also has some important managerial implications. First, it shows that social and environmental practices pay-off in terms of impact on the TBL. This means that in order to become more sustainable, managers should adopt both types of practices. However, an important aspect should be considered: whereas social practices have a positive effect on social and operational performance, they do not have any statistically significant relationship with environmental performance. To improve environmental performance, environmental practices are the most appropriate ones. Managers should also be aware that, having high levels of environmental and social performance leads to high levels of operational performance. This suggests that being a sustainable company (i.e., high social performance, high environmental performance) contributes to achieve operational improvements. Finally, another important managerial implication is that environmental practices only have a positive effect on the operational dimension of the TBL if they in fact lead to an improvement in the environmental and/or social performance. This suggests that it is not only important to implement these practices but to make sure that they lead to effective results.

Limitations and future research

Besides the abovementioned theoretical contributions and managerial implications, there are some limitations that need to be highlighted. First, this study focuses on the causal relationship between sustainable practices and the TBL. However, since the research methodology used is cross-sectional, it ignores a possible recursive relationship. It could be possible that improved performance leads to higher levels of implementation of sustainable practices. Although cross-sectional data may be considered as a limitation, it is a widely adopted methodology in the operations management literature when exploring relationships between constructs. Future research should use panel data to further study the proposed framework. Second, our study has focused on better understanding the relationship between environmental and social practices on the TBL performance dimensions given the mixed results found in the literature. Future research should go a step further and adopt a contingency perspective that takes contextual variables into account. Third, social performance is analysed by only focusing on the internal community, which might result on a partial measure of social performance. Future research should measure social performance also including the external community. Fourth, we have focused on operational performance and neglected the impact that environmental and social practices might have on economic performance. While we posit that the use of more energy-efficient processes might lead to reduced costs or reduced pollution, we neglected the negative impact that its implementation might have on economic performance due to the cost of implementation. Further research should measure the financial impact of green investments. Fifth, data were collected only in Spain, and therefore a possible bias caused by culture and national institutions should be taken into account. Finally, performance was measured using perceptual measures. That is, the improvement the buying firm perceives on the different sustainability dimensions. Future studies should include objective measures such as carbon dioxide emissions and/or number of accidents.

References

Angell, LC., and Klassen, R.D. (1999). Integrating environmental issues into the mainstream: an agenda for research in operations management. *Journal of Operations Management*, 17, 575–598.

Aragon-Correa, J.A., and Sharma, S. (2003). A contingent resource-based view of proactive corporate environmental strategy. *Academy of Management Review*, 28, 71–88.

Azzone, G., and Noci, G. (1996). Measuring the environmental performance of new products: an integrated approach. *International Journal of Production Research*, 34, 3055–3078.

Bagozzi, R.P., Yi, Y., and Phillips, L.W. (1991). Assessing construct validity in organizational research. *Administrative Science Quarterly*, 36, 421–458.

Barney, J.B. (1991). Firm resources and sustained competitive advantage. *Journal of Management*, 17, 99–120.

Bloomberg (2003). Clean energy helps Wal-Mart reach elusive sustainability goal, available at: http://www.bloomberg.com/news/2013-03-04/clean-energy-growth-helps-wal-mart-hit-a-sustainability-goal-early.html.

Bowen, F., Cousins, P., Lamming, R., and Faruk, A. (2001). The role of supply management capabilities in green supply. *Production Operations Management*, 10(2), 174–189.

Brown, K. (1996). Workplace safety: a call for research. *Journal of Operations Management*, 14(1), 157–171.

Brown, K., Willis, P.G., and Prussia, G.E. (2000). Predicting safe employee behavior in the steel industry: development and test of a sociotechnical model. *Journal of Operations Management*, 18(4), 445–465.

Cagliano, R., Golini, R., and Longoni, A. (2010). The role of NFWO in sustainability strategies: an OM perspective. *Proceedings of the European Operations Management Association*, ed. R. Sousa, Catholic University of Portugal, Porto, 1–10.

Carter, C.R., and Carter, J.R. (1998). Interorganizational determinants of environmental purchasing initial evidence from the consumer products industries. *Decision Sciences*, 29(3), 659–684.

Chin, W. (1998). *The Partial Least Squares Approach to Structural Equation Modeling*. New Jersey, NJ: Lawrence Erlbaum Associates Publisher.

Colby, S., Kingsley, T., and Whitehead, B. (1995). The real green issues. *McKinsey Quarterly*, 2, 132–143.

Cruz, J.M., and Wakolbinger, T. (2008). Multiperiod effects of corporate social responsibility on supply chain networks, transaction costs, emissions, and risk. *International Journal of Production Economics*, 116(1), 61–74.

de Giovanni, P. (2012). Do internal and external environmental management contribute to the triple bottom line? *International Journal of Operations and Production Management*, 32(3), 265–290.

de Ron, A.J. (1998). Sustainable production: the ultimate result of a continuous improvement. *International Journal of Production Economics*, 56–57, 99–110.

Dobos, I., and Floriska, A. (2007). The resource conservation effect of recycling in a dynamic Leontief model. *International Journal of Production Economics*, 108, 334–340.

Elkington, J. (1994). Towards the sustainable corporation: win-win-win business strategies for sustainable development. *California Management Review*, 36(2), 90–100.

Elkington, J. (1998). *Cannibals with Forks: The Triple Bottom Line of the 21st Century*. Stoney Creek: New Society Publishers.

Florida, R. (1996). Lean and Green: the move to environmentally conscious manufacturing. *California Management Review*, 39(1), 80–105.

Gimenez, C., Sierra, V., and Rodon, J. (2012). Sustainable operations: their impact on the triple bottom line. *International Journal of Production Economics*, 140, 149–159.

Golicic, S.L., and Smith, C.D. (2013). A meta-analysis of environmentally sustainable supply chain management practices and firm performance. *Journal of Supply Chain Management*, 49(2), 78–95.

Golini, R., Longoni, A., and Cagliano, R. (2014). Developing sustainability in global manufacturing networks: the role site competence on sustainability performance. *International Journal of Production Economics*, 147, 448–459.

Gualandris, J., Golini, R., and Kalchschmidt, M. (2014). Do supply management and global sourcing matter for firm sustainability performance? *Supply Chain Management: An International Journal*, 19(3), 258–274.

Hair, J.F., Black, W.C., Babin, B., and Anderson, R.E. (2009). *Multivariate Data Analysis*. Upper Saddle River: Pearson Prentice Hall.

Hair, J.F., Hult, G.T.M., Ringle, C.M., and Sarstedt, M. (2017). *A Primer on Partial Least Squares Structural Equation Modeling (PLS-SEM)*. Thousand Oaks: Sage.

Hart, S.L. (1995). A natural-resource-based view of the firm. *Academy of Management Review*, 20(4), 986–1014.

Hoffman, A.J., and Ventresca, M.J. (1999). The institutional framing of policy debates: economics versus the environment. *Administrative Behavioural Science*, 42(8), 1368–1391.

Jarvis, C.B., MacKenzie, S.B., Podsakoff, P.M., Mick, D.G., and Bearden, W.Q. (2003). A critical review of construct indicators and measurement model misspecification in marketing and consumer research. *Journal of Consumer Research*, 30(2), 199–218.

Kleindorfer, P.R., Singhal, K., and van Wassenhove, L. (2005). Sustainable operations management. *Production Operations Management*, 14(4), 482–492.

KPMG (2008). KPMG International Survey of Corporate Responsibility Reporting 2008, available at: www.kpmg.com/Global/en/IssuesAndInsights/ArticlesPublications/Pages/Sustainability-corporate-responsibility-reporting-2008-aspx

Lindell, M.K., and Whitney, D.J. (2001). Accounting for common method variance in cross-sectional research designs. *Journal of Applied Psychology*, 86(1), 114–121.

Longo, M., Mura, M., and Bonoli, A. (2005). Corporate Social Responsibility and Corporate Performance: the case of Italian SMEs. *Corporate Governance*, 5(4), 28–42.

Margolis, J.D., and Walsh, J.P. (2003). Misery loves companies: rethinking social initiatives by business. *Administrative Science Quarterly*, 48(2), 268–305.

Markley, M.J., and Davis, L. (2007). Exploring future competitive advantage through supply chain. *International Journal of Physical Distribution and Logistics Management*, 37(9), 763–774.

Marshall, R.S., Cordano, M., and Silverman, M. (2005). Exploring individual and institutional drivers of proactive environmentalism. *Business Strategy and the Environment*, 14(2), 92–109.

Maxwell, D., Sheate, W., and van der Vorst, R. (2006). Functional and systems aspects of the sustainable product and service development approach for industry. *Journal of Cleaner Production*, 14(17), 1466–1479.

Maxwell, D., and van der Vorst, R. (2003) Developing sustainable products and services. *Journal of Cleaner Production*, 11(8), 883–895.

McKinnon, D.P., Lockwood, C.M., Hoffman, J.M., West, S.G., and Sheets, V. (2002). A comparison of methods to test mediation and other intervening variable effects. *Phsycology Methods*, 7(1), 83–104.

Miller, L., and Smith, K. (1983). Handling non-response issues. *The Journal of Extension*, 21, 45–50.

Min, H., and Galle, W.P. (2001). Green purchasing practices of US firms. *International Journal of Operations and Production Management*, 21(9), 1222–1238.

Orlitzky, M., Schmidt, F.L., and Rynes, S.L. (2003). Corporate social and financial performance: a meta-analysis. *Organizational Studies*, 24(3), 296–319.

Pagell, M., and Gobeli, D. (2009). How plant managers' experiences and attitudes toward sustainability relate to operational performance. *Production and Operations Management*, 18(3), 278–299.

Peng, D.X., and Lai, F. (2012). Using partial least squares in operations management research: a practical guideline and summary of past research. *Journal of Operations Management*, 30, 467–480.

Penrose, E.T. (1959). *The Theory of the Growth of the Firm*. New York: John Wiley & Sons.

Peteraf, M.A. (1993). The cornerstones of competitive advantage: a resource-based view. *Strategic Management Journal*, 14(3), 179–191.

Podsakoff, P.M., MacKenzie, S.B., Lee, J.Y., and Podsakoff, N.P. (2003). Common method biases in behavioral research: a critical review of the literature and recommended remedies. *Journal of Applied Psychology*, 88(5), 879–903.

Preacher, K.K., and Hayes, A.F. (2004). SPSS and SAS procedures for estimating indirect effects in simple mediation models. *Behavioural Research Methods*, 36, 717–731.

Pullman, M.E., Maloni, M.J., and Carter, C.G. (2009). Food for thought: social versus environmental sustainability programs and performance outcomes. *Journal of Supply Chain Management*, 45(4), 38–54.

Rao, P. (2002). Greening the supply chain: a new initiative in South East Asia. *International Journal of Operations and Production Management*, 22(6), 632–655.

Rao, P., and Holt, D. (2005). Do green supply chains lead to competitiveness and economic performance? *International Journal of Operations and Production Management*, 25(9), 898–916.

Sancha, C., Gimenez, C., and Sierra, V. (2016). Achieving a socially responsible supply chain through assessment and collaboration. *Journal of Cleaner Production*, 112(3), 1934–1947.

Schoenherr, T., and Swink, M. (2012). Revisiting the arcs of integration: cross-validations and extensions. *Journal of Operations Management*, 20, 99–115.

Seuring, S., and Muller, M. (2008). From a literature review to a conceptual framework for sustainable supply chain management. *Journal of Cleaner Production*, 16(15), 1699–1710.

Starik, M., and Rands, G.P. (1995). Weaving an integrated web: multilevel and multisystem perspectives of ecologically sustainable organizations. *Academy Management Review*, 20(4), 908–935.

Suhaiza, H.M.Z., Tarig, K.E., Chin-Chun, H., and Keah, C.T. (2012). The impact of external institutional drivers and internal strategy on environmental performance. *International Journal of Operations and Production Management*, 32(6), 721–745.

Surroca, J., Tribó, J.A., and Waddock, S. (2010). Corporate responsibility and financial performance: the role of intangible resources. *Strategic Management Journal*, 31(5), 463–490.

The Huffington Post (2012). Wal-Mart working conditions, available at: http://www.huffingtonpost.com/tag/walmart-working-conditions

Theyel, G. (2000). Management practice for environmental innovation and performance. *International Journal of Operations and Production Management*, 20(2), 249–266.

Vachon, S., and Klassen, R.D. (2008). Environmental management and manufacturing performance: the role of collaboration in the supply chain. *International Journal of Production Economics*, 111(2), 299–315.

Waddock, S.A., and Graves, S.B. (1997). The corporate social performance-financial performance link. *Strategic Management Journal*, 18(4), 303–319.

Waley, N., and Whitehead, B. (1994). It's not easy being green. *Harvard Business Review*, 72(3), 46–52.

Wernerfelt, B. (1984). A resource-based view of the firm. *Strategic Management Journal*, 5(2), 171–180.

Wheeler, D., Fabig, H., and Boele, R. (2002). Paradoxes and dilemmas for stakeholder responsive firms in the extractive sector: lessons from the case of Shell and Ogoni. *Journal of Business Ethics*, 39(3), 297–318.

Wilkinson, A., Hill, M., and Gollan, P. (2001). The sustainability debate. *International Journal of Operations and Production Management*, 21(12), 1492–1502.

World Business Council for Sustainable Development (1999). *Corporate Social Responsibility: Meeting Changing Expectations*, WBCSD.

World Commission on Environment and Development (1987). *Our Common Future*. New York, NY: Oxford University Press.

Zhu, Q., and Sarkis, J. (2004). Relationships between operational programs and performance among early adopters of green supply chain management programs in Chinese manufacturing enterprises. *Journal of Operations Management*, 22(3), 265–289.

Zhu, Q., Sarkis, J., and Geng, Y. (2005). Green supply chain management in China: pressures, programs and performance. *International Journal of Operations and Production Management*, 25(5), 449–468.

Zhu, Q., Sarkis, J., and Lai, K. (2007). Initiatives and outcomes of green supply chain management implementation by Chinese manufacturers. *Journal of Environmental Management*, 85(1), 179–189.

Appendix A. Measures

Environmental practices

The company has implemented environmentally friendly practices to manage the following aspects:

Int1	Energetic resources
Int2	Raw materials and waste materials
Int3	Production processes

Social practices

The company has implemented socially responsible practices to manage the following aspects:

Int4	Employees' health and safety
Int5	Employees' social progress
Int6	Employees' career development and promotion paths
Int7	Work–life balance policies

Environmental performance

Please indicate the improvement on the following performance dimensions with respect to two years ago:

EnvPer1	The company has reduced pollution and waste materials.
EnvPer2	The company has improved the fulfilment of environmental legislation.
EnvPer3	The company has increased the recycle levels.
EnvPer4	The company has improved its environmental reputation.

Social performance

Please indicate the improvement on the following performance dimensions with respect to two years ago:

SocPer1	The company has improved its social reputation.
SocPer2	The company has reduced the number of industrial accidents in the one-year period.
SocPer3	The company has improved safety and labour conditions in its facilities.

Operational performance

Please indicate the improvement on the following performance dimensions with respect to two years ago:

OpPer1	The company has improved its product/service quality.
OpPer2	The company has reduced its delivery times to clients.
OpPer3	The company has reduced its total costs.
OpPer4	The company has reduced purchasing costs.

Appendix B. Measurement assessment

This Appendix summarizes the measurement assessment analysis. As in the model, there are both reflective and formative indicators, we need to distinguish between them in the measurement assessment. Testing the measurement model for reflective indicators includes estimating the convergent and discriminant validities.

Following the recommendations of Hair et al. (2009), convergent validity of the measurement model was assessed using three measures: item reliability, construct reliability and Average Variance Extracted (AVE). Item reliability was evaluated by the size of the loadings of the measures on their corresponding constructs. In order to have high convergent validity, high factor loadings are needed. One indicator of social performance was not included in further analysis because it loaded on a factor distinct from the intended factor. Table A shows that all loadings are higher than the threshold value of 0.70 (Hair et al., 2017). Reliability was assessed using Cronbach alpha and composite reliability indicators. For all constructs, both indicators score values higher than the 0.70 suggested threshold (see Table 3.1.3). The AVE, which is a summary indicator of convergence, was higher than 0.60 for all constructs, showing that convergent validity was adequate.

Discriminant validity was analysed comparing the square root of the AVE for each construct with the correlation between the construct and the remaining constructs. Table 3.1.4 provides support for sufficient discriminant validity since the square root of the AVE of each construct is higher than its correlations.

All in all, the measurement model results provided support for convergent and discriminant validities of the reflective measures used.

To evaluate the quality of the formative construct (i.e., operational performance), we checked the following criteria: (1) multicollinearity between indicators, (2) indicators' relative importance, and (3) indicators' absolute importance (see Table 3.1.5). High multicollinearity between the construct indicators means that there is redundant information. All VIF's are lower than the suggested boundary of 5, showing that multicollinearity is not an issue. In fact, the highest value equals 1.748. The indicators' relative and absolute importance was checked by looking at the indicators' outer weight and outer loadings, respectively. An indicator should be retained if it is significant. In the case it is not significant but the corresponding loading is relatively high (>.5), it should also be retained. Based on this, we decided to keep all four indicators.

Finally, as data were collected from a single person at a single point in time, an additional threat to our study could have been common method variance (CMV). To prevent and minimize CMV, in the questionnaire we placed the dependent variables after the independent ones (Podsakoff et al., 2003). To evaluate if CMV influences results, we relied on the following statistical procedures: (1) to analyse the correlation matrix between the different constructs (Lindell and Whitney's, 2001), (2) to examine the correlations between the constructs and a marker variable (Bagozzi et al., 1991), and (3) to perform the Harmans single factor (one-factor) test (Podsakoff et al., 2003). Table 3.1.4 shows that none of the correlations values between constructs surpasses the suggested threshold (i.e., r =.90). Table 3.1.6 shows that none of our constructs is related to the marker variable (i.e., a variable that is theoretically unrelated to the constructs under study). In addition, if the Pearson correlation coefficient is squared, we obtain the maximum percentage of variance shared by the construct and the marker variable (R^2). A high

Table 3.1.3 Measurement features for reflective indicators

Construct		Item descriptive			Component assessment				
		Item	Mean	Std Dev	Factor Loadings	% Variance	Cronbach Alpha	AVE	Composite Reliability
Practices	Environmental	Int1	5.30	1.268	0.829	67.64	0.754	0.673	0.860
		Int2	5.76	0.979	0.825				
		Int3	5.58	1.228	0.812				
	Social	Int4	6.26	0.835	0.740	64.84	0.800	0.644	0.878
		Int5	5.33	1.082	0.851				
		Int6	4.98	1.414	0.849				
		Int7	4.74	1.517	0.775				
Performance	Environmental	EnvPer1	5.62	1.278	0.889	68.68	0.877	0.680	0.914
		EnvPer2	5.83	1.288	0.870				
		EnvPer3	5.67	1.416	0.774				
		EnvPer4	5.38	1.413	0.823				
	Social	SocPer1	not included 5.72	not included	n.a	84.64	0.800	0.838	0.912
		SocPer2	5.97	1.401	0.920				
		SocPer3		1.053	0.920				

Table 3.1.4 Pearson correlation between factors

	Environmental Practices	Social Practices	Environmental Performance	Social Performance
Environmental Practices	0.820			
Social Practices	0.002	0.802		
Environmental Performance	0.482***	0.252***	0.825	
Social Performance	0.282***	0.335***	0.509***	0.916

Note: * $p < 0.10$; ** $p < 0.05$; *** $p < 0.001$; Square root of AVE in the diagonal

Table 3.1.5 Measurement features for formative indicators

Construct	Item	Mean	Std Dev	VIF (max)	Stand. Loadings	Weight	Lower bound (95%)	Upper bound (95%)
Operational Performance	OpPer1	5.69	1.094	1.748	0.779	0.543	0.200	0.875
	OpPer2	5.03	1.405		0.501	−0.106	−0.372	0.134
	OpPer3	4.71	1.427		0.601	0.088	−0.199	0.349
	OpPer4	4.22	1.519		0.829	0.412	0.221	0.599

Table 3.1.6 Marker variable

	Correlation	R^2
Environmental Practices	0.035	0.001
Social Practices	−0.033	0.001
Environmental Performance	−0.048	0.002
Social Performance	−0.047	0.002

R^2 would signal the presence of CMV. In our case, the highest R^2 value equals 0.22%. Finally, we loaded all the variables into an exploratory factor analysis (EFA) to perform the Harmans test and the results suggested that CMV is not present. In summary, all the different applied procedures to test for CMV suggest that it is not a threat to the study.

Appendix C. Structural analysis

This Appendix details the steps used to conduct the structural analysis and test both the direct and the indirect effects hypotheses. We used PLS-SEM to estimate the model path relationships (standardized regression coefficients). Since the estimation of the relationships is based on OLS regression, before looking at the results of the structural model, it is necessary to check for multicollinearity issues. If multicollinearity is present, estimations might be biased. As shown in Table 3.1.7, VIFs between constructs are low, showing that multicollinearity is not present in the model.

As the model includes two types of effects (i.e., direct and indirect), we first analyse direct effects and then indirect effects. The results of the direct effects estimation can be seen in Figure 3.1.2.

The estimated path coefficients allow us to compute the direct, indirect and total effects. This decomposition enable us to check for the possible mediating effects of the variables environmental and social performance in the relationship between internal practices (i.e., social and environmental) and operational performance. To test for the mediating effects, we compute and test indirect effects by the products of coefficients (McKinnon et al., 2002) and run the Sobel test (Preacher and Hayes, 2004). Table 3.1.8 shows the results of the mediation analysis.

Table 3.1.7 VIF between constructs

	Dependent Variable		
Predictor	*Environmental Performance*	*Social Performance*	*Operational Performance*
Environmental Practices	1.418	1.566	1.685
Social Practices	1.418	1.566	1.498
Environmental Performance	–	–	1.709
Social Performance	–	–	1.445

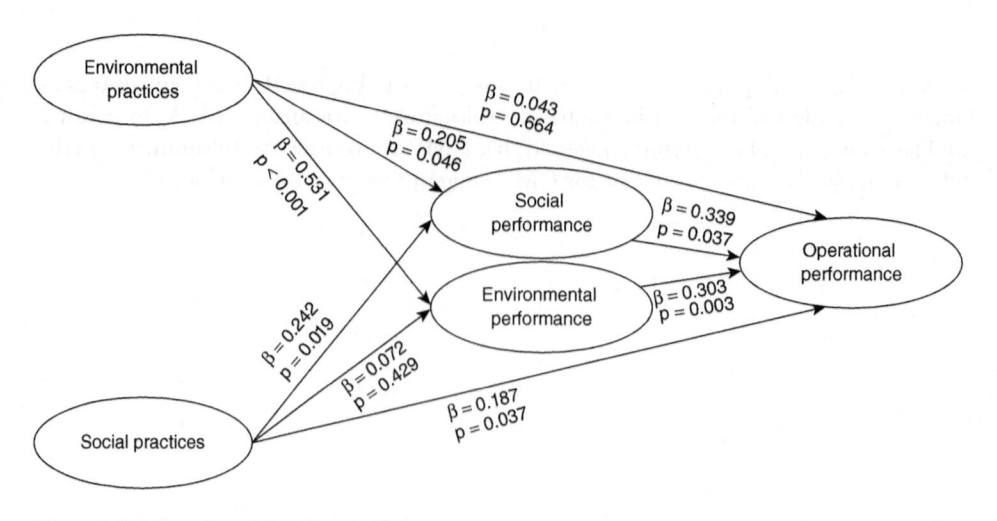

Figure 3.1.2 Results of the direct effects

Table 3.1.8 Results of the mediation effects

	Direct effect coefficients (β)			Indirect effect (mediation)	
	a	*b*	*c'*	*Ab*	*Sobel test*
EnvPract -> Env Perf -> Op Perf	0.531 (0.001)[1]	0.303 (0.003)	-0.043 (0.664)	0.161	2.74 (0.0062)
SocPract -> Env Perf -> Op Perf	0.072 (0.429)	0.303 (0.003)	0.187 (0.037)	n/a	n/a
EnvPract -> Soc Perf -> Op Perf	0.205 (0.046)	0.339 (0.029)	-0.043 (0.664)	0.069	1.79 (0.074)
SocPract -> Soc Perf -> Op Perf	0.242 (0.019)	0.339 (0.029)	0.187 (0.037)	0.082	2.026 (0.043)

(1) p-value

For a mediating effect to be significant, the following conditions need to be fulfilled. First, both the direct effect between the independent and the mediating variable (*a*) and the mediating and the dependent variable (*b*) need to be significant. Second, the Sobel test for the *ab* product needs to be also significant.

In the case of environmental performance as a mediating variable (H5a and H5b), results show that both hypotheses need to be rejected. In H5a, we posited that environmental performance is a partial mediator between internal environmental practices and operational performance. Although *a* (β=0.531, p<0.001) and *b* (β=0.303, p=0.003) are both significant and the Sobel test is also significant (z=2.74, p=0.0062), the estimated direct effect between internal environmental practices and operational performance, controlling for the mediator, (*c'*) is not (β=-0.043, p=0.664). This suggests that environmental performance is not a partial mediator but a full mediator in the relationship, providing no support for H5a. Regarding H5b which postulates that environmental performance is a partial mediator in the relationship between internal social practices and operational performance, results show that *a* (β=0.072, p=.429) is not significant. Therefore, H5b is to be rejected.

In the case of social performance acting as a mediator (H6a and H6b), Table 3.1.8 shows that H6a, which hypothesized that social performance is a partial mediator between internal environmental practices and operational performance is not supported. Results show that all conditions are met: *a* (β=0.205, p=0.046) and *b* (β=0.339, p=0.029) are both significant and the Sobel test (z= 1.79, p=0.074) is also significant. However, the estimated direct effect between internal environmental practices and operational performance, controlling for the mediator, (*c'*) is not significant (β=-.043, p=.664), suggesting that social performance is a full mediator, rather than a partial mediator, in this relationship. Finally, H6b hypothesized that the relationship between internal social practices and operational performance is partially mediated by social performance. Results in Table 3.1.8 show that *a* (β=0.242, p=0.019), *b* (β=0.339, p=0.029), and the Sobel test (z= 2.026, p=0.043) are significant. In addition, as the estimated direct effect between internal social practices and operational performance, controlling for the mediator (*c'*), is also significant (β=0.187, p=0.037), we can state that social performance partially mediates the studied relationship. This provides support for H6b. In addition, the comparison between the coefficients for the direct versus the indirect path (c'=0.187 vs. ab=0.082) suggests that 30% of the effect of internal social practices on operational performance is mediated by social performance.

3.2 Disclosing the invisible

Measurement and disclosure pitfalls of carbon dioxide emissions

Nils Niehues and Andreas Dutzi

Introduction

Carbon dioxide emission reporting is the most standardized reporting item in the area of corporate social responsibility (CSR) (Williams, 2013; Alejandra Gonzalez-Perez, 2013; Gond and Moon, 2011; Carroll, 1999). This includes global guidelines and high attention by various stakeholders. From a societal point of view, the signing of the Kyoto Protocol (Kyoto-Protokoll, 1997) was one milestone illustrative of perceived importance. The relevance has not been reduced over the decades, as scientific (IPCC, 2014) perception and the willingness of governments show (United Nations, 2015). Therefore, carbon emissions are part of the GRI framework, which is the leading standard for sustainability reporting issues (GRI, 2013). Carbon accounting already has a considerable record of evolving methods of standardized reporting (WBCSD and WRI, 2004; WBCSD and WRI, 2010), and sector-specific reporting guidelines to date are fragmentary. So, although carbon accounting is one of the most highly evolved CSR measurement items, there are still some serious measurement problems that allow management to make only fragmentary disclosures of carbon emissions. Prior studies developed theoretical hypotheses that explain management discretion to some extent, but there is still no general model of voluntary carbon disclosure. Hence, the shortcomings of the carbon reporting described in this chapter most likely also apply to other items in the field of CSR reporting.

The main part of the chapter is divided into three sections. As current literature for carbon accounting and sustainability disclosure often lacks a sound theoretical model (Stechemesser and Guenther, 2012), this chapter shows which theories can explain voluntary disclosure in that field and develops a comprehensive theoretical model based on disclosure quality. The respective theories in use – namely, stakeholder theory, legitimacy theory, institutional theory, and agency theory – have been derived by means of a recent literature review on carbon disclosure (Hahn et al., 2015). Subsequently, the complexity involved in recording a carbon inventory and interpreting disclosure is shown. Knowledge about the management's reporting motivation and the complexity of carbon inventory reporting is especially important to an understanding of current reporting and assurance practices, which are analysed next. We then highlight the shortcomings of incomplete reports that are disconnected from the two-degree target. Finally, we review current research in the field of carbon disclosure, focusing on comparisons between financial and environmental performance. The summary suggests open fields for research.

Theoretical explanation of CSR disclosure strategies

Stakeholder theory

The fact that current empirical work often invokes stakeholder theory without further specification shows a lack of theoretical understanding (Cotter and Najah, 2012). Of course, voluntary disclosure is disclosure for the stakeholders of companies. Parmar (Parmar et al., 2010) pointed out that stakeholder theory should be used as a theoretical framework within which other theories must be employed. The general idea of stakeholder theory is that a company must maintain dialogue with its various stakeholders and take their needs into account in the firm's value-creation process. This is required to achieve financial profits (Freeman, 1984). The argument is based on the notion that because a company works in a network of stakeholders from which the company gains benefit and/or upon which it depends, it must work within their interests as well (Freeman and Liedtka, 1991).

The theoretical backing for carbon disclosure within the stakeholder theory is that certain stakeholders expect companies to reduce their impact on global warming over time, and that carbon disclosure can be seen as evidence of this success. The management of the disclosing company can choose between different levels of depth and quality of disclosure. The resulting patterns of voluntary disclosure can be explained not fully by stakeholder theory directly, but by various theories beneath the stakeholder framework.

Legitimacy theory

Legitimacy theory explains companies' CSR actions as activities in which a company must engage in order to keep its "licence to operate" (Deegan, 2002; Suchman, 1995) or "right to operate" (Hart and Milstein, 2003). This licence to operate results from an "implicit social contract" (Patten, 1991) between the company and the society as a whole. Within this implicit contract, the society has an expectation that the company serves the society while it generates profits. Concerns raised by society about the business acumen of a management team lead to pressure on the firm. The firm has to react (Cho and Patten, 2007; Deegan, 2002; Gray et al., 1995; Ramanathan, 1976; Souza et al., 2004). If a company breaches the social contract, it is likely that society will take actions to penalize that company. Awareness of the penalizing power a society wields helps ensure that the company behaves within the confines of the implicit social contract. If environmental, social, and governance (ESG) disclosure is used to prove that the firm follows the requirements of society, it is likely that this disclosure is communicating only biased information and uses a biased verbal description for the required facts (Deegan and Rankin, 1997; Maines et al., 2002; Milne and Patten, 2002; Patten, 1991; Shocker and Sethi, 1973). Furthermore, as the disclosure is a reaction to public pressure, it is likely that the firm discloses only the required information (Cho and Roberts, 2010). However, if the information disclosed is seen as not sufficient, or the demand of the stakeholder increases over time, the disclosure improves to meet new requirements over time as well (Cavana and Becker, 2016; Stanny, 2013).

The power of the legitimacy argument is driven by the effective influence of the stakeholder on the company. ESG disclosure is often explained by legitimacy arguments, as the carbon debate is a relevant part of public debate (Patten, 1991). Prior studies suggest that research media exposure can be internationalized, with company size and company sector as legitimacy proxies, while profitability is not connected to legitimacy arguments (Yunus et al., 2016). The branch is relevant to the legitimacy discussion, as regulations, public debates, and so on, are often connected with entire sectors of industry (Wackernagel and Rees, 1997).

Legitimacy theory is powerful when it comes to explaining the content of stakeholder communication, but it does not state much about the reporting threshold. However, the organizational setting of environmental reporting in the communication department could be one indicator that supports the legitimacy theory (Windolph, 2013). The legitimacy argument is supported as company disclosure practise is criticized by disclosing only biased information. Additionally, the disclosure is often incomplete and lacks external assurance (Andrew and Cortese, 2013; Blacconiere and Patten, 1994; Patten, 1992). Applying this theory to carbon disclosure practices, we should assume the two-degree target as the expectation of society. One could expect a linkage between the licence to operate and a strategy connected with the setting of scientific targets. This is not currently the case, however (Patten, 2002). This finding indicate either that societal demand points in the wrong direction or that the threat of penalties is not sufficiently credible to force companies to behave in keeping with the targets of society.

Institutional theory

Institutional theory names three core factors that explain why actions and organizational structures of companies become homogeneous over time. These factors are known as "isomorphic" processes and include coercive, mimetic, and normative actions (DiMaggio and Powell, 1983). Coercive isomorphism describes a behaviour or reaction on the part of companies faced with external pressure. If external forces such as regulators, markets, or other stakeholders pressure companies to disclose information, it is likely that firms with similar stakeholders will also disclose similar reports (GRI et al., 2015; Stubbs and Higgins, 2014). Coercive isomorphism is fostered by the relevance and/or dependency of a single stakeholder or group(s) of stakeholders, the homogeneity of the competition, and the homogeneity of the stakeholder groups, for example customers, who pass requirements along to their suppliers (WBCSD and WRI, 2004). This is officially fostered as several standard-setters explicitly recommend adopting commonly used practices (CDP et al., 2011).

Mimetic isomorphism refers to the processes firms undertake in the face of uncertainty. The main argument is that, during phases of uncertainty, companies (especially their upper-echelon, decision-making bodies) behave in ways similar to companies that they perceive as successful. The process of blindly copying best practices occurs regardless of whether respective actions benefit the company. The following uncertainty factors might foster mimetic isomorphism.

- Uncertainty of the goal. While there seems to be consensus in science and society to limit the global warming to two degrees, the implications for the business world broken down to each single company are widely uncertain (CDP, 2015; United Nations, 2015; IPCC, 2014), even though sector ambitions do exist (CDP, 2015).
- Uncertainty of the approach or how to reach the target. Uncertainty is even higher, as business models and technologies are subject to rapid change.
- Uncertainty of future actions by stakeholder and regulators, especially if stakeholders send signals that change will happen, but the exact road map is unclear (CDP, 2015; ECOpoint Inc., 2015; United Nations, 2015).

In addition, processes of normative isomorphism ensure that companies solve problems homogeneously over time. If people are taught similarly about how to solve specific problems, it is likely that the problems will be approached similarly. Consequently, employees with a high level of education, specialist job role profiles with typical career paths, or domination of education provider and consulting firms tend to support normative isomorphism. These conformities are further supported by bureaucratic processes and regular interaction among specialists, for example, at industry conferences or programmes of cross-company training (WBCSD and WRI, 2004).

Prior studies used the example of the CDP to validate the application of institutional theory. Results showed that institutional forces increase the amount of reported data, even though this is not perceived as enabling stakeholders to identify carbon-efficient companies (Jira and Toffel, 2013; Kolk et al., 2008). Institutional theory as well as legitimacy theory, however, fail to explain fully why companies would exceed the reporting requirements and disclose a full environmental report.

Agency theory

Generally speaking, the ability to gain green rents based on environmentally friendly behaviour is a function of market efficiency. Relying on agency theory, managers should send a signal to shareholders to reduce information asymmetry. A valid signal could be a carbon report demonstrating that the company is carbon-efficient or is at least in the process of reducing its emissions. Based on this voluntary disclosure, companies expect to participate in green rents. As companies have an incentive to send environmentally friendly signals to the market, the most environmentally friendly companies disclose comparable information to permit investors to distinguish between environmentally friendly companies and less environmentally friendly companies (Akerlof, 1970).

To ensure that the signal is strong and robust, companies can strive for external, ideally reasonable, assurance from an audit company with a solid reputation, which ensures the trustworthiness of the audit statement. At a minimum, the signal itself should contain industry-specific KPIs based on an industry reporting standard aligned with the GHGP. The communication is ideally embedded within the financial reports. One reason why shareholders would be willing to grant green rents to environmentally friendly companies is the litigation-cost hypothesis. This applies if the carbon report includes information that reduces the risk of subsequent legal threat (Healy and Palepu, 2001).

Carbon disclosure model

As described, voluntary carbon disclosure can be explained by various theories and arguments under the stakeholder umbrella. The different options as to how companies report, and as to how stakeholders respond to companies' reporting, are shown in Figure 3.2.1. The different categories of no report/satisfying minimum expectation, the aim of copying the benchmark with limited effort or of striving for best-in-class reporting, could be explained by different theories, namely legitimacy theory and the aim to retain the licence to operate, the institutional isomorphism and the agency theory with the signal argument to earn green rents.

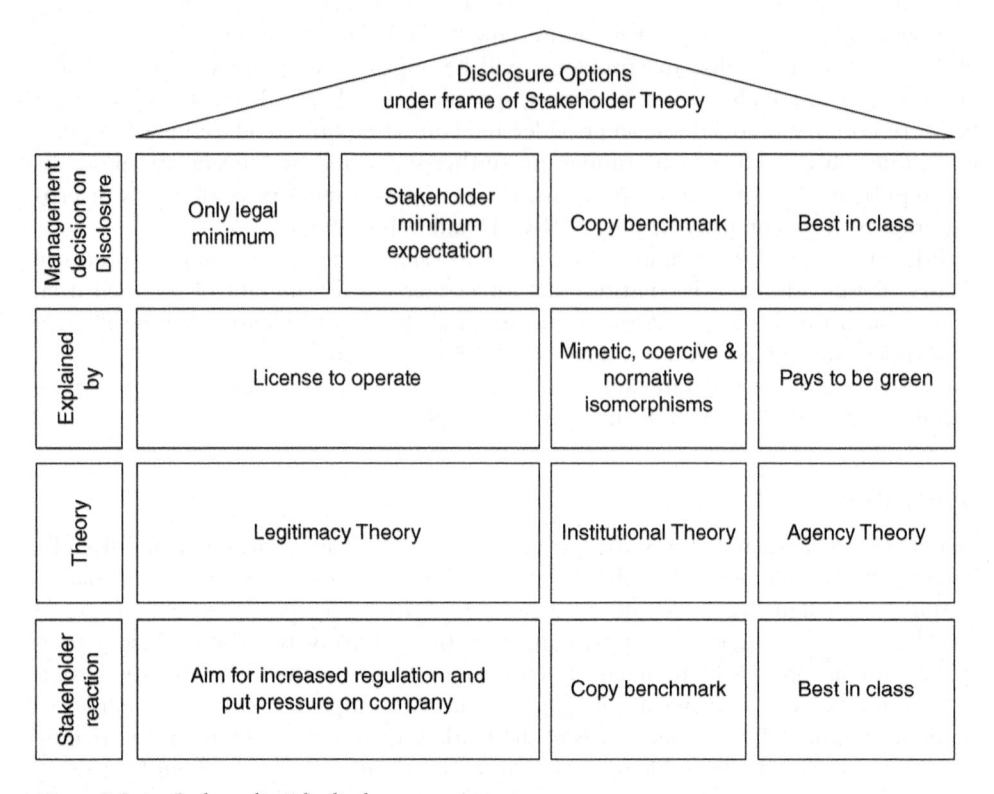

Figure 3.2.1   Carbon dioxide disclosure options

Even though this model is presented in a static way, the interactions between stakeholder, peer companies, and the reporting company over time has an impact on the disclosure patterns over time.

Complexity of carbon disclosure

Recording the full value chain

The GHGP defines three different scopes for reporting (Figure 3.2.2). It is important to understand that reporting covers not only the emissions caused by a company's activities (scope 1), but also emissions arising during the production of energy, especially electricity consumed (scope 2), and emissions from subcontracted goods and services (scope 3 upstream) or emissions caused during the lifecycle of product usage (scope 3 downstream) (WBCSD and WRI, 2004). This complete view is especially important, as otherwise outsourcing (insourcing vice versa) activities would have a significant impact on measured carbon performance without altering total emissions. The result of such an outsourcing strategy causes a shift in emissions from scope 1 to scope 3 upstream. A carbon report based on scope 1 emissions only is thus biased.

In contrast to financial reporting, which generally covers only the activities of the entities controlled by the reporting company, carbon reporting has a much broader scope. This has strong implications for the challenges around complete reporting and the availability of the required data. Accounting from upstream and downstream emissions can be compared with the complexity of accounting for warranties and off-balance-sheet financing options. Looking into the content of scope 3 emissions, we have to keep in mind that all emissions "from cradle to gate" (WBCSD and WRI, 2011) have to be reported. These emissions can be further classified into categories. The stakeholder requires knowledge about which categories are relevant for a certain industry to judge whether a carbon inventory is complete (WBCSD and WRI, 2004; WBCSD and WRI, 2011). Information which is not accessible from the reporting company needs to be estimated. As scope 3 emissions are usually higher than the scope 1 and 2 emissions, the underlying measurement error is significant (Downie and Stubbs, 2011; Downie and Stubbs, 2012).

The dynamic process involved in the production of carbon emissions makes measurements of these emissions a complex undertaking, and hence cost-intensive. Additionally, a completeness check of the kind is possible in accounting with regard to the connection of balance sheet and profit and loss is not possible, as the measuring process occurs dynamically (IAASB, 2011). Indirect calculations of emissions, for example, based on operational data, can be performed based on different assumptions and formulas, resulting in deviating numbers. Scope 3 emissions often need to be estimated with even less accurate calculation schemes for endless numbers of suppliers and customers affected by allocation keys and potential fraud (Andrew and Cortese, 2011; Milne and Grubnic, 2011; Lewis et al., 2014). All these issues very clearly document the complexity of compiling

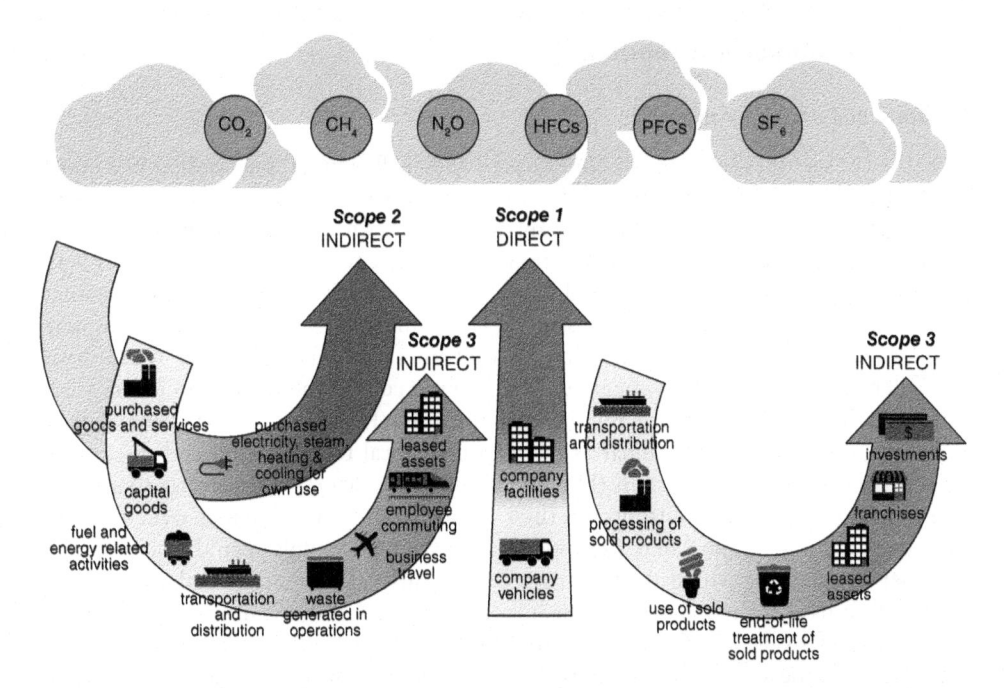

Figure 3.2.2 Overview of carbon dioxide emissions by scope (WBCSD and WRI, 2011)

data on own carbon emissions, as well as the emissions along the entire value chain and the need to disclose the underlying reporting error. Reporting an estimation error that does not plausibly account for the underlying reporting error can also be interpreted as a sign of "green-washing".

Standards and KPIs

As carbon reporting requires chemical, technical, and, to some extent, accounting skills, several standards and approaches have evolved from the various communities based on their respective priorities (Bowen and Wittneben, 2011; Ascui, 2014). These standards face the needs from companies based in all countries of the world across all industries and all local regulations (Goldsmith and Basak, 2001; Hartmann et al., 2013). Therefore, overarching standards (e.g., GHGP) call for detailed industry standards that should also be specified to respective industry-specific regulations. As these standards vary, the CDP reviews reporting and audit standards with regard to the extent to which they can be seen as acceptable for carbon disclosure (CDP, 2016a; CDP, 2016b). As carbon disclosure is an evolving field of reporting, many industries lack specifications (Greene and Lewis, 2016).

Comparing companies over time or with peers calls for intensity-based KPIs. So in addition to the complexity of creating a comparable carbon inventory, one must find a common denominator that reflects the output of a company, ideally also defined within an industry sector (Eccles and Serafeim, 2012). The judgement of companies' carbon performance and target-setting should follow a science-based target approach; this can be also applied in various ways (based targets, 2016).

Limitations on carbon reporting

Disclosure and assurance practice

While the last section showed how complicated and challenging the recording of a complete and reliable carbon inventory for companies is, this section describes the current reporting practice and its shortcomings relative to the effort to communicate reliable carbon-inventory figures. The issues within the current reporting practise start with very basic items. Even for own scope 1 and 2 emissions, a significant number of companies (15 per cent in a 2005–2009 sample size of 431 companies) fail to report a complete inventory (Liesen et al., 2014). Identifying companies with an incomplete footprint is still challenging, however, as companies often (19 per cent of the FTSE 350 in the years 2010–2013) fail to disclose their reporting boundaries (Kasim et al., 2016). As already companies' own reporting boundaries seem to be critical to evaluation and disclosure, scope 3 is reported even less often (Downie and Stubbs, 2011). This implies that companies could benefit from outsourcing their resource-intensive activities over time, as this reduces absolute scope 1 and 2 emissions. An extreme example would be companies like Uber or AirBnB, which do not own/control any transportation/real estate assets and therefore have no scope 1 or 2 emissions except the emissions from administration (San-salvador-del valle and Gomez-Bezares, 2016).

In line with the overall poor reporting practice is the voluntary usage of assurance services, which usually cover only scopes 1 and 2, and which is mostly done on a limited assurance level only (Busch and Hoffmann, 2011; Kennedy et al., 2015). This implies that the auditor is not required to evaluate or monitor the control systems nor the sampling and estimation methods (IAASB, 2011). Plausibility checks from stakeholders are made difficult as companies often fail to report the previous-year, like-for-like comparison and choose reporting years/periods other than the financial year. Comparability is also limited in terms of relevant KPIs. Most companies report only their scope 1 and 2 emissions compared to revenue or total number of employees instead of showing KPIs which are relevant in their industry. Both KPIs have limited ability to enable steering. This is especially interesting as the majority of companies identify carbon emissions as one of the core risks, but only a minority of companies use carbon inventory as a steering KPI or include carbon emissions in their risk reporting (Kasim et al., 2016).

To date, companies' KPIs and targets are usually not aligned with the two-degree target. For example, there is no company in the automotive industry that has incorporated the two-degree scenario in its reported strategy (Nicholls et al., 2015; Baker, 2016). Unfortunately, stakeholder pressure seems not to be strong enough to force companies to disclose better information over time. An analysis between 1998 and 2010 showed that, for example, the oil industry did not improve its reporting practises (Chi et al., 2013). From a communication point of view, companies are far away from a true and fair view. Apart from the issues around real fraud, companies do not focus their disclosure on materiality but communicate unbalanced information with biased wording (Gray, 2006; Arena et al., 2014; Comyns et al., 2013; Comyns and Figge, 2015).

Research on disclosure practice

Literature reviews about carbon accounting from Hahn (Hahn et al., 2015) and Stechemesser (Stechemesser and Guenther, 2012) document that the current research focusses on the question of whether environmental actions pays off. Conceptually, the arguments for the pays-to-be-green literature are cost and risk reduction from reduced resource usage and benefits from brand and reputation gains (Porter et al., 1995) and against the Friedman (Friedman, 1962, 1970) quote that "Business of Business is Business", and therefore should focus only on maximizing profits instead of transferring environmental costs to the firm. This source actually advocates greenwashing communication if it is perceived as beneficial. After reviewing the complexity of carbon disclosure and the respective reporting practice, it is not unexpected that the currently dominant quantitative reporting practice comes to mixed results in meta-studies – especially as these quantitative studies are always criticized for using poor measures, lacking theoretical foundation, and failing to use relevant moderator variables (Albertini, 2013; Dixon-Fowler et al., 2013; Endrikat et al., 2014). Looking in greater detail into the measures used to operationalize green performance, such as the amount of disclosure or the indices measured by the amount of disclosure, it is obvious that the results of these studies cannot be interpreted in the way in which they aim to be interpreted. As the amount of disclosure is mainly dependent on stakeholder salience (Guenther et al., 2015), the amount of disclosure bears no correlation to underlying green performance (Chi et al., 2013; Doda et al., 2015; Kennedy et al., 2015; Krause and June, 2015), and sometimes even correlates negatively, which is especially interesting as some environmental leadership indices are mainly ratings based on the amount of disclosure (Patten, 2002; Cho and Patten, 2007; Cho et al., 2012). The next section summarizes this chapter and gives recommendations for future research and practitioners.

Summary and recommendations

This review has shown that legitimacy, institutional, and agency theory are helpful to explain the existence of different voluntary carbon-reporting strategies. However, only agency and, to some extent, institutional theory intend to convince stakeholders to perceive the company in a manner that is as environmentally friendly as possible. To provide a carbon inventory, a sound understanding of various disciplines is required. This results from complexity in reporting along the entire value chain and the dynamic nature of the creation of carbon emissions. External analysts thus need detailed information to make judgements about the environmental impact of the reporting company and respective trends.

The current reporting practice fails to provide sufficient information to judge the carbon efficiency of companies. The problem of insufficient data, however, is typically ignored by the dominant research stream in the field comparing financial and carbon performance. This absence of critical feedback permits companies to claim green performance without the need to provide evidence. Therefore, we recommend focusing more research on ways of identifying reports that aiming to achieve comparability and enable quantitative-focused researchers and investors to identify high-quality reports. In addition, researchers should focus on exploring how currently available information can be used to judge how companies perform compared to scientific targets.

References

Akerlof, G. A. (1970). The market for "lemons": quality uncertainty and the market mechanism. *The Quarterly Journal of Economics*, 84(3): 488–500.

Albertini, E. (2013). Does environmental management improve financial performance? A meta-analytical review. *Organization and Environment*, 26(4): 431–457.

Alejandra Gonzalez-Perez, M. (2013). *International Business, Sustainability and Corporate Social Responsibility*. Bingley, Yorkshire: Emerald Group Publishing.

Andrew, J., and Cortese, C. (2011). Carbon disclosures: comparability, the carbon disclosure project and the Greenhouse Gas Protocol. *Australian Accounting, Business and Finance Journal*, 5(4): 6–18.

Andrew, J., and Cortese, C. (2013). Free market environmentalism and the neoliberal project: the case of the Climate Disclosure Standards Board. *Critical Perspectives on Accounting*, 24(6): 397–409.

Arena, C., Bozzolan, S., and Michelon, G. (2014). Environmental reporting: transparency to stakeholders or stakeholder manipulation? An analysis of disclosure tone and the role of the Board of Directors. *Corporate Social Responsibility and Environmental Management*, 361(May), n.p.

Ascui, F. (2014). A review of carbon accounting in the social and environmental accounting literature: what can it contribute to the debate? *Social and Environmental Accountability Journal*, 34(1): 6–28.

Baker, C. (2016). Emission impossible? – Which car makers are driving into trouble?, CDP. www.cdsb.net/FTSE350

Blacconiere, W. G., and Patten, D. M. (1994). Environmental disclosures, regulatory costs, and changes in firm value. *Journal of Accounting and Economics*, 18(3): 357–377.

Bowen, F., and Wittneben, B. (2011). Carbon accounting: negotiating accuracy, consistency and certainty across organisational field. *Accounting, Auditing and Accountability Journal*, 24(8): 1022–1036.

Busch, T., and Hoffmann, V. H. (2011). How hot is your bottom line? Linking carbon and financial performance. *Business and Society*, 50(2): 233–265.

Carroll, A. B. (1999). Corporate Social Responsibility. *Business and Society*, 38(3): 268–295.

Cavana, R. Y., and Becker, C. S. (2016). An exploratory analysis of legitimation strategies used in sustainability reporting of negative incidents. In EURAM Conference Proceeding 2016.

CDP (2015). CDP policy briefing: business and the Paris agreement. Technical report.

CDP (2016a). Guidance for companies reporting on climate change on behalf of investors and supply chain members 2016.

CDP (2016b). What third-party verification standards are appropriate when reporting to CDP's climate change program?

CDP, Bureau Veritas, LRQA Lloyd's Register Quality Assurance, PwC, and TÜ V Nord (2011). Carbon Disclosure Project verification of climate data. Technical report.

Chi, W., Dhaliwal, D., Li, O. Z., and Lin, T.-H. (2013). Voluntary reporting incentives and reporting quality: evidence from a reporting regime change for private firms in Taiwan. *Contemporary Accounting Research*, 30(4): 1462–1489.

Cho, C. H., Guidry, R. P., Hageman, A. M., and Patten, D. M. (2012). Do actions speak louder than words? An empirical investigation of corporate environmental reputation. *Accounting, Organizations and Society*, 37(1): 14–25.

Cho, C. H., and Patten, D. M. (2007). The role of environmental disclosures as tools of legitimacy: a research note. *Accounting, Organizations and Society*, 32(7–8): 639–647.

Cho, C. H., and Roberts, R. W. (2010). International Journal of Accounting Information Systems Environmental reporting on the internet by America's Toxic 100: Legitimacy and self- presentation. *International Journal of Accounting Information Systems*, 11(1): 1–16.

Comyns, B., and Figge, F. (2015). Greenhouse gas reporting quality in the oil and gas industry. *Accounting, Auditing and Accountability Journal*, 28(3): 403–433.

Comyns, B., Figge, F., Hahn, T., and Barkemeyer, R. (2013). Sustainability reporting: the role of 'Search', 'Experience' and 'Credence' information. *Accounting Forum*, 37(3): 231–243.

Cotter, J., and Najah, M. M. (2012). Institutional investor influence on global climate change disclosure practices. *Australian Journal of Management*, 37(2): 169–187.

Deegan, C. (2002). Introduction: the legitimising effect of social and environmental disclosures – a theoretical foundation. *Accounting, Auditing and Accountability Journal*. https://doi.org/10.1108/09513570210435852

Deegan, C., and Rankin, M. (1997). The materiality of environmental information to users of annual reports. *Accounting, Auditing and Accountability Journal*, 10(4): 562–583.

DiMaggio, P. J., and Powell, W. W. (1983). The Iron Cage revisited: institutional isomorphism and collective rationality in organizational fields. *American Sociological Review*, 48(2): 147–159.

Dixon-Fowler, H. R., Slater, D. J., Johnson, J. L., Ellstrand, A. E., and Romi, A. M. (2013). Beyond "Does it pay to be green?": a meta-analysis of moderators of the CEP–CFP relationship. *Journal of Business Ethics*. https://doi.org/10.1007/s10551-012-1268-8

Doda, B., Gennaioli, C., Gouldson, A., Grover, D., and Sullivan, R. (2015). Are corporate carbon management practices reducing corporate carbon emissions? *Corporate Social Responsibility and Environmental Management* (September): n.p.

Downie, J., and Stubbs, W. (2011). Evaluation of Australian companies' scope 3 greenhouse gas emissions assessments. *Journal of Cleaner Production*: 1–8.

Downie, J. and Stubbs, W. (2012). Corporate carbon strategies and greenhouse gas emission assessments: the implications of scope 3 emission factor selection. *Business Strategy and the Environment*, 21(6): 412–422.

Eccles, R. G., and Serafeim, G. (2012). The impact of corporate sustainability on organizational processes and and performance. National Bureau of Economic Research, Cambridge. Retrieved from http://www.nber.org/papers/w17950

ECOpoint Inc. (2015). Emission Standards: United States.

Endrikat, J., Guenther, E., and Hoppe, H. (2014). Making sense of conflicting empirical findings: a meta-analytic review of the relationship between corporate environmental and financial performance. *European Management Journal*, 32(5): 735–751.

Freeman, R. E. (1984). *Strategic Management: A Stakeholder Approach*, volume 1. Cambridge: Cambridge University Press.

Freeman, R. E., and Liedtka, J. (1991). Corporate social responsibility: a critical approach. *Business Horizons*, (July–August): 92–98.

Friedman, M. (1962). Capitalism and freedom: the relation between economic freedom and political freedom. In *Capitalism and Freedom*, 7–17.

Friedman, M. (1970). The social responsibility of business is to increase its profits. *The New York Times Magazine* (32), 13 September.

Goldsmith, P. D., and Basak, R. (2001). Incentive contracts and environmental performance indicators. *Environmental and Resource Economics* (Parkinson 1996): 259–279.

Gond, J.-P., and Moon, J. (2011). Corporate social responsibility in retrospect and prospect: exploring the life-cycle of an essentially contested concept. *ICCSR Research Paper Series*, 59: 1–40.

Gray, R. (2006). Does sustainability reporting improve corporate behaviour? Wrong question? Right time? *Accounting and Business Research*, 36 (suppl. 1): 65–88.

Gray, R., Kouhy, R., and Lavers, S. (1995). Corporate social and environmental reporting. *Accounting, Auditing and Accountability Journal*, 8(2): 47–77.

Greene, S., and Lewis, A. (2016). GLEC Framework for Logistics Emissions Methodologies.

GRI (2013). *G4 Sustainability Reporting Guidelines*. Global Reporting Initiatives, Amsterdam, version 3 Edition.

GRI, CDP, Basacik, L., Kutner, M., Buck, B., Dreyfus, R., Espinach, L., Hagen, S., and Kriege, K. (2015). Linking GRI and CDP: Water. Technical report, Global Reporting Initiative.

Guenther, E., Guenther, T., Schiemann, F., and Weber, G. (2015). Stakeholder relevance for reporting: explanatory factors of carbon disclosure. *Business and Society*: 1–37.

Hahn, R., Reimsbach, D., and Schiemann, F. (2015). Organizations, climate change, and transparency: reviewing the literature on carbon disclosure. *Organization and Environment*, 28(1): 80–102.

Hart, S. L., and Milstein, M. B. (2003). Creating sustainable value. *Academy of Management Executive*, 17(2): 56–67.

Hartmann, F., Perego, P., and Young, A. (2013). Carbon accounting: challenges for research in management control and performance measurement. *Abacus*, 49(4): 539–563.

Healy, P. M., and Palepu, K. G. (2001). Information asymmetry, corporate disclosure, and the capital markets: a review of the empirical disclosure literature. *Journal of Accounting and Economics*, 31(1–3): 405–440.

IAASB (2011). *ISAE 3000 – Assurance Engagements Other Than Audits or Reviews of Historical Financial Information*. Retrieved from https://www.ifac.org/system/files/.../IAASB_ISAE_3000_ED.pdf

IPCC (2014). Summary for policymakers provisionally approved. *Technical report*. October, IPCC.

Jira, C. F., and Toffel, M. W. (2013). Engaging supply chains in climate change. *Manufacturing and Service Operations Management*, 15(4): 559–577.

Kasim, T., Baker, R., Cooke, D., and Molloy, J. (2016). Comply or explain: a review of FTSE 350 companies' environmental reporting and greenhouse gas emission disclosures in annual reports. Technical report, December, CDSB.

Kennedy, K., Obeiter, M., and Kaufman, N. (2015). Putting a price on carbon: a handbook for U.S. *policymakers*. Retrieved from www.wri.org/sites/default/files/carbonpricing_april_2015.pdf

Kolk, A., Levy, D., and Pinkse, J. (2008). Corporate responses in an emerging climate regime: the institutionalization and commensuration of carbon disclosure. *European Accounting Review*, 17(4): 719–745.

Krause, E., and June, M. O. (2015). Carbon pricing gains popularity with governments, businesses. Retrieved 23 November 2015, from http://www.wri.org/print/43020

Kyoto-Protokoll, UN Secretary-General (1997). 1997 Kyoto Protocol to the UN Framework Convention on Climate Change (UNFCCC), 2303 UNTS 148.

Lewis, A., Ehrler, V., Auvinen, H., Maurer, H., Davydenko, I., Burmeister, A., Seidel, S., Lischke, A., and Kiel, J. (2014). Harmonising carbon footprint calculation for freight transport chains. In *Transport Research Arena*, 10, Paris. Retrieved from http://tra2014.traconference.eu/papers/pdfs/TRA2014_Fpaper_17406.pdf

Liesen, A., Hoepner, A. G. F., Patten, D. M., and Figge, F. (2014). Corporate disclosure of greenhouse gas emissions in the context of stakeholder pressures: an empirical analysis of reporting activity and completeness. *Accounting, Auditing and Accountability Journal*. SSRN Electronic Journal. 10.2139/ssrn.2307876.

Maines, L. A., Bartov, E., Mallett, R., Schrand, C. M., Skinner, D. J., and Vincent, L. (2002). Recommendations on disclosure of nonfinancial performance measures. *American Accounting Association*, 16(4): 353–362.

Milne, M. J., and Grubnic, S. (2011). Climate change accounting research: keeping it interesting and different. *Accounting, Auditing and Accountability Journal*, 24(8): 948–977.

Milne, M. J., and Patten, D. M. (2002). Securing organizational legitimacy. *Accounting, Auditing and Accountability Journal*, 15(3): 372–405.

Nicholls, M., Faria, P., Labutong, N., Wasmuth, K., Pineda, A. C., Delgado, P., Tornay, C., Huusko, H., Aden, N., and Russel, S. (2015). *Mind the Science, Mind the Gap*. Technical report, May. We Mean Business coalition, Paris.

Parmar, B. L., Freeman, R. E., Harrison, J. S., Wicks, A. C., and Colle, S. (2010). Stakeholder theory: the state of the art. *The Academy of Management Annals*, 4(1): 403–445.

Patten, D. M. (1991). Exposure, legitimacy, and social disclosure. *Journal of Accounting and Public Policy*, 10(4): 297–308.

Patten, D. M. (1992). Intra-industry environmental disclosures in response to the Alaskan oil spill: a note on legitimacy theory. *Accounting, Organizations and Society*, 17(5): 471–475.

Patten, D. M. (2002). The relation between environmental performance and environmental disclosure: a research note. *Accounting, Organizations and Society*, 27: 763–773.

Porter, M. E., Linde, C. V. D., and Porter, M. E. (1995). Green and competitive: ending the stalemate. *Harvard Business Review*, 28(6): 119–134.

Ramanathan, K. V. (1976). Toward a theory of corporate social accounting. *Accounting Review*, 51(3): 516–528.

San-salvador-del valle, C., and Gomez-Bezares, F. (2016). 1542 – Distribution of the value generated by the economic activity of an organization: model and application to the companies in the IBEX 35. In *EURAM*, volume 53: 1689–1699.

Shocker, A. D., and Sethi, S. P. (1973). An approach to incorporating societal preferences in developing corporate action strategies. *California Management Review*, 15(4): 97–105.

Souza, J. D. D., Baginski, S., Beneish, D., Biddle, G., Elliott, J., Hopkins, P., Johnson, M., Maines, L., Connor, K. O., Pae, S., Pratt, J., Salamon, J., Shevlin, T., Skinner, D., Smith, A., Sprinkle, G., Stanford, M., Swieringa, B., Tasker, S., and Wahlen, J. (2004). Voluntary disclosure in a multi-audience setting: an empirical investigation. *American Accounting Association*, 79(4): 921–947.

Stanny, E. (2013). Voluntary disclosures of emissions by US firms. *Business Strategy and the Environment*, 22(3): 145–158.

Stechemesser, K., and Guenther, E. (2012). Carbon accounting: a systematic literature review. *Journal of Cleaner Production*, 36: 17–38.

Stubbs, W., and Higgins, C. (2014). Integrated reporting and internal mechanisms of change. *Accounting, Auditing and Accountability Journal*, 27(7): 1068–1089.

Suchman, M. C. (1995). Managing legitimacy: strategy and approaches. *Academy of Management Review*, 20(3): 571–610. Retrieved from http://citeseerx.ist.psu.edu/viewdoc/download?doi=10.1.1.108.2768&rep=rep1&type=pdf

United Nations (2015). Adoption of the Paris Agreement. *Technical report*, December, United Nations, Paris.

Wackernagel, M., and Rees, W. E. (1997). Perceptual and structural barriers to investing in natural capital: economics from an ecological footprint perspective. *Ecological Economics*, 20(1): 3–24.

WBCSD and WRI (2004). *The Greenhouse Gas Protocol: A Corporate Accounting and Reporting Standard*. Technical report, World Business Council for Sustainable Development; World Resource Institute, Conches–Geneva.

WBCSD and WRI (2010). *GHG Protocol Corporate Value Chain (Scope 3) and Product Life Cycle Standards*. Technical report, Scope 3.

WBCSD and WRI (2011). *Corporate Value Chain (Scope 3) Accounting and Reporting Standard*. Technical report, Washington.

Williams, O. F. (2013). *Corporate Social Responsibility: The Role of Business in Sustainable Development*. London: Routledge.

Windolph, S. E. (2013). Motivations, organizational units, and management tools. *Taking Stock of the Why, Who, and How of Implementing Corporate Sustainability Management* (August): 157.

Yunus, S., Elijido-Ten, E., and Abhayawansa, S. (2016). Determinants of carbon management strategy adoption: evidence from Australia's top 200 publicly listed firms. *Managerial Auditing Journal*, 31(2): 156–179.

3.3 Social entrepreneurship and social impact assessment

The case of euforia

Florian Hoos

Introduction

The ultimate goal of social entrepreneurial activities is to develop a positive social impact on society. As a result, measuring and reporting to what extent social impact has been created through a social entrepreneurial activity and reporting it to stakeholders is becoming increasingly important (Miller & Wesley, 2010; Kroeger & Weber, 2014; Nicholls, 2009, 2010). At the same time, there are no generally accepted principles to develop a social impact measurement system, and there are no compulsory reporting standards. The current context makes it impossible to apply a one solution fits it all to design social impact measurement systems. In addition, the variety of different social missions that social entrepreneurs follow, such as fighting poverty, improving health conditions, fighting climate change, and so on, might also generally require different measurement designs and indicators that are reported to stakeholders (i.e., depending on the type of the social entrepreneurial mission). Therefore, social entrepreneurs have to individually decide how they want to measure and report their social mission achievement (e.g., Austin et al., 2006; Dacin et al., 2010; Nicholls, 2009) and how many resources they want to invest into this activity. To contribute to the emerging field of social impact assessment, I provide a case of the social enterprise euforia. The organization implemented its own social impact measurement system with the help of two researchers during a three-year project. The case illustrates advantages and drawbacks of different designs for internal and external use, and illustrates conclusions from the three-year project.

Background: social impact assessment

One of the fundamental differences between social entrepreneurship and traditional entrepreneurship is that social entrepreneurs primarily pursue a social mission instead of profit-maximization goals (e.g., Dacin et al., 2011; Mair, Battilana, & Cardenas, 2012; Peredo & McLean, 2006). As a result, social entrepreneurs do *not* solely focus on traditional financial reporting tools such as international financial reporting standards (e.g., Achleitner, Lutz, Mayer, & Spiess-Knafl, 2013; Kroeger & Weber, 2014). Instead, social entrepreneurs focus on reporting that they successfully achieve their social mission based on new reporting systems called social impact measurement systems.

Due to this trend, several institutions provide, or are about to develop, social reporting standards that should guide the development of social impact measurement systems. However, none of these initiatives has achieved to develop generally accepted principles for social impact measurement as they exist in the domain of financial reporting (i.e., IFRS, US-GAAP, etc.). In other words, social impact measurement is not mandatory for social entrepreneurs, and it therefore remains a voluntary effort to prove social mission achievement based on an organization's individually designed impact measurement system.

The lack of standardization for social impact measurement results in a myriad of different tools, metrics, and approaches that are used to measure social impact (see, e.g., Foundation Center 2016 for an extensive list). These approaches range from simple and tailor-made qualitative interviews and survey studies, which do not require respecting any scientific standards, to very sophisticated field experimental approaches (Kroeger & Weber, 2014). Since the latter approaches are extremely resource-intensive, and require sophisticated knowledge of experimental designs and econometrics, many social entrepreneurs lean towards presenting their impact based on anecdotes and expected outcomes, without rigorously measuring their impact.

Recently, however, social entrepreneurs started facing a situation where foundations, philanthropists, and social impact investors increasingly couple their willingness to fund social entrepreneurial activities with the requirement to implement a social impact measurement system (Lehner, 2013; Kroeger & Weber, 2014). The case of euforia shows how the trade-off between a foundation's requirements to measure social impact, the organization's willingness to use a sophisticated impact measurement system, and the need for a simple and implementable tool was managed during a three-year project.

The case of euforia

On 5 May 2007, Jerónimo Calderon, together with two co-founders, signed the charter to found euforia as a Geneva-based non-partisan, non-profit education organization under Article 60 in the Swiss Civil Code. Article 3.1 of euforia's charter defines its vision as follows: "euforia envisions developing a society where every young person realizes the importance of global challenges and possesses the necessary means and motivation to be a local change agent". In Article 3.2, euforia's stated mission is

> to mobilize youth potential by creating innovative and participatory events. euforia's approach is defined by a willingness to make youth more active in sustainable development by offering them concrete opportunities to become engaged, or immediate support for their own projects.

Since its founding in 2007, euforia – a Swiss social initiative "by youth, for youth" – and hundreds of volunteers have administered dozens of events and other activities that have offered concrete opportunities for over 3,500 youth to make a social impact. euforia and its co-founders have been recognized for catalysing social change both within Switzerland and internationally. As an organization, euforia earned a UNESCO project distinction as part of the United Nations Decade of Education for Sustainable Development, while Jerónimo was named an Ashoka Fellow and World Economic Forum Global Shaper, speaking at the Annual Forum in Davos in 2012. Furthermore, as it has grown, euforia has attracted support from a range of national and international partners, including non-governmental organizations (NGOs), Swiss and international foundations, and major Swiss corporations.

Table 3.3.1 Schedule for imp!act 2013 in Geneva (Switzerland)

Day 1:

The programme begins in the evening with a public conference at the University of Geneva, introducing the concept of social entrepreneurship as a tool for sustainable development and offering a unique opportunity for participants to meet young people who are involved in this area. Next, a "World Café" event is organized for participants to identify social and ecological ideas and projects of interest to them.

Day 2:

The second day focuses on the youth participants and their ambitions. Their ideas are matched with social entrepreneurs' existing and inspiring projects, then we give them their first project management tools and begin a giant brainstorming session, the first step in planning the concrete project. The day closes with a presentation of the projects ("Pitch Festival") and forming teams around the winning ideas.

Day 3:

The third day is dedicated to transitioning to action. Participants have the opportunity to test and try out their project plans. For example, they must go out and test their ideas and dreams in a real context.

Day 4:

On the fourth day, youth participants consolidate their projects with support and advice from experts specialized in project management, social entrepreneurship, sustainable development, fundraising, communications or other key areas. In 2012, experts such as Mr. Acher, founder of "Association Cinetransat", and Mr. Claudio Deuel, "Delegate for Youth in the City of Geneva", also shared their knowledge and know-how at imp!act. After meeting the experts, the participants present their finalized projects to a panel of judges who evaluate their pertinence and chance for long-term success. The day ends with a party.

Day 5:

The fifth day is dedicated to evaluating the event and offering feedback, but also to the next steps through which the different projects will progress, on both a personal and a team level. The objective is to craft action plans to maintain the same energy and pace of development for the projects.

Despite this tremendous success, euforia only had a rudimentary social impact measurement system in 2013. As many other social enterprises, they simply asked participants of their events in post-event surveys a few open questions during phone interviews or based on paper-pencil questionnaires, and used quotes to prove their social impact. Only in late 2013, when euforia received funding from a Swiss foundation that included a budget to develop a social impact measurement system, the organization started to develop their own sophisticated social impact measurement system.

The main target for the impact assessment was euforia's flagship training programme called imp!act – a five-day programme to motivate youth to make a social impact through their own activities. During imp!act, euforia trains youth aged 18 to 28 years and connects them to specific opportunities for social engagement. From a Swiss training programme, it has since grown to accommodate youth from other countries including Italy, France, Spain, Germany, Portugal, Austria, England, Russia, Colombia, Argentina, Mexico, Brazil, Greece, and Turkey, with up to 50 youth attending a given event. imp!act prepares youth for social engagement either as changemakers seeking to make more sustainable day-to-day choices, as volunteers within established organizations, or as co-founders of new social initiatives. By calling upon youth participants to develop their own social projects in groups, imp!act events are based on experiential learning. As such, imp!act relies on its own staff and volunteers, as well as on experienced mentors from partner non-governmental and community organizations, to lead training sessions and provide coaching for participants.

Designing a social impact measurement system for euforia

The development of a social impact measurement system for euforia started when euforia received funding from a Swiss foundation for its flagship programme called imp!act, and two other related programmes. At this time, the aim was to develop a social impact measurement system that could be used to prove euforia's impact externally to their stakeholders.

The process of developing euforia's social impact measurement system started with structuring the potential impacts that euforia could have. This was done based on several workshops with members from the organization, moderated by two researchers (including the author). The major objective of these workshops was to develop a stakeholder map, which made it necessary to list all stakeholders who are potentially influenced by euforia's activities. The vast list of stakeholders, which included the Cantons of Geneva, Vaud, and Zurich (i.e., the Swiss states in which euforia operated at the time), politicians, donors, euforia staff, imp!act participants, the general public, etc., was then reduced by the researchers, based on the decision by euforia to focus on imp!act participants for their social impact measurement system. In a second step, euforia together with the researchers defined the different impact dimensions that would be the result of participating in the imp!act event. After multiple iterations, today, euforia measures its impact on participants of the imp!act events based on four dimensions which ultimately form a pyramid, namely *outreach, empowerment, changemaking,* and *multiplying* (see Figure 3.3.1). It was very important for euforia to develop their own visualization of their impact measurement system. Therefore, the researchers made multiple propositions in different workshops, which were then internally reworked, until euforia members and the researchers were satisfied with the results.

At this point, euforia and the researchers decided to include dimensions that contained both output and outcome measures. Outputs are direct results of euforia's activities, while outcomes are indirect, and more long-term results of euforia's activities. *Outreach* (i.e., the first dimension in the pyramid), for instance, is measured based on the number of people who participate in an imp!act event, and is therefore an output measure. In other words, it is an automatic and direct result of an imp!act event. The definition of *outreach*, for instance, is based on euforia's mission to be a visible actor for a better society which reaches out to people, connects them, involves them, and shows them ways to contribute to a better society.

Despite many organizations that stop here with their impact measurement system and thereby focus on output measures only, and despite many donors (foundations, European funds, philanthropists, etc.) who just ask social entrepreneurs to measure the output of their activities (e.g., the number of participants who attended a training programme, training hours delivered, and other output-based measures), euforia decided to go beyond the output level and defined three further (outcome) dimensions.

Those additional three dimensions of the pyramid – *empowerment, changemaking, multiplying* – measure outcomes (not outputs). They are indirect (or postponed) results of the imp!act event which is the characteristic of an outcome measure. Consider the example of a social entrepreneur who distributes mosquito nets to fight malaria. One potential direct output measure is the number of mosquito nets distributed. However, the number of mosquito nets distributed, does not measure to what extent malaria infections were reduced thanks to the social entrepreneur's activities – this would be the intended outcome. In the worst case, people who received mosquito nets will use them to go fishing,

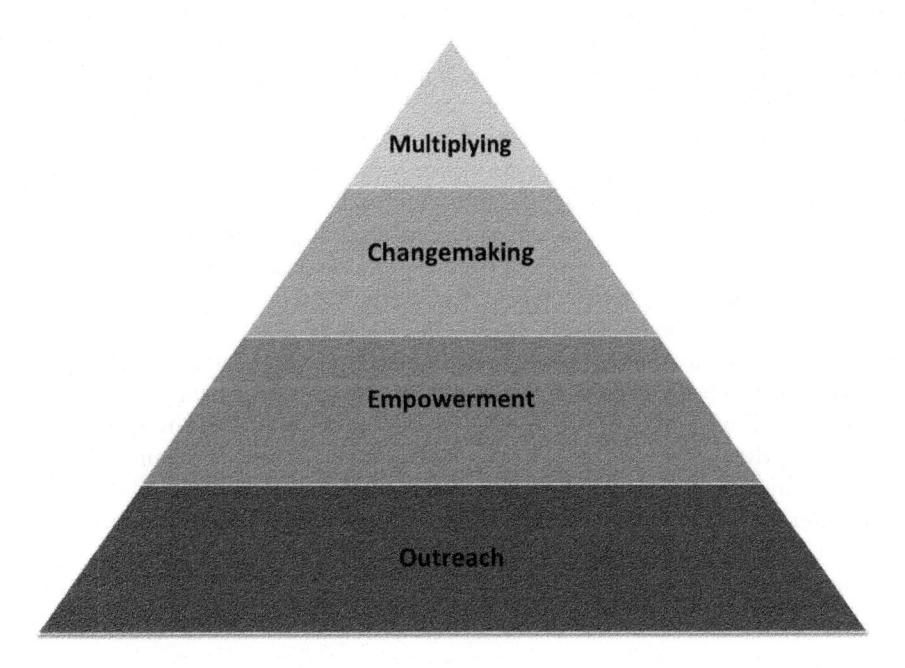

Figure 3.3.1 The impact dimensions of euforia

instead of sleeping under them to be protected from mosquitos. In that case, there is still a measurable output – the number of nets distributed – while the outcome (a reduction of malaria infections) is non-existent. This is why euforia wanted to focus on the outcome – instead of the output – in their pyramid, and defined the following three additional levels: *empowerment, changemaking, multiplying*.

The pyramid dimension *empowerment* describes that euforia aims at creating the belief in people that they can positively change society. Here, euforia aims at equipping participants with the necessary skills to become contributors to a better society. The point of *changemaking* is to identify those empowered participants who are capable of changing habits and lifestyles for the positive after the imp!act event, thereby showing concrete action. The final aspect of the pyramid measurement model is *multiplying*. euforia defines multiplayers as those participants whose actions after the imp!act event have motivated others to make a positive impact or change. The three dimensions describe outcomes that euforia aims to have with its activities.

After the definition and visualization of euforia's impact dimensions, workshops continued to define euforia's measurement system design. Many social entrepreneurs focus on post-tests only. In other words, they measure the impact of their activities only after, for instance, a training event. Two potential issues arise from this measurement design. First, it is impossible to judge the development of any measured key performance indicator thanks to the social entrepreneur's activities. If, for instance, IQ is only measured after an intelligence training, and the achieved value is 130, then this does not inform us whether a person improved his/her IQ thanks to the training programme or not. It simply tells us that the person has a high IQ. Therefore, euforia decided to measure outcomes based on the comparison of the same measures before and after the imp!act event based on a pre-test, post-test design. The pre-test questionnaire would be distributed before the participants took part in the imp!act event. The post-test questionnaire would be distributed to the participants, usually three months after the imp!act event. The pre- and post-test questionnaires contain items from the scientific literature or self-developed scales to measure key performance indicators representing dimensions on which euforia tries to have an impact through their imp!act event.

Table 3.3.2 shows the KPIs (e.g., teamwork leadership skills), the pyramid dimension to which KPIs belong (e.g., empowerment), the type of scale (e.g., a seven-point Likert scale from "totally disagree" to "totally agree"), the (scientific) reference, and the time of measurement (e.g., pre-test and post-test, or one time measurement only).

For instance, the pyramid dimension *empowerment* involves creating the belief in people that they can positively change society and to equip them with the right skills. It is measured based on the following five KPIs: "Team work leadership skills", "Transformational leadership style", "Motivation to lead", "Changemaker skills", "Bravery/Courage", and "Entrepreneurial intention". They are almost all measured based on items taken from the scientific literature. For instance, the KPI "Team work leadership skills" is measured based on established items first proposed by Podsakoff et al. (1990): "I have a clear understanding of where we are going when I work in a team", "I am able to get a team

Table 3.3.2 Questionnaire for euforia

KPI (Dimension)	Number of items in questionnaire	Type of scale	(Scientific) Source	Measurement
General satisfaction	6	Likert-scale	Self-developed	Post-test
Team work leadership skills *(Empowerment)*	3	Likert-scale	Adapted from Podsakoff et al. (1990)	Pre- and post-test
Transformational leadership style *(Empowerment)*	3	Likert-scale	Adapted from Podsakoff et al. (1990)	Pre- and post-test
Motivation to lead *(Empowerment)*	3	Likert-scale	Adapted from Chan and Drasgow (2001)	Pre- and post-test
Changemaker skills *(Empowerment)*	4	Likert-scale	Self-developed	Pre- and post-test
Bravery / Courage *(Empowerment)*	4	Likert-scale	IPIP scales	Pre- and post-test
Entrepreneurial intention *(Empowerment)*	1	Likert-scale	Oosterbeek et al. (2010)	Pre- and post-test
Sustainable lifestyle *(Changemaking)*	5	Likert-scale	Astebro & Hoos (2016)	Pre- and post-test
Social entrepreneurial skills *(Changemaking)*	7	Yes/No	Astebro & Hoos (2016)	Pre- and post-test
Responsible action in own life *(Changemaking)*	1	Open question	Self-developed	Pre- and post-test
Responsible action to influence others *(Multiplying)*	1	Open question	Self-developed	Pre- and post-test

committed to my dream", and "I am always seeking new opportunities when I work in a team". Those items are measured based on a seven-point Likert scale and the average score over the three items forms a pre-test score, and – after the imp!act event – a post-test score. Comparing the two scores shows the development in the KPI "Team work leadership skills". Based on this pre-test pot-test design, euforia measures the impact of each imp!act event in a standardized manner. Besides the KPIs that are measured pre- and post- the imp!act event, euforia also measures participants general satisfaction with the imp!act event. Although this is a very subjective measure and informs euforia more about the pleasure people have taken in the event, and does not tell euforia about the social impact achieved, many external stakeholders still rely on those satisfaction measures.

Once euforia's impact had been visualized, and KPIs were defined, the researchers assisted euforia during one year in developing and administering online surveys. During this time, euforia meambers were trained "on the job" to perform the social impact measurement, until they felt able to independently perform euforia's social impact assessment. The training on the job included the use of survey software, the download and cleaning of the data, and training in basic statistical methods. The amount of training was comparable to a first-year PhD programme in a major European business school. The objective was to empower euforia staff to be able to perform the social impact measurement themselves, and to further develop it in the future. The final step of the project was that euforia performed its social impact measurement independently and presented the final results to the researchers.

Discussion and conclusions

The development of a social impact measurement system for euforia showed that it is possible to use a very rigorous social impact measurement system that goes far beyond qualitative post-test designs in which the impact of a social entrepreneur is only measured after an activity, such as an event or a training program, for instance, based on telephone interviews. Major learnings from the case included the following:

1   Social impact measurement systems should be created together with (instead of for) a social entrepreneurial organization. This facilitates internal implementation and further use.
2   Social impact measurement systems should be adapted to the resources, knowledge, and skills of a social entrepreneurial organization. Ideally, euforia would have used randomized control trials (RCTs) to respect the highest scientific standards. However, the organization would have been unable on all three dimensions (i.e., resources, knowledge, and skills) to implement and execute RCTs.
3   It is a long-term process to find the right level of detail for measurable impact dimensions and the scientific rigor of KPIs, and to visualize them to increase acceptance within the organization. During the process, it is important that staff of an organization is trained on the job to use a social impact measurement system, and to raise importance about social impact measurement within an organization.
4   A social impact measurement system is as useful for external stakeholders as for internal stakeholders (e.g., for quality control purposes).

The first learning describes the challenge for external consultants (including the author) to adapt the measurement system design and KPIs to the needs of social entrepreneurs, so that an organization can use the social impact measurement system after the consulting project. Very often, social entrepreneurs' websites contain a report on social impact that had been conducted by an external party. However, those reports are often one-time reports, and stand in contrast to the idea of continuous social impact measurement and reporting. They also contribute very little to the general acceptance and implementation of social impact measurement systems in social entrepreneurial organizations.

The second learning describes one of the main challenges for researchers who are used to achieving the highest scientific rigour when they design social impact measurement systems. In principle, the most sophisticated social impact measurement system for euforia would have been a field experimental design (or RCT) with random assignment to a treatment group (for imp!act participants) and a control group (those that do not take part in the imp!act event). The design of euforia's measurement does not respect this design since it does not use a control group and random assignment. This also means that the highest scientific standards were not achieved. As Kroeger and Weber (2014, p. 517) point out in their review of existing approaches to measure social impact: "perhaps the most sophisticated approaches are experimental and quasi-experimental research designs, such as randomized control trials (RCTs) or the difference-in-differences technique" (see also Banerjee, 2007). The final measurement system design for euforia is based on a compromise between a certain level of academic rigour and sophistication, and the need of implementing a social impact measurement system within a young and innovative social entrepreneurial organization for continuous social impact measurement. This compromise was also reached because many funders and donors do not apply the most rigorous scientific standards to evaluate the quality of a social impact measurement system and the measured impacts, for instance, for their funding decisions. With the compromise applied by euforia, they are still a leading organization when it comes to rigour and sophistication for their social impact measurement system, by at the same time being able of using the measurement system without external support.

The third point of learning occurred during the project. The social impact measurement system turned out to be extremely useful for internal communication. For the first time, euforia was able to translate its impact into a visually presented form (i.e., the pyramid), to name its impact dimensions (outreach, empowerment, changemaking, multiplying), and to translate its impact into numbers (instead of some selected post-test interview quotes from participants). This facilitated the communication about a rather intangible impact, and enhanced the discussions about improvements of euforia's impact.

The last learning is that continuous social impact measurement is not limited to a tool for external reporting, but can also be used for internal quality control and management purposes. It turned out that many external stakeholders were positively surprised by the rigour of the social impact measurement system. In fact, euforia's social impact measurement proved to be a competitive advantage to receive funding and support from some stakeholder. At the same time, euforia leaders and staff stressed that the result of implementing a social impact measurement tool was also that internal processes such as quality control for events were improved.

A number of research implications and recommendations for social entrepreneurs and their stakeholders emerge from these findings. From a social entrepreneur's perspective, the reported case is important because some social entrepreneurs seem to have a natural reflex to reject impact measurement systems, not because they are not useful, but because they require a great deal of resources. The euforia case shows that it is possible to define and execute a process with the explicit objective of an implementation of the social impact measurement system into the organization's processes. The latter comes along with potential benefits for external reporting and funding opportunities, but it also helps to improve internal processes and quality management. This result is also useful to foundations and philanthropists who are the main players financing impact measurement (or external monitoring and evaluation) in the early stages of a social enterprise. They can insist on the implementation of social impact measurement systems within organizations, so that they continuously improve their respective impact, instead of just requiring an externally developed monitoring and evaluation report.

From a research perspective, the case contributes to the very limited evidence on *how* social impact measurement systems are developed within an organization. So far, the literature focuses on arguing why social impact measurement should be done and why it is important (Nicholls, 2009, 2010), whether it should be universal to all social entrepreneurs or organization-specific (Kroeger & Weber, 2014), and which measurement designs should be used (Kroeger & Weber, 2014). In addition, there is literature on the extent to which social impact reporting influences external decision-makers such as impact investors (Achleitner et al., 2013). The case study of *how* euforia developed an impact measurement system (together with external support) shows that despite some arguments for generally accepted social impact measurement principles, organization-specific processes are useful for the acceptance and internal use of social impact measurement, and to clearly define an organization's impact dimensions. The euforia case also shows that developing a social impact measurement system is more comparable to the development of a management control tool for internal use (i.e., like a balanced scorecard), then to the financial reporting process, where data is aggregated into annual reports, mainly for the use of external stakeholders. A potential area for future research is to explore to what extend social impact assessment is used within an organization as a management tool relative to the use as a reporting tool for external stakeholders, and whether it is possible to develop social impact measurement systems that are useful for both purposes.

References

Achleitner, A.-K., Lutz, E., Mayer, J., & Spiess-Knafl, W. (2013). Disentangling gut feeling: Assessing the integrity of social entrepreneurs. *VOLUNTAS: International Journal of Voluntary and Nonprofit Organizations*, 24(1), 93–124.

Astebro, T. B., & Hoos, F. (2016). The effects of a training program to encourage social entrepreneurship. *HEC Paris Research Paper No. SPE-2016-1128*. Available at SSRN: https://ssrn.com/abstract=2715384 or http://dx.doi.org/10.2139/ssrn.2715384.

Austin, J., Stevenson, H., & Wei-Skillern, J. (2006). Social and commercial entrepreneurship: Same, different, or both? *Entrepreneurship Theory and Practice*, 30(1), 1–22.

Chan, K.-Y., & Drasgow, F. (2001). Toward a theory of individual differences and leadership: Understanding the motivation to lead. *Journal of Applied Psychology*, 86(3), 481–498.

Dacin, P. A., Dacin, M. T., & Matear, M. (2010). Social entrepreneurship: Why we don't need a new theory and how we move forward from here. *Academy of Management Perspectives*, 24(3), 37–57.

Dacin, P. A., Dacin, M. T., Matear, M., & Tracey, P. (2011). Social entrepreneurship: A critique and future directions. *Organization Science*, 22(5), 1203–1213.

Foundation Center (2016). Available online at http://trasi.foundationcenter.org/browse.php (accessed 12 May 2017).

Kroeger, A., & Weber, C. (2014). Developing a conceptual framework for comparing social value creation. *Academy of Management Review*, 39(4), 513–540.

Lehner, O. M. (2013). Crowd-funding social ventures: a model and research agenda. *Venture Capital: An International Journal of Entrepreneurial Finance, 15*(4), 289–311.

Mair, J., Battilana, J., & Cardenas, J. (2012). Organizing for society: a typology of social entrepreneuring models. *Journal of Business Ethics, 111*(3), 353–373.

Miller, T. L., & Wesley, C. L. (2010). Assessing mission and resources for social change: an organizational identity perspective on social venture capitalists' decision criteria. *Entrepreneurship Theory and Practice, 34*(4), 705–733.

Nicholls, A. (2009). We do good things, don't we? "Blended value accounting" in social entrepreneurship. *Accounting, Organizations and Society, 34*(6/7), 755–769.

Nicholls, A. (2010). Institutionalizing social entrepreneurship in regulatory space: reporting and disclosure by community interest companies. *Accounting, Organizations and Society, 35*(4), 394–415.

Oosterbeek, H., Van Praag, M., & Ijsselstein, A. (2010). The impact of entrepreneurship education on entrepreneurship competencies and intentions: an evaluation of the junior achievement student mini-company program. *European Economic Review, 54*(3), 442–454.

Peredo, A. M., & McLean, M. (2006). Social entrepreneurship: a critical review of the concept. *Journal of World Business, 41*(1), 56–65.

Podsakoff, P. M., MacKenzie, S. B., Morrman, R. H., & Fetter, R. (1990). Transformational leader behaviors and their effects on followers' trust in leader, satisfaction, and organizational citizenship behaviors. *Leadership Quarterly, 1*(2), 107–142.

3.4 Mechanisms and tools for measuring and reporting sustainability in the hotel industry

A practical dimension

Piotr Zientara and Paulina Bohdanowicz-Godfrey

Introduction

The pursuit of sustainability is regarded as a moral imperative facing mankind in the 21st century. The underlying ethical principle here is that human action should not lead to the depletion of natural resources and the destruction of the natural environment. It is, therefore, conceived as being one of the ethical universals or, in other words, "norms, principles, policies, or goals that are not a function of time or place" (Cummings & Patel, 2009, p. 58). Crucially, sustainability lies at the heart of the triple bottom line (TBL) concept, which implies that any company that adopts such framework should be simultaneously focused on its financial, social, and environmental performance (Chapman & Milne, 2003; Milne & Gray, 2009). Thus, sustainability is intertwined (and associated) with corporate social responsibility (CSR) – itself part of business ethics (Velasquez, 1998). This means that responsible companies should seek to reduce their environmental impacts and to further the development of a fair and equitable society. Moreover, they should pay special attention to social auditing,[1] which is the "process of defining, observing, and reporting measures of the ethical behavior and social impact of an organization in relation to its aims and those of its stakeholders" (Zadek, 1994, p. 632). In other words, they have a moral obligation to inform the public about their social and environmental performance, which, in turn, requires disclosing accurate information (Herremans, Nazari, & Mahmoudia, 2016). Measuring sustainability, however, poses a challenge to any multinational firm (see also Azapagic, 2003).

This holds true also for international hotel chains, which operate numerous properties that vary in management/ownership structure, size, service classification, geographic location, and socio-political context. The principal difficulty lies in consistently guaranteeing methodological rigour (with appropriate performance metrics to the fore) and in seamlessly incorporating environmental and social matters in management systems (Searcy, 2009; Székely & Knirsch, 2005). To that end, a hotel firm needs to use a standardized methodology, to apply a uniform approach across the entire portfolio, to install precise measurement tools, and to ensure compliance with data-collection procedures (Kaspersen & Johansen, 2016).

This accent on accurateness and reliability reflects the fact that sustainability measurement and reporting have been subjected to the principles of financial accounting (Potter, 2005; Power, 1994, 1996). Central to this approach is the idea of auditability, which implies that organizational phenomena that are internally recorded (captured) and externally reported (communicated) should be verifiable by third parties or, in other words, auditable. In turn, auditability renders it possible to benchmark a hotel firm's social and environmental performance against external criteria and, by extension, to make meaningful within-industry comparisons. That is greatly facilitated by specialist tools developed for the industry by, among others, the International Tourism Partnership.

This chapter focuses on the hotel industry, which, arguably, can be seen as being at the cutting edge of sustainability measuring (indeed, in recent years, the entire industry, with international hotel chains to the fore, has made great progress in this respect, which in itself merits recognition). It first offers a theoretical background. Then, it examines industry-wide standardization initiatives and shows how particular hotel companies cope with the challenge by means of environmental performance assessment tools (systems). It uses an example of Hilton's LightStay tool to provide insights into practical applications. Subsequently, it discusses the future of sustainability measurement. In this context, a case is made for so-called smart feedback and this highlights a distinction between "outputs" and "outcomes" – key themes that are beginning to feature saliently on the managerial agenda (if not yet in the academic literature). There is little doubt that, given that more and more firms see sense in creating "as much value as possible for stakeholders, without resorting to trade-offs" (Freeman Harrison, Wicks, Parmar, & de Colle, 2010, p. 28), the issue of measuring and reporting sustainability is likely to take centre stage in the deliberations on modern-day business praxis, thereby attracting a lot of attention from academics and practitioners alike. And this chapter, while disseminating best practice, aims to contribute to this debate.

The quintessence of sustainability and corporate social responsibility

As mentioned in the introduction, there is a strong ethical dimension to sustainability and corporate social responsibility (CSR). Business ethics is "a specialized study of moral right and wrong [that] concentrates on moral standards as they apply particularly to business policies, institutions, and behaviors" (Velasquez, 1998, p. 13). Crucially, issues of ethics are conceived as having a potential effect on *others* (Solomon & Hanson, 1985). This, in turn, evokes Schwartz's (1996) circular framework of values, which features, among other values,[2] universalism, and benevolence. These two values focus on the general welfare of *others*,[3] with which both sustainability and CSR are also concerned.

Thus, given that there are three basic dimensions (social, environmental, and economic) to sustainability (Hall, Gössling, & Scott, 2015), its pursuit implies not only preserving biodiversity and tackling global warming, which "is a serious threat to the quality of life on earth" (Depoers, Jeanjean, & Jérôme, 2016, p. 445), but also generating prosperity for all and, by implication, building a fair and equitable society. Such a society does not countenance mass poverty, worker exploitation, gaping income inequality, and discrimination on ground of sex, sexual orientation, race, or religion. Accordingly, sustainability is seen as an ethical universal (Cummings & Patel, 2009). This concept is central to what Donaldson and Dunfee (1999, p. 243) term "hypernorms", by which they mean fundamental, universal standards of human behaviour that "cannot be overridden by local customs, norms or laws". In practice, this means that a company that wholeheartedly embraces sustainability (or CSR) should, for example, employ and promote women even if this is frowned upon in a local culture.

Nonetheless, it is important to realize that sustainability and CSR have evolved from different backgrounds – from, respectively, the idea of sustainable development (Hailey, 1998) and stakeholder theory (Freeman et al., 2010). Specifically, the former is about ensuring that humanity "meets the needs of the present without compromising the ability of future generations to meet their own needs" (United Nations, 1987, p. 43), and the latter holds that "organizations should be managed in the interest of all their constituents, not only in the interest of shareholders" (Laplume, Sonpar, & Litz, 2008, p. 1153). It follows that, while corporate sustainability reflects a paradigmatic shift in the business–society relationship, CSR represents a major shift in the conceptualization of the company's *raison d'être* (see also Garavan & McGuire, 2010). However, it is undeniable that, as argued by Montiel (2008), both CSR and corporate sustainability share the same commitment and are progressing towards a common future.

In this context, it is necessary to ask how firms view sustainability/CSR and the attitude to it they adopt. In fact, evidence has accumulated that more and more companies regard sustainability/CSR as a core value. In other words, they embed it into their organizational cultures (Swanson, 2014). And for this to happen, it is essential, above all, to set "the tone at the top" (Collier & Esteban, 2007, p. 20), whereby a chief executive officer and senior management explicitly and repeatedly declare that sustainability/CSR is a core value and that, consequently, the company will seek to achieve the goal of sustainable, stakeholder-centric operation. That, in turn, aims at a shared vision capability (Senge, 1990), which comes to the fore whenever the management explains to all employees what the organization stands for and what it aspires to attain in order to actively involve them in the shared pursuit of these aspirations.

All of which is of great relevance since it determines the place of sustainability/CSR in business praxis. Indeed, adoption of a strategic approach to sustainability/CSR means, in essence, that it permeates through the whole organization, thereby underpinning all managerial decisions and organizational practices (Bohdanowicz & Zientara, 2008). Accordingly, a company that sees sustainability/CSR as a centrepiece of its organizational culture (rather than as an "add-on") will be highly unlikely to act irresponsibly even if operating in a jurisdiction where, say, environmental rules are lax or poorly enforced (as is often the case in some developing countries). Crucially, such a company will go to great lengths to inform the public of its social and environmental performance, which, as already noted, calls for accurate measurement and effective communication.

Measuring and reporting sustainability: the nature of the challenge

However, measuring and reporting corporate emissions, resource use and contributions to social causes is *per se* an inherently complex undertaking (Adams, Hill, & Roberts 1998; Morhardt, Baird, & Freeman, 2002; Skouloudis, Evangelinos, & Kourmousis, 2009; Yadava & Sinha, 2016). This is due to the sheer scale and complexity of the task (especially in multi-unit enterprises), in general, and to lack of standardization and problems with methodological rigour (accuracy of measurement, appropriate performance metrics, compliance with data-collection procedures, etc.), in particular. There is also evidence that – given non-negligible differences between industry sectors in terms of *modus operandi* and between same-sector firms in terms of business models – sustainability-related issues are not conceived in the same way (Azapagic, 2003).

Therefore, to aid companies in measuring and communicating social and environmental performance, the Global Reporting Initiative (GRI) and the Carbon Disclosure Project (CDP) were developed. The former is a CSR reporting guideline (Morhardt et al., 2002; Vigneau, Humphreys, & Moon, 2015; Yadava & Sinha, 2016), while the latter "is a not-for-profit organization created in 2000 at the initiative of a group of institutional investors interested in incorporating information on businesses' carbon emissions into their analyses and assessments" (Depoers et al., 2016, p. 446). Nonetheless, both initiatives, much as they are helpful in their own right, are not devoid of certain inherent flaws. As for the former, there is a real risk that companies might focus on the improvement of reporting practices rather than enhance actual CSR performance. This is because, as argued by Vigneau et al. (2015), excessive (and disproportionate) importance is attached to documenting CSR action rather than to evaluating and, crucially, extending its beneficent impacts. As regards the latter, participants, being allowed to disclose information on their greenhouse gas emissions either in corporate reports or via the Carbon Disclosure Project, usually go for the former and tend to cherry-pick data so as to portray their company's decarbonization record in a more positive light (Depoers et al., 2016). It follows that the public does not get a full picture of a company's carbon footprint (see also below).

Other related initiatives, such as the Global Compact (GC) or the Fair Labor Code (FLC), are not free from certain deficiencies, either. In particular, this goes for the former, which is, in essence, about procedures rather than outcomes, and mandates self-reporting about implementation rather than implementation *per se* (Behnam & MacLean, 2011). Besides, with its principles regarded as generic and imprecise (so as to encompass firms from various industry sectors), it is problematic to have high expectations of the former. As regards the latter, its enforcement mechanisms are not particularly robust (it is extremely rare, for example, to see a factory that flouts these rules punished by being ousted from the programme). Another problem is CSR-washing, defined as "the successful use of a false CSR claim to improve a company's competitive standing" (Pope & Wæraas, 2016, p. 175). Indeed, some firms increasingly resort to CSR-washing, *de facto* deceiving their stakeholders, with customers to the fore. Arguably, there is a world of difference between reporting *unintentionally* inaccurate data on greenhouse gas emissions, say, due to lack of precise measurement tools (lack of professionalism), and between doing so *intentionally* (dishonesty). Although the magnitude of this unethical practice is contested, it is, by no means, infrequent.

Undoubtedly, any form of corporate dishonesty related to measurement and reporting should be exposed and denounced. For example, meaningful information can be inferred from comparisons with companies that tend to report their environmental and social performance completely and accurately. It follows that firms should be held accountable for their reporting practices, ideally by non-governmental organizations (NGOs) and other pressure groups. Members of such bodies usually have great expertise in the technicalities of reporting praxis. Yet, irrespective of what might be done in this respect, one thing is certain: a company that sees sustainability or CSR as a core value will be highly unlikely, in line with the logic presented at the end of the previous section, to resort to selective reporting.

That, in turn, bears indirectly on another issue, namely, on the relationship between sustainability reporting characteristics and stakeholder engagement strategy, which, arguably, remains understudied (Herremans et al., 2016). What underlies this line of research is the fundamental premise of stakeholder theory, which states that organizations need to establish and maintain a relationship with their stakeholders. Central to this relationship is communication (Bourne, 2009), which serves to ensure that stakeholders get to know a company's performance. This usually takes the form of a sustainability/CSR report (Morsing & Schultz, 2006). Yet there is much more to communication than that. In fact, at its core lies a dialogue with stakeholders (Golob & Podnar, 2014; Hess, 2008), which is now done via online discussion forums and interaction on social media. The overarching idea behind stakeholder dialogue is to engage stakeholders[4] (Greenwood, 2007) with a view to ensuring that their voice is heard and that their needs are met.[5] If conceived in radical terms, engagement entails empowering stakeholders (through joint decision-making) which, in practice, leads to stakeholder-driven changes in organizational behaviour (Herremans et al., 2016). And there are studies that have focused on how different stakeholder engagement strategies affect sustainability reports (e.g., Herremans et al., 2016; Manetti, 2011; Manetti & Toccafondi, 2012).

Specificity of measuring and reporting sustainability in the hotel industry

All of which is of great relevance to the hotel sector, which, due to its idiosyncratic *modus operandi*, produces considerable environmental impacts (Erdogan & Baris, 2007). It is true that noteworthy progress has been made in this respect, but the fact remains that there is still ample scope for environmental performance improvement. The same can be said about employee wellbeing and community welfare. Indeed, even though overall working conditions in many facilities can be described as good, the quality of typical jobs is relatively low. At the same time, hotel employees endure certain industry-specific inconveniences, such as, for example, unsocial hours (and resulting problems with work–life balance), emotional labour,[6] and seasonality-related job insecurity. These sectorial characteristics are hardly conducive to greater social and environmental sustainability. Yet growing numbers of travellers and tourists, while deciding where to stay, take into account a hotel's social and environmental credentials (Han & Yoon, 2015; Green Hotelier, 2014) – a tendency that is part of a broader drive towards "responsible holidays" (Leslie, 2012).

Unsurprisingly, extensive research has been undertaken into how – and to what effect – (mainly environmental) sustainability is pursued in hotel properties varying in size, ownership, location, and classification (Álvarez-Gil, Burgos-Jimenez, & Cespedes-Lorente, 2001; De Burgos-Jiménez, Cano-Guillén, & Céspedes-Lorente, 2002; Fraj, Matute, & Melero, 2015; Jacob, Florido, & Aguiló, 2010; Molina-Azorín, Claver-Cortés, Pereira-Moliner, & Tarí, 2009; Smerecnik & Andersen, 2011). However, far less attention has been paid to hotels' social performance (Bohdanowicz & Zientara, 2009). Crucially, a few studies pertaining to the former line of research have focused specifically on the question of measurement and benchmarking (Bohdanowicz-Godfrey & Zientara, 2015; Chong & Ricaurte, 2014; Sloan, Legrand, & Chen, 2009). In this context, Chong and Ricaurte (2014, p. 8) note that "the value of benchmarking performance against prior years and current competitors, as well as the use of accepted benchmarks at aggregate levels, is proven and widely understood within the hotel industry". But they go on to say that "benchmarks must make sense" (p. 8). In practice, this means that one should be particularly cautious about making environmental performance-based comparisons between properties and drawing definitive conclusions on that basis. This is because, for example, a hotel's overall utility (energy and water) consumption hinges on a variety of variables, which makes comparisons problematic even within the *same* market segment and geographic location. For instance, a meaningful comparison would involve juxtaposing an economy hotel with a swimming pool and a restaurant (frequented not only by hotel guests, but also by local residents) and located in the city centre with an economy hotel without such amenities and located on the outskirts.

The environmental variables in question include weather (rather than climate as such), the handling of laundry,[7] the presence of specific amenities (swimming pools, golf courses, restaurants, conference halls, etc.), the size and layout of public areas, the very design of the building, the range and character of operating practices, occupancy rates, and space utilization (it is important to note that some of these aspects have not been fully explored and standardized; of which more below). Things seem less complex when it comes to water consumption, which "is closely linked to energy and food production, and best addressed in accommodation, the locus of most tourism consumption" (Gössling, 2015, p. 243). Yet, even though fewer factors are at work, which *per se* makes between–hotel comparisons more meaningful, the problem lies in calculating total or *direct* and *indirect* water consumption. In the words of Gössling (2015, p. 243):

> current use of indicators is largely focused on direct water use, i.e. the volume of local water consumed per tourist per day, which is usually restricted to accommodation. This excludes other areas of water consumption – such as activities, shopping or services – as well as indirect (or imported/embodied) water needed for the production of infrastructure, fuels and foodstuffs.

The implication is that hotel firms, while measuring and reporting their "water footprint", typically centre only on *direct* water consumption at particular facilities, which does not present the full picture (Hadjikakou, Chenoweth, & Miller, 2013). Given the nature of the challenge, it should come as no surprise that efforts have recently been made to create a standardized methodology.

Industry-specific initiatives aimed at methodological standardization and performance monitoring

Even though, in the past, there existed standardized methodologies for measuring and communicating resource use and carbon emissions (for example, carbon measurement in line with the recommendations of the Greenhouse Gas Protocol), their practical utilization posed certain challenges. In fact, most companies found them too complicated and, accordingly, decided to simplify them or to use other (i.e., their own) methodologies. What really made it hard (if not impossible) to compare *two* sustainability (or CSR) reports was the fact that some reports provided key performance indicators, some focused on absolute quantities, and others on percentage change. To complicate things further, some reports covered the entire portfolio, while others included only an owned and/or managed portfolio.[8] Besides, although relevant data were gathered on a yearly basis, the use of technology was limited. In sum, lack of methodological rigour and standardization-related problems slowed down progress towards greater social and environmental sustainability in the entire industry. That is why action has of late been taken to address these issues. As a result, several relevant initiatives were created, including the development of methodologies (the Hotel Carbon Measuring Initiative and the Hotel Water Measuring Initiative), benchmark indexes (the Hotel Sustainability Benchmark Index and the Hotel Footprinting Tool) and customer-facing self-assessment tools (TripAdvisor GreenLeaders programme).

Further to the above, consultants and individual hotel companies have developed their own environmental performance monitoring and assessment tools, such as Green Hotels Global, Accor's OPEN, Hilton's LightStay, InterContinental Hotel

Table 3.4.1 A comparison of selected initiatives and tools available within the hotel sector (Arup, 2014; Chong & Ricaurte, 2014; Green Hotelier, 2014; Green Hotels Global, 2017; Hilton Worldwide, 2010, 2015; IHG, 2017; ITP & Greenview, 2017; ITP, 2015, 2017; TripAdvisor, 2017)

Criteria	Hotel Carbon / Water Measuring Initiative (HCMI / HWMI)	Hotel Footprinting Tool (HFT) and Cornell Hotel Sustainability Benchmark	TripAdvisor Green Leaders	LightStay	GreenEngage	Green Hotels Global
Type of tool	Methodology standardizing CO_2 / water measurement and reporting procedures	Footprint calculation and benchmarking to reference database	Self-assessment	Reporting, monitoring, benchmarking, current practices, improvement suggestions	Reporting, monitoring, benchmarking, current practices, improvement suggestions, internal certification	Reporting, monitoring, current practices
Beneficiary stakeholders	Sector globally	Sector and customers via website	Customers in selected countries via website	Hilton and their stakeholders via internal channels	Intercontinental Hotel Group and their stakeholders	Marriott and their stakeholders
Development stakeholders	International Tourism Partnership and World Travel & Tourism Council with 23 global hotel companies	Cornell University, International Tourism Partnership, Greenview (based on HCMI and HWMI)	TripAdvisor, Carbon Trust, UK Green Building Council, the United Nations Environment Programme	Internal with consultancy support (DNV GL)	Internal with consultancy support (Arup)	External: Carbon Accounting
Initiation	2012 and 2016	2015	2013	2002 /2010	2011	2011
Participation status / Utilization level	Voluntary / HCMI adopted by 21500 units by 2016	Voluntary / input from 13 hotel companies	Voluntary / 6900 corporate units in 2016	Mandatory brand standard / entire portfolio	Mandatory brand standard / entire portfolio	Mandatory brand standard / entire portfolio
Key focus areas	Carbon / Water	Energy / Carbon / Water	Environmental activities	Environment + social	Environment	Environment
Incorporation of HCMI and HWMI	N/A	Yes	N/A	Yes	Yes	Yes

(continued)

Table 3.4.1 (continued)

Criteria	Hotel Carbon / Water Measuring Initiative (HCMI / HWMI)	Hotel Footprinting Tool (HFT) and Cornell Hotel Sustainability Benchmark	TripAdvisor Green Leaders	LightStay	GreenEngage	Green Hotels Global
Output and outcome metrics	Output: per m^2, occupied room	Output: per m^2, per m^2 of meeting space, per occupied room	Output: activities	Output: energy, CO_2, water, waste per m^2 or occupied room, volunteering hours, CSR activities; Outcome: people impacted	Output: energy, CO_2, water, waste per occupied room, or cost, environmental practices	Output: energy, CO_2, water, waste per m^2, occupied room, m^2 meeting hour, environmental practices
Quality assurance	N/A	Annual, external upon data collection via Cornell	Only if required	Internal and external of data input	External of certification level and of data input	Internal via provider
Reporting frequency	N/A	Annual for database	Ad hoc	Monthly for environmental, ad hoc for social	Monthly for environmental	Monthly for environmental
Purpose of reporting	N/A	To update the database and refine the index	To customers via website	Internal for decision making, external for customer decision making, data used in external corporate reports and compliance	Internal for decision making, external through request for proposals, and for corporate reporting	Internal for decision making, external for corporate reporting
Proprietary features	N/A	Benchmarking for hotel operators, Footprinting for customers to inform offsetting needs	Levels of compliance, Channel for hoteliers to market their green efforts to travellers	Improvement suggestions, Action plans, Projects gallery, Meeting calculator	Customised improvement suggestions, Water risk mapping, Internal levels of compliance, Communication of certification levels via booking website	Includes budget & project planning tool, Supports alignment with APEX / ASTM standards for green meetings & events

Group's GREENengage, and Wyndham Worldwide's Green Toolbox, to name a few (Bohdanowicz & Zientara, 2008; Bohdanowicz-Godfrey & Zientara, 2015). A typical performance assessment system draws on a combination of measurement (i.e., environmentally sensitive and operational "inputs") and performance (i.e., industry-specific "outputs", usually in the form of indicators, such as carbon footprint per room or per square metre). Critically, the actual usefulness of such a tool hinges on the quality and accuracy of the input data on water and energy consumption, carbon emissions and waste generation, food and beverage and events data, and even revenue. Performance is then presented in tabular or graphical form either as absolute figures or as indicators on per available or occupied room, per property unit area, or using units of other services offered or sometimes even revenue. All this, in turn, enables management to get an understanding of how their hotel performs against industry norms, competitors with similar characteristics (or other establishments within the portfolio) or against itself over time (Hawkins & Bohdanowicz, 2011). These tools are primarily used for internal benchmarking of CSR activities and decision-making; however, the information collected is typically used for external reporting and communication. Table 3.4.1 presents a comparison of a selected sectoral and hotel-specific tools.

A practical example of a sustainability monitoring platform in the hotel industry – Hilton LightStay

Most of the hotel-commissioned tools undergo continued development to support the growing reporting needs of the evolving sustainability strategy. Hilton's LightStay is an example of such evolution. It started as a simple digital monitoring instrument of energy consumption and costs, and through a number of iterations developed into a comprehensive platform for measuring and reporting the environmental and, crucially, social performance of all hotels within Hilton brands.

LightStay measures energy, water, waste, and carbon impacts throughout 200 areas of hotel operations, including housekeeping, paper product use, food waste, chemical storage, air quality, and transportation (Hilton Worldwide, 2015). It supports monitoring of performance against annual goals at a local and regional level, and provides feedback to the users using various key performance metrics in graphical and tabular form, as well as through visual comparisons of achievements to tangible events, that is, comparing reductions in carbon emissions to the number of cars removed from the roads. Through these reporting and trending features, LightStay provides operators with the relevant data to help them identify focus areas and take action to improve a hotel's performance on an ongoing basis. In order to enable more measurable impact of the environmental strategy, it includes best practice sharing through networking and internal benchmarking.

In 2011, Hilton announced Travel with Purpose, its

> corporate responsibility commitment to providing shared value to its business and communities by creating opportunities for individuals to reach their full potential; strengthening communities where Hilton operates; and preserving environments through the measurement, analysis and improvement of the company's use of natural resources.
>
> (Hilton, 2017)

As a consequence, by the end of 2011, the measurement of sustainability performance became a brand standard for Hilton's entire portfolio, on a par with service, and evaluated accordingly as part of regular, property-level reviews.

All hotel teams are required to track and complete efficiency projects in energy, water, and waste management each year, thereby ensuring continuous improvement. LightStay has the capability to propose improvements based on individual property needs and characteristics, and taking into account the initiatives they have already put in place. Best practice sharing is supported by the relevant business teams to help standardize good operational practices across the portfolio. The implementation and validity of LightStay was verified by KEMA-Registered Quality, Inc., a management systems design company, through a series of third-party audits, helping Hilton achieve ISO9001, ISO14001, and ISO 50001 certification (Hilton Worldwide, 2011, 2014).

To enable better communication with the customers, the "meeting impact calculator" that measures the environmental impact of any meeting or conference held at a property (based on HCMI 1.0 methodology) was developed. This report provides corporate customers with hotel-specific carbon, water, and waste data, as well as information about their operational practices, thus enabling them to consider the impact of hotel stays and meetings when making purchasing decisions (and to include it in their own sustainability reporting).

The latest version of LightStay (released in 2015) is equipped with a function that can forecast future energy and water usage levels. This feature enables hotel operating teams, owners, and management groups to understand the discrepancies between forecasted and actual performance, to take corrective action (in order to influence future performance) and, last but not least, to grasp the benefits accruing from assorted efficiency projects. The tool now offers comprehensive monitoring of all key performance indicators within the framework of Travel with Purpose. Social and community measures were fully integrated into tracking and reporting to ensure internal and external transparency. Chief among them are hours employees spend volunteering (their skills in educating youth or supporting local youth centres) or items donated to charitable causes. Additionally, the tool makes it possible to track participation levels in international and company-instigated environmental and social campaigns. Based on the above, it is fair to say that LightStay bears all the hallmarks of a *comprehensive* platform for measuring and reporting sustainability and, by this token, stands out among similar tools used by other hotel firms.

Future of sustainability measurement

While talking about the future of sustainability measurement, it is important to realize the emergence of two important phenomena. On the one hand, there is a growing recognition that the question of sustainability measurement may well go beyond data collection, benchmarking, and standardization. In fact, what is at issue is smart feedback, which is part of a wider trend that has recently come to the fore as a result of the propagation of objects with a baked-in internet connection (thereby making previously "dumb" things "smart"). With smart grid or smart home becoming a reality, there is increased talk of smart feedback in environmental management. In the hotel context, this might take the form of intelligent systems that not only analyse data in view of a property's characteristics, but also come up with – and apply – relevant solutions. For instance, if a hotel, which includes, say, a swimming pool, a large garden, and wet cooling towers, uses too much water, a smart system should propose a water-efficient solution that would consist of purifying the water from the pool and the cooling towers and, subsequently, in reusing it for watering the landscape.

On the other hand, it is essential to recognize the difference between outputs and outcomes. The term "output" implies quantifiable achievements related to reductions in energy use (in kilowatt-hours) or water use (in litres) or in greenhouse gas emissions (in kilograms of carbon dioxide equivalent). By contrast, the term "outcome" conveys different information, suggesting a broader consequence of what has been achieved. For example, a particular hotel may well reduce its use of water by a given quantity (in litres per room or square metre or guest night), which, as such, represents an output. Yet one may speak of an outcome when considering how this achievement affects, say, overall water supply in a local community. This differentiation matters since, increasingly, calls are made for linking hard data to societal phenomena (in a wider context of sustainable development), rather than focusing on them for the sake of benchmarking. In other words the idea is to show how a particular reduction, say, in water use impacts not only on a hotel's environmental performance, but also on the situation of local residents or the flora and fauna of the area. The same principle should apply to social and economic performance measurement. Although a certain volume of guidelines on how to describe outcomes to make them benchmarkable exists (i.e., LBG standard managed by Global Citizenship in the realm of volunteering), there is a need for further focus in this area.

Although, undoubtedly, thinking in terms of outcomes is highly unlikely to replace analyses of outputs, it might help shift focus from *narrow* indicators to *wider* issues of societal character. By reflecting the essence of sustainability efforts, this *per se* might be conceived as being more in tune with a strategic approach to CSR, whereby it is embedded in organizational culture and treated as a core value (rather than as an add-on). And this is exactly what some hotel companies – including Scandic and Hilton (Bohdanowicz & Zientara, 2008; Bohdanowicz, Zientara, & Novotna, 2011) – actually did. A company that embeds CSR in its culture adopts a holistic or a whole-business view of CSR, meaning that it furthers sustainability not because this may translate into reputational or financial gains (i.e., an instrumental approach), but because this is morally right (i.e., a normative approach). Seen in this way, sustainability measurement and reporting becomes a moral imperative rather than just another managerial task.

Conclusions

As great pressure is put on multinational companies to behave responsibly towards the environment and society, some of them – in line with a stakeholder conception of the firm – decide to see sustainability/CSR as a core value. This means, among other things, that measuring and reporting a company's social and environmental performance are likely to occupy a prominent position in modern-day business practice. In other words, since the public has a right to know how corporations fare not only financially, but also socially and environmentally, accurate measurement and truthful reporting are bound to figure high on the managerial list of priorities. That is part of a wider tendency, namely, of the need to establish and maintain a relationship with their stakeholders. Central to this relationship is communication, which, when it comes to social and environmental performance, takes the form of a sustainability/CSR report (Morsing & Schultz, 2006).

Yet, as has been argued, at the core of the communicative process lies a dialogue with stakeholders (Golob & Podnar, 2014), which, in turn, serves to engage them and, by extension, to encourage them to participate in organizational matters (Greenwood, 2007; Herremans et al., 2016).

The implication is that sustainability, if it is to be effectively pursued, calls for joint managerial effort and stakeholder involvement. That is particularly true of the hotel sector, which, as an integral part of the tourism industry, has a special interest in the preservation of the natural environment and the welfare of local communities. Indeed, due to its specific nature and idiosyncratic *modus operandi* – that is, constant interaction between employees and guests, above-average consumption of resources, significance to many local economies, and so on – hotel facilities are well placed to engage a broad spectrum of stakeholders (staff, customers, local inhabitants) in organizational pursuit of sustainability. In this chapter, we have focused on this sector (especially, its corporate segment) since, arguably, it appears to be at the cutting edge of sustainability measurement and reporting.

In fact, as we have attempted to demonstrate in the course of the chapter, the hotel industry has made great strides towards more precise measurement and more accurate reporting of sustainability. As the experience of hotel companies that are at the cutting edge of sustainability shows, it should be literally embedded into every aspect of organizational operation. This should be accompanied by the articulation (by an executive and/or senior management) of bold objectives (i.e., science-based targets or net-positive goals) and, crucially, by the dissemination of appropriate procedures (i.e., best practice) to individual plants or facilities (depending on the industry sector) within a company's portfolio. That should be done through the introduction of brand standards or, alternatively, engagement programmes. At the same time, much should be made of industry-wide initiatives aimed at methodological standardization, in general, as well as environmental performance assessment systems, in particular. Now commonly used in top hotel chains, these tools should, as we have pointed out, evolve into comprehensive platforms that would, apart from measuring a property's contribution to environmental conservation and social causes, provide smart feedback and analysis of "outcomes" (rather than only "outputs").

We believe that the insights offered by this chapter are of particular interest to hoteliers seeking to improve measurement and disclosure of their properties' sustainability record. Yet these insights should also inspire academics to conduct more research into how sustainability is measured and reported and, at the same time, to contribute to the ongoing debate on how firms view CSR. In particular, researchers might wish to ascertain – using a longitudinal (rather than cross-sectional) design – whether hotel firms' social and environmental performance affects the attitudes and behaviours of their stakeholders, with customers and employees to the fore. Furthermore, it might be instructive to find out how different stakeholder engagement strategies impact on sustainability reports – a research area that, as mentioned earlier, remains understudied.

In essence, pursuit of sustainability raises fundamental questions about the role of business in society. And multinational hotel firms, with their global reach and important financial resources, are particularly well placed to promote the development of a fair, equitable, and environmentally friendly society.

Notes

1 In the late 1990s, such terms as "social auditing" and "social accounting" came to be replaced with a single acronym – SEAAR, or "social and ethical accounting, auditing and reporting" (Zadek, Pruzan, & Evans, 1997).
2 The other values featuring in the circular framework of values are conformity, tradition, security, power, achievement, hedonism, stimulation, and self-direction.
3 Given their focus, universalism and benevolence are categorized as self-transcendent values (one of the four higher-order value dimensions).
4 Bourne (2009) defines stakeholder engagement as "practices, processes and actions that an organisation must perform to involve stakeholders in any organisational activity to secure their involvement and commitment, or reduce their indifference or hostility" (p. 93).
5 When it comes to corporate communication and stakeholder engagement, it is important to note that Morsing and Schultz (2006) came up with three distinct communication strategies: informing, responding, and involving. Building on this distinction, Bowen, Newenham-Kahindi, and Herremans (2010) proposed three community engagement strategies (transactional, transitional, and transformational). An informing strategy, like a transactional engagement, is a one-way communication process, whereby an organization informs the target audience. A responding strategy, like transitional community engagement, relies on two-way communication, whereby an organization takes into account stakeholder suggestions. An involving strategy, like transformational engagement, is a two-way communication process that entails joint decision-making or joint management of a project.
6 Prevalent in service occupations (Lewis & McCann, 2004), emotional labour is defined as the "management of feeling to create a publicly observable facial and bodily display" (Hochschild, 1983, p. 7). Hence, an employee is expected to smile when interacting with a client even if they are upset or angry (Chu, Baker, & Murrmann, 2012).
7 Chong and Ricaurte (2014, p. 15) point out that there are two analytical approaches to measuring the contribution of laundry wash to a hotel's energy usage: the bottom-up approach and the top-down approach. "The bottom-up approach adds up the amount of laundry used, determines drivers of this laundry use, and looks at the energy per unit of laundry (which may vary based on technology)." The top-down approach "looks at total energy use and attempts to infer the energy used for laundry based on variation in laundry use across hotels".
8 The Carbon Disclosure Project addressed this issue by requiring reporting in absolute figures and including the emissions of supplier and franchised entities. As regards social performance reporting, most companies accurately reported on their philanthropic activities. The problem lies in reporting non-monetary performance measures.

References

Adams, C. A., Hill, W. Y., & Roberts, C. B. (1998). Corporate social reporting practices in Western Europe: Legitimating corporate behavior? *The British Accounting Review, 30*(1), 1–21.

Álvarez-Gil, M. J., Burgos-Jimenez, J., & Cespedes-Lorente, J. J. (2001). An analysis of environmental management, organizational context and performance of Spanish hotels. *Omega, 29*(6), 457–471.

ARUP. (2014). *IHG's Green Engage programme reaches global proportions.* Retrieved 29 May 2017, from http://www.arup.com/news/2014_10_october/29_october_ihgs_green_engage_programme/.

Azapagic, A. (2003). Systems approach to corporate sustainability: A general management framework. *Process Safety and Environmental Protection, 81*(5), 303–316.

Behnam, M., & MacLean, T. L. (2011). Where is the accountability in international accountability standards? A decoupling perspective. *Business Ethics Quarterly, 21*(1), 45–72.

Bohdanowicz, P., & Zientara, P. (2008). Corporate social responsibility in hospitality: Issues and implications, a case study of Scandic. *Scandinavian Journal of Hospitality and Tourism, 8*(4), 271–293.

Bohdanowicz, P., & Zientara, P. (2009). Hotel companies' contribution to improving the quality of life of local communities and the well-being of their employees. *Tourism and Hospitality Research, 9*(2), 147–158.

Bohdanowicz, P., Zientara, P., & Novotna, E. (2011). International hotel chains and environmental protection: Analysis of Hilton's we care! programme (Europe, 2006–2008). *Journal of Sustainable Tourism, 19*(7), 797–816.

Bohdanowicz-Godfrey, P., & Zientara, P. (2015). Environmental management and online environmental performance assessment tools in the hotel industry: Theory and practice. In C. M. Hall, S. Gössling, & D. Scott (Eds.), *The Routledge Handbook of Tourism and Sustainability* (pp. 342–356). Abingdon: Routledge.

Bourne, L. (2009). *Stakeholder Relationship Management.* Farnham: Gower.

Bowen, F., Newenham-Kahindi, A., & Herremans, I. (2010). When suits meet roots: The antecedents and consequences of community engagement strategy. *Journal of Business Ethics, 95*(2), 297–318.

Chong, H. G., & Ricaurte, E. E. (2014). Hotel sustainability benchmarking study. *Cornell Hospitality Report, 14*(11), 1–29.

Chu, K. H., Baker, M. A., & Murrmann, S. K. (2012). When we are onstage, we smile: The effects of emotional labor on employee outcomes. *International Journal of Hospitality Management, 31*(3), 906–915.

Collier, J., & Esteban, R. (2007). Corporate social responsibility and employee commitment. *Business Ethics: A European Review, 16*(1), 19–33.

Cummings, L., & Patel, C. (2009). Managerial attitudes toward a stakeholder prominence within a Southeast Asian context. In M. J. Epstein (Ed.), *Studies in Managerial and Financial Accounting* (pp. 1–219). Bingley: Emerald.

De Burgos-Jiménez, J., Cano-Guillén, C. J., & Céspedes-Lorente, J. J. (2002). Planning and control of environmental performance in hotels. *Journal of Sustainable Tourism, 10*(3), 207–221.

Depoers, F., Jeanjean, T., & Jérôme, T. (2016). Voluntary disclosure of greenhouse gas emissions: Contrasting the Carbon Disclosure Project and corporate reports. *Journal of Business Ethics, 134*(3), 445–461.

Donaldson, T., & Dunfee, T. W. (1999). *Ties that Bind: A Social Contacts Approach to Business Ethics.* Boston: Harvard Business School Press.

Erdogan, N., & Baris, E. (2007). Environmental protection programs and conservation practices of hotels in Ankara, Turkey. *Tourism Management, 28*, 604–614.

Fraj, E., Matute, J., & Melero, I. (2015). Environmental strategies and organizational competitiveness in the hotel industry: The role of learning and innovation as determinants of environmental success. *Tourism Management, 46*, 30–42.

Freeman, R. E., Harrison, J. S., Wicks, A. C., Parmar, B. L., & de Colle, S. (2010). *Stakeholder Theory: The State of the Art.* Cambridge: Cambridge University Press.

Garavan, T., & McGuire, D. (2010). Human resource development and society: Human resource development's role in embedding corporate social responsibility, sustainability, and ethics in organizations. *Advances in Developing Human Resources, 12*(5), 487–507.

Golob, U., & Podnar, K. (2014). Critical points of CSR-related stakeholder dialogue in practice. *Business Ethics: A European Review, 23*(3), 248–257.

Gössling, S. (2015). New performance indicators for water management in tourism. *Tourism Management, 46*, 233–244.

Green Hotelier (2014). *TripAdvisor GreenLeaders launches in Europe.* Retrieved 23 August 2016, from http://www.greenhotelier.org/our-themes/policy-certification-business/tripadvisor-greenleaders-launches-in-europe/.

Green Hotels Global. (2017). *The Hotel Industry Environmental Database*. Retrieved 29 May 2017, from https://www.greenhotelsglobal.com/.

Greenwood, M. (2007). Stakeholder engagement: Beyond the myth of corporate responsibility. *Journal of Business Ethics*, 74(4), 315–327.

Hadjikakou, M., Chenoweth, J., & Miller, G. (2013). Estimating the direct and indirect water use of tourism in the eastern Mediterranean. *Journal of Environmental Management*, 114, 548–556.

Hailey, J. (1998). Management education for sustainable development. *Sustainable Development*, 6(1), 40–48.

Hall, C. M., Gössling, S., & Scott, D. (Eds.) (2015). *The Routledge Handbook of Tourism and Sustainability*. Abingdon: Routledge.

Han, H., & Yoon, H. (2015). Customer retention in the eco-friendly hotel sector: Examining the diverse processes of post-purchase decision-making. *Journal of Sustainable Tourism*, 23(7), 1095–1113.

Hawkins, R., & Bohdanowicz, P. (2011). *Responsible Hospitality: Theory and Practice*. Woodeaton, Oxford: Goodfellow Publishers.

Herremans, I. M., Nazari, J. A., & Mahmoudia, F. (2016). Stakeholder relationships, engagement, and sustainability reporting. *Journal of Business Ethics*, 138(3), 417–435.

Hess, D. (2008). The three pillars of corporate social reporting as new governance regulation: Disclosure, dialogue, and development. *Business Ethics Quarterly*, 18(4), 447–482.

Hilton. (2017). *Corporate Responsibility*. Retrieved 2 April 2017, from http://cr.hiltonworldwide.com/.

Hilton Worldwide. (2010). *Hilton Worldwide unveils "LightStay" sustainability measurement system*. Retrieved 29 May 2017, from http://news.hiltonworldwide.com/index.cfm/newsroom/detail/3094/.

Hilton Worldwide. (2011). *Hilton Worldwide earns ISO 9001 and ISO 14001 certifications for quality and environmental management*. Retrieved 29 May 2017, from http://news.hiltonworldwide.com/index.cfm/news/hilton-worldwide-earns-iso-9001-and-iso-14001-certifications-for-quality-and-environmental-management/.

Hilton Worldwide. (2014). *Hilton Worldwide achieves ISO 50001 certification*. Retrieved 29 May 2017, from http://news.hiltonworldwide.com/index.cfm/news/hilton-worldwide-achieves-iso-50001-certification/.

Hilton Worldwide. (2015). *Hilton Worldwide unveils upgrades to corporate responsibility reporting across its global portfolio*. Retrieved 29 May 2017, from http://news.hiltonworldwide.com/index.cfm/news/hilton-worldwide-unveils-upgrades-to-corporate-responsibility-reporting-across-its-global-portfolio-/.

Hochschild, A. R. (1983). *The Managed Heart*. Berkeley: University of California Press.

Intercontinental Hotel Group. (2017). *IHG Green Engage™ system*. Retrieved 29 May 2017, from https://www.ihgplc.com/responsible-business/environmental-sustainability/ihg-green-engage-system/.

International Tourism Partnership (2015). *ITP launches Hotel Water Measurement Initiative*. Retrieved 29 May 2017, from http://tourismpartnership.org/news/itp-launches-hotel-water-measurement-initiative/.

International Tourism Partnership. (2017). *Issues we address*. Retrieved 29 May 2017, from http://tourismpartnership.org/issues-we-address/.

International Tourism Partnership and Greenview. (2017). *Hotel Footprinting Tool*. Retrieved 29 May 2017, from https://www.hotelfootprints.org/.

Jacob, M., Florido, C., & Aguiló, E. (2010). Environmental innovation as a competitiveness factor in the Balearic Islands. *Tourism Economics*, 16(3), 755–764.

Kaspersen, M., & Johansen, T. R. (2016). Changing social and environmental reporting systems. *Journal of Business Ethics*, 135(4), 731–749.

Laplume, A. O., Sonpar, K., & Litz, R. A. (2008). Stakeholder theory: Reviewing a theory that moves us. *Journal of Management, 34*(6), 1152–1189.

Leslie, D. (2012). Tourism, tourists and sustainability. In D. Leslie (Ed.), *Tourism Enterprises and the Sustainability Agenda across Europe* (pp. 15–34). Farnham: Ashgate.

Lewis, B. R., & McCann, P. (2004). Service failure and recovery: Evidence from the hotel sector. *International Journal of Contemporary Hospitality Management, 16*(1), 6–17.

Manetti, G. (2011). The quality of stakeholder engagement in sustainability reporting: Empirical evidence and critical points. *Corporate Social Responsibility and Environmental Management, 18*(2), 110–122.

Manetti, G., & Toccafondi, S. (2012). The role of stakeholders in sustainability reporting assurance. *Journal of Business Ethics, 107*(3), 363–377.

Milne, M., & Gray, R. (2013). W(h)ither ecology? The triple bottom line, the global reporting initiative, and corporate sustainability reporting. *Journal of Business Ethics, 118*(1), 13–29.

Molina-Azorín, J. F., Claver-Cortés, E., Pereira-Moliner, J., & Tarí, J. J. (2009). Environmental practices and firm performance: An empirical analysis in the Spanish hotel industry. *Journal of Cleaner Production, 17*(5), 516–524.

Montiel, I. (2008). Corporate social responsibility and corporate sustainability. Separate pasts, common futures. *Organization Environment, 21*(3), 245–269.

Morhardt, J. E., Baird, S., & Freeman, K. (2002). Scoring corporate environmental and sustainability reports using GRI 2000, ISO 14031 and other criteria. *Corporate Social Responsibility and Environmental Management, 9*(4), 215–233.

Morsing, M, & Schultz, M. (2006). Corporate social responsibility communication: Stakeholder information, response and involvement strategies. *Business Ethics: A European Review, 15*(4), 323–338.

Potter, B. N. (2005). Accounting as a social and institutional practice: Perspectives to enrich our understanding of accounting change. *ABACUS, 41*(3), 265–289.

Power, M. (1994). *The Audit Explosion*. London: Demos.

Power, M. (1996). Making things auditable. *Accounting, Organizations and Society, 21*(2–3), 289–315.

Schwartz, S. H. (1996). Value priorities and behavior: Applying of theory of integrated value systems. In C. Seligman, J. M. Olson, & M. P. Zanna (Eds.), *The Psychology of Values: The Ontario Symposium* (pp. 1–24). Hillsdale: Erlbaum.

Searcy, C. (2009). Setting a course in corporate sustainability performance measurement. *Measuring Business Excellence, 13*(3), 49–57.

Senge, P. M. (1990). *The Fifth Discipline*. New York: Currency Doubleday.

Skouloudis, A., Evangelinos, K., & Kourmousis, F. (2009). Development of an evaluation methodology for triple bottom line reports using international standards on reporting. *Environmental Management, 44*(2), 298–311.

Sloan, P., Legrand, W., & Chen, J. S. (2009). *Sustainability in the Hospitality Industry: Principles of Sustainable Operations*. Oxford: Elsevier.

Smerecnik, K., & Andersen, P. (2011). The diffusion of environmental sustainability innovations in North American hotels and ski resorts. *Journal of Sustainable Tourism, 19*(2), 171–196.

Solomon, R. C., & Hanson, K. (1985). *It's Good Business*. New York: Harper & Row.

Swanson, D. L. (2014). *Embedding CSR into Corporate Culture*. New York: Palgrave MacMillan.

Székely, F., & Knirsch, M. (2005). Responsible leadership and corporate social responsibility: Metrics for sustainable performance. *European Management Journal, 23*(6), 628–647.

TripAdvisor. (2017). *Green Hotels: The GreenLeaders Programme from TripAdvisor*. Retrieved 2 April 2017, from Available at: https://www.tripadvisor.co.uk/GreenLeaders/.

United Nations (1987). *Our Common Future*. Report of the World Commission on Environment and Development.

Velasquez, M. G. (1998). *Business Ethics: Cases and Concepts*. Englewood Cliffs: Prentice Hall.

Vigneau, L., Humphreys, M., & Moon, J. (2015). How do firms comply with international sustainability standards? Processes and consequences of adopting the Global Reporting Initiative. *Journal of Business Ethics, 131*(2), 469–486.

Yadava, R. N., & Sinha, B. (2016). Scoring sustainability reports using GRI 2011 guidelines for assessing environmental, economic, and social dimensions of leading public and private Indian companies. *Journal of Business Ethics, 138*(3), 549–558.

Zadek, S. (1994). Trading ethics: Auditing the market. *Journal of Economic Issues, 28*(2), 631–645.

Zadek, S., Pruzan, P., & Evans. R. (Eds.) (1997). *Building Corporate Accountability: Emerging Practices in Social and Ethical Accounting and Auditing*. London: Earthscan Publications.

3.5 The growth of social banks

A new measurement approach

Nikolas Höhnke and Susanne Homölle

Introduction

Since the beginning of the financial crisis in 2007, banking journals and newspapers have reported on the enormous growth of so-called 'social banks' in Germany. Social banks, also known as ethical, green, sustainable, or alternative banks, are credit institutions that integrate social and environmental issues into their core business model and provide financial services to individuals and organizations that create a positive social or environmental impact (Weber 2014). In addition to hypotheses about the reasons for their growth and the prediction of further growth, the quantification has been a central part of the media landscape. The range of growth reported in the media reaches from lower double-digit percentages to 30% per year (Lumma and Jauernig 2010; Benedikter 2011; RBSC 2012; ZEB 2012; Remer 2014). Accordingly, social banks must have grown by a factor of between 2.59 and 13.78 for the period 2007 to 2016. Especially in times of stagnant or even shrinking markets, it seems that the business model of social banks has proved successful.

However, a closer look at these reports discovers several issues that attack the objectivity and validity of the data. Apart from the vagueness of the objects of the 'analyses' and the time distribution of the data, the growth measure used in these 'studies' is inappropriate. Following a convention in the field of banking, customer deposits and total assets are often used as measures to quantify banks' size and growth (e.g., Lumma and Jauernig 2010; Benedikter 2011; Jauernig 2014; Remer 2014). Even if the relevant literature quotes several arguments that deny the usefulness of customer deposits and total assets as valid proxy variables for bank size, using total assets has emerged as a common standard in practice and science. Total assets and customer deposits can be interpreted as a measure of services produced and sold in previous periods (output) or as the capability to produce and sell further services in following periods (input) (Baxmann 1995). Both scales are thus an expression of purely commercial (selling) efforts, so that they are useful proxies only for companies with a purely commercial purpose.

Social banks, however, arrange their business model in the sense of the triple bottom line approach (Benedikter 2011; Weber 2014; GABV 2016), which is based on an equal consideration of economic, ecological, and social aspects in all corporate activities (Jamali 2006). The representation of a social bank's total activities by only using total assets and customer deposits is not appropriate, because these proxies merely reflect one of three equally important aspects. Following this line of argumentation, existing proxies cannot be useful to measure the growth of companies with multidimensional objectives like those of social banks. Another, more specific measurement approach for the growth of social banks has been unavailable in the literature so far.

Social banks face the same challenges as the companies they finance. Customer demand for sustainable products and services is on the rise (Future Business Council 2015). Furthermore, customers are willing to pay more for these products (Nielsen 2014). In consequence, companies have the incentive to be perceived as sustainable. Therefore, 'sustainability reporting has become a mainstream practice in the communication of corporate commitment to and performance on sustainability issues' (Boiral et al. 2017, Introduction, para. 1). However, the extension of sustainability disclosures is discussed critically (Cho et al. 2015), because the gap between disclosures and real business practices reveals greenwash tendencies. Greenwashing leads to a general uncertainty among customers, and in consequence to damage to virtuous companies (Chen and Chang 2013). To face these problems, there is an enormous public and scientific debate that deals with sustainable production, reporting, and greenwashing. However, this debate has rarely included social banking, even though social banks seem to show comparable demand growth and face the greenwashing strategies of conventional banks. This gap is surprising, because social banking could be a relevant tool to reduce customers' uncertainty, and not just for financial products. One major function of financial intermediaries is screening of their investment counterparties to reduce depositors' uncertainty about risk and (in this case) about sustainability as well. Social banks could be reliable information providers to overcome the problems of information asymmetries between customers and companies in general. However, due to the lack of a scientific foundation regarding the size and growth of social banks, the impact of social banks on the overall development of sustainability is unclear.

Therefore, the objective of this paper is to develop a valid measure of growth for social banks that reflects the specific characteristics and needs of sustainably focused cooperation.

The development of an appropriate growth measure fulfils three major purposes. First, it allows a critical reflection of the conventional growth measures as well as the properness of the reported growth values. Second, it enables a sound description of the development of the market and a differentiated judgement of social banks' contribution to a sustainable economy. Finally, a more detailed model enables the separation of inherent components and thus a better explanation of the drivers of and obstacles to social banks' growth.

Since we are considering a very specific form of credit institution, the term 'social bank' is defined in more detail and differentiated from related concepts in the next section. The requirements for a new and more suitable growth measurement approach are deduced from the relevant literature on companies' and banks' growth. We then explain the intermediation approach as our basic model of banking, before we show the conception and our way of operationalizing the new measure. Afterwards, the developed measure is demonstrated using GLS Bank as an example. The chapter ends with a concluding discussion.

Social banking

The term 'social banking' might be easily confused with the modern phenomenon of social media banking. Social media banking, such as peer-to-peer-lending, includes several forms of direct lending between private parties without central mediators like financial institutions that offer transformation services (Bachmann et al. 2011). In this chapter, we concentrate on social banking – also called sustainable, ethical, or green banking – and hence on financial intermediation. The intermediary acts as a third party between lenders and borrowers.

The literature offers no generally accepted definition of the term 'social banking' (Weber and Remer 2011). Many more or less similar definitions are available. One reason for the existence of various similar but not fully equal understandings could be that while social banks have quite similar objectives and business areas, these objectives and business areas arise from different ideological origins (Franz 2007; De Clearck 2009). A taxonomy of social banking based on individual ideological background would consequently lead to a higher divergence than a taxonomy based on concrete objectives or actual business lines. As will be shown later, a growth measure should reflect a bank's objectives. Therefore, it seems indispensable to define social banks by referring to their objectives and observed business areas instead of their ideological origin.

Most definitions of social banking have one aspect in common: they emphasize the importance of a multidimensional system of corporate objectives. Apart from the usually dominating financial or profit orientation in banking, ecological and social objectives are taken into account and elevated to an equal rank (Benedikter 2011; Weber 2014; GABV 2016; ISB 2016). The recognition of these three equally ranked dimensions meets the so-called triple bottom line approach.[1] Some authors go one step further and suggest that profits are an unnecessary by-product in the process of social and environmental impact creation (Weber 2014). However, ignoring profits seems to conflict with the going concern principle (Baxmann 1995). For example, profits are needed for the compensation of loan defaults, for raising equity, or to create reserves.

Weber (2014, p. 265) concretizes the role of social banks in the creation of social and ecological impact as follows: 'Social banks provide financial services to individuals and organizations that create social, environmental or sustainability benefits.' These financial services consist primarily of taking deposits and distributing loans (FEBEA 2012), but also of other investments or even gifts (Weber and Remer 2011). Thus, social banks enable social and environmental impact by financing individuals and organizations that create this impact.

To sum up, three aspects are part of our working definition of social banking: the differentiation from social media banking, the triple bottom line approach, and the core business areas. A social bank is thus defined as a financial intermediary (bank) that primarily takes deposits and other kinds of debt to distribute them in the form of loans and other investments to individuals and organizations, with the objectives of creating social and environmental impact on the real economy and gaining at least sufficient profit for securing the bank's going concern.

This definition describes the core idea of social banking, but will not guarantee a clear differentiation between truly sustainably focused financial institutions and those that merely pretend to be. However, San-Jose et al. (2011) found significant differences between social banks and other financial institutions in the placement of the assets themselves as well as the transparency of their asset placement. Social banks provide at least aggregated information about their asset placement in various categories. Some institutions even disclose all their investments separately to enable full transparency. This level of transparency is necessary to guarantee that investments do not contravene their self-imposed positive and negative asset placement criteria. The clear exclusion of investments with a negative social or ecological impact, the focus on investments in the real economy with a positive social or ecological impact and a high level of transparency to secure investment selection are concrete criteria to identify a social or ecological objective and thus a social bank.

Growth measure

Requirements for growth measures

A theoretically sound normative measurement approach needs comprehensible criteria to evaluate the quality of the measure. As the research strand of banks' growth quantification is a special part of the literature about the quantification of companies' growth, we use criteria from both research strands. According to Zahn (1971), three requirements are important for the development of a growth measure for all types of companies:

(A) reflection of reality as far as possible,
(B) representation of corporates' objectives (and success definition) and
(C) operationalizability.

These three requirements can be assigned to two subgroups. The reflection of reality (A) and the representation of objectives (B) are criteria that are mainly important for the theoretical conception of the measure. They must even be fulfilled in purely normative approaches. We call this group 'conceptual requirements'.

The fulfilment of operationalizability (C) goes beyond the conception. It lifts a purely normative approach to a functional level by transferring the conceptual approach to a practicable figure. Operationalizability thus belongs to a group called 'application-oriented requirements'.

Both groups are supplemented by bank-specific growth measurement requirements. In the banking literature, we find further conceptual requirements (Osthues–Albrecht 1974; Tebroke 1994):

(D) the measure has to be applicable to all banks in the sample and
(E) it has to represent all areas and characteristics of these banks.

Requirement D enables interbank comparisons and complements the conceptual requirements. The demand for representation of all areas and characteristics of a bank (E) can be subsumed under requirement A. A comprehensive representation of the total bank business reflects the reality of banking. Therefore, the major challenge is the combined representation of the lending and deposit-taking business of banks (Osthues–Albrecht 1974).

Tebroke (1994) formulates two further application-oriented requirements:

(F) the measure should be easy to operate and
(G) the necessary data should be generally accessible (especially for an external analyst).

Both requirements are complementary conditions to the need for general operationalizability. C is the compulsory main condition because, first of all, a growth measure must be operationalizable. Afterwards, one can examine whether F and G are fulfilled.

Our line of argumentation ends up with two groups of requirements, one for the conception and one for the operationalization, which enable a stepwise and comprehensible judgement on growth measures. Table 3.5.1 provides a final overview of both groups of requirements.

Table 3.5.1 Requirements for growth measures

Conceptual requirements		
(A)	To reflect reality as well as possible	
(B)	To represent the corporate definitions of objectives (and success)	
(D)	To be applicable to all banks in the sample	

Application-oriented requirements		
(C)	*Main condition*	To be operational
(F)	*Complementary conditions*	To be easy to operate
(G)		To use generally accessible data

Banking paradigms

The banking literature mainly offers two theoretical models of a bank, the so-called production approach and the intermediation approach (Subramanyam and Reddy 2008; Kipesha 2013; Hartmann-Wendels et al. 2015). The production approach is a bank-specific adaptation of Gutenberg's production theory and goes back to the 1950s (Deppe 1964). The entire banking growth research strand has been based on this banking paradigm so far. Deppe (1964) was the first to develop a theoretically founded growth measurement approach, which has been the basis of subsequent research projects (Deppe 1964; Osthues-Albrecht 1974; Tebroke 1994; Baxmann 1995). According to the production approach, the creation of banking services consists of three elements: first, the input of dispositive, elementary, and financial production factors; second, the production itself, where the factors are combined and used; and third, the output of financial products and services, like loans or savings accounts (Deppe 1964). In the bank-specific factor system elementary factors, such as labour and physical assets, and dispositive factors, for example the bank organization, are combined in the so-called technical-organizational sphere (TOS), which is separated from the liquidity-financial sphere representing all financial inputs; that is, capital (Deppe 1964; Tebroke 1994). Basically, the production approach assumes that the pursuit of profits is the sole objective of banks (Deppe 1964; Baxmann 1995). All production factors are used to create financial services, which in turn will create profits. This assumption does not fit the definition of social banking and its multidimensional objective system. Growth measures based on this paradigm infringe requirement B, mentioned earlier.

The intermediation approach is a younger concept of a bank's service creation and has been the dominant banking paradigm for most efficiency studies (Lang and Welzel 1996; Altunbas et al. 2001). However, a growth measurement theory for the intermediation paradigm is still missing. In contrast to the production approach, banks are not production corporations but intermediaries between depositors and borrowers. This description already illustrates the major difference between these paradigms: deposits are inputs in the intermediation approach, whereas they are outputs in the production approach (Subramanyam and Reddy 2008). In addition to deposits and other kinds of debt, labour, physical capital, and equity are inputs (Thakor and Boot 2008). Inputs can be classified as internal or external. Deposits and other liabilities like bonds are external. Their availability depends on the financial market. Labour and physical assets are internal inputs, which enable the intermediary to transform deposits, for instance into loans. Even if the equity is part of the liabilities side of the balance sheet and can be seen as part of the funding, we merge it with labour and physical assets and classify it as part of the so-called internal-organization sphere (IOS) because of its function in the transformation process. In comparison to debt, equity is more expensive from a long-term perspective. Therefore, banks have the incentive to finance investments by debt rather than by equity. However, by regulatory requirements, banks are forced to back up risk positions on the asset side of the balance sheet with sufficient equity. That means that equity is needed only in the case of the transformation of deposits into assets. Therefore, equity is comparable to the other elements of the IOS.

The IOS can be seen in Figure 3.5.1, which shows an intermediation approach model of banking.

Fundamentally, the present intermediation approach is not able to reflect the whole range of possible banking activities, such as investment banking (Hartmann-Wendels et al. 2015) or proprietary trading. However, neither investment banking nor proprietary trading contributes to social banks' objectives, because the creation of profits by price changes in securities does not create an additional social or environmental value. Thus, the inclusion of these services is not necessary at all for a growth measurement approach to social banks. Other special services like consulting or mergers and acquisitions for social businesses are not reflected either, even if they could create a positive impact. This limitation is not very restrictive, because these services are only an insignificant part of social banks' business. According to the European Federation of Ethical and Alternative Banks (FEBEA 2012), the core business model is commercial banking. Therefore, the model shown in Figure 3.5.1 is able to reflect the core banking business of social banks and fulfils requirement A, above.

Furthermore, as stated, the objective of social banks is the maximization of social and environmental impact. Since social banks reach that objective by transforming deposits into (for example) loans to organizations that create this impact, the intermediation model is able to reflect corporate objectives (requirement B) as well.

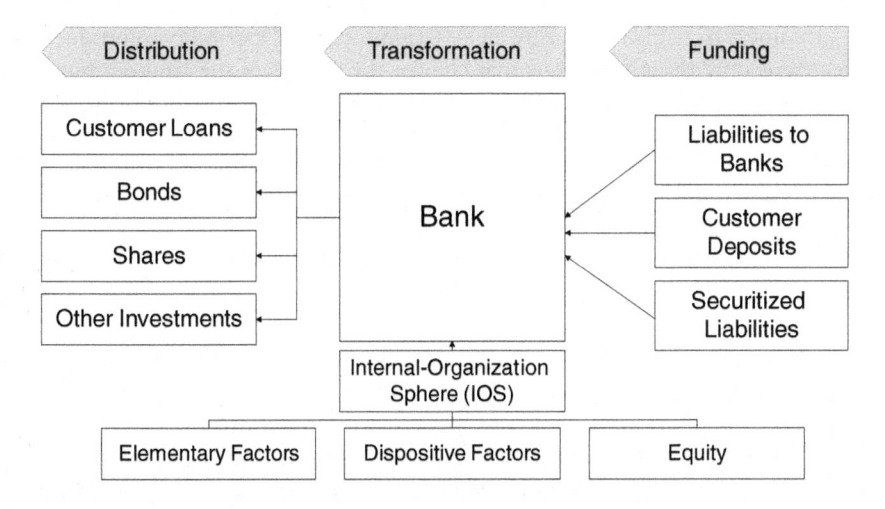

Figure 3.5.1 Intermediation approach

Finally, we do not see any lack of suitability of the model for the entire group of social banks (requirement D).

Since all conceptual requirements for the development of growth measures are met by the intermediation model, we prefer to use the intermediation approach, even if the entire literature on the measurement of banks' growth arises from the production approach.

Conception

Looking at the human body, everyone has a clear idea of what is meant by the term 'growth' and how it could be quantified. A person has a size at a certain point in time, which can be quantified with an ordinary measuring tape in centimetres, inches, feet, or something similar. If a subsequent measurement leads to a higher result, the body has grown. As there is no possibility of continuous measurement of (a body's) growth, it is quantified by a comparative static approach. Absolute growth, $G_{a,t}$, is the difference between the sizes at two points in time, ΔS_t:

$$G_{a,t} = \Delta S_t = S_t - S_{t-n}, \tag{1}$$

where n is the number of periods between the two points in time.

To compare the growth of two bodies or banks, we need a relative (instead of an absolute) growth figure, $G_{r,t}$, which is also called the growth rate:

$$G_{r,t} = \frac{\Delta S_t}{S_{t-n}}. \tag{2}$$

Basically, banks' growth can be interpreted as the variation of banks' capability to create banking services (Deppe 1964). Zahn (1971) states that a suitable measure of the growth of a company should represent the extent of target achievement. As already mentioned, in the production approach financial services are produced for one reason, namely profits. Therefore, it is not reasonable to measure all variations of banks' capability to produce banking services, but only those variations that change the output of the banking business in line with its objective to earn profits. Generalizing this interpretation of banks' growth leads to the following statements. A bank's growth is the (positive) variation of the capability to reach its objective. A bank's size, S_t, is hence the capability to reach its objective, $CAP_{Obj,t}$, at a point in time, t. In the following, we will skip the subscript t for ease of notation, so that

$$S = CAP_{Obj}. \tag{3}$$

Taking into account social banks' objectives is the first step to fulfilling requirement B for the development of growth measures. According to the definition of social banks, their objective is to supply capital to individuals and organisations that show a positive social or environmental impact on the real economy. Therefore, the size of social banks at a point in time is the capability to provide individuals and organizations with loans, other investments, and gifts by funding deposits and transforming them. This capability can be split into two sub–capabilities: the capability to take deposits and other liabilities (CAP_{Dep}) and the capability to transform these deposits and distribute them in form of loans and other investments (CAP_{Loa}).

Therefore, CAP_{Dep} depends on the demand for deposit contracts on the market. Independent of the subsequent transformation and distribution process, banks are free to collect as many deposits as they want, whereas CAP_{Loa} is not limited merely by the demand for loans but by the internal transformation as well. As can be seen in Figure 3.5.1, the transformation requires equity, elementary factors and dispositive factors. The transformation of deposits will only take place if a loan is distributed. Moreover, a loan can only be granted if the internal organization ensures the transformation. Thus, transformation is a basic element of the capability to distribute loans and make other investments, CAP_{Loa}.

If one sub–capability exceeded the other one and we chose the higher capability as a measure of the bank's size, an overestimation of total capability, CAP_{Obj}, would occur, because the surplus of the higher capability could never be realized. For example, if a social bank took €1 billion of deposits and wanted to hand out the same amount in loans, but had only enough equity or demand for loans to distribute €100 million, the total capability of the bank would be overestimated by €900 million if we referred to CAP_{Dep} as the measure of CAP_{Obj}. In this case, only €100 million of deposits would be transformed into loans. The total capability, CAP_{Obj}, is thus determined by the bottleneck of the intermediation process, so that

$$S = \min\left\{CAP_{Dep}; CAP_{Loa}\right\}. \tag{4}$$

Two cases might occur. In the first case, the bank collects more funds than it can distribute (see example above). The surplus capital must be held as liquidity or invested in assets that do not support the social bank's objective. The second case implies that the bank holds more 'impact assets' than debt. The deficit has to be balanced by equity or provisions. Even if all of these assets contribute to the bank's objective, this impact is not created by its function as an intermediary; that is, as the result of the transformation.

A description and almost an operationalisation of CAP_{Dep} can be derived from the intermediation model. The capability to collect deposits is the sum of all the borrowed capital of the bank, BC, at a point in time:

$$CAP_{Dep} = BC. \tag{5}$$

The variable BC includes all liabilities to customers and banks as well as securitized liabilities, because the sum of these liabilities is the result of the social bank's funding activities, which is displayed by the intermediation approach model. Other liabilities such as provisions arise from business activities but not from a social bank's funding activities and are thus not included in CAP_{Dep}.

The capability of social banks to distribute loans and other investments, CAP_{Loa}, is the sum of all existing assets at a point in time that support the bank's objective, A_{Obj}:

$$CAP_{Loa} = A_{Obj}. \tag{6}$$

If one expected that a social bank only held assets that supported its social or environmental objectives, A_{Obj} would be equal to its total assets, TA. However, in addition to the information about social banking's growth measured by total assets, some reports highlight the enormous growth of customer deposits in a short time period, especially in the years after the start of the financial crisis in 2007 (Remer 2014). If a direct transfer of these deposits to target-oriented assets was not possible, these deposits could just be held as liquid assets without any social, ecological or even financial impact, or be invested in other assets without any support for their social or ecological objectives. Therefore, we deduct the assets with no direct support for the bank's objectives, A_{noObj}, from the total assets to get the sum of target-oriented assets, A_{Obj}.

Nevertheless, the exclusion of every asset that is neither a loan to nor another investment in social or ecological impact organizations would be wrong. Some assets, like bank buildings, are necessary for the work of the social bank. We define such non-financial assets as a bank's buildings as an investment in its own social organization, which creates a positive social or ecological impact in the end. Thus, non-financial assets, which are needed for the core bank business, A_N, must not be subtracted from total assets.

In addition to A_N, some of the financial assets with no support for the bank's objectives, A_{noObj}, are necessary to fulfil the regulatory requirements or the transformation functions of social banks. One central function of a bank as a financial intermediary is maturity transformation; that is, the collection of short-term deposits and their distribution in the form of long-term loans and other investments. Due to the usual lack of matching maturities of deposits and assets, banks are forced to hold a certain amount of liquid assets, $LIQA_N$, such as cash or deposits with central banks, to be able to pay out customers who withdraw their deposits. These liquidity reserves decrease the amount of assets that are evaluated as not supporting the bank's objectives. To sum up, target-oriented assets are calculated as follows:

$$A_{Obj} = TA - \left(A_{noObj} - A_N - LIQA_N \right). \tag{7}$$

Inserting (6), (7) and (8) into (5) leads to

$$S = \min \left\{ BC; TA - \left(A_{noObj} - A_N - LIQA_N \right) \right\}. \tag{8}$$

To complete the design of our growth measure for social banks, the absolute growth, G_a, and relative growth, G_r, can be calculated by inserting (8) into (1) and (2), respectively.

The intermediation approach model seems to be the best available form of modelling social banking's core (commercial) business. To reflect reality as well as possible (see requirement A), both lending and deposit-taking are included in our measure as defined above. Since only assets that enable a social bank to achieve its objectives are taken into account, requirement B is also fulfilled. As investment banking and proprietary trading are not consistent with social banks' business model, these business lines are not included in our measure. The conceptual approach should thus be applicable to all social banks. For this reason, the final conceptual requirement D is also met.

Operationalization

One challenge to the operationalizability of (8) is the assignment of assets to A_{Obj} or A_{noObj}. The general assignment of loans, bonds and shares is especially critical. Although most social banks disclose positive and negative investment criteria, it is far from clear whether social banks only hold assets from counterparties that create a social and environmental impact. Their positive criteria describe individuals and organizations in which the social bank would invest, for instance renewable energy projects. The negative criteria close out investment opportunities that create social or environmental damage, for example atomic power plants. However, there is no evidence as to whether social banks invest in projects that are neither included by their positive criteria nor excluded by their negative criteria, such as a medium-sized carpentry business or a private household. As long as no further evidence exists, we assume that all loans to customers, bonds, and shares are A_{Obj}.

Therefore, as can be seen in Table 3.5.2, the variables TA, BC, A_{noObj} and A_N can be operationalized by a concrete balance sheet item or as the sum of several items.

$LIQA_N$ needs further specification. It consists of two parts. First, in accordance with article 19.1 of the statute of the European Central Bank (ECB), financial institutions must hold deposits with their national central banks. According to ECB regulation no. 2818/19, these so-called minimum reserves are determined by multiplying the reserve base by the current reserve rate. Since 2012, the reserve rate has been fixed at 1%. The reserve base, $RB_{M<2}$, mainly consists of deposits and securitized liabilities to non-banks with an agreed maturity or period of notice of up to two years (ECB 2016). A separate balance sheet item for these deposits and securitized liabilities does not exist, but the

Table 3.5.2 Variables and balance sheet items

Variables	Abbreviations	Calculation on the Basis of Balance Sheet Items	
Total assets	TA	Total assets	
Borrowed capital (funding result)	BC	Sum of	Liabilities to banks
			Liabilities to customers
			Securitized liabilities
			E.g. Profit participation certificates
Assets with no support for bank's objectives	A_{noObj}	Sum of	Cash
			Receivables from banks
			Intangible fixed assets
			Property and equipment
			Other assets
			Provisions
Non-financial assets needed	A_N	Sum of	Intangible fixed assets
			Property and equipment
Liquid assets needed ($LIQA_N$)	$0.01 \cdot RB$	Sum of	Savings accounts and other funds entrusted: payable on demand
			Savings accounts and other funds entrusted: 1 to 3 months
			Savings accounts and other funds entrusted: 3 months to 1 year
			¼ of savings accounts and other funds entrusted: 1 to 5 years
			Securitized liabilities with a maturity < 2 years
	$0.0321 \cdot TA$	Total assets	

notes to the financial statement generally offer a differentiated presentation of all liabilities and their maturities. The liabilities are often divided into five groups: 'on demand', '1 to 3 months', '3 months to 1 year', '1 to 5 years', and 'longer than 5 years'. For our analysis, the first three groups and part of '1 to 5 years' must be summarized to get the reserve base. As there is no possibility for external analysts to further split up the '1 to 5 years' item, we assume a uniform distribution of maturities between 1 and 5 years and divide the value of this item by 4. Finally, the reserve base, $RB_{M<2}$, is multiplied by the current reserve rate of 0.01 to get the first part of $LIQA_N$.

Second, in 2008 the Basel Committee on Banking Supervision (BCBS 2008) published the *Principles for Sound Liquidity Risk Management and Supervisory*, which include different key figures, such as the Liquidity Coverage Ratio, *LCR*. Their purpose is 'to ensure that a bank maintains an adequate level of unencumbered, high-quality liquid assets that can be converted into cash to meet its liquidity needs for a 30 calendar day time horizon under a significantly severe liquidity stress scenario' (BCBS 2010, p. 3), which means that

$$LCR = \frac{HQLA}{TNCO_{30}} \geq 100\%.$$ (9)

HQLA is the stock of high-quality liquid assets and $TNCO_{30}$ denotes the total net cash outflows over the next 30 days.

As external analysts cannot determine the $TNCO_{30}$ of a bank, the following argumentation falls back on a statistically based generalization. To reach a minimum ratio of 1 (*LCR* = 1), *HQLA* has to be as high as $TNCO_{30}$. The quantification of *HQLA* is as complicated as that for $TNCO_{30}$. The European Banking Authority (EBA 2014), however, published average values, which enable a generalised approach. The average *HQLA* of a sample of 322 European banks corresponds to approximately 12.5% of total assets. This percentage leads to an average *LCR* of 116.7% (EBA 2014). An *LCR* of 100% would *ceteris paribus* require *HQLA* to be approximately 10.71% (= 100 · 12.5% / 116.7) of total assets. However, by definition, *HQLA* might consist not only of cash or deposits with central banks, but also of, for example, high-quality bonds on high-liquid markets. Just 30% of *HQLA* must be cash or deposits with central banks (article 17.1.b. of EU 2015/61). The remaining 70% could consist of different bonds and stocks with certain risk-specific value adjustments. Combining the 10.71% of *HQLA* and the 30% requirement for purely liquid assets, approximately 3.21% of total assets must (at least) be held as purely liquid assets.

As the minimum reserves are not accepted as *HQLA* (article 10.1.b.iii. of (EU) 2015/61), $LIQA_N$ can be calculated as follows:

$$LIQA_N = 0.01 n RB_{M<2} + 0.0321 n TA.$$ (10)

Within this specification all variables of (8) are operationalized by surrogates from a social bank's financial statement and its notes. Table 3.5.2 summarizes the variables and their quantification methods. The *general* operationalizability of our measure is obvious, so that the main condition (C) of the application-oriented requirements is also met. Since all data can be extracted from financial statements, the general accessibility of data (G) is given as well. Furthermore, no complex collection or processing of data is needed, so that requirement F is fulfilled too.

Example

GLS Bank is a credit union located in Bochum, Germany. It has been part of several media reports about the growth of social banks in Germany (Benedikter 2011; Weber and Remer 2011; Remer 2014). GLS Bank fulfils the previously notified criteria for social banks. It publishes at least aggregated information for all its assets and does not invest in organizations that contravene its negative criteria (San-Jose et al. 2011).

All data needed for the quantification of GLS Bank's growth within the intermediation approach model are extracted from its financial statements from 2006 to 2015.

Figure 3.5.2 points out that since 2006, CAP_{Loa} has been lower than CAP_{Dep}. This means that according to (5), the capability to provide ecologically and socially oriented individuals and organizations with loans and other investments, CAP_{Loa}, has defined the size of GLS Bank continuously for the period under review.

Since 2006, the gap between CAP_{Dep} and CAP_{Loa} has increased constantly. Growth quantifications with a focus on depositors (e.g., Jauernig 2014; Remer 2014) could thus lead to overestimations of GLS Bank's growth. However, even the lower CAP_{Loa} has risen continuously since 2006, so that GLS Bank's size has multiplied by a factor of approximately 5.42 in nine years.

A check of GLS Bank's disclosure reports from 2014 and 2015 reveals no limitation of CAP_{Loa} due to a lack of equity, as only approximately 63% of the equity was needed to meet regulatory requirements. Furthermore, indications of a limitation of CAP_{Loa} due to a lack of dispositive or elementary factors are not apparent, at least in GLS Bank's annual reports. Therefore, we assume that CAP_{Loa} is limited by the (non-)availability of suitable investment opportunities.

Figure 3.5.3 illustrates the development of GLS Bank's relative growth per year. Between 2006 and 2010, the growth rate, G_r, increased to a peak of 31.18%. Afterwards, a continuous flattening down to a level of 13.14% in the last year can be observed. Figure 3.5.3 also shows the mean growth rate of 20.81% over the entire observation period.

In the media reports, social banks' growth is illustrated by the development of total assets, TA, customer volume, CV,[2] and deposits, CD (Benedikter 2011; Jauernig 2014; Remer 2014). Figure 3.5.4 shows the relative growth of these figures for the period from

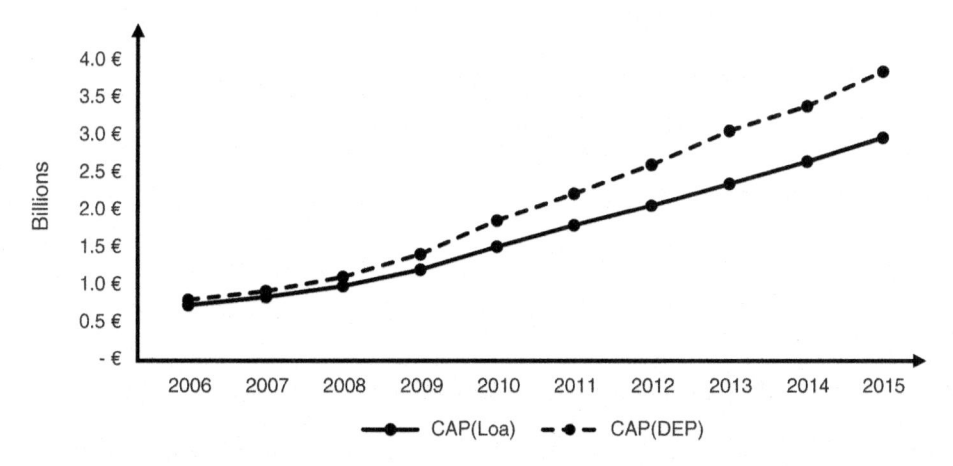

Figure 3.5.2 CAP_{Loa} and CAP_{Dep}

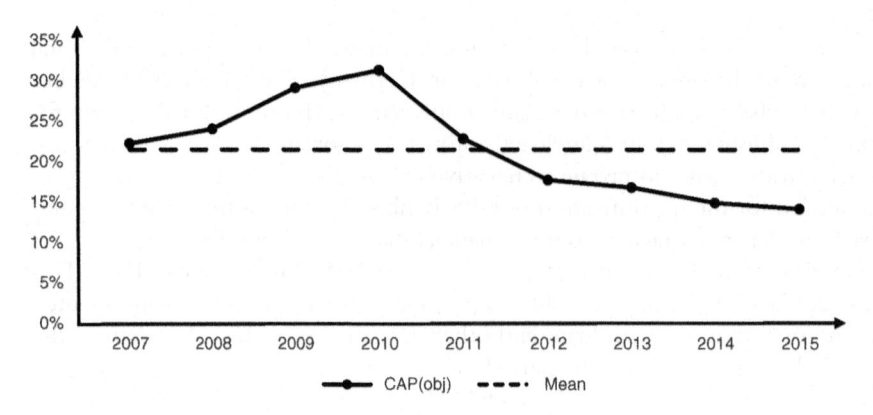

Figure 3.5.3 Relative growth G_r

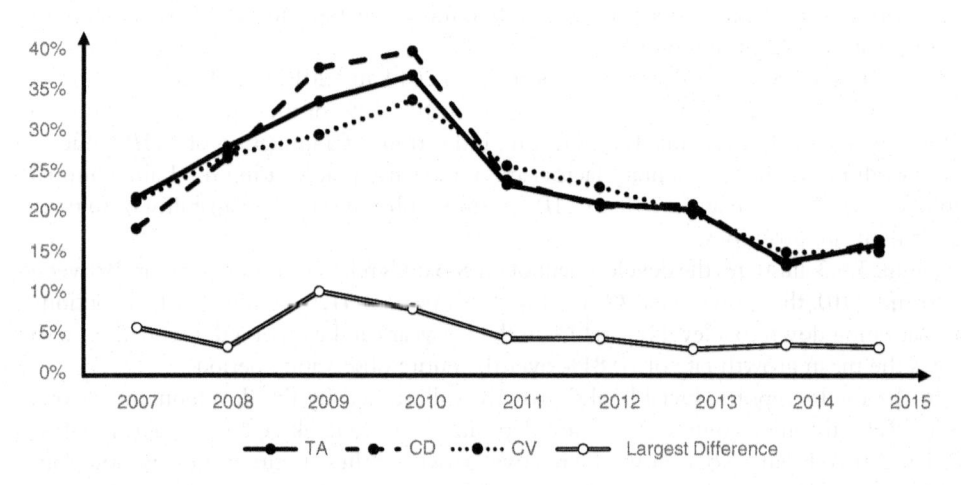

Figure 3.5.4 Relative growth of *TA*, *CD*, and *CV*

Table 3.5.3 Differences between conventional growth measures and G_r

Growth measures based on	Difference to G_r		
	Minimum	Mean	Maximum
Total assets	0.2814%	2.5721%	5.4773%
Customer deposits	0.9029%	3.4713%	8.7306%
Customer volume	−0.1840%	2.0689%	5.3728%

2006 to 2015 and the maximum difference between these three conventional measures in each year.

All variables follow the same trend. In times of trend change (2009–2010), the maximum difference rises to a peak of approximately 8.66% in 2009.

If we compare Figure 3.5.3 with Figure 3.5.4, the growth curves seem to be quite similar. However, there are differences between our measure of social bank growth, G_r, and the conventional measures used so far. Table 3.5.3 shows the largest, smallest, and mean deviations between the relative growth of *TA*, *CD*, and *CV*, on the one hand, and G_r on the other.

Each of the measures used in the media leads to an average overestimation of GLS Bank's growth compared with our intermediation-based growth measure, G_r.

In this example, the growth rate based on customer volume, *CV*, seems to be the best proxy for our more complex growth rate, G_r, due to the lowest mean difference (and in absolute values the lowest maximum and minimum differences). The customer volume includes information about loans and thus does not only reflect funding, but also distribution activity, which is represented by CAP_{Loa}. In all nine years, CAP_{Loa} determines bank size in our model. If, however, bank size was primarily determined by CAP_{Dep}, debt-oriented proxies like customer deposits could be more suitable.

Discussion and conclusions

In this chapter, we develop a measure of social banks' growth based upon a slightly revised intermediation approach. This growth measure fulfils all the requirements deduced. From a theoretical point of view, our model thus goes far beyond the conventional growth measures for social banks. Our model includes both the investment and funding side of the banking business and differentiates between assets with and without the support of a bank's objectives. As a result, we improve the validity of growth measures by eliminating several sources of potential growth overestimation.

However, our measure requires more data and is more complex than conventional measures. Thus, our model could include a higher level of error, which might endanger the reliability of the measure. Nevertheless, since most of the model consists merely of public information and quite easy calculations (the sum of balance sheet positions), we consider its potential error as insignificant. Only $LIQA_N$ must be operated by generalizations, which implies an inherent estimation error. To minimize that error, we recommend that subsequent research should ask a sufficient number of social banks for their required amount of purely liquid assets and compare this with our estimation.

The separation of the investment and funding sides of banking basically enables an explanation of how and why social banks have grown. As reasons for more or higher deposits could be completely independent from those for more or higher investment opportunities, a non-separated approach would miss out several aspects of growth determination. Instead, CAP_{Loa} and CAP_{Dep} offer the possibility to explore social banks' growth in total. The division and designation of the components of CAP_{Loa} and CAP_{Dep} form the first explicit conceptual step towards identifying and evaluating the drivers and obstacles of CAP_{Loa} and CAP_{Dep} growth.

The GLS Bank example affirms that the use of growth measures focused on bank funding could lead to a general overestimation of social banks' growth. This provides the first evidence that the media reports have been too optimistic so far. For banks that limit their investment opportunities by self-imposed criteria and at the same time collect a large amount of deposits, it seems to be reasonable that CAP_{Loa} is the bottleneck and thus defines the bank's size. However, even the lower CAP_{Loa} multiplied in size by a factor of 5.42 between 2006 and 2015. As a result, we identify a mean overestimation of relative growth between approximately 2.0% and 3.5% per year comparing CAP_{Loa} with customer deposits, total assets and customer volume.

At first glance, especially the overestimation of growth using customer volume, CV, does not seem to be high enough to justify greater measurement efforts. However, for several reasons the potential overestimation could be even higher. First, between 2006 and 2016, the average annual relative growth of GLS Bank's customer deposits (approximately 23.3%) just slightly outperformed the growth of customer loans (approximately 21.3%). If the out-performance of customer deposits were higher, the overestimation of social bank growth measured by CV would automatically increase. If other social banks show such a relationship of customer deposits to customer loans, even the use of CV would lead to a higher overestimation of growth. Since there has been no concrete empirical evidence of the growth of a sufficient number of social banks so far, we recommend using our theoretically sound but complex model until a suitable simple surrogate for all social banks can be derived.

Second, in the present approach we assume that all financial assets (e.g., loans, bonds, and shares) are A_{Obj}, meaning that all belong to counterparties that create a social or environmental impact. Even if social banks disclose negative criteria to close out some investment areas and positive criteria to describe their predominant fields of investment, there is ambiguity over how to deal with investments that are neither excluded by their negative criteria nor included by their positive criteria, such as private customer credits or government bonds. A generally accepted norm for the valuation of a social or ecological positive impact asset does not exist. However, San-Jose et al. (2011) analysed the asset placement of GLS Bank, among others. They found that 37.53% of GLS Bank's financial assets do not have any additional social value. If social banks really invest in organisations without a clear positive impact, CAP_{Loa} will be lower than in our estimation. As a consequence, the suitability of passively oriented growth measures further decreases. Future research should thus identify clear selection criteria for assets with a positive social or ecological impact to define social banks' investment spectrum. This would enable a sound quantification of A_{Obj}.

We conclude that our measurement approach needs subsequent research to confirm or improve the operationalization of $LIQA_N$ and A_{Obj} (or A_{noObj}). Nevertheless, it already demonstrates an improvement in comparison to conventional measures by eliminating sources of overestimation and enabling the mapping of different growth scenarios as well as the derivation of potential growth drivers and obstacles.

Apart from the possibility of quantifying absolute and relative growth, a single point-in-time inspection of CAP_{Loa} could be interpreted as the sustainable impact of social banks; that is, their contribution to individuals or organisations with a positive impact on society and the environment. Independent of its source, CAP_{Loa} is the distributed amount of money that individuals and organizations could use to create a positive social or ecological contribution.

We understand our conceptual contribution as the basis for subsequent empirical research in the field of social banking. In this chapter, we have paid special attention to the explanation of growth and the detailed quantification of social banks' social and environmental impact.

Notes

1 The triple bottom line approach was invented by Elkington (1997) and has been frequently picked up, quoted, and reviewed for the past two decades, e.g., Jeurissen (2000), Hubbard (2006), and Slaper and Hall (2011).
2 Customer volume is the sum of all customer deposits and loans.

References

Altunbas, Y., et al., 2001. Efficiency in European banking. *European Economic Review*, 45(10), 1931–1955.

Bachmann, A., et al., 2011. Online peer-to-peer lending? A literature review. *Journal of Internet Banking and Commerce*, 16(2), 1–18.

Baxmann, U., 1995. *Kreditwirtschaftliche Betriebsgrößen*. Stuttgart: Deutscher Sparkassenverlag.

BCBS, Basel Committee on Banking Supervision, 2008. *Principles for Sound Liquidity Risk Management and Supervisory*. Basel: The Stationery Office.

BCBS, Basel Committee on Banking Supervision, 2010. *Basel III: International Framework for Liquidity Risk Measurement, Standards and Monitoring*. Basel: The Stationery Office.

Benedikter, R., 2011. *Social Banking and Social Finance: Answers to the Economic Crisis*. New York: Springer.

Boiral, O., Heras-Saizarbitoria, I., and Brotherton, M., 2017. Assessing and improving the quality of sustainability reports: The auditors' perspective. *Journal of Business Ethics* [online].

Chen, Y., and Chang, C., 2013. Greenwash and green trust: The mediation effects of green consumer confusion and green perceived risk. *Journal of Business Ethics*, 114(3), 489–500.

Cho, C., et al., 2015. Organized hypocrisy, organizational façades, and sustainability reporting. *Accounting, Organization and Society*, 40, 78–94.

De Clearck, F., 2009. Ethical banking. In: Zsolnai, L., Boda, Z., Fekete, L., eds., *Ethical Prospects: Economy, Society and Environment*. Berlin: Springer, 209–227.

Deppe, H.-D., 1964. Der Bankbetrieb als Gegenstand von Wachstumsanalysen. *Zeitschrift für Betriebswirtschaft*, 34, 353–381.

EBA, European Banking Authority, 2014. *Second Report on Impact Assessment for Liquidity Measures under Article 509(1) of the CRR*. London: The Stationery Office.

ECB, European Central Bank, 2016. *How to Calculate the Minimum Reserve Requirements* [online]. Available from: https://www.ecb.europa.eu/mopo/implement/mr/html/calc.en.html [Accessed 10 August 2016].

Elkington, J., 1997. *Cannibals with Forks: The Triple Bottom Line of 21st Century Business*. Oxford: John Wiley and Sons.

FEBEA, European Federation of Ethical and Alternative Banks, 2012. *What Really Differentiates Ethical Banks from Modern Banks?* Available from: http://www.febea.org/sites/default/files/definition_ethical_bank-en.pdf [Accessed 10 May 2016].

Franz, F., 2007. *Ethisch-ökologische Kreditinstitute: Vergleichende Analyse im deutschsprachigen Raum*. Saarbrücken: VDM Verlag Dr. Müller.

Future Business Council, 2015. *The Next Boom: A Surprise New Hope for Australia's Economy?* Melbourne: The Stationery Office.

GABV, Global Alliance for Banking on Values, 2016. *Our Principles*. Available from: http://www.gabv.org/about-us/our-principles [Accessed 10 May 2016].

Hartmann-Wendels, T., Pfingsten, A., and Weber, M., 2015. *Bankbetriebslehre*. 6th edn. Heidelberg: Springer.

Hubbard, G., 2006. Measuring organizational performance: beyond the triple bottom line. *Business Strategy and the Environment*, 18(3), 177–191.

ISB, Institute for Social Banking, 2016. *Our Definition of Social Banking*. Available from: http://www.social-banking.org/the-institute/what-is-social-banking/ [Accessed 10 May 2016].

Jamali, D., 2006. Insights into triple bottom line integration from a learning organization perspective. *Business Process Management Journal*, 12, 809–821.

Jauernig, C., 2014. Sustainable growth: social banking on the rise [online]. Münster: ZEB. Available from: https://www.bankinghub.eu/banking/sales/sustainable-growth-social-banking-rise [Accessed 4 May 2016].

Jeurissen, R., 2000. Book review of: John Elkington, *Cannibals with Forks: The Triple Bottom Line of 21st Century Business. Journal of Business Ethics*, 23(2), 229–231.

Kipesha, E., 2013. Production and intermediation efficiency of microfinance institutions in Tanzania. *Research Journal of Finance and Accounting*, 4(1), 149–159.

Lang, G., and Welzel, P., 1996. Efficiency and technical progress in banking: empirical results for a panel of German cooperative banks. *Journal of Banking and Finance*, 20, 1003–1023.

Lumma, K., and Jauernig, C., 2010. Nachhaltig krisenfest: Auch Genossenschaftsbanken können vom Erfolg der Social Banks lernen. *Bankinformation*, 2, 10–11.

Nielsen, 2014. *Nielsen Global Survey of Corporate Social Responsibility: Doing Well by Doing Good.* Diemen: The Stationery Office.

Osthues-Albrecht, H., 1974. *Der Einfluss der Betriebsgröße auf Kosten und Erlöse von Kreditinstituten.* Wiesbaden: Gabler.

RBSC, Roland Berger Strategy Consultants, 2012. Green banking: sustainable banking offers financial institutions high growth potential. Available from: http://www.rolandberger.com/media/pdf/Roland_Berger_taC_Green_Banking_E_20121120.pdf [Accessed 10 May 2016].

Remer, S., 2014. The social banking landscape in Europe. *Global Social Policy*, 14, 267–269.

San-Jose, L., Retolaza, J., and Gutierrez-Goiria, J., 2011. Are ethical banks different? A comparative analysis using the radical affinity index. *Journal of Business Ethics*, 100(1), 151–173.

Slaper, T., and Hall, T., 2011. The triple bottom line: what is it and how does it work? *Indiana Business Review*, 86(1), 4–8.

Subramanyam, T., and Reddy, C. S., 2008. Measuring the risk efficiency in Indian commercial banking: a DEA approach. *East–West Journal of Economics and Business*, 11(1), 76–105.

Tebroke, H., 1994. *Größe und Fusionserfolg von Genossenschaftsbanken.* Köln: Müller Botermann Verlag.

Thakor, A., and Boot, A., 2008. *Handbook of Financial Intermediation and Banking.* Amsterdam: Elsevier Science.

Weber, O., 2014. Social banking: concept, definition and practice. *Global Social Policy*, 14, 265–267.

Weber, O., and Remer, S., 2011. Social banking: Introduction. In: Weber, O., and Remer, S., eds., *Social Banks and the Future of Sustainable Finance.* Abingdon: Routledge, 1–14.

Zahn, E., 1971. *Das Wachstum industrieller Unternehmen.* Wiesbaden: Gabler.

ZEB, 2012. *Social Banking Study 2012: Management Summary.* Available from: https://www.zeb.eu/lightbox_popup/nojs/1915/popup [Accessed 10 May 2016].

Part 4

Choices, incentives, guidance, and ethics

4.1 An experimental study on corporate social responsibility in junior managers' project choice in an energy-producing company

Introduction

While in the 1990s shareholder value orientation was prevalent in management literature, today's focus has shifted towards a more stakeholder-oriented perspective (Carroll & Buchholtz, 2014). Attracting, keeping, and developing highly skilled employees are major challenges for companies, which must find ways to attract and retain their workforce (Hiltrop, 1999). Skilled employees are a critical success factor for companies competing on a global scale (Porter, 1986). Human resources are part of all activities of a company and are therefore essential to gain a sustainable competitive advantage (Barney & Wright, 1997; Bartlett & Ghoshal, 2002). One critical factor in attracting and retaining talent is the corporate social responsibility (CSR) footprint of the corporation, which entails a balance of social, environmental, and economic goals (Székely & Knirsch, 2005). Employees want to work for companies with strong corporate values that are in line with their own and that go beyond a mere financial orientation. This phenomenon is known as *person–organization fit* (Cable & Judge, 1996). Individual and corporate values should be congruent to satisfy employees' expectations, motivate them, and keep them on board (Cable & Judge, 1996). The reputation of a company and an industry can be affected by CSR and, in particular, corporations holding lower ranks in employer attractiveness rankings face challenges when attracting and retaining the employees needed for their future operations. Energy companies belong to this group (Trendence Institute, 2015). In particular, since BP and EXXON caused environmental disasters, the energy industry has been assessed as inferior in employer attractiveness compared to other sectors.

Traditionally, there are various means to enhance a company's reputation as perceived by employees. Examples are above-average payment, flexible working hours, or home office solutions (Hiltrop, 1999). In addition to these employee-targeted measures, CSR emerged as a potential source of competitive advantage and differentiation in the labour market (Backhaus, Stone, & Heiner, 2002).[1] Greening and Turban (2000) argue that CSR can be used as a positive signal in attracting talent. A positive perception of a firm's CSR activities enhances its attractiveness and supports its legitimacy even when engaging in debatable production processes, such as the oil industry (de Roeck & Delobbe, 2012). A positive effect is most effectively conveyed when CSR performance is transparent and traceable for employees, for example through the disclosure of CSR indicators (Greening & Turban, 2000). Mahoney, Thorne, Cecil, and LaGore (2013) suggest that there are two reasons for publishing CSR indicators in CSR reports. The first is to use them as a tool to signal superior commitment to CSR, and the second reason is to use CSR for greenwashing of corporate activities. If the energy industry's CSR activities are perceived as 'greenwashing', or if a company's social commitment in the energy-producing regions does not seem very sustainable, these conflicting messages can weaken stakeholders' commitment towards the enterprise (Brammer, Millington, & Rayton, 2007).

While an ever-increasing body of research deals with how CSR is perceived by potential employees, so far little research addresses the role of CSR in junior managers' project choices. Junior managers, unlike potential employees, actively shape the future CSR profile of a company. Considering this stakeholder group explicitly is therefore relevant both from a research perspective and from a practitioner's perspective, regarding the short-term practical impact of their actions.

We, therefore, examine whether junior managers consider the impact of projects on the company's CSR performance valuable and important, especially if they would personally work on these projects. Dedicating their labour and time to a topic or project is within the span of control of a junior manager, and it is a clear proof of commitment to such topics. This paper demonstrates how junior managers perceive and prioritize CSR activities within a German subsidiary of a global energy-producing company. Additionally, we focus on how junior managers trade off financial consequences both for the enterprise and for themselves in the form of remuneration with the implications for the CSR dimensions of a business project. We aim to address the following research questions:

- Are projects with CSR objectives relevant to next-generation managers in general?
- Which CSR topics are perceived as most attractive; which ones are seen as least attractive?
- How do next-generation managers evaluate personal and material advantage versus social responsibility aspects?

To answer these questions, we conducted an online experiment with junior managers of the German subsidiary of an energy company. We used a so-called process-tracing technique, which monitors the junior managers' information acquisition and weighting processes. We created a decision scenario with multiple project options, in which junior managers selected the most and least attractive project. Information about these projects included financial dimensions of the project as well as the projects' impact on CSR. The process-tracing technique monitors how often and to what extent managers use the information given. Our research is based on realistic project scenarios and resembles employees' decision-making situations of the day-to-day business of employees in an international corporation in the energy sector.

The results show that the junior managers' project evaluation depends on financial as well as on CSR dimensions. In our sample, the employees accessed project information rather holistically and traded off financial consequences of their project choice with social and environmental ones. Overall, however, financial aspects were considered most important. Our results also suggest that male participants focus more on financial aspects than female participants.

In sum, our results underpin that CSR dimensions affect the project choices of junior managers. We thus argue that companies that engage in CSR should not only measure their CSR activities but also need to communicate them to their employees while making transparent how individual project choices impact CSR activities of the firm.

Theoretical implications

The concept of CSR

The European Commission (EC) defines CSR as '*a concept whereby companies decide voluntarily to contribute to a better society and a cleaner environment*' (EC, 2001, p. 5). Different stakeholders' needs like the ones of employees, customers, suppliers, shareholders, or non-governmental organizations should be integrated into the decision-making process by the corporation's management. Thereby, a broad societal acceptance should be reached. The present study focuses on employees as stakeholders. CSR information is usually provided through a sustainability report. Through this report, the essential stakeholder dialogue is held, and it serves to promote the acceptance of corporate policies (Jamali, 2008). The Global Reporting Initiative (GRI) has established a comprehensive list of attributes describing the CSR footprint of corporations in their Reporting Guidelines (GRI, 2013). These reporting guidelines have reached the status of a '*de facto* standard' and include the criteria selected for this study. CSR components are usually categorized into three broad categories, *people, planet,* and *profit,* also called the *triple bottom line.* In this context, *people* means social and humanitarian commitment; *planet* refers to a commitment to the environment; and *profit* represents the economic component aiming to ensure long-term corporate success. This study addresses all three categories of CSR.

CSR and decision-making

CSR affects different stakeholders' decision-making. Consumer research, for example, found that customers are willing to pay mark-ups for ethical products (De Pelsmacker, Driesen, & Rayp, 2005) and are more loyal to firms they perceive as responsible (Martinez & del Bosque, 2013). In a similar vein, investors tend to shun 'sin stocks', that is, stocks of companies that produce vice products (like alcohol and tobacco), which shows that ethical considerations also play a role for investment decisions (Hong & Kaspercyk, 2009). Related more closely to our set-up, previous research found that CSR plays a role in employer selection decisions. Through CSR, organizations can create a unique employee value proposition, which constitutes a critical resource that is harder to obtain or imitate for a competitor than, for example, higher compensation (Bhattacharya, Sen, & Korschun, 2008; Tymon, Stumpf, & Doh, 2010). Hence, CSR is seen as an important instrument in the retention and recruitment strategy of many companies. Potential employees are not seeking a workplace that solely maximizes income, but instead they additionally derive utility from non-monetary aspects, like the CSR profile of an employer (Tymon et al., 2010). Thus, CSR has the potential to increase work motivation and to lower employee turnover (Redington, 2005). Naturally, the interest in CSR differs across individuals and some personal characteristics have been found to be correlated to caring for CSR.

CSR and employee characteristics

CSR initiatives have only little impact on some people, but might be important for others (Bhattacharya & Sen, 2004). According to Sen, Bhattacharya, and Korschun (2006), factors determining how strongly employees respond to CSR initiatives are: the nature of the individual job, gender, age, tenure at the company, as well as the perceived importance of the project by the individual.

Concerning gender differences in the perception of CSR importance, findings are mixed. Panwar, Hansen, and Anderson (2010), for example, reveal that male students are more satisfied that the US forest products industry fulfills its socio-environmental responsibilities than female students. Kraft and Singhapakdi (1995) find that female students rate social responsibility as more important in determining organizational effectiveness than male students. In a similar vein, Marz, Powers, and Queisser (2003) reported that females perceive CSR as more meaningful compared to males, especially when it comes to its social dimension. Furthermore, female customers are characterized as the typical consumers of green products (Gilg, Barr, & Ford, 2005; Brécard, Hlaimi, Lucas, Perraudeau, & Salladarré, 2009; Lee, 2009). On the contrary, other studies do not find any difference in actual purchasing between men and women (Chen & Chai, 2010). Similarly, Kahreh, Babania, Tive, and Mirmehdi (2014) also do not identify gender differences in respect to CSR. In a nutshell, there seems to be some evidence that CSR is more important to women than men.

Regardless of gender, age can be a factor that influences individuals' orientation towards CSR (Ramasamy & Yeung, 2009). Ethical behaviour, in general, is positively related to age (Ruegger & King, 1992) because elderly people typically have higher ethical standards and are less influenced by their environment than younger people (Peterson, Rhoads, & Vaught, 2001).

Additionally, education affects individuals' perceptions of companies' CSR measures. In particular, perception is influenced by the institutions where individuals received their education. These shape individuals' attitudes towards CSR concepts and tools, and determine whether CSR is perceived as a fundamental part of a company's success (Sobczak, Debucquet, & Havard, 2006). Mixed effects of the overall length of education have been found. Some studies conclude that higher education is associated with higher moral sensitivity (e.g., Stevens, Harris, & Williamson, 1993), while other studies demonstrate that there is no such effect (Loe, Ferrell, & Mansfield, 2000). In our research, we poll participants' gender, age, and business experience, and indeed observe differences in project choice between male and female managers.

Methodology

Participants

The study was conducted with employees from the German subsidiary of an internationally operating energy company. All participants of this study belong to this company's talent pool, which means that they form the potential next-generation's management team. All 63 employees registered in the company's talent pool were invited to participate in the study. In the invitation letter, no further information was provided in order to avoid any bias, meaning that mainly employees with a strong positive or negative attitude towards CSR participated. A time frame of four weeks was set within which the participants should respond. After two weeks, a reminder was sent out to all participants. Finally, 56 employees took part in this study. The participants' age ranged between 26 and 46 years (*mean* = 34.90 years), and they had between 3 and 26 years of professional experience (*mean* = 13.68 years). Five of the recorded 56 data sets contained either data recording errors or were otherwise not properly completed. Thus, ultimately, data of 51 participants could be analysed (21 female and 30 male participants).

Research process and design

The study was conducted as an online experiment. In a first step, a link to the website was sent to the participants. The participants were instructed to complete the experiment in one go and to avoid any interruption during the execution. When opening the link, the participants were first familiarized with the specifics of the tool (MouselabWEB) used for this experiment, mainly how to uncover hidden information and how to move to the next step of the experiment. Subsequently, participants were provided with a case description, which consisted of information about four different projects that the company would want to launch. Participants were asked to identify the project they would preferably engage in and to name the one they considered least attractive. Furthermore, participants were asked to allocate their working time to at least two of the four projects.

The CSR criteria selected to describe each of the project profiles constitute a well-balanced set of aspects across the triple bottom line (people, planet, and profit). All attributes were taken from the GRI list of criteria. The people aspect was split into two different subsets (internal view towards employees; external view towards stakeholder outside of the organization). The final criteria used in this study were selected together with the management of the company with whom we conducted this research. The 'bonus' criterion was necessary to build up a trade-off scenario between individual economic benefit and CSR contributions.

Each of the four projects' profiles was designed to generate improvements in different CSR domains (people, planet, and profit), with each project being superior in one domain. Project A (see Table 4.1.1) provides major improvements in the 'planet'-domain (emission reduction and higher use of renewable energy); Project B provides superior contributions to the 'profit'-domain, both for the company and the individual project member (bonus); Project C focuses on the 'people'-domain (promotion of education in the civil society and auditing suppliers); and Project D addresses the 'people'-domain with a particular focus on the company's employees (sickness rate and gender diversity). Achievements were chosen to be 2 to 2.5 times higher in the domains of focus (e.g., in the environmental improvements of Project A) than the corresponding figures for the remaining projects. Additionally, for each project, a probability of success was defined. This probability was kept constant across options to avoid any influence of an anticipated project success on the decision. The resulting pattern is summarized in Table 4.1.1. For reasons of simplicity, the following synonyms will be used throughout this article: Project A – Environment Project, Project B – EBIT Project, Project C – Society Project, Project D – Employee Project.

In order to analyse not only the outcome of the decision-making process (the resulting choices) but also the actual decision-making process, a tool to monitor the process itself and the related information acquisition was used. The open source software tool MouselabWEB provided the functionality required. This tool logs the participant's activities during the decision-making process. Similar to eye-tracking systems that log where the participant is looking, MouselabWEB records the movement of the cursor while the participant is conducting the experiment. When the user accesses the relevant decision page, the matrix above (Table 4.1.1) is displayed with all project profile values being hidden. By moving the cursor over the respective cell of the matrix, the value becomes visible. When the user moves the cursor off the cell, the information disappears again. The respective events (cursor over a cell, cursor off a cell) are logged including a timestamp (granularity one millisecond) and stored in a data set. With these data we can see which

Table 4.1.1 Decision scenario and stimuli values (translated, originally in German)

Criteria	Project A	Project B	Project C	Project D
Profit increase (in M €)	4.5	9	5	5.8
Expected success probability of the project (in %)	80–85	80–85	80–85	80–85
Bonus (in €)	6,000	8,500	6,200	5,900
Reduction of CO_2 emissions (in %)	20	8	10	9
Increased use of renewable energies (in %)	34	14	19	15
Reduction of sickness caused absence rate of employees (in %)	8	7	9	19
Increase of women's share in the management (in %)	11	8	9	28
Increase of the rate of audited suppliers (in %)	24	23	56	29
Increase of the education sponsorship (in %)	9	8	22	12

information has been acquired, how often, for how long, and in which sequence. Cell openings below the cognitive threshold (< 200 milliseconds) were removed from the data set because conscious recognition of the respective data is not possible in time frames below 200 ms and can therefore not be part of the information integration process for the task under consideration. As suggested by previous research in cognitive psychology, the importance of a piece of information correlates with the frequency of accessing the respective cell to integrate it into the decision-making process (Wedell & Senter, 1997). The simple rule is: the more often a particular data cell is opened, the more important this information is for the participant in his or her decision-making process. We also monitor the cells' opening time, but this measurement is a less reliable indicator since cells' opening times are subject to a person's individual processing speed (see also Sohn, Sohn, Klaas-Wissing, & Hirsch, 2015). Although the frequency of accessing data is a reliable measurement for the importance of this information for the decision-maker, we asked the participants in a post-experimental questionnaire to indicate the importance they attribute to each criterion on a scale from 0 (not important at all) to 100 (extremely important). Thereby, a comparison between the subjectively perceived importance of each criteria and the observed attention distribution could be made. It was not possible to go back and modify the project selection after submitting choices. Based on the information provided, participants were asked to make three decisions:

- select the most attractive project;
- select the least attractive project;
- distribute their project engagement in percent among at least two out of the four projects.

Finally, in a post-experimental questionnaire, some demographic data (age, gender, years of business experience) were collected from the participants.

Results

The intensity of accessing a specific attribute relates to the importance of this information for the decision-making process of the participant. As can be seen from Figure 4.1.1, the frequency of cell openings for an attribute ranges from 16 to 30 openings across all four projects. The cells that received most attention are the ones describing the financial impacts of the project – profit increase. This reflects, not at all surprisingly, the classic business case view on projects, a view that the participants as members of the talent pool are used to and have already applied many times in their business career. The expected success probability of the project is rated as important by most participants in the post-experimental questionnaire. However, the attribute was designed with identical values for all projects and was therefore obviously irrelevant for differentiating or prioritizing the projects. Consequently, it attains the least attention. The second highest level of attention was attributed to the bonus received upon successful completion of the project. Due to the immediate impact on the decision-maker, it is again not surprising that this criterion received the second highest attention rate. The attention distribution for the remaining CSR criteria shows a slight preference for environmental criteria and is rather balanced for the remaining ones. To test whether the differences in information acquisition between the financial and CSR attributes are significant, we built a hierarchical model. A base model consisting of a random participant factor is compared to a model that includes the factor attribute. The latter improved the model fit, $X^2(8) = 76.65$, $p < 0.01$. We also found that the profit increase attribute received significantly more attention than the remaining attributes (all $p < 0.05$), except when compared to the bonus attribute ($p = 0.73$).

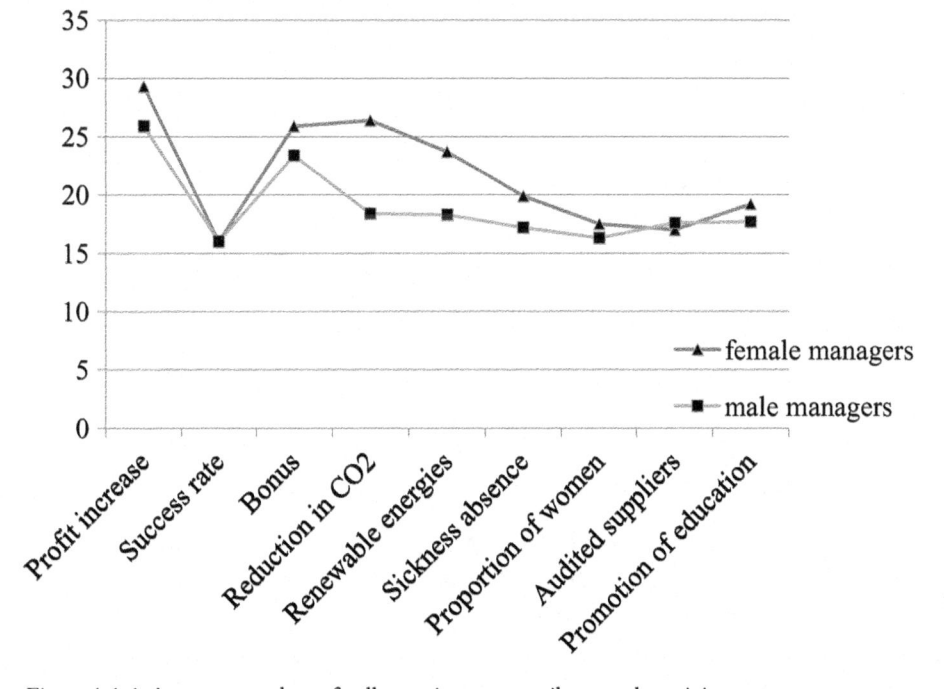

Figure 4.1.1 Average number of cell openings per attribute and participant

A similar pattern can be identified in the post-experimental questionnaire concerning participants' subjective rating of the importance of different attributes (Figure 4.1.2). Profit increase remains the most important attribute, the attribute *proportion of women* is considered of least importance, while the attribute *promotion of education* is considered relevant to participants. The latter phenomenon can be explained by the fact that the company was already running a project that deals with the *promotion of education* of under-privileged people. Thus, the study most likely benefits from a 'recognition' effect. A one-way ANOVA shows that the importance ratings indeed differ across the attributes, $F(8) = 19.48$, $p < 0.01$.

The first research question can be answered with the findings. In the respective energy corporation, CSR topics are relevant to management talent. The participation rate of 91% (56 respondents from a baseline of 61 invitees) in the experiment is high. The intensity with which data were acquired during the study is also quite high compared to our experience from other studies. Cell opening frequencies above 2.5 for a single piece of information on average are an indicator for very intensive data acquisition. Thus, monitoring the decision process allows measuring the effort participants invested and leads to the straightforward conclusion that CSR criteria matter to young managers. In line with previous research, however, financial information and its impact on the decision-maker (e.g., bonus) play the most important role in the pre-decisional phase of the judgement process (Schauß, Hirsch, & Sohn, 2014).

The second research question moves beyond the decision-making process and to the choices made by participants (irrespective of how participants came to their conclusions) (see Figure 4.1.3). The EBIT Project (largest profit increase for the corporation, largest bonus for the employee) is considered most attractive, and the Employee Project (female share in management and reduction of sickness rate) is seen as least attractive.

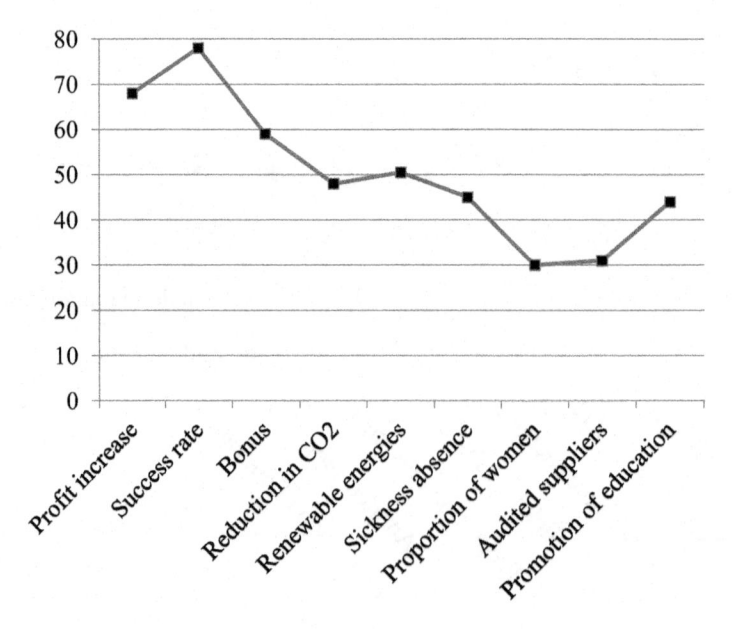

Figure 4.1.2 Relative subjective weighting (mean) of project information (scale 0 – unimportant, 100 – very important)

The explanation for the most attractive project is analogous to the interpretation of attention distribution. In contrast, the selection of projects that are considered least attractive is more interesting and also more surprising. The results indicate that the Employee Project is consistently rarely rated as attractive and at the same time is most frequently rated as unattractive.

In contrast, the EBIT Project is considered attractive most often, but at the same time, it is ranked as the second most unattractive one. The participants obviously form two distinct groups when rating this project: one group strongly welcomes this project; the other group strongly rejects it. The Environmental Project and the Societal Project are perceived as less controversial. The environmental project is rated most frequently as unattractive but also below-average as attractive. This tendency is in line with the trend that sustainability, which in recent years has been a synonym for environmental efforts, nowadays covers the broader context of all three CSR domains with the consequence that the environmental aspects lose their dominance in the sustainability discussion (Crane & Matten, 2010).

Research question three looks at the trade-off between monetary or self-serving aspects of projects versus projects with other beneficiaries than the decision-maker. The results are somewhat ambiguous. The self-serving EBIT Project is judged most attractive overall, supporting the idea of opportunistic decision-making. Following this line of justification, the Employee Project should be ranked second, since the project benefits participants personally. The data show clearly that this is not the case. Therefore, purely selfish motives are not sufficient to explain the choices made by the participants. When further analysing the data with respect to the demographics of the group of participants, it becomes evident that there is a gender difference regarding the choice of the least and most attractive project.

Figure 4.1.4a depicts the choices separated for female and male participants. Roughly 50% of men choose the EBIT Project as most attractive; by contrast, women consider this project least frequently as the most attractive one. The reverse applies to the Employee Project.

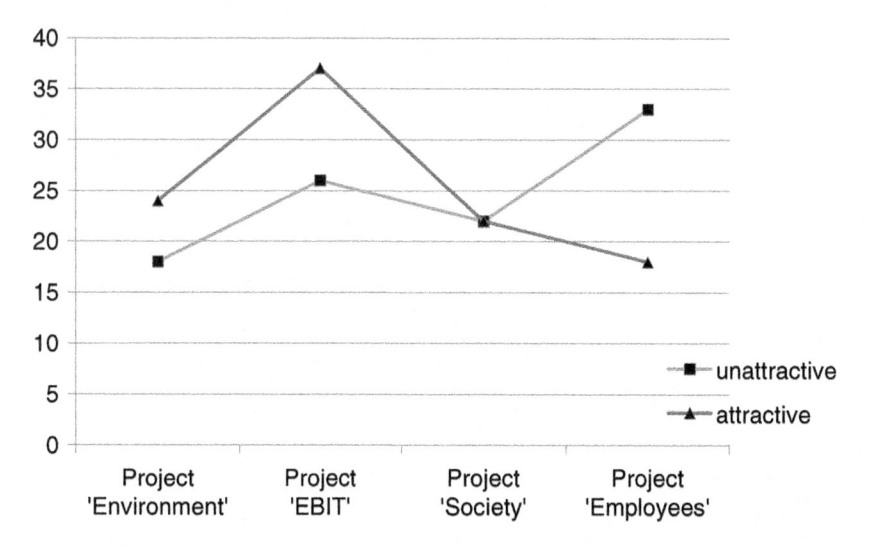

Figure 4.1.3 Percentage of employees who have rated the project as the most attractive/ unattractive

Women regard this project (on a similar level as the Environmental Project) as particularly attractive, whereas men rate this project most attractive in only 10% of the cases. Thus, women renounce a larger bonus much more frequently than men for the sake of CSR activities. The attractiveness of the employee project for female managers is certainly also determined by the fact that the improvement of the female share in management is an explicit goal of this project. It is likely that the female talent directly benefits from such a project. Due to the relatively small sample, the difference between male and female managers in choosing the most attractive project is not statistically significant, $X^2(3) = 6$, $p = 0.11$.

A similar pattern can be observed when considering the distribution of workload among the respective projects (Figure 4.1.4b).[2] It can be noted that women spread their preferences more widely and that they balance the allocation of their resources for the respective projects, whereas male managers prefer the EBIT Project. To test for gender differences, we calculate a mixed model ANOVA with the type of project as a within-subjects factor and gender as a between-subjects factor. We find a marginally significant interaction between the factors, showing that male and female managers differ in their preferences for the distribution of workload across the four projects, $F(3) = 2.41$, $p = 0.08$.

In summary, the analyses show a tendency towards gender-specific behaviour. Female participants perceive projects that generate clear value for CSR performance of corporations more attractive in comparison to male participants, who prefer projects that primarily support the individual and corporate financial benefits.

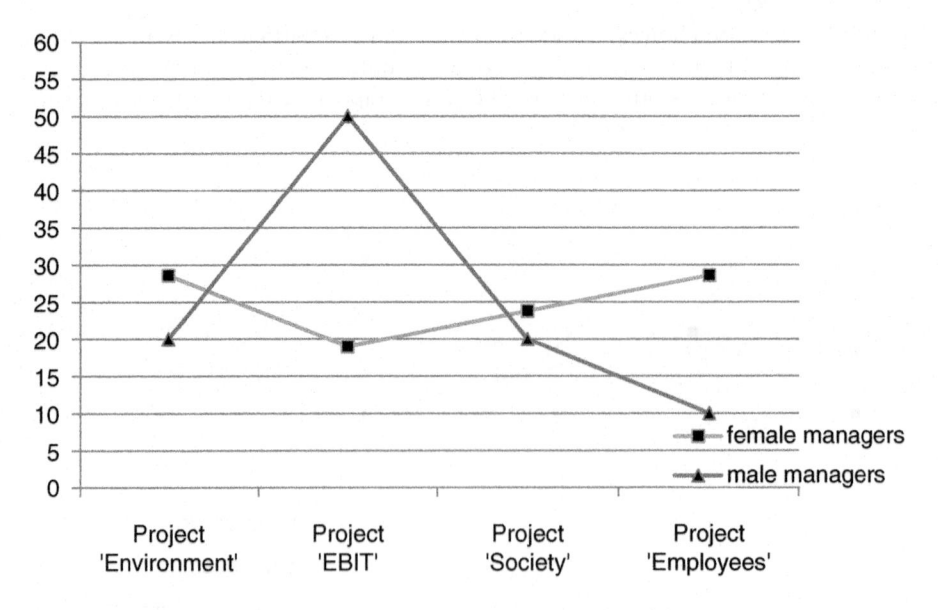

Figure 4.1.4a Percentage of projects rated as the most attractive one for male and female managers

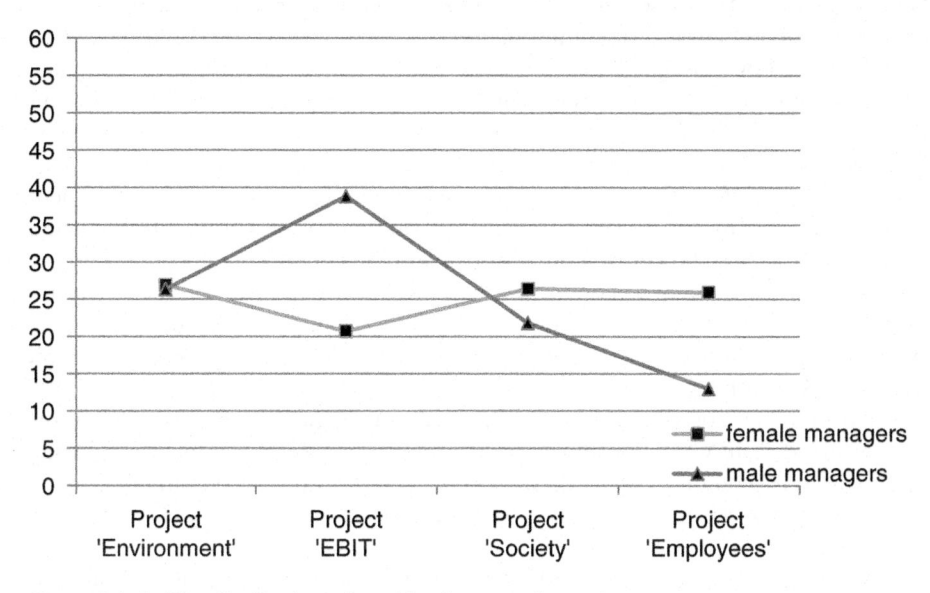

Figure 4.1.4b The distribution of workload among the projects

Conclusions and recommendations for practice

The study has shown that CSR aspects are relevant to junior managers when deciding to engage in potential projects. This is primarily indicated by the effort participants invested in the decision-making process. Although the overall attitude towards participating in projects that improve CSR-related aspects is positive, the group of participants is not homogeneous in their choices. Our study shows that gender differences can be observed and that some CSR topics trigger controversial reactions among participants; either they are rated as particularly attractive or as particularly unattractive. Previous research addressed gender differences concerning the importance of CSR and we provided evidence that in decision-making similar to our set-up, male and female managers decide differently. We thus present additional evidence that women care more about CSR than men (Kraft & Singhapakdi, 1995; Burton & Hegarty, 1999; Marz et al., 2003; Gilg et al., 2005; Brécard et al., 2009; Lee, 2009). Moreover, our study shows that when weighting personal monetary advantages (bonus) together with improving the company's financial position (profit domain) against improvements in the other domains (people, planet), the majority of participants pursues the more traditional opportunistic approach and opts for the profit domain. Consequently, our results align with previous research, which found that despite the fact that consumers report positive attitudes towards ethical products, CSR has little influence on their actual consumption behaviour (Devinney, Auger, Eckhardt, & Birtchnell, 2006; Öberseder, Schlegelmilch, & Gruber, 2011; White, MacDonnell, & Ellard, 2012).

CSR initiatives can provoke a variety of reactions among employees and in the worst case can split the workforce into groups. Even a seemingly unique social commitment can be misunderstood. Definitions of *why* or *how* to run CSR projects should be easily derivable from the corporate strategy and involve an accessible and understandable message. Thereby, the organizational commitment of an employee to the company can be further enhanced. For example, while the study was conducted, the topic of *educational support* was an ongoing project in this corporation. Since this issue received attention on a corporate level, employees potentially committed to it, thereby supporting the company's management decision. Clearly and deliberately selecting the areas of CSR engagement should be part of strategic considerations and theme hopping should be avoided. The CSR strategy has to be consistent with the overall strategic direction of the company and has to follow a clear direction in the medium and long-term.

Employees are most likely to commit to projects with clearly quantifiable monetary advantages for the company and themselves. This finding is in line with standard economic theory suggesting that monetary rewards are a powerful predictor of employee motivation (Aguinis, Joo, & Gottfredson, 2013). The underlying motivation can be 'following the managerial mainstream', or in other words the 'managerial desirability'. If a company wants to seriously incorporate CSR domains other than the profit domain into their strategy, a strong managerial commitment to these aspects, as well as proper communication, is required (Collier & Esteban, 2007). One possible approach to unite the monetary value-driven decision logic with CSR domains could be to quantify forms of capital (human capital, environmental capital, intellectual capital, social capital) that are addressed through CSR projects, preferably in monetary units. Decision-makers could then base their decisions on hard facts and comparable information rather than on a combination of hard factors (e.g., money) and unquantified and subjective soft factors (e.g., employee satisfaction).

Asking employees, and more specifically the future management team, about their preferences concerning CSR topics reveals the value system of the company workforce. It may help to find groups or clusters of staff with unique or distinct value systems. In our case, the male participants considered the project that would improve the female share in management as the least attractive one. This could be due to male employees seeing their career opportunities being reduced by such a project or by just not being interested in the opportunities offered to women within the company. Irrespective of the reasons or motivation the fact that different value systems in different subgroups of the company's workforce prevail is undisputed and should be addressed by the company's management. If diversity, fairness, and solidarity belong to the value set of the company, projects should be selected through a process that guarantees support by the vast majority of the workforce. Alternatively, a company should opt to choose a balanced portfolio of initiatives to satisfy different internal stakeholder groups.

The environmental dimension of corporate responsibility is certainly the most intensively discussed one in public media and also in the self-presentation of company's CSR initiatives. Information on environmental sustainability is also strongly demanded by the general public (Babiak & Trendafilova, 2010). This has been the case for the last one to two decades. Despite the necessity of addressing environmental aspects of a company's business operation, including the implementation of remediation measures, the topic does not receive an extraordinary dominant attention or a dominant preference in our study. The reason is that nowadays the planet domain in CSR is perceived either as overstretched or already as an essential part of standard operating procedure improvements. In plain terms, the hype about emission reduction has decreased, and respective efforts are already taken for granted. Social- or people-related topics have recently caught up with environmental dimensions and receive more attention. Additionally, in the past, 'sustainability' and 'environmental measure' were considered synonyms, whereas today it is better understood by employees and the civil society that the concept of CSR covers more than the planet domain. Addressing dimensions other than the planet domain becomes more and more important for a company, and again, a well-balanced portfolio of initiatives in all three CSR domains is nowadays expected by stakeholders.

Another recommendation for practice relates to the way of communicating CSR initiatives. One of the obvious goals of communicating CSR projects is to improve the overall corporate image. The recommended approach in CSR management is to start with a materiality analysis and to subsequently report and improve the most relevant topics accordingly. However, this procedure might lead to a rather unbalanced, one-dimensional portfolio of CSR projects that might not be easy to communicate and may appear rather unattractive to many stakeholders. Moreover, the approach to 'follow the general trend' when selecting the right topics might trigger little attention. According to the company with whom we conducted this study, engagement in corporate volunteering was difficult to implement as those institutions that would benefit from such corporate volunteering are already flooded by volunteering offers. Image and attention can rather be achieved by new, creative ideas for CSR in the people- or society-domain. Actively incorporating employees in the selection process for CSR initiatives can only be strongly recommended – a top-down managerial approach will most likely create less buy-in.

Notes

1 According to Schnietz and Epstein (2005), good reputation for CSR can even prevent stock declines during a corporate crisis.
2 Concerning the distribution of workload, participants were asked to distribute 100% of their available project working time between at least two projects. The aim of this request is to facilitate a relative weighting of the projects on the participant's part. If the participant distributes the project working time evenly between two projects, one can assume that both are equally important to him/her. With regards to the selection of the most attractive project, the participant is obliged to choose a project. Thus, the distribution of workload practically acts as a smoothing filter for the distribution of attractiveness.

References

Aguinis, H., Joo, H., & Gottfredson, R. K. (2013). What monetary rewards can and cannot do: How to show employees the money. *Business Horizons, 56*(2), 241–249.

Babiak, K., & Trendafilova, S. (2011). CSR and environmental responsibility: Motives and pressures to adopt green management practices. *Corporate Social Responsibility and Environmental Management, 18*(1), 11–24.

Backhaus, K. B., Stone, B. A., & Heiner, K. (2002). Exploring the relationship between corporate social performance and employer attractiveness. *Business and Society, 41*(3), 292–318.

Barney, J. B. & Wright, P. M. (1997). On becoming a strategic partner: The role of human resources in gaining competitive advantage. *Human Resource Management (1986–1998), 37*(1), 1–25.

Bartlett, C. A., & Ghoshal, S. (2002). Building competitive advantage through people. *MIT Sloan Management Review, 43*(2), 34–41.

Bhattacharya, C. B., & Sen, S. (2004). Doing better at doing good: When, why, and how consumers respond to corporate social initiatives. *California Management Review, 47*(1), 9–24.

Bhattacharya, C. B., Sen, S., & Korschun, D. (2008). Using corporate social responsibility to win the war for talent. *MIT Sloan Management Review, 49*(2), 37–44.

Brammer, S., Millington, A., & Rayton, B. (2007). The contribution of corporate social responsibility to organizational commitment. *The International Journal of Human Resource Management, 18*(10), 1701–1719.

Brécard, D., Hlaimi, B., Lucas, S., Perraudeau, Y., & Salladarré, F. (2009). Determinants of demand for green products: An application to eco-label demand for fish in Europe. *Ecological Economics, 69*(1), 115–125.

Burton, B. K., & Hegarty, W. H. (1999). Some determinants of student corporate social responsibility orientation. *Business and Society, 38*(2), 188–205.

Cable, D. M., & Judge, T. A. (1996). Person–organization fit, job choice decisions, and organizational entry. *Organizational Behavior and Human Decision Processes, 67*(3), 294–311.

Carroll, A. B., & Buchholtz, A. K. (2014). *Business and Society: Ethics, Sustainability, and Stakeholder Management*. Stamford, CT: Cengage Learning.

Chen, T. B., & Chai, L. T. (2010). Attitude towards the environment and green products: Consumers' perspective. *Management Science and Engineering, 4*(2), 27–39.

Collier, J. & Esteban, R. (2007). Corporate social responsibility and employee commitment. *Business Ethics: A European Review, 16*(1), 19–33.

Crane, A., & Matten, D. (2010). *Business Ethics: Managing Corporate Citizenship and Sustainability in the Age of Globalization*. Oxford: Oxford University Press.

De Pelsmacker, P., Driesen, L., & Rayp, G. (2005). Do consumers care about ethics? Willingness to pay for fair-trade coffee. *Journal of Consumer Affairs, 39*(2), 363–385.

De Roeck, K. & Delobbe, N. (2012). Do environmental CSR initiatives serve organizations' legitimacy in the oil industry? Exploring employees' reactions through organizational identification theory. *Journal of Business Ethics, 110*(4), 397–412.

Devinney, T. M., Auger, P., Eckhardt, G., & Birtchnell, T. (2006). *The Other CSR: Consumer Social Responsibility*. Cambridge: Cambridge University Press.

European Commission (2001). *GREEN PAPER: Promoting a European Framework for Corporate Social Responsibility* [online]. Brussels, Commission of the European Communities. Available from: http://eur-lex.europa.eu/LexUriServ/site/en/com/2001/com2001_0531en01.pdf. [Accessed 10 June 2013].

Gilg, A., Barr, S., & Ford, N. (2005). Green consumption or sustainable lifestyles? Identifying the sustainable consumer. *Futures, 37*(6), 481–504.

Global Reporting Initiative (GRI) (2013). *G4 Sustainability Reporting Guidelines* [online]. Available from: https://www.globalreporting.org/resourcelibrary/GRIG4-Part1-Reporting-Principles-and-Standard-Disclosures.pdf. [Accessed 5 May 2014].

Greening, D. W., & Turban, D. B. (2000). Corporate social performance as a competitive advantage in attracting a quality workforce. *Business and Society, 39*(3), 254–280.

Hiltrop, J. M. (1999). The quest for the best: Human resource practices to attract and retain talent. *European Management Journal, 17*(4), 422–430.

Hong, H., & Kacperczyk, M. (2009). The price of sin: The effects of social norms on markets. *Journal of Financial Economics, 93*(1), 15–36.

Jamali, D. (2008). A stakeholder approach to corporate social responsibility: A fresh perspective into theory and practice. *Journal of Business Ethics, 82*(1), 213–231.

Kahreh, M. S., Babania, A., Tive, M., & Mirmehdi, S. M. (2014). An examination to effects of gender differences on the corporate social responsibility (CSR). *Procedia: Social and Behavioral Sciences, 109*, 664–668.

Kraft, K. L., & Singhapakdi, A. (1995). The relative importance of social responsibility in determining organizational effectiveness: Student responses II. *Journal of Business Ethics, 14*(4), 315–326.

Lee, K. (2009). Gender differences in Hong Kong adolescent consumers' green purchasing behavior. *Journal of Consumer Marketing, 26*(2), 87–96.

Loe, T. W., Ferrell, L., & Mansfield, P. (2000). A review of empirical studies assessing ethical decision making in business. *Journal of Business Ethics, 25*(3), 185–204.

Mahoney, L. S., Thorne, L., Cecil, L., & LaGore, W. (2013). A research note on standalone corporate social responsibility reports: Signaling or greenwashing? *Critical Perspectives on Accounting, 24*(4), 350–359.

Martínez, P., & del Bosque, I. R. (2013). CSR and customer loyalty: The roles of trust, customer identification with the company and satisfaction. *International Journal of Hospitality Management, 35,* 89–99.

Marz, J. W., Powers T. L., & Queisser, T. (2003). Corporate and individual influences on managers' social orientation. *Journal of Business Ethics, 46*(1), 1–11.

Öberseder, M., Schlegelmilch, B. B., & Gruber, V. (2011). "Why don't consumers care about CSR?" A qualitative study exploring the role of CSR in consumption decisions. *Journal of Business Ethics, 104*(4), 449–460.

Panwar, R., Hansen, E., & Anderson, R. (2010). Students' perceptions regarding CSR success of the US forest products industry. *Social Responsibility Journal, 6*(1), 18–32.

Peterson, D., Rhoads, A., & Vaught, B. C. (2001). Ethical beliefs of business professionals: A study of gender, age and external factors. *Journal of Business Ethics, 31*(3), 225–232.

Porter, M. E. (1986). *Competition in Global Industries.* Boston, MA: Harvard Business School Press Books.

Ramasamy, B., & Yeung, M. (2009). Chinese consumers' perception of corporate social responsibility (CSR). *Journal of Business Ethics, 88,* 119–132.

Redington, I. (2005). *Making CSR Happen: The Contribution of People Management.* London: Chartered Institute of Personnel and Development.

Ruegger, D., & King, E. W. (1992). A study of the effect of age and gender upon student business ethics. *Journal of Business Ethics, 11*(3), 179–186.

Schauß, J., Hirsch, B., & Sohn, M. (2014). Functional fixation and the balanced scorecard: Adaption of BSC users' judgment processes. *Journal of Accounting and Organizational Change, 10*(4), 540–566.

Schnietz, K. E., & Epstein, M. J. (2005). Exploring the financial value of a reputation for corporate social responsibility during a crisis. *Corporate Reputation Review, 7*(4), 327–345.

Sen, S., Bhattacharya, C. B., & Korschun, D. (2006). The role of corporate social responsibility in strengthening multiple stakeholder relationships: A field experiment. *Journal of the Academy of Marketing Science, 34*(2), 158–166.

Sobczak, A., Debucquet, G., & Havard, C. (2006). The impact of higher education on students' and young managers' perception of companies and CSR: An exploratory analysis. *Corporate Governance: The International Journal of Business in Society, 6*(4), 463–474.

Sohn, M., Sohn, W., Klaas-Wissing, T., & Hirsch, B. (2015). The influence of corporate social performance on employer attractiveness in the transport and logistics industry: Insights from German junior talent. *International Journal of Physical Distribution and Logistics Management, 45*(5), 486–505.

Stevens, R. E., Harris, O. J., & Williamson, S. (1993). A comparison of ethical evaluations of business school faculty and students: A pilot study. *Journal of Business Ethics, 12*(8), 611–619.

Székely, F., & Knirsch, M. (2005). Responsible leadership and corporate social responsibility: Metrics for sustainable performance. *European Management Journal, 23*(6), 628–647.

Trendence Institute (2015). Trendence Graduate Barometer 2015 – *German Business Edition* [online]. Berlin. Available from: http://www.trendence.com/fileadmin/trendence/content/Unternehmen/Rankings/tGrad15_DE_Ranking_BUS_DE.pdf [Accessed 25 May 2015].

Tymon, W. G., Stumpf, S. A., & Doh, J. P. (2010). Exploring talent management in India: The neglected role of intrinsic rewards. *Journal of World Business, 45*(2), 109–121.

Wedell, D. H., & Senter, S. M. (1997). Looking and weighting in judgment and choice. *Organizational Behavior and Human Decision Processes, 70*(1), 41–64.

White, K., MacDonnell, R., & Ellard, J. H. (2012). Belief in a just world: Consumer intentions and behaviors toward ethical products. *Journal of Marketing, 76*(1), 103–118.

4.2 Design options for sustainability-oriented incentive systems

Robert Huber, Bernhard Hirsch, and Matthias Sohn

Incentive systems and sustainability

Corporate sustainability (CS) is a long-term, three-dimensional concept that, for the purpose of sustainable development, encompasses three dimensions: financial, environmental, and social (Loew et al., 2004; Bansal, 2005). Sustainable business thus means that a company's activities are geared not only to the (short-term) goals of one dimension but also to the (medium-term or long-term) goals of all three sustainability dimensions (Dyllick & Hockerts, 2002). This notion of sustainability is also referred to as the triple bottom line concept (Elkington, 1997). One way for companies to connect CS with corporate target-setting is through sustainability-oriented incentive systems. In corporate management, incentive systems are important tools that can be used to influence the behaviour of current and future managers in such a way that their behaviour complies with company targets (Winter, 1997).

At first glance, incentive systems and sustainability seem largely unrelated. In recent years, however, two developments, in particular, have led business research and corporate practice to increasingly focus on the overlap of both topics. In Germany, for example, an act in 2009 on the appropriateness of management board compensation (*Gesetz zur Angemessenheit der Vorstandsvergütung, VorstAG*) established a clear connection between the concept of sustainability and incentive systems for listed German companies. As a result of this change in regulatory framework conditions, companies now face the challenge of incorporating sustainability components into their incentive systems (von Werder, 2011). On the other hand, the strategic relevance of corporate sustainability is steadily growing, and this trend can be observed in the continuous increase in sustainable business models (Lacy et al., 2010). Adopting a sustainable business model, however, also requires companies to implement economic, environmental, and social sustainability targets into their management control systems (Boons & Lüdeke-Freund, 2013; Schaltegger et al., 2016).

Despite the practical relevance of the interrelation between incentive systems and sustainability, academic research on this topic is still scarce (see, for a similar overview, Huber & Hirsch, 2017). Some studies concentrate – with mixed results – on a potential link between pay structure (long-term versus short-term orientation) and different performance measures of sustainability or corporate social performance (e.g., Deckop et al., 2006; Mahoney & Thorn, 2006; Walls et al., 2012; Kolk & Perego, 2014). A related body of research examines associations between measures of sustainability performance and executive compensation (e.g., Stanwick & Stanwick, 2001; Cordeiro & Sarkis, 2008; Berrone & Gomez-Mejia, 2009; Cai et al., 2011). Those studies provide empirical insights into whether higher corporate social and/or environmental performance results in higher executive pay. Corresponding findings are mixed, and no explicit relationship has yet been found (Stanwick & Stanwick, 2001; Berrone & Gomez-Mejia, 2009). Research also shows that although companies do incorporate aspects of sustainability into their strategies and target-settings, these aspects are very rarely linked to incentive systems (Merriman & Sen, 2012). Because of scarce and ambiguous research and a lack of practical guidance about how to create sustainability-oriented incentive systems, our book chapter identifies, systematizes, and discusses the options available for creating such systems (see, similarly, Huber, 2014). We thereby contribute to the literature by providing a systematic overview of options for creating sustainability-oriented incentive systems and give guidance to practitioners as to how to translate them into practice. This chapter is structured as follows. We next present options for creating sustainability-oriented incentive systems, which is followed by a discussion of how to incorporate such systems into business practice. We conclude with a summary of our findings.

Options for creating sustainability-oriented incentive systems

Literature distinguishes between two key interpretations of the concept of sustainability. The first and somewhat narrower interpretation focuses on the long-term time component (e.g., Friedl & Döscher, 2009). According to this interpretation, compensation structures need to be geared toward long-term objectives, particularly by assessing performance over several years or deferring compensation (von Werder, 2011). Accordingly, incentive systems in line with this interpretation are referred to as *pecuniary-oriented incentive systems* throughout this chapter. The other interpretation of the concept of sustainability focuses on the triple bottom line of corporate sustainability. This means that environmental and social aspects are considered in addition to financial aspects (e.g., Seyboth & Thannisch, 2010). Accordingly, incentive systems created to be sustainable, on the basis of this three-dimensional interpretation, are referred to in this chapter as *CS-oriented incentive systems*.

Depending on the interpretation of sustainability, literature relating to the subject proposes different options for creating sustainability-oriented incentive systems. Based on the individual elements of incentive systems, we will present a systematic overview of the options discussed in the literature for designing such incentive systems.

Incentives and payout policy

When creating incentive systems, it is necessary to determine which incentives to use to reward manager behaviour and when these incentives are paid. To foster the long-term aspect of sustainability, firms should provide not only short-term but also long-term incentives. In contrast to short-term incentives (e.g., annual bonus), long-term incentives are not paid out immediately; therefore, they involve a greater degree of uncertainty. They are designed to encourage managers to develop behavioural patterns that are long-term oriented. One way to create a long-term incentive is to defer parts or all of a manager's incentive-related compensation to later years (deferred incentive; e.g., Lange & Walth, 2011). Another tool to foster managers' long-term orientation is a bonus-malus system. Bonus-malus systems involve a degree of uncertainty because bonus payments already earned can potentially be reduced by a future malus payment (Evers et al., 2010). Share-based incentive schemes can also be an effective tool to encourage long-term motivation (e.g., Friedl & Döscher, 2009). The long-term effect of such incentives comes from the uncertainty that results from the share price risk over time (Hoffmann-Becking & Krieger, 2009). The prospect of incentives that involve uncertainty due to repayment obligations can also be conducive to managers' long-term motivation (e.g., Lange & Walth, 2011). Through repayment agreements, incentives that have already been paid out can be reclaimed if longer-term targets are not reached or if agreements, e.g., good governance, are violated. An example of such an incentive system would be so-called clawback compensation schemes (Hol et al., 2010). Finally, long-term incentives can also be created by tying the granting of an incentive to a personal investment in company shares (e.g., Evers et al., 2010). In this case, again, incentives that are tied to personal investments in shares result in uncertainty because the final value of the incentive can only be determined after a waiting period has expired and also depends on how the share prices have developed until that point.

In order to strengthen CS, companies can also use environmental and social incentives, which should be integrated into traditional financial incentives (Gade, 2007; Berrone & Gomez-Mejia, 2009). Using environmental (awards, training, etc.) and social incentives (health courses, flexible working hours, etc.) might allow companies to influence manager behaviour accordingly if corresponding manager needs exist.

Assessment criteria

A second key aspect in regard to designing incentive systems is to define evaluation criteria that properly assess manager performance. With the right assessment criteria, firms can foster the long-term aspect of sustainability. Performance can be assessed on the basis of multi-year averages of evaluation criteria (multi-year performance appraisal; e.g., Friedl & Döscher, 2009). This approach requires deciding whether multi-year performance appraisals should be based on a comparison of actual performance indicators with past or future performance targets (Lange & Walth, 2011).

The selection of evaluation criteria can also be used to create CS-oriented incentive systems. This can be done by incorporating not only traditional financial criteria but also environmental and social criteria into the incentive scheme. Potential criteria that are very frequently mentioned include carbon footprint, energy efficiency (e.g., Evers et al., 2010), employee satisfaction (e.g., von Werder, 2011), and employee health and safety (e.g., Seyboth & Thannisch, 2010).

Reward function

The reward function is the connection between the incentive criteria and the incentive. The functional connection can be configured such that a specific upper limit (cap) is applied to the incentive. This means that an agreed maximum for variable compensation cannot be exceeded. It ensures that a company does not have to pay excessive variable compensation (usually bonus payments) as a result of unexpected developments (Götz & Friese, 2010). This issue has been raised in the banking and insurance industry – especially after the financial crisis – where excessive bonuses were paid while taxpayers' money was needed to keep banks and insurers afloat. A prominent example is the American International Group (AIG), which required taxpayer money to avoid bankruptcy and paid out approximately one billion dollars in variable compensation to the management in the same year. This provision thus ensures that the company's long-term sustainable capital resources are not put at risk. It is therefore propagated by many professional investors, researchers, and the general public (Eurosif & EIRIS, 2010) and is consistent with the idea of sustainability as a long-term concept.

With regard to CS, the reward function itself is not an option to promote sustainable behaviour. This is because the reward function as a mathematical relation only establishes the connection between assessment criteria and incentives.

Target group

The target group determines the addressee of a certain incentive scheme. From a long-term point of view, one could argue that target group continuity provides a potential starting point for strengthening an incentive system's orientation towards financial sustainability. This is particularly true because a long-term approach in the personnel sector – that is, a high degree of continuity and/or low fluctuation – is usually explicitly desired. The aspect of continuity, however, does not create any long-term sustainable incentive structures or behavioural incentives. The choice of a target group itself thus does not provide an option for incorporating sustainability. Instead, to strengthen the sustainability orientation of an organization, the focus should be on (1) the individual and (2) the organizational culture:

(1) If managers have a sustainability-oriented attitude, the achievement of sustainability targets becomes more likely. Empirical findings show that the effectiveness of CS-oriented incentive systems is influenced significantly by the personal attitudes, goals, and values of the managers towards sustainability (Huber & Hirsch, 2017). Organizational citizenship behaviour, for example, which is a construct that covers good behaviour in an organization – such as altruism, conscientiousness, sportsmanship, and courtesy (Organ, 1988) – is not only linked to job satisfaction but also to long-term business success (van Dyne et al., 1994). Additionally, the perceived importance of ethics and social responsibility for organizational effectiveness varies across individuals (Singhapakdi et al., 1996) and has a mediating role in the effectiveness of CS-targeted incentive schemes on employee attraction and retention (Huber & Hirsch, 2017). This is especially the case for millennials. Corresponding research suggests that young job-seekers not only care about CS but also weigh corporate signals of CS against conditions of employment, such as their (potential) salary (Sohn et al., 2015). This means that young job-seekers and employees forgo individual monetary benefits by working for companies that are high performers from a corporate social responsibility perspective. Additionally, a recent survey shows that millennials intend to work longer with those employers that engage with social issues, which could lead to long-term financial success (Deloitte, 2017).
(2) The role of the organizational culture or climate on employee attitudes and behaviours has gained momentum in business ethics research. An ethical working climate can be defined as a climate in which employees have shared perceptions of what constitutes ethical conduct (Martin & Cullen, 2006); an ethical culture can be defined as concrete aspects of the organizational context that stimulate ethical conduct (Weaver et al., 1999; Kaptein, 2008). Both can have a positive effect on employee attraction and retention and moderate the effect of sustainability-oriented incentive schemes on employee behaviour. This moderating role depends on whether CS and compliance are actually integrated into core business processes and strategy or simply serve as green-washing (Collier & Esteban, 2007).

Table 4.2.1 Options to create sustainability-oriented incentive systems

Element	Pecuniary-oriented incentive systems (long-term approach)	CS-oriented incentive systems (triple bottom line)
Incentives and payout policy	• Deferred incentive availability • Bonus–malus arrangement • Repayment obligation • Personal investment	• Environmental incentives • Social incentives
Assessment criteria	• Multi-year performance appraisal	• Environmental assessment bases • Social assessment bases
Reward function	• Upper limit (cap)	• ---
Target group	• --- (instead: Focus on individual and organizational culture)	• --- (instead: Focus on individual and organizational culture)

Table 4.2.1 provides a systematic overview of the options discussed for creating sustainability-oriented incentive systems on the basis of the individual elements of incentive systems. We differentiate between whether options apply to the creation of pecuniary-oriented incentive systems or CS-oriented incentive systems.

Discussion of options for creating sustainability-oriented incentive systems

In the following section, we discuss which of the options described above should be given priority in company practice. In our framework, the options are considered according to three different aspects. First, they are assessed in terms of how they contribute to corporate sustainability. Second, we consider the degree to which the options help to meet regulatory requirements. Finally, we discuss, based on findings from behavioural research, whether the implementation of the options can be expected to have positive or negative effects on manager behaviour and ultimately on (sustainable) business practice.

Implementing corporate sustainability

The purpose of sustainability-oriented incentive systems is to draw managers' attention to sustainability goals and thus to contribute to sustainable corporate development (Epstein & Roy, 2001). In order to foster corporate sustainability as a long-term, three-dimensional concept, sustainability-oriented incentive systems should account for both long-term and triple bottom line aspects of corporate sustainability.

Obviously, the six options described for creating incentive systems oriented towards financial sustainability help to develop long-term mindsets and behavioural patterns among managers. As a result, all these options can be used to foster the long-term aspect of sustainability. However, the simultaneous application of all options would result in complexity or transparency problems. Lange & Walth (2011) and Wilke and Schmid (2012), for example, note that incentive systems in corporate practice have become less comprehensible due to their complexity. In order to be effective, incentive systems should be simple enough for managers to understand. As a result, the six options described should be used selectively rather than simultaneously.

Incorporating environmental and social incentives into corporate incentive systems does not, by itself, contribute to sustainable corporate development. It neither creates long-term sustainable incentive structures nor helps to achieve sustainability goals. In combination with environmentally and/or socially oriented assessment criteria, however, it is possible to indirectly foster socially and environmentally oriented behaviour. Because managers usually have very diverse needs, environmental and social incentives should only be offered on an individual level (Winter, 1997).

The integration of environmental and social assessment criteria into corporate incentive systems plays a significant role in achieving sustainable business development. Employees can only be expected to fully support sustainability goals if these goals are also integrated into their incentive schemes (Berrone & Gomez-Mejia, 2009). It is important, however, to keep in mind that simultaneously pursuing economic, environmental, and social targets entails possible goal conflicts. For example, sourcing production material globally may lead to greater transportation efforts and thus increased greenhouse gas emissions. Sourcing locally might be more expensive but could also be less detrimental to the environment. Nonetheless, we argue that sustainability-oriented assessments that include environmental as well as social targets are the preferred way to translate CS strategy into practice. DHL Deutsche Post, for example, uses an employee survey to rate the leadership behaviour of superiors as an assessment basis for executives. The company also includes ecological assessment criteria, such as the carbon efficiency index, in its incentive scheme for top managers (Deutsche Post AG, 2016). Similarly, the BMW group's incentive schemes for top management include non-financial assessment criteria, such as reducing greenhouse gas emissions, fostering diversity in management, or business activities specifically targeted at CS. Of course, at BMW, the incentive scheme for top management addresses not only CS but also financial sustainability, as 20% of the variable compensation is paid out in stocks to foster long-term thinking in top management (BMW AG, 2016).

Meeting regulatory and other requirements

The options for creating sustainability-oriented incentive systems should be chosen and deployed on the basis of, among other things, the extent to which regulatory frameworks require them to be implemented. In this section, we present the most important regulations in Germany, complemented by recent initiatives from the US and UK.

In Germany, both the German Stock Corporation Act and the German Corporate Governance Code (DCGK) mention multi-year performance appraisals and specify a cap on variable compensation. In addition, the German Corporate Governance Code suggests the use of bonus–malus arrangements. For companies that are subject to the regulations of the German Stock Corporation Act, the option of deferred incentive availability should also be considered when issuing stock options. Therefore, with due regard for the standards of good and responsible corporate management established in the German Corporate Governance Code, we recommend that companies give priority to the options of multi-year assessments, caps on variable compensation, and bonus–malus arrangements. If the German Stock Corporation Act is relevant, the option of deferred incentive availability should also be used where applicable. All these measures are designed to strengthen managers' long-term orientation.

There are also regulatory measures in the US and the UK that encourage or even require companies to implement deferred compensation or bonus-malus incentive schemes. In the US, clawback provisions became popular with the Sarbanes–Oxley Act of 2002 as a reaction to the accounting scandals at Enron and WorldCom. These incentive schemes allow companies to "claw back" variable compensation in the case of financial restatements that result from noncompliance or misconduct. Clawbacks were voluntarily adopted by US companies on a large scale (Chen et al., 2013). Clawback schemes became mandatory with the Dodd–Frank Act of 2010 as a reaction to the financial crisis of 2007/2008; such schemes also focus on financial restatements and fraud. In the UK, clawback compensation schemes became mandatory for banking and insurance companies in January 2015 and allow companies to reclaim incentives that date back up to six years. These schemes are not limited to financial restatements but apply to a wider range of managerial misconduct and myopia. The Bank of England proposes that firms can require managers to pay back previously earned compensation when the company or the relevant business unit suffers a material failure of risk management. Accordingly, there is a strong consensus that bonus-malus schemes, especially clawbacks, are suitable tools to foster long-term mindsets among managers. This applies to continental Europe, the UK, and the US. All these regulatory initiatives, however, aim at incentive systems oriented towards financial sustainability and not CS.

Concerning CS, subsection 8 of the German Sustainability Code and reporting principle G4-51 of the Global Reporting Initiative (GRI) recommend integrating environmental and social assessment criteria into corporate incentive systems. This option is also proposed or postulated by influential lobby groups (Eurosif & EIRIS, 2010; World Business Council for Sustainable Development, 2010). Against this background, we also recommend integrating environmental and social assessment criteria in managerial incentive schemes.

Influence on the goals of incentive systems

In general, incentive systems serve four purposes: attraction, cooperation, motivation, and retention (Winter, 1997). For the purposes of effective incentive systems, priority should be given to using those options that have positive effects – or at least have no negative effects – on these functions.

Options for creating pecuniary-oriented incentive systems can be expected to have a negative effect on manager attraction and motivation. This is because incentives are capped, deferred, or involve additional uncertainty that managers aim to avoid. Deferred incentive availability, for example, can be less effective because the direct causality between a manager's own actions and the resulting consequence become less apparent (Hohenstatt & Kuhnke, 2009). At the same time, the prospect of a cap on variable compensation can be expected to have a negative effect on manager attraction and motivation because of the lack of any further incentive once the limit has been reached (Anthony & Govindarajan, 2007). On the other hand, however, bonus-malus arrangements, repayment obligations, and personal investments can be expected to generate additional motivation because managers will try to clear negative accounts and avoid having to make repayments. This will ultimately increase company value. Further, the use of options for creating pecuniary-oriented incentive systems could positively affect manager retention. Bonus-malus arrangements that provide, for example, a personal account that will expire when a manager leaves the company create an incentive to stay

Table 4.2.2 Assessment of the options available for creating sustainability-oriented incentive systems

Option	Implementation of corporate sustainability	Compliance with regulations and other requirements	Influence on the functions of incentive systems
Options for gearing incentive systems towards financial sustainability	Creation of long-term sustainable incentive structures (long-term approach)	Compliance with: Section 87 Paragraph 1 Sentence 3, German Stock Corporation Act Section 193 Paragraph 2 No. 4, German Stock Corporation Act Subsection 4.2.3 German Corporate Governance Code, the Dodd–Frank-Act of 2010, Bank of England Prudential Regulation Authority	Likely negative effect on manager attraction and motivation Likely positive effect on manager cooperation and retention
Environmental and social incentives	Possible indirect contribution to achieving sustainability goals (triple bottom line)		Potential to increase manager attraction, motivation, cooperation, and retention
Environmental and social assessment bases	Direct contribution to achieving sustainability goals (triple bottom line)	Compliance with: Subsection 8 German Sustainability Code GRI reporting principle G4-51	Potential to increase manager attraction, motivation, cooperation, and retention

(golden handcuffs; Anthony & Govindarajan, 2007). Whether there are incentives to stay, however, depends on the specific agreements, i.e., whether and to what extent a manager's claims expire if they leave the company early, depending on whether this leave is voluntary or involuntary. A significant effect on managers' willingness to cooperate is not to be expected, as these options mainly concern a person's individual situation (e.g., deferred bonus payments, repayment obligation), which means that there is usually no need to strive for closer interaction with other colleagues. The option of personal investment could possibly be an exception to this rule. A manager holding company shares is keen to see an increase in the price of these shares and thus in company value. Because all areas and managers contribute directly or indirectly to such a development, this option, as a group incentive, could have a stimulating effect on the degree of mutual coordination and cooperation between departments and managers.

For the option of environmental and social incentives, no definite statement can be made on the effectiveness of incentive systems. This is because the effects of environmental and social incentives very much depend on the individual manager's needs (Gade, 2007). It is clear, however, that managers' needs become more diverse over time and increasingly concern non-financial areas (e.g., Fay & Thompson, 2001). In addition, the relevant literature reports positive effects of environmental and social incentives (Govindarajulu & Daily, 2004; Berrone & Gomez-Mejia, 2009) and recommends using such incentives (Steinle et al., 1997; Dyckhoff & Souren, 2008). Thus, this option has the potential to help increase manager attraction, cooperation, motivation, and retention. We therefore recommend using environmental and social incentives, which should be integrated with economic incentives.

No general statement can be made on whether the option of environmentally and socially oriented assessment is suitable to increase managers' sustainability-oriented behaviour. Research shows that both corporate sustainability efforts and direct manager participation in sustainability projects can have a positive influence on manager behaviour (attraction, cooperation, motivation, retention). An ever-increasing body of research suggests that employees derive utility from the congruence of personal and corporate values, known as Person-Organization-Fit Theory (Sen & Bhattacharya, 2001; Ambrose et al., 2008). In a similar vein, signalling theory suggests that information about a firm's CS policies and programs signals organizational values and norms (Greening & Turban, 2000). These signals make companies more attractive to those employees who themselves value CS. On the other hand, in this context, the importance of the type of CS activity (Bhattacharya et al., 2008) and personal attitudes towards sustainability (Petersen, 2004; Berens et al., 2007) are often stressed. Accordingly, managers might prefer a diverse set of targets that include environmental and social aspects, especially for those managers who care about CS. This would ultimately increase these managers' motivation and retention. On the basis of these findings, we argue that environmental and social evaluation criteria have the potential to increase manager attraction, cooperation, motivation, and retention. Table 4.2.2 provides a summary of the most significant results of the discussion.

Conclusions

Today, companies need to meet different stakeholders' demands in regard to sustainable business practices, including demands from managers, customers, investors, or regulators. Accordingly, companies integrate sustainability into their business models and need to translate these strategic goals into practice using incentive schemes that make managers act in a way that complies with corporate sustainability goals. The above discussion shows that in order to put corporate sustainability into practice, companies should consider integrating not only financial but also environmental and social assessment criteria into their incentive systems. Such an approach is geared toward CS. This is also in line with recommendations in Subsection 8 of the German Sustainability Code and GRI reporting principle G4-51. The integration of environmental and social assessment criteria can also have positive effects on manager behaviour. In addition, companies should integrate environmental and social incentives into their incentive systems. This option can positively affect manager behaviour when the incentives are in line with managers' individual needs. In order to foster sustainable corporate development, companies should also use selected options in order to create long-term sustainable incentive structures. Due to relevant regulations in the German Stock Corporation Act and/or the German Corporate Governance Code, as well as outside Germany (e.g., the Dodd–Frank Act of 2010), the options of multi-year performance assessment, caps on compensation, bonus-malus arrangements, and, if applicable, deferred incentive availability are particularly relevant. When using these options, however, it is important to keep in mind potential negative effects on manager attraction and motivation. Finally, we argue that companies need to select a subset of the available measures targeting financial sustainability and combine them with environmental and social assessment criteria, when applicable. Otherwise, the incentive schemes might become too complex. Managers need to understand the connection among their actions, the incentive system, and corporate goals and strategy. If the incentive schemes are too complex, the intended behavioural patterns might not result.

References

Ambrose, M.L., Arnaud, A., & Schminke, M. (2008). Individual moral development and ethical climate: The influence of person–organization fit on job attitudes. *Journal of Business Ethics*, 77(3), 323–333.

Anthony, R.N., & Govindarajan, V. (2007). *Management Control Systems*, 12th edn. Boston: McGraw Hill/Irwin.

Bansal, P. (2005). Evolving sustainably: A longitudinal study of corporate sustainable development. *Strategic Management Journal*, 26(3), 197–218.

Berens, G., van Riel, C.B., & van Rekom, J. (2007). The CSR-quality trade-off: When can corporate social responsibility and corporate ability compensate each other? *Journal of Business Ethics*, 74(3), 233–252.

Berrone, P., & Gomez-Mejia, L.R. (2009). The pros and cons of rewarding social responsibility at the top. *Human Resource Management*, 48(6), 959–971.

Bhattacharya, C.B., Sen, S., & Korschun, D. (2008). Using corporate social responsibility to win the war for talent. *MIT Sloan Management Review*, 49(2), 37–44.

BMW AG (2016). *Annual Report 2015*. München: BMW AG.

Boons, F., & Lüdeke-Freund, F. (2013). Business models for sustainable innovation: State of the art and steps towards a research agenda. *Journal of Cleaner Production*, 45, 9–19.

Cai, Y., Jo, H., & Pan, C. (2011). Vice or virtue? The impact of corporate social responsibility on executive compensation. *Journal of Business Ethics*, 104, 159–173.

Chen, M., Greene, D., & Owers, J. (2013). The costs and benefits of CEO clawback provisions: Theory and evidence. Working paper, Available at SSRN 1980406.

Collier, J., & Esteban, R. (2007). Corporate social responsibility and employee commitment. *Business Ethics*, *16*(1), 19–33.

Cordeiro, J.J., & Sarkis, J. (2008). Does explicit contracting effectively link CEO compensation to environmental performance? *Business Strategy and the Environment*, *17*(5), 304–317.

Deckop, J.R., Merriman, K.K., & Gupta, S. (2006). The effects of CEO pay structure on Corporate Social Performance. *Journal of Management*, *32*(3), 329–342.

Deloitte (2017). *The 2017 Deloitte Millennial Survey*. Retrieved from: https://www2.deloitte. com/global/en/pages/about-deloitte/articles/millennialsurvey.html

Deutsche Post AG (2016). *2015 Annual Report*. Bonn: Deutsche Post AG.

Dyckhoff, H., & Souren, R. (2008). Nachhaltige Unternehmensführung: Grundzüge industriellen Umweltmanagements. Berlin et al.: Springer.

Dyllick, T., & Hockerts, K. (2002). Beyond the business case for corporate sustainability. *Business Strategy and the Environment*, *11*(2), 130–141.

Elkington, J. (1997). *Cannibals with Forks: The Triple Bottom Line of 21st Century Business*. Oxford: Capstone Publishing.

Epstein, M.J., & Roy, M.-J. (2001). Sustainability in action: Identifying and measuring the key performance drivers. *Long Range Planning*, *34*(5), 585–604.

Eurosif & EIRIS (2010). *Remuneration. Theme report*. Paris/London: Eurosif & EIRIS.

Evers, H., Köstler, R., & Weckes, M. (2010). Managervergütung in der Praxis: Hinweise zum Umgang mit dem VorstAG. In: Hans-Böckler-Stiftung (Ed.), *Angemessene Vorstandsvergütung: Informationen zur Bemessung der Vorstandsvergütungen durch den Aufsichtsrat*, 4th edn. (pp. 22–79). Düsseldorf: Hans-Böckler-Stiftung.

Fay, C.H., & Thompson, M.A. (2001). Contextual determinants of reward systems' success: An exploratory study. *Human Resource Management*, *40*(3), 213–226.

Friedl, G., & Döscher, T. (2009). Langfristige Anreize in der DAX 30-Vorstandsvergütung. *Der Aufsichtsrat*, *6*(3), 36–38.

Gade, C. (2007). *Ökologieorientierte Anreizgestaltung: Erklärung ökologieschonenden Arbeitsverhaltens und Gestaltung ökologieorientierter Anreizsysteme*. München/Mering: Hampp.

Götz, A., & Friese, N. (2010). Empirische Analyse der Vorstandsvergütung im DAX und MDAX nach Einführung des Vorstandsvergütungsangemessenheitsgesetzes. *Corporate Finance biz*, *1*(6), 410–420.

Govindarajulu, N., & Daily, B.F. (2004). Motivating employees for environmental improvement. *Industrial Management and Data Systems*, *104*(4), 364–372.

Greening, D.W., & Turban, D.B. (2000). Corporate social performance as a competitive advantage in attracting a quality workforce. *Business and Society*, *39*(3), 254–280.

Hoffmann-Becking, M., & Krieger, G. (2009). Leitfaden zur Anwendung des Gesetzes zur Angemessenheit der Vorstandsvergütung (VorstAG). *NZG – Neue Zeitschrift für Gesellschaftsrecht*, *12*(26), 1–12.

Hohenstatt, K.-S., & Kuhnke, M. (2009). Vergütungsstruktur und variable Vergütungsmodelle für Vorstandsmitglieder nach dem VorstAG. *ZIP – Zeitschrift für Wirtschaftsrecht*, *30*(42), 1981–1989.

Hol, H., Kurznack, L., Logger, E., & van Tilburg, R. (2010). *Sustainable remuneration: A guide for linking sustainable goals to executive incentives*. Retrieved from: https://www.haygroup.com/ Downloads/nl/misc/Sustainable_Remuneration_-_A_guide_for_linking_sustainable_goals_ to_executive_incentives.pdf

Huber, R. (2014). *Nachhaltigkeitsorientierte Anreizsysteme: Eine empirische Analyse zu Gestaltung und Verhaltenswirkungen*. Lohmar: Eul.

Huber, R., & Hirsch, B. (2017). Behavioral effects of sustainability-oriented incentive systems. *Business Strategy and the Environment*, *26*(2), 163–181.

Kaptein, M. (2008). Developing and testing a measure for the ethical culture of organizations: The corporate ethical virtues model. *Journal of Organizational Behavior*, *29*(7), 923–947.

Kolk, A., & Perego, P. (2014). Sustainable bonuses: Sign of corporate responsibility or window dressing? *Journal of Business Ethics, 119*(1), 1–15.

Lacy, P., Cooper, T., Hayward, R., & Neuberger, L. (2010). *A new era of sustainability: CEO reflections on progress to date, challenges ahead and the impact of the journey toward a sustainable economy.* Retrieved from: https://www.unglobalcompact.org/docs/newsevents/8.1/UNGC_Accenture_CEO_Study_2010.pdf

Lange, R., & Walth, A. (2011). Anreizsysteme für Top-Manager im Lichte der regulatorischen Rahmenbedingungen. *Zeitschrift für Controlling und Management, 55*(3), 31–35.

Loew, T., Clausen, J., Braun, S., & Ankele, K. (2004). *Bedeutung der internationalen CSR-Diskussion für Nachhaltigkeit und die sich daraus ergebenden Anforderungen an Unternehmen mit Fokus Berichterstattung.* Münster/Berlin: N.N.

Mahoney, L.S., & Thorn, L. (2006). An examination of the structure of executive compensation and Corporate Social Responsibility: A Canadian investigation. *Journal of Business Ethics, 69*(2), 149–162.

Martin, K., & Cullen, J. (2006). Continuities and extensions of ethical climate theory: A meta-analytic review. *Journal of Business Ethics, 69*(2), 175–194.

Merriman, K.K., & Sen, S. (2012). Incenting managers toward the triple bottom line: An agency and social norm perspective. *Human Resource Management, 51*(6), 851–871.

Organ, D.W. (1988). *Organizational Citizenship Behavior: The Good Soldier Syndrome.* Lexington: The Free Press.

Petersen, D.K. (2004). The relationship between perceptions of corporate citizenship and organizational commitment. *Business and Society, 43*(3), 296–319.

Schaltegger, S., Hansen, E., & Lüdeke-Freund, F. (2016). Business models for sustainability: Origins, present research, and future avenues. *Organization and Environment, 29*(1), 3–10.

Sen, S., & Bhattacharya, C.B. (2001). Does doing good always lead to doing better? Consumer reactions to Corporate Social Responsibility. *Journal of Marketing Research, 38*(2), 225–243.

Seyboth, M., & Thannisch, R. (2010). Empfehlungen für eine angemessene Vorstandsvergütung. In: Hans-Böckler-Stiftung (Ed.), *Angemessene Vorstandsvergütung: Informationen zur Bemessung der Vorstandsvergütungen durch den Aufsichtsrat,* 4th edn. (pp. 7–21). Düsseldorf: Hans-Böckler-Stiftung.

Singhapakdi, A., Vitell, S.J., Rallapalli, K.C., & Kraft, K.L. (1996). The perceived role of ethics and social responsibility: A scale development. *Journal of Business Ethics, 15*(11), 1131–1140.

Sohn, M., Sohn, W., Klaas-Wissing, T., & Hirsch, B. (2015). The influence of Corporate Social Performance on employer attractiveness in the transportation and logistics industry: Insights from German Junior Talent. *International Journal of Physical Distribution and Logistics Management, 45*(5), 486–505.

Stanwick, P.A., & Stanwick, S.D. (2001). CEO compensation: Does it pay to be green? *Business Strategy and the Environment, 10*(3), 176–182.

Steinle, C., Bruch, H., & Neu, M. (1997). Ökologiebezogene Anreizgestaltung in Unternehmungen – Konzept, empirisches Schlaglicht und Praxisempfehlungen. *Zeitschrift für Umweltpolitik & Umweltrecht, 20*(2), 255–279.

van Dyne, L., Graham, J.W., & Dienesch, R.M. (1994). Organizational citizenship behavior: Construct redefinition, measurement, and validation. *Academy of Management Journal, 37*(4), 765–802.

von Werder, A. (2011). Neue Entwicklungen der Corporate Governance in Deutschland. *Schmalenbachs Zeitschrift für betriebswirtschaftliche Forschung, 63*(1), 48–62.

Walls, J.L., Berrone, P., & Phan, P.H. (2012). Corporate governance and environmental performance: Is there really a link? *Strategic Management Journal, 33*(8), 885–913.

Weaver, G.R., Treviño, L.K., & Cochran, P.L. (1999). Integrated and decoupled Corporate Social Performance: Management commitments, external pressures, and corporate ethics practices. *The Academy of Management Journal, 42*(5), 539–552.

Wilke, P., & Schmid, K. (2012). *Entwicklung der Vorstandsvergütung 2011 in den DAX-30-Untemehmen: Trends in der Vorstandsvergütung seit Einführung des Gesetzes zur Angemessenheit der Vorstandsvergütung*. Düsseldorf: Hans-Böckler-Stiftung.

Winter, S. (1997). Möglichkeiten der Gestaltung von Anreizsystemen für Führungskräfte. *Die Betriebswirtschaft, 57*(5), 615–629.

World Business Council for Sustainable Development (2010). *People Matter Reward: Linking Sustainability to Pay*. Geneva: World Business Council for Sustainable Development.

4.3 Sustainability reporting
Do the Global Reporting Initiative Guidelines provide clear guidance?

Rüdiger W. Waldkirch and Bernhard Hirsch

Introduction

Most companies are confronted with increasing expectations. Today, there is a broad stakeholder demand that companies base their decisions not only on economic arguments but also consider the impacts of their behaviour on the environment and society as a whole. In addition to behaving responsibly, companies are currently expected to provide an account or reckoning of their behaviour (e.g., Gray, Owen, & Adams, 1996; Gray, Owen, & Maunders, 1987). The demand for such information to be publicly disclosed has increased considerably over the last decades (e.g., Berthelot, Cormier, & Magnan, 2003; Burritt & Schaltegger, 2010; Lamberton, 2005).

In their efforts to report on sustainability (performance), companies can only rely on limited guidance (e.g., Gray 2001, 2010). This is partly because sustainability reporting is "an unstable and moving set of practices" (Bebbington, 2009, p. 189) and is plagued by complexity and ambiguity (e.g., Adams & Whelan, 2009; Boesso, Kumar, & Michelon, 2013). Several initiatives have developed principles to fill the gap. Today, the Global Reporting Initiative's G4 Sustainability Reporting Guidelines (hereafter "GRI Guidelines") are regarded as the *de facto* standard for sustainability reporting (e.g., Brown, de Jong, & Lessidrenska, 2009; Etzion & Ferraro, 2010; KPMG, 2017; Moneva, Archel, & Correa, 2006).

This chapter challenges the widespread assumption that the GRI Guidelines fulfil their purpose as a framework for voluntary sustainability reporting to a high degree. In general, reporting frameworks should prescribe the function of disclosures, facilitate the development of consistent reporting standards, and, first and foremost, provide good guidance on preparing corporate reports (e.g., Deegan & Unerman, 2006; Peasnell, 1982; Thomas & Ward, 2009). From our contractarian perspective, we find that the GRI Guidelines provide limited guidance for two reasons. First, the GRI Guidelines do not follow the theories widely used to analyse corporate reporting and thus do not thoroughly conceptualize reporting as a relational problem between a company and its reporting addressees. Second, the GRI Guidelines neglect the incentives present in the situation, and thus leave the questions open as to what companies disclose in their sustainability reports and what information stakeholders can reasonably expect from voluntary corporate reporting. To remedy these shortcomings, we suggest revising the GRI Guidelines. We recommend incorporating the idea of mutual gains by refining the *materiality* principle and introducing a cost–benefit perspective for sustainability reporting.

Apart from the GRI Guidelines and their further development, this chapter makes several more general contributions. First, we propose a new approach for analysing voluntary corporate reporting and relate it to the literature. Second, we adopt the economic theory of morality and apply it to the field of corporate reporting. Third, this chapter highlights the importance of incentives for sustainability reporting and underscores the restrictions they place on any voluntary reports.

This chapter unfolds as follows. The next section outlines the conceptual background for our study. The third section describes the GRI Guidelines by indicating their main objectives, proposed addressees, and core principles. Thereafter, we analyse the consistency of the GRI standards and how consequently the GRI Guidelines incorporate the idea of mutual gains. We then give guidance as to how to further improve the GRI Guidelines. We end with concluding remarks.

Conceptual background

The literature on voluntary corporate reporting offers several theoretical bases for discussing the GRI Guidelines. Scholars of sustainability reporting rely primarily on stakeholder thinking and/or legitimacy theory (e.g., Gray, Kouhy, & Lavers, 1995; Joseph, 2012). At its core, stakeholder thinking proposes the idea that a company serves all of its stakeholders (e.g., Freeman, Harrison, Wicks, Parmar, & de Colle, 2010; Friedman & Miles, 2006). Reporting corporate information is one aspect of such stakeholder engagement (e.g., Burrit & Schaltegger, 2010; Cooper & Owen, 2007; Deegan, 2002). Central to legitimacy theory is the idea that companies depend on a general perception that they operate within the norms, rules, and value systems of the society (e.g., Dowling & Pfeffer, 1975; Suchman, 1995). Accordingly, corporate reporting helps companies gain, maintain, or repair their legitimacy (e.g., Cho & Patten, 2007; Lindblom, 2010).

In contrast, information economics and/or agency theory dominates the literature on financial reporting (e.g., Healy & Palepu, 2001; Lambert, 2001; Mattessich, 2006; Verrecchia, 2001). Key to information economics and agency theory are incentive problems that arise from information asymmetries in the relationship between financial investors and companies. Reporting serves to alleviate these problems by providing potential investors with credible information about the companies' value (aka decision usefulness) and shareholders with the information needed for monitoring corporate management (aka stewardship) (e.g., Gjesdal, 1981).

Although a profound divide appears to run through the literature on voluntary corporate reporting, there is also a great deal of overlap between them (e.g., Chen & Roberts, 2010; Deegan, 2002; Gray et al., 1995). For our purposes, it is sufficient to emphasize that all these theories focus the relationship between a company and its (potential) investors, its stakeholders, or society at large. All provide resources to the company, for example, in form of money, work, infrastructure, or legitimacy, which then renders service in return, for example, in form of dividends, taxes, or jobs. We follow suit but use a different approach that helps to bridge the perceived gap between theories on (voluntary) financial and sustainability reporting.

Our contractarian approach builds upon the economic theory of morality as developed by Homann (2002, 2003). This theory combines the idea of mutual consent to a social contract from moral philosophy (e.g., Hobbes, 1947; Hume, 1967) with the idea of social dilemmas, for example, (one- and two-sided) prisoners' dilemma types of social interactions. It has inspired numerous publications on the notion of corporate social responsibility (e.g., Pies, Beckmann, & Hielscher, 2014; Beckmann, Hielscher, & Pies,

2012; Lin-Hi & Suchanek, 2011; Pies, Hielscher, & Beckmann, 2009; Waldkirch, 2001, 2002) as well as in other fields (e.g., Wagner-Tsukamoto, 2005, 2007).

We apply the economic theory of morality to the case of voluntary reporting and use a trust game (e.g., Dasgupta, 1988; Lin-Hi & Suchanek, 2011; Snijders, 1996) to illustrate the relational problem that underlies accounting practices, including voluntary sustainability reporting. Pictured in Figure 4.3.1, the trust game in our approach serves a different purpose compared to how it is used in game theory and/or institutional economics. In game theory, the trust game depicts the patterns of a specific situation and thus helps to explain how real people behave. This enables researchers to define an optimal strategy for these particular circumstances. In economic analyses, one-sided prisoners' dilemmas, such as the trust game, typically characterize situational information and incentive patterns. These analyses are focused on contracts or institutions that change the rules of the game, and players are enabled to realize mutual gains from interaction (similar to Pies et al., 2009).

Contrary hereto, in this chapter, the trust game serves as an "ideal type" (Weber, 1949), a "searchlight" (Popper, 1972), or a heuristic for understanding the function and the characteristic features of voluntary corporate reporting (for the concept of heuristics, see Waldkirch, Meyer, & Homann, 2009). It models an interaction between two players, the resource provider (RP) and the accounting entity (AE). The RP moves first by deciding whether to trust or distrust the AE. If the RP decides to distrust the AE, the game ends with an ordinal payoff of zero to both players (III). However, if the RP chooses to trust the AE, thereby choosing to invest resources (e.g., by providing legitimacy to the AE, buying their products, etc.), it is now the AE's turn to decide whether to honour or breach the RP's trust. If the AE chooses to honour the RP's trust (e.g., by providing information about sustainability performance, by providing a product with the advertised characteristics, etc.), the game reaches endpoint I, in which the RP reaches a higher payoff than in the first scenario (a > 0). If the AE chooses to breach the RP's trust, the game ends in endpoint II, in which the RP does comparably worse (0 > b), and the AE will receive a payoff of t.

"Our" trust game poses two closely related questions. First, does the AE have sufficient incentives to honour the RP's trust, that is, does the AE prefer s to t? Second, is the RP confident about the AE's trustworthiness? Has he found sound reasons to believe that the AE has an interest in honouring his trust? One could conceive of the trust game as a one-sided situation, in which only the RP is vulnerable because the AE can "exploit" the RP's investment by dishonouring his trust. However, if one thinks

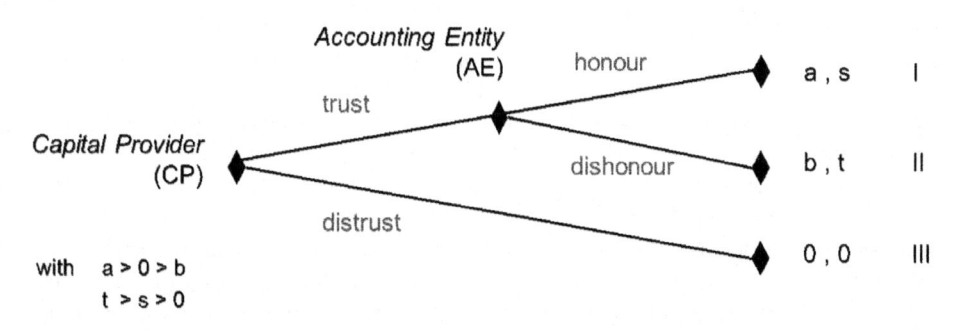

Figure 4.3.1 Trust game

in terms of mutual gains and the players' efforts to achieve mutual gains, the story is truly two-sided. That is, if the RP decides not to trust the AE and thus not to invest his resources, this decision also becomes a problem for the AE because his potential gains from the interaction are forfeited. Anticipating this relational problem, the AE has an interest not only in discovering the assumptions that the RP has made about him but also in actively influencing the RP's expectations about whether he might breach the RP's trust. The AE has an interest in investing in the RP's expectations – for example, by sending a credible signal about his trustworthiness, a signal that will enable the RP to believe that, even after receiving his investment, it is in the AE's best interest to honour his trust. In our view, voluntary reporting on corporate sustainability should be regarded as an investment into the trustworthiness of the reporting company as a signal to all of its stakeholders that helps to build the necessary trust, the "investor confidence" (Sutton, 1997).

Having outlined the basic features of the trust game, which highlights the interactional problem that voluntary sustainability reporting should help solve, we now turn briefly to two of its basic assumptions and their implications for voluntary sustainability reporting.

First, any social science attempting to derive proposals for altering laws, regulations, and ultimately changing the behaviour of companies or individuals confronts a legitimacy problem: Where does it derive moral legitimacy from? To which source(s) does it turn to judge what is morally right or wrong? Our contractarian approach provides a constructive answer to these questions of moral justification. In a globalized world, the moral legitimacy of rules (and ultimately, actions) can only come from the mutual consent of all individuals, who are the ultimate source of values (e.g., Buchanan, 1975; Brennan & Buchanan, 1985; Homann, 2002, 2003). Buchanan (1995) proposed another, now positive, argument to support this normative argument: as individuals always have discretionary leeway, they will veto, boycott, or act against the rules if these are not in their own best interests. Thus, the mutual consent of all is a criterion for moral legitimacy as well as for the stability and viability of rules. In our illustrative game, both players, RP and AE, can consent to a change in rules, which decreases AE's payoff t to t' at endpoint II to the extent necessary to induce RP to trust AE to honour the contract (s > t'); compared to the only other feasible solution (III), both would gain (for RP, a > 0; for AE, s > 0).

This is a major point of deviation from stakeholder thinking and legitimacy theory that bears consequences for the theoretical reconstruction of voluntary corporate reporting. If stakeholder theory seeks judgement on moral legitimacy, it applies diverse ethical theories but rarely the criterion of mutual consent (e.g., Freeman et al., 2010; Friedman & Miles, 2006). Additionally, legitimacy theory appears to regard legitimacy and organizations' search for it as an object of observation rather than something for which the theory should provide moral justification (e.g., Suchman, 1995).

Second, the multiple layers of formal societal institutions provide companies with both constraints and freedoms (e.g., Suchanek, 2001; Homann & Suchanek, 2005). Relevant contracts are necessarily incomplete (e.g., Suchanek & Waldkirch, 1999). Within the constraints set by laws, regulations, and market competition, each company finds room for manoeuvre and decides alone which course of action to take. Although the constraints are by and large set in such a way that the self-interested behaviour of companies furthers the interests of the others at the same time, the granted freedoms also open up the possibility for corporate behaviour to the detriment of others. To further reduce the risk of potential exploitation, society has developed informal institutions, including the notions of corporate responsibility and accountability, as a correlate of the granted freedoms. In accordance with our illustrative trust game, we define accountability as the (formally voluntary) duty of an accounting entity to account for his or her actions to the resource providers in ways relevant to their decisions to trust.[1] The trust game clarifies that our definition refers not only to the "duty" of the accounting entity but that accountability is ultimately in his or her enlightened, long-term self-interest. In our view, voluntary reporting is an incentive-compatible commitment to disclose information on corporate behaviour and its impact.[2] The incentive constraint places a clear limit on what companies voluntarily report and what stakeholders can expect from their sustainability reports. For example, it is not reasonable to expect companies to voluntarily disclose information that leads to a competitive disadvantage.

This limited exploration of our approach provides a heuristic to analyse the power of frameworks in guiding voluntary corporate disclosure, such as the GRI Guidelines. The trust game states that the objective of reporting is to help both players achieve mutual gains by providing the necessary information to encourage the RP to trust the AE. This determination raises three related questions:

RQ1 (Objective): Does the GRI framework define its objective consistently with the idea of disclosing information to facilitate mutual gain for the AE and the RP?

Disclosing information levels asymmetries that potentially exist between the provider and the recipient of the information. Corporate reporting is widely seen as an integral part of the many relations a company has with the actors in its environment. However, different reporting theories have focused on different relations and, thus, different report recipients. Our approach sees all resource providers as the addressees for reporting and confirms that this role is by no means limited to financial investors.

RQ2 (Addressees): Does the framework define all resource providers as the addressees of reporting?

Disclosing information has no value in itself but instead serves to alleviate a relational problem. Our approach closely ties voluntary reporting to the RP's decision to trust the AE, particularly the RP's assessment of the AE's trustworthiness. Thus, we formulate the following as our third research question:

RQ3 (Disclosed Information): Do the framework's principles help the RP trust the accounting entity?

The Global Reporting Initiative's G4 Sustainability Reporting Guidelines

The Global Reporting Initiative (GRI) was created to align methods of sustainability reporting with those of financial reporting and to institutionalize non-financial reporting as a routine practice (e.g., Haller & Ernstberger, 2006; Levy, Brown, & de Jong, 2010; Woods, 2003). The GRI Guidelines were first published in 1999/2000, but have undergone multiple revisions since then. Our analysis is based on their current version, the G4 Sustainability Reporting Guidelines (GRI 2013a, 2013b).

Objective

The GRI developed its guidelines against the backdrop of a society moving towards sustainability. As stakeholders' expectations have been increasing and more companies have embraced sustainability as a matter of course, a need arises for transparency about corporate impacts on sustainable development. Thus, the GRI defines the purpose of its guidelines as to "offer an international reference for all those interested in the disclosure (. . .) of the environmental, social and economic performance and impacts of organizations" (GRI, 2013a, p. 5). Furthermore, the GRI Guidelines "help reporters prepare sustainability reports that matter, contain valuable information about the organization's most critical sustainability-related issues" (ibid., p. 3). By doing so, the GRI hopes that reporting on these issues "helps organizations to set goals, measure performance, and manage change to make their operations more sustainable" (ibid., p. 3).

Addressees

The GRI Guidelines do not explicitly define the addressees of sustainability reporting. They talk about a "diverse range of stakeholders" (GRI, 2011, p. 2) or "markets and society" (GRI, 2013a, p. 3) to be informed on sustainability matters. These and other definitions can be found throughout publications by the GRI. One principle of the GRI Guidelines indicates that the definitions are not meant to be conclusive but instead act as a placeholder on the conceptual level, which must be filled by the AE in the process of application. *Stakeholder inclusiveness* calls for the identification of all stakeholders and helps with their identification through a minor revision of Freeman's (1984) original definition. A stakeholder is anybody who "can reasonably be expected to be significantly affected" by the AE's behaviour or "can reasonably be expected to affect the ability of the organization to successfully (. . .) achieve its objectives" (both: GRI, 2013a, p. 9). This includes different groups of stakeholders, of which shareholders, employees, suppliers, customers, vulnerable groups within local communities, and civil society are mentioned as examples. Given the lack of limitations on the stakeholder definition, the GRI Guidelines acknowledge that the "reasonable expectations and interests of a wide range of stakeholders" (GRI, 2013b, p. 9) should be considered by the AE and that their demands for information could be as heterogeneous as their different roles. Some examples are as follows: financial investors desire financial information concerning the current and future potential of the company to generate net cash inflows. Employees want information indicating the security of their jobs and/or the opportunity for a high year-end bonus as well as a pay increase in the next year. Additionally, the public wishes to know about the corporation's impacts on the environment and the ways the company is involved with society on a local level.

Disclosed information

The GRI Guidelines distinguish between two sets of principles (GRI, 2013a, 2013b). The first set, the report content, provides guidance for selecting the topics to be covered in the sustainability report. The second set, report quality, aims to ensure the quality and appropriate presentation of the disclosed information.

Report content is defined with the help of four principles. First, as described above, *stakeholder inclusiveness* requires the reporting entity to identify its stakeholders and the sustainability report to explain how the company has responded to their reasonable expectations and interests (GRI, 2013a, p. 16). Second, the *sustainability context* calls for a presentation of the company's performance in the wider context of sustainability (ibid., p 17): How does the company contribute to the improvement or deterioration of the economic, environmental, and social conditions at the local, regional, or global level? The principle highlights two aspects that are especially important for sustainability issues: location and time. The location aspect acknowledges that corporate impacts are not limited to a given range or level and that looking only at a certain range or level runs the risk of failing to notice a relevant impact on another level. The time aspect highlights that it might take a long time for any impact to show. Third, *materiality* demands that the information in a report cover aspects that "[r]eflect the organization's significant economic, environmental, and social impacts" (EES impacts) or that would "[s]ubstantively influence the assessments and decisions of stakeholders" (GRI, 2013a, p. 17). This definition shows that the principle has essentially two defining features: the EES impacts and relevance. The EES impacts aspect suggests including all significant EES impacts in the report, whereas the idea of relevance proposes to report information that substantively influences the stakeholders' view of the company and its behaviour. In defining *materiality*, the GRI Guidelines link both aspects with an "or" (ibid.). Fourth, *completeness* aims to create an all-encompassing and comprehensive sustainability report. The covered subjects should be "sufficient to reflect significant" EES impacts and "enable stakeholders to assess the reporting organization's performance" (both: ibid., p. 17). In addition, the principle contains two further dimensions (GRI, 2013b, p. 12f.): the boundary dimension asks reporting entities to describe where the impact occurs (i.e., inside or outside of the organization), and the time dimension requires the reporting of all EES impacts within the reporting period, along with any future impacts, when they are "reasonably foreseeable and may become unavoidable or irreversible" (ibid., p. 13).

The quality of a sustainability report should be ensured by six principles. First, the *balance* principle demands that the report reflects both "positive and negative aspects of the organization's performance to enable a reasoned assessment of overall performance" (GRI, 2013a, p. 17). Second, *comparability* calls for disclosed information to be consistently selected, compiled, and reported. It also requires information to be "presented in a manner that enables stakeholders to analyse changes in the organization's performance over time and that could support analysis relative to other organizations" (ibid., p. 18). Third, to comply with *accuracy*, the reported information should be "sufficiently accurate and detailed for stakeholders to assess the reporting organization's performance" (ibid., p. 18). The fourth principle, *timeliness*, calls for information to be reported on a regular schedule and in time for stakeholders to make informed decisions (ibid., p. 18). Fifth, *clarity* demands sustainability information to be "available in a manner that is understandable and accessible to stakeholders using the report" (ibid., p. 18). Sixth, *reliability* is defined as follows: "The organization should gather, record, compile, analyse and disclose information and processes used in the preparation of a report in a way that they can be subject to examination and that establishes the quality and materiality of the information" (ibid., p. 18).

Analysis and discussion

Objectives

As the objective stated by the GRI indicates, the GRI Guidelines ultimately serve the normative agenda of changing corporate behaviour. By offering practical guidance on sustainability reporting, they intend to facilitate corporate change and push its operations towards an increased level of sustainability. The normative idea of sustainability, which gained acceptance in European forestry as early as the 18th century (Wiersum, 1995), was introduced to the general public by Brundtland's (1987) report on *Our Common Future*. For reasons of practicality, the GRI Guidelines make use of the three-pillar model of sustainability, which was developed and popularized by John Elkington (1998). According to the triple bottom line (TBL) concept, an adequate evaluation of a company's success requires ecological and social criteria to be taken into account alongside the traditional financial bottom line (see further Joseph, 2012; Savitz & Weber, 2006; Westing, 1996). Thus, for the GRI, sustainability reports primarily concern the economic, environmental, and social impacts of a company's everyday activities.

Evaluating the GRI guidelines' objective against our first research question, two issues draw our attention. First, the idea of sustainability, as translated by the TBL concept for practicality reasons, is proposed as the ultimate yardstick for selecting the information that should be provided. Second, the objective is formulated rather independently from the AE and the RP. Although the GRI states clearly that its guidelines help an AE prepare meaningful sustainability reports, it remains unclear why providing sustainability reports is in the interests of an AE and RP.

Addressees

The GRI Guidelines state that "a wide range of stakeholders" (GRI, 2013b, p. 9) are interested in sustainability reports, and that the reports should address their reasonable expectations. However, ultimately, the GRI Guidelines call for the managers of the reporting entity to define the report's addressees in a stakeholder discourse. This fuzzy definition reflects the current status of stakeholder theory, in which no general agreement on the definition of stakeholders has yet been reached (e.g., Freeman et al., 2010; Friedman & Miles, 2006). The current fuzziness is not surprising, given the purpose of stakeholder thinking and its sibling, sustainability reporting: persuading corporate managers to provide information to readers beyond the group of readers they have firmly in mind, that is, the financial investors. It serves as a reminder that hitherto neglected stakeholder groups might have a legitimate interest in information on corporate sustainability. In our view, the fuzziness does not pose a problem, as reporting *what* should be reported is more important than *who* asked for the information.

Disclosed information

Our RQ3 raises the question of whether the GRI Guidelines' principles are aligned with the relationship between an RP and AE, especially in supporting RPs' decision to trust AE. In this regard, we observe an inconsistency within the GRI's report-content-related principles. These principles reflect a mélange of the two central ideas of stakeholder thinking and sustainability. As developed earlier, stakeholder thinking calls for management issues to be reconstructed as a relational problem, that is as an issue affecting the relationship between a company and its stakeholders, and for stakeholders to be included in corporate decision-making with regard to these issues. The GRI's *stakeholder inclusiveness* and the relevance aspect of *materiality* are consistent with this view: both express the idea of a relational setting. The idea of sustainability is usually developed not in a relational, two-person setting but in the context of a decision-maker and his decision to allocate depletable, natural resources – essentially leaving the consequences of the allocation decision on someone other than the decision-maker undiscussed. Several GRI Guidelines' principles reflect this notion: the EES impacts aspect of *materiality*, the scope dimension of *completeness*, and the *sustainability context*. As with sustainability thinking, the GRI Guidelines do not bridge the gap between the impacts that corporate decision-making has had, or will have, on the environment, the economy, and society and its effect on the stakeholders. Thus, we argue that the influence of the two central ideas creates a set of inconsistent principles that the GRI fails to distil into a coherent whole. The inconsistency is most apparent from the fact that *materiality* is defined by the twin aspects of relevance and EES impacts. It is interesting to note that the last revision of the GRI Guidelines has brought a change in the order of the report content principles. Whereas the version from 2011 initially introduces materiality, the G4 version presents it as the third principle after *stakeholder inclusiveness* and the *sustainability context* (GRI, 2011, 2013a, 2013b). Although this step strengthens the internal consistency, tension remains. In this context, it can be argued that the GRI Guidelines are not well aligned with reporting theories, including stakeholder thinking or legitimacy theory, which all suggest a strict relational problem-setting.

This inconsistency matters from a theoretical standpoint and a practical viewpoint. Even if a company initiates and engages in a comprehensive dialogue with all its stakeholders and addresses all raised issues in its report, the report does not necessarily meet all requirements of the *materiality* principle. Although it is safe to assume that the report fulfils the relevance aspect of the principle, its EES impact aspect might not be satisfied. For example, corporative behaviour might have a significant, long-range impact on certain environmental conditions with which stakeholders are not concerned. In this case, the GRI Guidelines require the company to report on its EES impact, although its stakeholders neither asked for information on this issue nor are concerned with it.

The GRI Guidelines inherit a problematic approach towards moral legitimacy derived from stakeholder thinking. The intention of stakeholder thinking and the GRI Guidelines, as the *stakeholder inclusiveness* principle notes, is to systematically include the hitherto-neglected groups of stakeholders as a source of legitimate interests and as rightful addressees of corporate information. The idea of mutual consent within our contractarian approach supports this aim but goes considerably further in requiring that the expressed interests (in the rules of the game) must be mutually beneficial to be legitimate. To put it differently, anyone may formulate legitimate interests, but for a voiced interest to be legitimate, it must pass a test for mutual benefits. Given that the GRI Guidelines neither explicitly formulate nor implicitly include the idea of mutual gains, the moral legitimacy, and the limitations of voluntary disclosure by companies in competitive markets cannot be convincingly established.

The idea of sustainability in combination with stakeholder thinking creates high expectations for sustainability reporting. The combination is likely to be understood by companies and stakeholders as requiring the disclosure of as much information about the company's impact on sustainability as is demanded. The GRI Guidelines' objective of achieving transparency through a complete disclosure of corporate impacts reinforces such a view. This understanding, however, creates a potential problem of information overload (Eppler & Mengis, 2004; Fries, McCulloch, & Webster, 2010; Ranganathan, 1998) for the addressees and an excessive burden for the reporting companies, and in practice, it also results in widespread disillusion because many companies report much less than expected (e.g., Joseph, 2012). Without the concept of mutual gains as a check on the moral legitimacy of information requests and the limitations of voluntary reporting, the GRI Guidelines do not provide corporate management and stakeholders with a clear-cut thought experiment that distinguishes between legitimate informational claims that should be fulfilled and non-legitimate information claims that should be rejected. In this regard, the GRI Guidelines are one-sided. They encourage stakeholders to express their information claims towards companies and managers to include these in their sustainability report, but they do not sufficiently help stakeholders and corporate management restrict claims to legitimate ones. Limiting the expectations and interests of stakeholders to which companies should respond in their reports to those that are "reasonable" (GRI, 2013a, p. 16), as is the case with the *stakeholder inclusiveness* principle, is little more than a reminder of the fact that companies are also confronted with unreasonable and illegitimate expectations, which corporate management must address.

One important insight of social contract theory is that to be viable, the social contract must be self-enforcing (Binmore, 1994; Suchanek, 2001). The GRI Guidelines acknowledge that incentives are important, as the *balance* principle indicates. Requiring both negative and positive aspects of performance to be reported by the corporation, the principle expresses a fear that self-interested companies may cherry-pick and provide a strategically distorted or greenwashed report to deceive their stakeholders. The literature has repeatedly emphasized that companies disclose information strategically, and thus what they report might diverge from their actual performance (e.g., Berthelot et al., 2003; Burrit & Schaltegger, 2010; Deegan & Rankin, 1996; Gray, 2001; Hess & Dunfee, 2007; Milne & Gray, 2013; Moneva et al., 2006). Although the GRI Guidelines address this imminent issue of incentive compatibility, some reservations remain. First, invoking the *balance* principle is by no means sufficient to overcome a problem of incentive compatibility as the persistence (or fear) of strategic corporate disclosure indicates. Second, the GRI Guidelines are one-sided. Although they acknowledge the incentive constraints of corporations, they are blind to the fact that stakeholders might also use information requests strategically, that is to further their own interests at the expense of the company or other stakeholders. As long as the GRI Guidelines do not address the incentives of both the AE and the RPs, an important aspect and restriction of voluntary reporting is missed. Against this backdrop, the argument that a balanced report creates trust is not convincing (GRI, 2014, p. 7).

Potential improvements

How can the GRI Guidelines be improved? We recommend incorporating the idea of mutual gains into a framework for voluntary sustainability reporting given that the concept is already present in scientific and public discourses about corporate responsibility (e.g., Beckmann et al., 2014; Homann, 2003; Lin-Hi & Suchanek, 2011; Pies et al., 2009, 2014). We suggest introducing it into the GRI Guidelines by subordinating – or at least shifting importance from – the EES impact aspect to the relevance aspect in defining *materiality*. In doing so, self-enforcement of the GRI standards can be strengthened. In addition, renaming this principle in terms of relevance should be considered.

This change would highlight the relational nature of reporting and increase the consistency of the GRI Guidelines. We furthermore recommend adding a principle or a constraint that requires a cost–benefit perspective for sustainability reporting. Is sustainability reporting to the benefit of both the RP and the AE? All these measures will sharpen the framework's heuristic and avoid unnecessary burdens on companies and stakeholders. These measures will also help ensure a focus on disclosing only meaningful and trust-facilitating information.

In addition, these changes would bring the GRI Guidelines more in line with the reporting framework proposed by the International Accounting Standards Board (IASB) and the US Financial Accounting Standards Board (FASB) for financial reporting in 2010 (IASB, 2010). Although closing the gap between these frameworks might not be appealing to all proponents of sustainability reporting, the IASB/FASB Framework demonstrates the applicability of our contractarian approach to reporting frameworks. The conceptual background of the IASB/FASB Framework is a principal-agent relationship into which the financial investor and the company enter voluntarily because their contractual provisions alleviate the information problem and facilitate a mutually beneficial exchange (van Mourik, 2014). The idea of mutual gains forges ahead with the IASB/FASB Framework's principle of relevance and cost constraint (IASB, 2010, QC35-39). The former links information disclosure closely to financial RPs' decisions (IASB, 2010, QC6, QC11), and thus implies a benefit for the RP. The latter weighs these benefits against the costs of financial reporting for the AE.

From our contractarian perspective, the principles concerning report quality appear to indicate the necessary aspects of the disclosed information to ensure that the information helps to facilitate the RP's trust decision. The information must be reported in ways that enable RPs to identify, understand, compare, and check the report's substance if the information is to be able to influence their trust decisions. With respect to sustainability reporting, the disclosure of information remains primarily voluntary, and there is no legal requirement for an audit. However, an increasing number of companies is using external assurance (e.g., Hess, 2008; KPMG, 2017). The GRI recommends such a step and allows companies to indicate its use of external assurance in their report (GRI, 2013b, p. 51).

Concluding remarks

This chapter analyses the dominant reporting framework for sustainability reporting, the GRI Guidelines, against the backdrop of a contractarian approach. This approach shares the central insight that reporting is a relational practice through which a company discloses information to encourage a trust decision by resource providers. Contrary to other reporting theories, however, the contractarian approach uses the criterion of (incentive-compatible) mutual gains to establish institutions' moral legitimacy and viability.

This chapter contributes to the literature in several ways. On a theoretical level, it outlines a new theory on voluntary corporate reporting. The presented contractarian approach is connected to earlier efforts in the field that introduced the idea of a social contract to accounting theory (e.g., Mathews, 2008/2009; Ramanathan, 1976). However, we suggest that the social contract tradition within moral philosophy has greater implications for corporate reporting and its theory than previously acknowledged. Second, this chapter applies for the first time the economic theory of morality developed by Homann (2002, 2003) to corporate reporting and shows that it can be fruitfully applied to this new research object. Third, it pinpoints the importance of incentives for sustainability reporting practices, which stakeholder thinking and legitimacy theory insufficiently recognize.

On a practical level, this chapter pinpoints several limitations of the current GRI Guidelines for guiding sustainability reporting and traces them back to the theories underlying sustainability reporting. First, the GRI Guidelines are not developed against the backdrop of a relational problem setting. Second, the GRI Guidelines underestimate the importance of mutual gains and incentive compatibility for the viability and legitimacy of institutions. As long as sustainability disclosure is a voluntary practice, companies may commit themselves to disclosing their "realistic" sustainability performance to the public. However, if they believe that such strategy could weaken their competitive position in the long run, they will abstain from making this individual self-commitment (similar to Pies et al., 2009). Without strengthening the idea of mutual gains within its principles, the GRI Guidelines create expectations that voluntary reporting cannot fulfil, but might be successfully addressed by changes of the rules of the game. In this context, the GRI's recommendation for a voluntary audit could be interpreted as an important step to signalling companies' credibility to stakeholders and credible self-commitments of industries in a sense that all players will disclose realistic sustainability performance information to the public.

Like any study, this research is not free of limitations. The chapter outlines the cornerstones of a contractarian reporting theory but must leave its more thorough development to future research.

Notes

1 This definition shares the central ideas of the definition proposed by Gray et al. (1987). However, the main difference rests in the fact that we derive our definition from the contractarian approach illustrated by the trust game.
2 On this account, the widespread notion that achieving accountability necessarily "hurts" – which can be found, for example, in Gray (2001) or Gilbert and Rasche (2007) – should be reconsidered.

References

Adams, C.A., & Whelan, G. (2009). Conceptualising future change in corporate sustainability reporting. *Accounting, Auditing and Accountability Journal, 22(1)*, 118–143.

Bebbington, J. (2009). Measuring sustainable development performance: Possibilities and issues. *Accounting Forum, 33(3)*, 189–193.

Beckmann, M., Hielscher, S., & Pies, I. (2014). Commitment strategies for sustainability: How business firms can transform trade-offs into win–win outcomes. *Business Strategy and the Environment, 23(1)*, 18–37.

Berthelot, S., Cormier, D., & Magnan, M. (2003). Environmental disclosure research: Review and synthesis. *Journal of Accounting Literature, 22*, 1–44.

Binmore, K.G. (1994). *Game Theory and the Social Contract*. Volume 1: *Playing Fair*. Cambridge: The MIT Press.

Boesso, G., Kumar, K., & Michelon, G. (2013). Descriptive, instrumental and strategic approaches to corporate social responsibility: Do they drive the financial performance of companies differently? *Accounting, Auditing and Accountability Journal, 26(3)*, 399–422.

Brennan, G., & Buchanan, J.M. (1985). *The Reason of Rules: Constitutional Political Economy*. Cambridge: Cambridge University Press.

Brown, H.S., de Jong, M., & Lessidrenska, T. (2009). The rise of the global reporting initiative: A case of institutional entrepreneurship. *Environmental Politics, 18(2)*, 182–200.

Brundtland, G.H. (1987). *Our Common Future*. Report of the World Commission on Environment and Development. Geneva: UN Document A/42/427.

Buchanan, J.M. (1975). *The Limits of Liberty: Between Anarchy and Leviathan*. Chicago: University of Chicago Press.

Buchanan, J.M. (1995). Individual rights, emergent social states, and behavioral feasibility. *Rationality and Society*, *7(2)*, 141–150.

Burrit, R.L., & Schaltegger, S. (2010). Sustainability accounting and reporting: Fad or trend? *Accounting, Auditing and Accountability Journal*, *23(7)*, 829–846.

Chen, J., & Roberts, R. (2010). Toward a more coherent understanding of the organization–society relationship: A theoretical consideration for social and environmental accounting research. *Journal of Business Ethics*, *97(4)*, 651–665.

Cho, C.H., & Patten, D.M. (2007). The role of environmental disclosures as tools of legitimacy: A research note. *Accounting, Organizations and Society*, *32(7–8)*, 639–647.

Cooper, S.M., & Owen, D.L. (2007). Corporate social reporting and stakeholder accountability: The missing link. *Accounting, Organizations and Society*, *32(7–8)*, 649–667.

Dasgupta, P. (1988). Trust as a commodity. In: D. Gambetta (Ed.), *Trust: Making and Breaking Cooperative Relations*. Oxford: Basil Blackwell, 49–72.

Deegan, C. (2002). Introduction: The legitimising effect of social and environmental disclosures – A theoretical foundation. *Accounting, Auditing and Accountability Journal*, *15(3)*, 282–311.

Deegan, C., & Rankin, M. (1996). Do Australian companies report environmental news objectively? An analysis of environmental disclosures by firms prosecuted successfully by the environmental protection authority. *Accounting, Auditing and Accountability Journal*, *9(2)*, 50–67.

Deegan, C., & Unerman, J. (2006). *Financial Accounting Theory*. London: McGraw-Hill.

Dowling, J., & Pfeffer, J. (1975). Organizational legitimacy: Social values and organizational behavior. *Pacific Sociological Review*, *18(1)*, 122–136.

Elkington, J. (1998). Accounting for the triple bottom line. *Measuring Business Excellence*, *2(3)*, 18–22.

Eppler, M.J., & Mengis, J. (2004). The concept of information overload: A review of literature from organization science, accounting, marketing, MIS, and related disciplines. *The Information Society*, *20(5)*, 325–344.

Etzion, D., & Ferraro, F. (2010). The role of analogy in the institutionalization of sustainability reporting. *Organization Science*, *21(5)*, 1092–1107.

Freeman, R.E. (1984). *Strategic Management: A Stakeholder Approach*. Boston: Financial Times Prentice Hall.

Freeman, R.E., Harrison, J.S., Wicks, A.C., Parmar, B., & de Colle, S. (2010). *Stakeholder Theory: The State of the Art*. Cambridge: Cambridge University Press.

Friedman, A.L., and Miles, S. (2006). *Stakeholders: Theory and Practice*. Oxford: Oxford University Press.

Fries, J., McCulloch, K., & Webster, W. (2010). The prince's accounting for sustainability project: creating 21st-century decision making and reporting system to respond to 21st-century challenges and opportunities. In A.G. Hopwood, J. Unerman, & J. Fries (Eds.), *Accounting for Sustainability: Practical Insights* (pp. 29–46). London: Earthscan.

Gilbert, D.U., & Rasche, A. (2007). Discourse ethics and social accountability: The ethics of SA 8000. *Business Ethics Quarterly*, *17(2)*, 187–216.

Gjesdal, F. (1981). Accounting for stewardship. *Journal of Accounting Research*, *19(1)*, 208–231.

Gray, R. (2001). Thirty years of social accounting, reporting and auditing: What (if anything) have we learnt? *Business Ethics: A European Review*, *10(1)*, 9–15.

Gray, R. (2010). Is accounting for sustainability actually accounting for sustainability . . . and how would we know? An exploration of narratives of organisations and the planet. *Accounting, Organizations and Society*, *35(1)*, 47–62.

Gray, R., Kouhy, R., & Lavers, S. (1995). Corporate social and environmental reporting: A review of the literature and a longitudinal study of UK disclosure. *Accounting, Auditing and Accountability Journal*, *8(2)*, 47–77.

Gray, R., Owen, D., & Adams, C. (1996). *Accounting and Accountability: Changes and Challenges in Corporate Social and Environmental Reporting.* London: Prentice Hall.

Gray, R., Owen, D., & Maunders, K. (1987). *Corporate Social Reporting: Accounting and Accountability.* Englewood Cliffs: Longman.

GRI (2011). Sustainability Reporting Guidelines. Boston: GRI.

GRI (2012). G4 Development. GRI Second G4 Public Comment Period. G4 Exposure Draft. Retrieved from: www.globalreporting.org/resourcelibrary/G4-Exposure-Draft.pdf

GRI (2013a). Reporting Principles and Standard Disclosures. Retrieved from: www.globalreporting.org/resourcelibrary/GRIG4-Part1-Reporting-Principles-and-Standard-Disclosures.pdf

GRI (2013b). Implementation Manual. Retrieved from: www.globalreporting.org/resourcelibrary/GRIG4-Part2-Implementation-Manual.pdf

GRI (2014). Ready to Report? Introducing sustainability reporting for SMEs. Retrieved from: www.globalreporting.org/resourcelibrary/Ready-to-Report-SME-booklet-online.pdf

Haller, A., & Ernstberger, J. (2006). Global Reporting Initiative: Internationale Leitlinien zur Erstellung von Nachhaltigkeitsberichten. *Betriebs-Berater, 61(46),* 2516–2524.

Healy, P.M., & Palepu, K.G. (2001). Information asymmetry, corporate disclosure, and the capital markets: A review of the empirical disclosure literature. *Journal of Accounting and Economics, 31(1–3),* 405–440.

Hess, D. (2008). The three pillars of corporate social reporting as new governance regulation: Disclosure, dialogue, and development. *Business Ethics Quarterly, 18(4),* 447–482.

Hess, D., & Dunfee, T. (2007). The Kasky-Nike threat to corporate social reporting: Implementing a standard of optimal truthful disclosure as a solution. *Business Ethics Quarterly, 17(1),* 5–32.

Hobbes, T. (1947). *Leviathan.* London: Dent & Sons.

Homann, K. (2002). *Vorteile und Anreize: Zur Grundlegung einer Ethik der Zukunft.* Tübingen: J.C.B. Mohr.

Homann, K. (2003). *Anreize und Moral: Gesellschaftstheorie, Ethik, Anwendungen.* Münster: LIT.

Homann, K., & Suchanek, A. (2005). *Ökonomik. Eine Einführung.* 2nd edn. Tübingen: J.C.B. Mohr.

Hume, D. (1967). *A Treatise of Human Nature.* Oxford: Oxford University Press.

IASB (2010). *Conceptual Framework for Financial Reporting 2010.* London: IASB.

IASB (2013). *Discussion Paper: A Review of the Conceptional Framework for Financial Reporting.* London: IASB.

Joseph, G. (2012). Ambiguous but tethered: An accounting basis for sustainability reporting. *Critical Perspectives on Accounting, 23,* 93–106.

KPMG (2017). *The KPMG survey of corporate responsibility reporting 2017.* Retrieved from: https://assets.kpmg.com/content/dam/kpmg/xx/pdf/2017/10/kpmg-survey-of-corporate-responsibility-reporting-2017.pdf

Lambert, R.A. (2001). Contracting theory and accounting. *Journal of Accounting and Economics, 32(1–3),* 3–87.

Lamberton, G. (2005). Sustainability accounting: A brief history and conceptual framework. *Accounting Forum, 29(1),* 7–26.

Levy, D.L., Brown, H.S., & de Jong, M. (2010). The contested politics of corporate governance: The case of the Global Reporting Initiative. *Business and Society, 49(1),* 88–115.

Lindblom, C. (2010). The implications of organizational legitimacy for corporate social performance and disclosure. In R. Grey, J. Bebbington, & S. Grey (Eds.), *Social and Environmental Accounting.* Volume II: *Developing the Field* (pp. 51–64). London: Sage.

Lin-Hi, N., & Suchanek, A. (2011). Corporate Social Responsibility als Integrationsherausforderung: Zum systematischen Umgang mit Konflikten zwischen Gewinn und Moral. *Zeitschrift für Betriebswirtschaft, 81(Supplement 1),* 63–91.

Mathews, M.R. (2008/2009). Further thoughts on mega-accounting and the need for standards. *Issues in Social and Environmental Accounting, 2(2),* 158–175.

Mattessich, R. (2006). The information economic perspective of accounting: Its coming of age. *Canadian Accounting Perspectives, 5(2)*, 209–236.

Milne, M.J., & Gray, R. (2013). W(h)ither ecology? The triple bottom line, the global reporting initiative, and corporate sustainability reporting. *Journal of Business Ethics, 118(1)*, 13–29.

Moneva, J.M., Archel, P., & Correa, C. (2006). GRI and the camouflaging of corporate unsustainability. *Accounting Forum, 30*, 121–137.

Peasnell, K.V. (1982). The function of a conceptual framework for corporate finance reporting. *Accounting and Business Research, 12(48)*, 243–256.

Pies, I., Beckmann, M., & Hielscher, S. (2014). The political role of the business firm: An ordonomic concept of corporate citizenship developed in comparison with the Aristotelian idea of individual citizenship. *Business and Society, 53(2)*, 226–259.

Pies, I., Hielscher, S., & Beckmann, M. (2009). Moral commitments and the societal role of business: An ordonomic approach to corporate citizenship. *Business Ethics Quarterly, 19(3)*, 375–401.

Ramanathan, K.V. (1976). Toward a theory of corporate social accounting. *The Accounting Review, 51(3)*, 516–528.

Ranganathan, J. (1998). Sustainability Rulers: Measuring Corporate Environment and Social Performance: Sustainable Enterprises Perspectives Series. Washington, DC: Word Resources Institute.

Savitz, A., & Weber, K. (2006). *The Triple Bottom Line: How Today's Best-Run Companies Are Achieving Economic, Social, and Environmental Success*. San Francisco: Jossey-Bass.

Snijders, C. (1996). *Trust and Commitments*. Amsterdam: Thela Thesis.

Suchanek, A. (2001). *Ökonomische Ethik*. Tübingen: Mohr.

Suchanek, A. (2004). What is meant by consent? In D. van Aaken, C. List, & C. Luetge (Eds.), *Deliberation and Decision: Economics, Constitutional Theory and Deliberative Democracy* (pp. 169–180). Aldershot: Ashgate.

Suchanek, A., & Waldkirch, R. (1999). *Das Konzept der offenen Verträge*. Working paper No. 128. Ingolstadt: Katholische Universität Eichstätt-Ingolstadt.

Suchman, M.C. (1995). Managing legitimacy: Strategic and institutional approaches. *Academy of Management Review, 20(3)*, 571–610.

Sutton, M. (1997). Financial reporting and investor protection. Retrieved from: www.sec.gov/news/speech/speecharchive/1997/spch201.txt

Thomas, A., & Ward, A.M. (2009). *Introduction to Financial Accounting*, 6th edn. Berkshire: McGraw-Hill.

van Mourik, C. (2014). The equity theories and the IASB Conceptual Framework. *Accounting in Europe, 11*, 219–233.

Verrecchia, R.E. (2001). Essays on disclosure. *Journal of Accounting and Economics, 32(1–3)*, 97–180.

Wagner-Tsukamoto, S. (2005). An economic approach to business ethics: Moral agency of the firm and the enabling and constraining effects of economic institutions and interactions in a market economy. *Journal of Business Ethics, 60(1)*, 75–89.

Wagner-Tsukamoto, S. (2007). An institutional economic reconstruction of scientific management: On the lost theoretical logic of Taylorism. *Academy of Management Review, 32(1)*, 105–117.

Waldkirch, R.W. (2001). Prolegomena for an economic theory of morals. *Business Ethics: A European Review, 10(1)*, 61–70.

Waldkirch, R.W. (2002). *Unternehmen und Gesellschaft: Zur Grundlegung einer Ökonomik von Organisationen*. Wiesbaden: DUV.

Waldkirch, R.W., Meyer, M., & Homann, K. (2009). Accounting for the benefits of social security and the role of business: Four ideal types and their different heuristics. *Journal of Business Ethics, 89(3)*, 247–267.

Weber, M. (1949). *The Methodology of the Social Sciences*. Glencoe: The Free Press.

Westing, A.H. (1996). Core values for sustainable development. *Environmental Conservation, 23(3)*, 218–225.

Wiersum, K.F. (1995). 200 years of sustainability in forestry: Lessons from history. *Environmental Management, 19(3)*, 321–329.

Woods, M. (2003). The Global Reporting Initiative. *The RPA Journal, 73(6)*, 60–65.

4.4 Sustainability and ethics in financial reporting

An empirical study of German, Austrian, and Swiss groups

Peter G. Kirchschläger and Michaela M. Schaffhauser-Linzatti

External accounting reports no longer address the commercial interests of shareholders only. Accelerated by the global financial crises and social developments, they changed their focus onto the much broader target group of stakeholders and their interest in new issues such as sustainability and ethical behaviour. On the one hand, groups themselves recognized their character as social institutions (Dillard & Murray, 2013) and their responsibility for humans, society, and the environment. Based on an instrument that the private sector has developed to live up to its responsibility, the horizon of addressees of external accounting reports was widened. Corporate social responsibility (CSR) conceptualizes the objects of responsibility of groups beyond the shareholders and includes internal and external stakeholders, employees, clients, suppliers, and the community (Braun, 2009). It entails standards concerning working conditions, environmental protection, sustainability, social aspects, and so on (Hilty & Henning-Bodewig, 2014), acknowledging the contribution of groups to the common good. This aspect receives even more emphasis in the further development of CSR in the concept of "public value" (Moore, 1995, 2013). On the other hand, other societal actors – including states and civil society – perceived the potential of groups in being complicit in or subject to the destruction of the environment and human rights violations (Kirchschlaeger, 2015b); the responsibility of groups (Kirchschlaeger, 2014) for sustainability corresponding to their own power and influence, and the risk of something like a "governance gap" (MacDonald, 2011, 549).

So far, management reports, and notes as qualitative parts of annual reports, have been extended within the existing legal frameworks worldwide to additionally cover these now necessary narratives and verbal explanations of environmental and social activities (Jamali, 2017). New approaches such as intellectual capital reporting or, far better accepted, sustainability reporting have been filling the still existing gap, however, on a voluntary basis (Schaffhauser-Linzatti, 2017; Kolk, 2004; see also, for a comprehensive literature overview of the so-called sustainability reporting, Choi and Ng, 2011; Jaeger, 2015; Morhardt, 2002; Leipziger, 2016). The demand for further, harmonizing steps triggered an intense discussion on whether to enforce voluntary information of the groups or legal requirements: while accounting literature traditionally discusses legal interpretations and application scopes (Kalbers, 2009; Singh & Vasudeva, 2013; Aminu & Oladipo, 2016), empirical evidence on how and to what extent financial reports reveal sustainability and ethical attitudes is scarce (Labelle et al., 2010; Tassadaq & Malik, 2015; Karaibrahimoglu & Cangarli, 2016).

The motivation of this chapter is to add another data-based contribution to this dispute. More precisely, it aims at revealing whether annual reports of groups contain information on sustainability and ethics, either demanded by law or published voluntarily. Consequently, it focuses on the information published, not on a mere legal comparison or compliance with prescribed regulations. Further, it is one of the first analyses to examine the German-speaking countries, the so-called DACH region – D-Germany, A-Austria, and CH-Switzerland. These countries are economically strong, seem similar, but are nevertheless embedded in different corporate laws and cultures. However, they are bound by a long common historical and economic tradition (Schedler & Summermatter, 2011), in contrast to the Anglo-American economic area on which most of the relevant studies focus (Burrit & Schaltegger, 2010). We conduct a full survey of all listed groups in the main stock indices of Germany, Austria, and Switzerland for the business year of 2015, and apply a qualitative text analysis according to the methodology of Mayring (2014), whether and to what extent groups report about sustainability and ethical issues. To do so, we concentrate on notes and management reports as part of the legally prescribed annual report due to their qualitative character. As nearly all groups of the sample also or exclusively report according to the International Financial Reporting Standards (IFRS) in addition to their national law, Management Commentary might serve as a corresponding regulation for qualitative reporting.

The chapter is structured as follows: the following section discusses the legal and ethical dimension of reporting. We then explain the applied methodology and describe the sample of the empirical study, while the results are presented and discussed thereafter. The conclusion summarizes the findings and leads to an outlook about how the presentation of sustainable corporate governance can be enforced and improved.

Legal and ethical dimensions

In order to guide the reader directly into the empirical analysis central for this specific research, this section emphasizes the legal and ethical dimensions of sustainability reporting.

Legal dimension

Groups have accounting and reporting duties according to their corresponding national Generally Accepted Accounting Principles (GAAP) (Sacer, 2015). As defined by IAS 27.4, a group consists of a parent company and all its subsidiaries, the parent having direct or indirect control over its subsidiaries (Deloitte, 2008). Groups that are listed on an international stock exchange mostly have to apply International Financial Reporting Standards (IFRS), their consolidated annual reports include at least a balance sheet, profit and loss account, notes, and a management report. Focusing on sustainability and ethics, a) notes and b) management report or c) Management Commentary are the main sources of information within the obligatory annual report and serve as a data base in this study. Hence, the corresponding legal requirements are briefly summarized; a comprehensive overview of national GAAPS and IFRS is given in Born (2011).

a)   Notes: The German *Handelsgesetzbuch (HGB)* prescribes in the sections 284, 313, and 314 on consolidated notes, among others, information on applied accounting and valuation principles, major deviations, evaluation of financial instruments, a statement of fixed assets and interest on production costs, long-term debt, risks, deferred taxes sales by region, employees, details on the auditors and board of directors, or shares and option plans in a very compact way. The Austrian *Unternehmensgesetzbuch*

(UGB), sections 265–266, and the Swiss *Obligationenrecht (OR)*, Art. 959c, 961 a,d, comprise similar regulations. According to *IFRS* the notes contain narrative descriptions or disaggregations of items the in balance sheet and profit and loss account, changes in equity or the cash flow statement "about items that do not qualify for recognition in those statements" (IAS 1.77-80A, 1.97-105, 1.112–138, further details in nearly all standards). To cover these comprehensive prescriptions, long manuals and check lists are provided by literature (ESMA, 2011; EFRAG, 2012) and auditing firms (KPMG, 2014; EY, 2014; PWC, 2014; Deloitte, 2014).

b)   Management Report: Following sections 289 and 315 HGB, the consolidated management report mainly contains business performance, situation, true and fair view, financial and non-financial indicators, information on employees and environmental issues, as far as essential, risks, the internal control and risk management system, research and development, important regional branches, management compensation, as well as equity and voting rights. Again very similar to Germany, the requirements for the consolidated management report in Austria and Switzerland are defined in section 267 UGB and sections 265 OR, respectively. The IFRS do not demand any management report.

c)   Management Commentary: The IASB and the IFRS Foundation (IFRS Foundation, 2016) introduced Management Commentary as a Practice Statement, not as a standard, which can be published voluntarily. As regards content it corresponds to the management report (Kirsch, 2006). Narratives shall present shareholders, investors, creditors and management a future-oriented qualitative decision basis and further explanations on the annual report (PwC, 2016). The so-called elements comprise information on the nature of the business, its objectives and strategies, resources, risks and relationships, results and prospects, as well as performance measures and indicators which are not prescribed in detail (IFRS Foundation, 2010). In case a group restrains from Management Commentary, it has to provide a management report under national GAAP instead.

Ethical dimension

In order to respect the character of reporting as communication of information between single communication partners and as language of the corporate communication to transmit information about the use of the resources, reporting needs to take into account two expansions: firstly, concerning the external reporting serving to inform external actors the results of the group's performance (Stolowy et al., 2013), the above-mentioned requirements regarding a broader horizon of stakeholders and addressees lead to an adaptation of the "external actors" which must be considered as communication partners. Secondly, the use of resources respectively the performance can be analysed also from a perspective of sustainability. The communication partners mentioned above are interested to know more about the ethical performance and the grade of sustainability of a group; they want to learn more about its "public value" (Moore, 1995, 2013).

A perspective of sustainability embraces the complementary combination of ecological, economic, and social goals (World Commission on Environment and Development, 1987). It takes into account that reporting as communication of information tackles also the ability of a group to create, provide, and maintain value in a sustainable manner. Looking at this interplay of the ecological, the economic, and the social dimension, more information in reporting is primarily needed in the areas of the ecological and social dimension of sustainability. (Of course, the economic dimension of sustainability gives an impulse for a long-term rather than short-term perspective in reporting economic data.)

The information about the ecological dimension could cover the contribution of a group to stop the acceleration of climate change, to the ending and preventing of ecological overshoot, to pollution-based on carbon dioxide emissions, etc. (Leipziger, 2016).

The social dimension becomes more tangible and applicable, applying as well the principle of responsibility and the principle of justice as using human rights as ethical frame of reference. The principle of responsibility knows different dimensions which can build with each other a variety of relations (Kirchschlaeger, 2014) in order to master the complexity of reality. The dimensions of responsibility can be defined and combined in different ways because of the relational character of responsibility. The understanding of responsibility knows a legal and an ethical meaning (Hoeffe, 2008). Groups are holders of both – of a legal and of an ethical responsibility – which interact with each other. Both responsibilities require freedom (Dierksmeier & Pirson, 2010; Dierksmeier, 2011; Wiemeyer, 2013) because an entity cannot be held responsible for an action or decision it is forced to. Corporate social responsibility belongs to the ethical responsibility of a group (Kirchschlaeger, 2015a; Williams, 2014, 1; Carroll, 1991). The significance of CSR becomes obvious if one imagines the following situation:

> A given company relocates to a country with unregulated market conditions, where a lack of ethical and ecological standards allows said company to operate at lower costs. The pressures of competition prompt others to follow this example, catapulting the host countries (which seek to retain capital, and maintain employment rates and tax revenues) into a competition over the lowest possible standard. This triggers a downward spiral that ends with the hypothetical 'worst case scenario' in which profits are privatized and the costs and consequences thereof socialized. On the slopes of an unbalanced global economy, this 'snowball effect' of a one-dimensional pursuit of profit threatens to launch an avalanche of precarious economic conduct.
> (Dierksmeier, 2012, 17)

Beyond that, the social dimension finds ethical guidance in the principle of justice (Kirchschlaeger, 2013a). Justice strives for equal treatment and for the attribution of what one is entitled to. Four concepts of justice can be differentiated (Koller, 2005). They enable the implementation of justice in a specific and individual situation and context: 1. exchange-justice (e. g., to perform services and to reciprocate); 2. political justice (fair and unbiased democratic opinion-forming and decision-making processes which respect the rights of every individual and enable social cooperation); 3. corrective justice (e.g., remedies in order to correct wrong-doings, punishment); 4. distributional justice (same distribution of common goods – education opportunities, access to the labour market, perspectives of income – or common burdens, e.g. taxes).

Of course, the choice of a specific concept of justice and the choice of the criterion applied to this specific concept – e.g., effort, need, or equality – influence the understanding of the principle of justice. In addition, all four concepts of justice can be understood from the perspective of "social justice" striving for a just order balancing the interests of groups and individuals and bringing them into a just relation (Glatzel, 2000). This differentiation of four concepts and the perspective of social justice broaden the concept of justice. With this differentiation, the following challenge arises: the same situation, decision, or action could be assessed as just and unjust at the same time – depending on the justice-concept of the perspective. Therefore, there is a necessity for clarification.

A first step for a solution (Kirchschlaeger, 2013a) entails understanding all four concepts with the perspective of social justice – the latter as a leading principle. Secondly, these four concepts of justice need to be combined in order to avoid a one-sided justice approach and in order to reach a holistic understanding of justice. All four concepts of justice are brought into a negative alignment. While positive cooperation would entail always the inclusion of all four concepts of justice, a negative conjunction embraces the necessity of inclusion of all four concepts of justice, respectively, the necessity to present rational reasons if one of several concepts of justice is not included. This way, justice is understood as omni-dynamic (referring to the cooperation of all four concepts). Thirdly, the above-mentioned principle of social justice is considered, which leads to an understanding of an omni-dynamic social justice (Kirchschlaeger, 2013a).

Finally, human rights serve as ethical frame of reference to the social dimension. Compared with other ethical theories, normative approaches, and value systems, human rights know a global acceptance without any competition (Kirchschlaeger, 2016). They can be justified morally (Kirchschlaeger, 2013), and protected in different dimensions (Kirchschlaeger, 2013c). As a minimum standard, they provide a clear focus and priority-setting to the social dimension of sustainability. Beyond that, they are practice-oriented, concrete, and – due to their legal and political dimension – they are applicable.

Methodology

Sustainability and ethical aspects in annual reports are almost exclusively expressed by verbal narratives which consequently demands the application of a qualitative text analysis for empirical research. Merkl-Davies et al. (2011) discuss the multitude of the required qualitative approaches. Focussing on accounting research, they offer a compound overview over existing methodologies and develop a taxonomy to guide researchers through the heterogeneous assumptions, methodological principles, and evaluation criteria. Therefore, quantitative and statistical analyses such as Leitner et al. (2007) or Baumueller and Kreuzer (2014) fall short. From a more social-scientific point of view, the objective hermeneutics by Oevermann (1979) or the discourse analysis by Jaeger (2015) only concentrate on one single category per analysed unit, in contrast to the multi-category requirements of this research; the international case-study design by Eisenhardt (1989) lacks inside information of the firm, and approaches such as that of Guthrie (2001) focus on a too-narrow issue like intellectual capital. That's why we decided for the content analysis suggested by Mayring (2014), as it allows for a high degree of freedom to determine the research design. The suggested eleven steps that can be individually adapted are described for the research question under consideration (see, for example, Schaffhauser-Linzatti & Ossmann, 2017), whereby some steps are summarized due to their close relationship.

Steps 1, 2, and 3: Definition of the material, analysis of the situation of origin, and formal characteristics of the material.

The study sample comprises listed groups within the DACH region. We include all 70 groups listed in the main index of each country's stock exchange, that is, the Austrian Traded Index ATX 20, the German Stock Index DAX 30, and the Swiss Market Index SMI 20 (see Table 4.4.1 for the sample). For these groups, we exclusively concentrate on the qualitative part of the consolidated annual reports, that is, the notes and the management report or Management Commentary, respectively, due to the narratives' characteristics of this research. These reports have to be published by law, so we can base our analysis on information in a standardized and comparable format. We are aware that groups increasingly offer more specific, qualitative reports on sustainability beyond their financial statements (Alonso et al., 2014). However, we nevertheless decided for the annual reports only in order to avoid any bias of voluntary publication which already indicates either a group's particular attention on sustainability and ethics, or even more distorting, the group's affinity to cover a topic for marketing reasons (Ottman, 2011; for a literature overview of green marketing, see Chamorro et al., 2009). To consider the latest legal changes, all reports refer to the fiscal year of 2015. In case of a fiscal year differing from the calendar year, 2014 was chosen. All notes and management reports/Management Commentaries were downloaded from the corresponding homepages in the English language. To increase readability, the homepages of the corresponding stock exchanges are quoted in the literature review only. The reports contain a cover sheet, an index, headers, subheadings and teasers, text, pictures, figures, and tables.

Steps 4 and 5: Direction of the analysis and theoretical differentiation of sub-components.

Each text is analysed by revealing how often previously determined issues are addressed. These issues are characterized by categories and subcategories (see Step 8).

Steps 6 and 7: Definition of the analysis techniques and the content analytical units.

The analysis is conducted manually. To do so, we abstain from running an automated search by a computer programme in order to gain more details and to take account of differentiated linguistic expressions. The analysed content units are chosen in accordance with the common research procedure of Mayring applications (f.e., Andringa, 2004; Bewernick et al., 2013; Bussmann et al., 2015). They comprise as smallest items single paragraphs including prefaces and statements, pictures, figures, tables, subheadings and teasers, purely financial instruments such as balance sheets and income statements embedded in the text, and directories, which, however, did not include information relevant for this study. Financial attachments were neglected. In a few cases, one content unit referred to two or more categories and subcategories, respectively. Anticipation the list of categories derived in Step 8, information on the economic and environmental categories are mostly given in terms of numbers and percentage information in tables/charts, while social aspects are mainly pointed out by text passages in the narratives' part.

Step 8: Analytical steps taken by means of the category system.

Mayring suggests choosing one of three different approaches, either *summarizing* the main contents within the analysed text; *explicating* the text by providing additional information; or *structuring* by filtering out specific aspects of the text. Due to the research question, this chapter applies the flexible and individually material-dependent *structuring*, that is, in line with Mayring, we first chose a standard definition as a starting point. As the legal regulations of neither notes nor management report/Management Commentary offer any applicable definition of sustainability, we decided to follow the Global Reporting Initiative (GRI 4, 2013). Currently, GRI 4 represents the most accepted sustainability reporting framework (Ortiz & Marin, 2014). It offers a very clear structure with a threefold division of economic, environmental, and social aspects as main categories and corresponding subcategories. Exhausting the underlying methodology which allows for flexible adaptations of any definitions to correspond to the research question, we add three ethical aspects in order to specify the social dimension. While the principle of responsibility and the principle of justice give access to the ethical dimension, human rights as a minimal standard – protecting essential elements and areas of human existence which a human needs for survival and for a life as a human being (Kirchschlaeger, 2013b) – support setting a clear focus and priorities (Kirchschlaeger, 2015b). The final eleven subcategories have been identified as follows:

- Economic category
  - Economic performance
  - Market presence
  - Indirect economic impacts
  - Procurement practices

- Environmental category
  - Materials and natural resources
  - Emissions, waste, and effluents
  - Environmental legal obligations and grievance mechanisms

- Social category
  - Labour practice and decent work
  - Human rights
  - Society
  - Product responsibility.

The economic category comprises the economic performance such as the organization's impacts on the economic conditions of its stakeholders, and on economic systems at local, national, and global levels, as well as market presence. Further, it refers to indirect economic impacts, among others, the organization's impacts on communities, local economies, development of significant infrastructure investments, changing the productivity of organizations, sectors, or the whole economy, economic development in areas of high poverty, economic impact of improving or deteriorating social or environmental conditions, availability of products and services for those on low incomes, enhancing skills and knowledge amongst a professional community or in a geographical region, or jobs supported in the supply chain or distribution chain. Also, procurement practices are included (GRI 4, 2013, 48 subs.).

Environmental issues are characterized according to GRI 4. Materials and natural resources relate to the organization's impact on living and non-living natural systems, including materials, energy, water, biodiversity, products and services, and transport (GRI 4, 2013, 52), while emissions, waste, and effluents include indicators on greenhouse gas emissions as well as ozone-depleting substances, NOX, SOX, and other significant air emissions (GRI 4, 2013, 5); environmental legal obligations and grievance mechanisms reveal effective or possible legal infringements. Their subcategories were summarized here, because they reflect the legal part in the environment section of the GRI 4 definition, either regulated by the law or internal rules of a group.

The social category was broadened in much detail in regard to the special focus on ethical behaviour. In general, it comprises the impacts the group has on the social systems in which it is embedded. The aspects in subcategory labour practice and decent work are directly derived from GRI 4 (p. 64) such as the definition of human rights (p. 70) which covers, among other things, incidents of human rights violations, and changes in stakeholders' ability to enjoy and exercise their human rights. The term "society" refers to impacts that an organization has on society and local communities (GRI 4, 2013, 76); product responsibility on products and services that directly affect stakeholders, and customers in particular (GRI 4, 2013, 80).

Steps 9 and 10: Controlling for the chosen categories (re-check) and application of content-analytical quality criteria.

After having coded the first ten reports (about 15% of the sample), Steps 4 to 8 were reviewed according to the previous coding experience by feedback loops, and thus the coding of the reports analysed so far were repeated according to the enhanced determination. The intercoder reliability was ensured by comparing the coding results of five reports conducted by two different researchers.

Step 11: Findings and interpretation of the results in relation to the main problem and issue are illustrated in the following section.

Results

Figure 4.4.1 shows the average percentage of economic, ecologic, and social content of the groups in each country. Following Mayring, the basis of the empirical content analysis is the definition of content units as defined in Step 8.

German groups publish 1,117 content units in their notes and management report/ Management Commentary on average. Thereof, 8.67% of the analysed units are identified as relevant for the underlying study, that is, they contain information on the defined categories and subcategories. About 60% of these relevant units include economic information, about 16% ecologic content, and 24% deal with social issues. Similarly, Austrian groups concentrate on economic factors by about 64% of all verbal information, while about 26% belong to social aspects, and with 10% only little interest is given to environmental issues. Swiss groups inform dominantly about economic factors, with 76% of the relevant content, only 6% about environmental aspects, and the remaining 18% about social issues.

In total, financial information is dominant, followed by social issues and environmental topics. While German groups publish most information on overall sustainability, comprising environment and ethics, with about 40%, Swiss groups turn to these issues only by less than 25%, Austria in between with 36%. Apart from different legal requirements, the direction of impact is obvious: financial information matters.

Figure 4.4.2 presents the detailed results of the empirical study.

In more detail, German groups inform by 57% of all relevant units on economic performance, none on market presence, and below 1% on indirect economic performance and procurement practices, each. While more than 8% each include information on materials and waste resources as well as emissions, waste, and effluents; environmental legal obligations and grievance mechanisms are negligible. As for social topics, labour practice and decent work comprise nearly the whole category.

In Austria, each group report contains 677 content units on average. Of the 8% relevant units, the majority of about 63% focuses on the economic performance, none on the market presence, and only two groups with a – therefore distorted – average of 1.5% on indirect market performance. While resources seem to be important by about 6.6%, emissions, waste, and effluents with 3%, procurement as well as environmental legal obligations below 1%, respectively, are not regarded as relevant. Contrarily, social issues regarding labour practice and decent work are highlighted, with about 23%, human rights, society, and product responsibility range below 2% each.

			economic category				environmental category			social category			
Company	Content units	relevant units in %	Economic Performance	Market Presence	Indirect Economic Impact	Procurement practices	Materials and Natural Resources	Emissions, Waste and Effluents	Environmental Legal Obligations and Grievance Mechanisms	Labor Practice and Decent Work	Human Rights	Society	Product Responsibility
Adidas	654	9,48%	38,71%				3,23%	1,61%	3,23%	48,39%		4,84%	
Allianz	607	4,94%	66,67%					13,33%		20,00%			
BASF	1223	11,53%	31,91%				17,02%	21,28%		25,53%		4,26%	
Bayer	1341	14,60%	20,89%			4,00%	15,11%	18,67%	0,89%	35,56%	1,33%	1,78%	1,78%
Beiersdorfer	422	11,14%	42,55%				23,40%			34,04%			
BMW	987	5,98%	47,46%				5,08%	6,78%		38,98%		1,69%	
Commerzbank	962	2,60%	76,00%							24,00%			
Continental	1276	12,38%	55,06%		0,63%		6,96%	9,49%	0,63%	13,29%		13,29%	0,63%
Daimler	1237	8,97%	41,44%				13,51%	23,42%		11,71%		9,91%	
Deutsche Bank	1928	4,36%	88,10%							11,90%			
Deutsche Börse	1188	7,15%	77,65%							22,35%			
Deutsche Lufthansa	1306	5,51%	83,33%							16,67%			
Deutsche Post	973	9,15%	62,92%				1,12%	3,37%		32,58%			
Deutsche Telekom	1370	9,85%	78,52%				2,22%	5,93%		6,67%		6,67%	
EON	1263	8,08%	47,06%				7,84%	3,92%		41,18%			
Fresenius Medical Care	836	12,87%	31,72%				19,26%	14,23%		34,80%			
Fresenius	1015	10,84%	26,30%				24,24%	19,55%		29,91%			
HeidelbergCement	1024	8,79%	53,90%				9,78%	9,99%		26,33%			
Henkel vz	1176	11,75%	29,98%				20,17%	18,35%		30,08%		1,42%	
Infineon Technologies	1506	8,43%	54,33%				20,51%	9,49%		15,67%			
Linde	1149	7,04%	59,79%				8,35%	5,56%		26,29%			
Merck	1078	12,36%	30,37%				20,50%	17,48%		31,65%			
Münchener Rückversicherungs-Gesell	1336	3,19%	69,20%				2,78%	1,50%		26,53%			
ProSiebenSat1 Media	1162	7,04%	77,84%				1,77%	0,86%		19,50%		0,03%	
RWE	774	8,97%	58,00%				17,34%	13,99%		10,67%			
SAP	1433	7,12%	64,42%				2,66%	1,40%		31,31%			0,21%
Siemens	651	7,68%	100,00%										
thyssenkrupp	1081	8,30%	74,68%				6,63%	8,33%		10,37%			
Volkswagen vz	1571	9,11%	47,99%				8,52%	13,23%		21,96%		8,30%	
Vonovia	800	10,49%	61,57%				6,01%	1,77%		25,57%		5,08%	
D - Germany	**1117,63**	**8,66%**	**56,61%**	**0,00%**	**0,02%**	**0,13%**	**8,80%**	**8,12%**	**0,16%**	**24,12%**	**0,04%**	**1,91%**	**0,09%**
ANDRITZ AG	629	16,53%	23,08%	8,65%			28,85%	6,73%		31,73%		0,96%	
BUWOG AG	926	12,74%	60,17%				10,17%	1,69%		16,95%		5,08%	5,93%
CA IMMOBILIEN INVEST SE	656	8,23%	62,96%				1,85%	1,85%	1,85%	31,48%			
CONWERT	434	4,15%	88,89%							11,11%			
DO&CO AKTIENGESELLSCHAFT	517	3,87%	60,00%							40,00%			
ERSTE GROUP BANK AG	1377	7,48%	14,56%				10,68%	10,68%	2,91%	34,95%	0,97%	25,24%	
IMMOFINANZ AG	846	5,44%	50,00%				19,57%			30,43%			
LENZING AG	749	7,08%	71,70%					1,89%	1,89%	24,53%			
OESTERREICHISCHE POST AG	599	8,85%	79,25%				3,77%	3,77%		13,21%			
OMV AG	475	2,11%	100,00%										
RAIFFEISEN BANK INTERNAT. AG	439	2,73%	33,33%							66,67%			
RHI AG	698	15,19%	46,23%				11,32%	9,43%		31,13%		1,89%	
SCHOELLER-BLECKMANN OILFIELD	417	2,88%	100,00%										
TELEKOM AUSTRIA AG	639	14,24%	87,78%				4,44%			6,67%			1,11%
UNIQA INSURANCE GROUP AG	634	2,05%	76,92%							23,08%			
VERBUND AG KAT. A	876	17,12%	34,00%	20,00%			22,00%	3,33%		20,67%			
VIENNA INSURANCE GROUP AG	970	2,58%	64,00%				4,00%			32,00%			
VOESTALPINE AG	578	5,02%	44,83%				6,90%	17,24%		31,03%			
WIENERBERGER AG	465	11,83%	98,18%							1,82%			
ZUMTOBEL GROUP AG	625	10,72%	65,67%			5,97%	8,96%	2,88%	4,48%	13,43%		1,49%	
A - Austria	**677,45**	**8,04%**	**53,08%**	**0,00%**	**1,43%**	**0,30%**	**6,63%**	**2,88%**	**0,56%**	**23,04%**	**0,05%**	**1,73%**	**0,35%**
ABB LTD N	347	14,12%	73,47%					4,08%	6,12%	16,33%			
ACTELION N	201	4,98%	100,00%										
ADECCO N	440	11,59%	74,51%				3,92%			21,57%			
CS GROUP N	812	4,56%	78,38%							21,62%			
GEBERIT N	694	8,50%	47,46%		1,69%		16,95%	8,47%		25,42%			
GIVAUDAN N	539	9,83%	58,49%					5,66%		35,85%			
JULIUS BAER	438	8,90%	58,97%							41,03%			
LAFARGEHOLCIM N	392	6,12%	83,33%				12,50%			4,17%			
NESTL N	342	8,77%	90,00%							10,00%			
NOVARTIS N	416	10,58%	63,64%				2,27%		11,36%	22,73%			
RICHEMONTAT N	386	8,81%	100,00%										
ROCHE GS	441	7,94%	94,29%						2,86%	2,86%			
SGS N	382	14,40%	83,64%				5,45%			10,91%			
SWATCH GROUP I	171	9,94%	47,06%							52,94%			
SWISS LIFE HOLDING AG N	631	6,81%	95,35%							4,65%			
SWISS RE N	341	9,09%	64,52%						12,90%	22,58%			
SWISSCOM N	606	15,35%	74,19%	1,08%	3,23%		6,45%	5,38%		9,68%			
SYNGENTA N	449	13,59%	65,57%						13,11%	21,31%			
UBS GROUP	772	3,63%	96,43%							3,57%			
ZURICH INSURANCE N	453	12,36%	71,43%							28,57%			
CH - Switzerland	**462,65**	**9,49%**	**76,04%**	**0,05%**	**0,29%**	**0,00%**	**2,38%**	**1,18%**	**2,92%**	**17,79%**	**0,00%**	**0,00%**	**0,00%**

Figure 4.4.1 Average percentage of economic, ecologic, and social content (own representation)

The Swiss results show that on average each group publishes 463 content units in its notes and management reports, thereof only 9.49% are regarded as relevant for the given analysis; 76% of all economic-related information belongs to the economic performance, while almost no information is given on the other economic categories or procurement practices. As for the environmental category, reporting is low, between 1% and 2%. In the field of social responsibility, only labour practice and decent work is given, with about 18%; no information on human rights, society, and product responsibility.

Analysing these details, is becomes obvious that the analysed groups seem to regard only two out of the eleven categories, that is, economic performance with about 57% and labour practice and decent work with about 24% relevant unity, as important for their

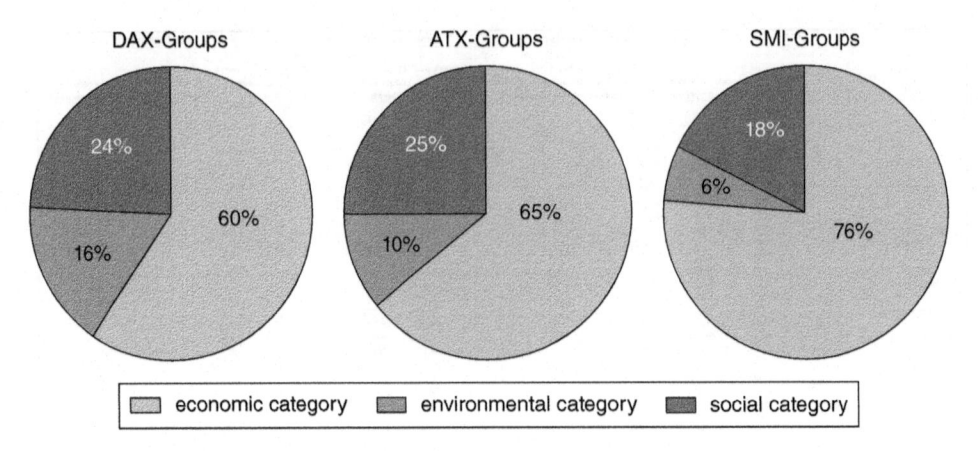

Figure 4.4.2 Results of empirical study (own representation)

business processes or their presentation to the external stakeholders. At least, all groups inform on emissions, waste, and effluents as well as on materials and waste resources, albeit not much – between 8% and 9%, respectively. On the other hand, only one group out of 70 is reporting on market presence, only two on procurement practices and human rights each, only five each on indirect economic impact and product responsibility. Also in relation to all relevant units, these subcategories may be seen as irrelevant. It is obvious that they are under-represented compared to the importance given in the GRI 4 and the literature.

Overall, the results confirm the focus already shown by the main categorization. Again, we reveal some differences among the three countries. Among others, German groups provide 2.5 times more information than Swiss groups and 1.7 times more than Austrian groups, measured in numbers of pages. Whereas the Swiss are leading in relevant text, with 19% more than German groups and 20% more than Austrian groups, measured in relevant units in percentages.

Conclusions

This chapter adds to the scarce empirical literature further evidence and one of the first analyses in the DACH region about whether, and to what extent, the overall sample of listed groups in Germany, Austria, and Switzerland informs about sustainability and ethics. In contrast to the more extensive research which concentrates on voluntary sustainability reports, we analyse legally prescribed annual reports, more specifically their narrative part of the notes and the management reports and Management Commentary, respectively, of the latest reporting year, 2015. By placing this emphasis, we want to contribute to the question of whether groups inform sufficiently about the corresponding issues within the given legal framework, whether these regulations have to be extended, or whether nudging voluntary publications might lead to satisfying results. We are aware of the fact that this short contribution cannot solve this fundamental dispute. However, by applying a qualitative text analysis according to Mayring, we reveal other data which are in line with our expectations based on past experience in the literature. Still, the majority of information, although published in the more qualitative orientation of the notes and management reports, comprises pure financial aspects and neglects sustainability and ethical issues in spite of an intensive academic and practical discussion on broad stakeholder information and the necessary widening of published issues in regard to sustainability. Groups give little information on social topics such as human rights, and even less on environmental issues. Based on the expected, however thoroughly weak and negative, results, our conclusions are threefold.

First, we learn that, apart from small differences, all groups in the DACH region, no matter under which regime, head in the same direction. On the one hand, this further implies that listed groups either do not care about sustainability and ethical issues in their operational business, or do not report on their respective behaviour. These facts cannot be filtered out by a pure desktop analysis of published annual reports. Based on our findings, a further research step should be to perform standardized and qualitative interviews with the sample groups to filter out the underlying reasons for these results.

Second, we identify an urgent need to enforce legal regulations that oblige economic entities to present their focus on issues of sustainability, respectively corporate social responsibility, justice, and human rights. Due to their ethical significance and relevance, and due to existing human rights law (Kirchschlaeger, 2017), sustainability, respectively corporate social responsibility, justice, and human rights, should no longer be treated by group reports as "nice to have". Further research should concentrate on more detailed juridical aspects in line with the question of which reporting instrument sustainability aspects should actually be embedded under the aspect of *division of labour*. It is indeed true that notes and management reports are not the first sources for stakeholders to look for information; sustainability reports are much more suitable for such content. At first glance, the selection of notes and management reports as a data base for this research seems to deter the interpretation of the study's empirical results. However, in accordance with the research question, only legally required information, and consequently obligatorily required reports, were consistent.

That is why, third, we do not derive the claim to enlarge reporting duties of annual reports, but to enlarge reporting duties in any suitable instrument. Further theoretical advancements should deepen research on where to best locate information, that is, how to optimize information policy in the field of sustainability reporting, from a stakeholder's point of view.

References

Alonso-Almeida, M., Llach, J., & Marimon, F. (2014). A Closer Look at the 'Global Reporting Initiative' Sustainability Reporting as a Tool to Implement Environmental and Social Policies: A Worldwide Sector Analysis. *Corporate Social Responsibility and Environmental Management*, 21, 318–335.

Aminu, A.A., & Oladipo, O.O. (2016). Application of Financial Ethics in Annual Financial Reporting of Banks. *Journal of Economic and Social Development*, 3(1), 66–75.

Andringa, E. (2004). The Interface between Fiction and Life: Patterns of Identification in Reading Biographies. *Poetics Today*, 25(2), 205–240.

Baumueller, J., & Kreuzer, C. (2014). *SWK-Spezial Bilanzanalyse*. Vienna: Linde Verlag Ges.m.b.H.

Bewernick, M., Schreyogg, G., & Costas, J. (2013). Charismatische Führung: Die Konstruktion von Charisma durch die deutsche Wirtschaftspresse am Beispiel von Ferdinand Piëch. *zfbf*, 65, 434–465.

Born, K. (2011). *Rechnungslegung international: IAS/IFRS im Vergleich mit HGB und US-GAAP*, 5th edn. Stuttgart: Schäffer-Poeschel Verlag.

Braun, H. (2009). Verantwortung. *Die Neue Ordnung*, 63, 244–252.

Burritt, R. L., & Schaltegger, S. (2010). Sustainability Accounting and Reporting: Fad or Trend? *Accounting, Auditing and Accountability Journal*, 23(7), 829–846.

Bussmann, S., Muders, P., Zahrt-Omar, C.A., Escobar, P.L.C., Claus, M., Schildmann, J., & Weber, M. (2015). Improving End-of-Life Care in Hospitals: A Qualitative Analysis of Bereaved Families' Experiences and Suggestions. *American Journal of Hospice and Palliative Medicine*, 32(1), 44–51.

Carroll, A.B. (1991). The Pyramid of Corporate Social Responsibility: Toward the Moral Management of Organizational Stakeholders. *Business Horizons*, 34(4), 39–48.

Chamorro, A., Rubio, S., & Miranda, F.J. (2009). Characteristics of Research on Green Marketing. *Business Strategy and Environment*, 18, 223–239.

Choi, S., & Ng, A. (2011). Environmental and Economic Dimensions of Sustainability and Price Effects on Consumer Responses. *Journal of Business Ethics*, 104(2), 269–282.

The Code of Obligations. Federal Act on the Amendment of the Swiss Civil Code (Part Five: The Code of Obligations), in force since 1 January 1912 (AS 27 317).

Commercial Code (Handelsgesetzbuch – HGB), in force since RGBl. I S. 219/1897, last amended BGBl. I S. 1578/2016.

Deloitte (2008). https://www.iasplus.com/en/binary/iasplus/0801buscomb.pdf (accessed 14 July 2017).

Deloitte (2014). IFRS compliance, presentation and disclosure checklist 2014. https://www.iasplus.com/en/ publications/global/models-checklists/2014/ifrs-checklist (accessed 17 February 2017).

Dierksmeier, C. (2011). The Freedom–Responsibility Nexus in Management Philosophy and Business Ethics. *Journal of Business Ethics*, 101(2), 263–283.

Dierksmeier, C. (2012). How Should We Do Business? Global Ethics in the Age of Globality. *10th Global Ethic Lecture and Inauguration of the Global Ethic Institute at the University of Tuebingen*, 18 April 2012. Tuebingen: Global Ethic Institute.

Dierksmeier, C., & Pirson, M. (2010). The Modern Corporation and the Idea of Freedom. *Philosophy of Management*, 9(3), 5–25.

Dillard, J., & Murray, A. (2013). Deciphering the Domain of Corporate Social Responsibility. In: Haynes, K., Dillard, J., & Murray, A. (eds.), *Corporate Social Responsibility: A Research Handbook*. London: Routledge, 10–27.

Eisenhardt, K. (1989). Building Theories from Case Study Research. *The Academy of Management Review*, 14(4), 532–550.

Entrepreneurial Code (Unternehmensgesetzbuch – UGB), in force since dRGBl. S 219/1897, last amended BGBl. I Nr. 120/2005.

European Financial Reporting Advisory Group (EFRAG) (2012). Towards a Disclosure Framework for the Notes to the financial statements. *Discussion Paper*. http://www.efrag.org/Assets/Download?assetUrl=%2Fsites%2Fwebpublishing%2FProject%20Documents%2F169%2F121015_Disclosure_Framework_-_FINAL1.pdf (accessed 15 February 2017).

European Securities and Markets Authority (ESMA) (2011). Consultation Paper, Considerations of materiality in financial reporting. *Brussels: ESMA*. https://www.esma.europa.eu/press-news/consultations/consultation-considerations-materiality-in-financial-reporting (accessed 26 September 2017).

EY (2014). International GAAP Disclosure Checklist: Based on International Financial Reporting Standards in issue at 28 February 2014. http://www.ey.com/Publication/vwLUAssets/EY_International_GAAP_Disclosure_Checklist/$File/EY-CTools-DC-March-2014.pdf (accessed 26 September 2017).

Frankfurt Stock Exchange – Deutscher Aktienindex 30. http://en.boerse-frankfurt.de/index/constituents/ DAX#Constituents (accessed 20 October 2016).

Glatzel, N. (2000). Soziale Gerechtigkeit – ein umstrittener Begriff. In: Nothelle-Wildfeuer, U., & Glatzel, N. (eds.), *Christliche Sozialethik im Dialog. Zur Zukunftsfähigkeit von Wirtschaft, Politik und Gesellschaft*. FS L. Roos. Grafschaft: Vektor Verlag, 139–150.

Global Reporting Initiative (GRI) (2013). G4 Sustainability Reporting Guidelines. https://www. globalreporting.org/resourcelibrary/GRIG4-Part1-Reporting-Principles-and-Standard-Disclosures.pdf (accessed 20 October 2016).

Guthrie, J. (2001). The Management, Measurement and the Reporting of Intellectual Capital. *Journal of Intellectual Capital*, 2(1), 27–41.

Hilty, R., & Henning-Bodewig, F. (eds.) (2014). *Corporate Social Responsibility. Verbindliche Standards des Wettbewerbrechts?* Berlin: Springer.

Hoeffe, O. (2008). *Lexikon der Ethik*. Munich: Beck.

IFRS (2016).http://www.ifrs.org/Current-Projects/IASB-Projects/Management-Commentary/ IFRS-Practice-Statement/Documents/Managementcommentarypracticestatement8December. pdf (accessed 19 October 2016).

IFRS Foundation (2010). IFRS Practice Statement. *Management Commentary*. http://www.ifrs. org/Current-Projects/IASB-Projects/Management-Commentary/IFRS-Practice-Statement/ Pages/IFRS-Practice-Statement.aspx (accessed 15 February 2017).

IFRS Foundation (2016a). International Financial Reporting Standards (IFRSs) including International Accounting Standards (IASs) and Interpretations as at 1 January 2016. http:// www.ifrs.org/IFRSs/Pages/IFRS.aspx (accessed 15 February 2017).

IFRS Foundation (2016b). http://www.ifrs.org/About-us/Pages/IFRS-Foundation-and-IASB. aspx (accessed 15 February 2017).

Jaeger, S. (2015). *Kritische Diskursanalyse: Eine Einfuehrung*, 7th edition. Muenster: Unrast.

Jamali, D. (ed.) (2017). *Comparative Perspectives on Global Corporate Social Responsibility*. Hershey, Pennsylvania: IGI Global.

Kalbers, L.P. (2009). Fraudulent Financial Reporting, Corporate Governance and Ethics: 1987–2007. *Review of Accounting and Finance*, 8(2), 187–209.

Karaibrahimoglu, Y.Z., & Cangarli, B.G. (2016). Do Auditing and Reporting Standards Affect Firms' Ethical Behaviours? The Moderating Role of National Culture. *Journal of Business Ethics*, 139, 55–75.

Kirchschläger, P.G. (2013a). Gerechtigkeit und ihre christlich-sozialethische Relevanz. *Zeitschrift für katholische Theologie*, 135(4), 433–456.

Kirchschlaeger, P.G. (2013b). *Wie können Menschenrechte begründet werden? Ein für religiöse und säkulare Menschenrechtskonzeptionen anschlussfähiger Begründungsansatz*. Muenster: LIT-Verlag.

Kirchschlaeger, P.G. (2013c). Die Multidimensionalitaet der Menschenrechte – Chance oder Gefahr für den universellen Menschenrechtsschutz? *MenschenRechtsMagazin*, 18(2), 77–95.

Kirchschlaeger, P.G. (2014). Verantwortung aus christlich-sozialethischer Perspektive. *ETHICA*, 22(1), 29–54.

Kirchschlaeger, P.G. (2015a). CSR zwischen Greenwashing und ethischer Reflexion – Menschenrechte als ethischer Referenzrahmen für Corporate Social Responsibility (CSR). *Zeitschrift für Wirtschafts- und Unternehmensethik*, 16, 264–287.

Kirchschlaeger, P.G. (2015b). Multinationale Konzerne und Menschenrechte. *ETHICA*, 23(3), 261–280.

Kirchschlaeger, P.G. (2016). *Menschenrechte und Religionen. Nichtstaatliche Akteure und ihr Verhältnis zu den Menschenrechten*. Paderborn: Ferdinand Schöningh Verlag.

Kirchschlaeger, P.G. (2017). Wirtschaft und Menschenrechte. In: Gabriel, I., Kirchschlaeger, P.G., & Sturn, R. (eds.), *Eine Wirtschaft, die Leben fördert. Wirtschafts- und unternehmensethische Reflexionen im Anschluss an Papst Franziskus*. Ostfildern: Patmos (in print).

Kirsch, H.-J. (2006). Stellungnahme zum Diskussionspapier. *Management Commentary*, http:// www.drsc.de/docs/press_releases/01_dpmc_kirsch_scheele.pdf (accessed 15 February 2017).

Kolk, A. (2004). A Decade of Sustainability Reporting: Developments and Significance. *International Journal of Environment and Sustainable Development*, 3(1), 51–64.

Koller, P. (2005). Zum Verhältnis von Domestischer und Globaler (Un)Gerechtigkeit: Vortrag an der Konferenz [The Diversity of Human Rights: Constitution and Human Rights]. InterUniversityCentre Dubrovnik, 3–10 September.

KPMG (2014). Guide to Annual Financial Statements – Disclosure Checklist. https://home.kpmg.com/content/dam/ kpmg/pdf/2014/09/guide-disclosure-checklist-sept14.pdf (accessed 17 February 2017).

Labelle, R., Makni Gargouri, R., & Francoeur, C. (2010). Ethics, Diversity Management, and Financial Reporting Quality. *Journal of Business Ethics*, 93(2), 335–353.

Leipziger, D. (2016). *The Corporate Responsibility Code Book*, third edition. Sheffield: Greenleaf Publishing.

Leitner, K.-H., Schaffhauser-Linzatti, M.M., Stowasser, R., & Wagner, K. (2007). The Impact of Size and Specialisation on Universities' Department Performance: A DEA Analysis Applied to Austrian Universities. *Higher Education*, 53(4), 517–538.

MacDonald, K. (2011). Re-Thinking "Spheres of Responsibility": Business Responsibility for Indirect Harm 2011. *Journal of Business Ethics*, 99, 549–563.

Mayring, Ph. (2014). Qualitative Content Analysis. *Theoretical Foundation, Basic Procedures and Software Solution.* https://www.psychopen.eu/fileadmin/user_upload/books/mayring/ssoar-2014-mayring-Qualitative_content_analysis_theoretical_foundation.pdf (accessed 26 September 2017).

Merkl-Davies, D., Brennan, N., & Vourvachis, P. (2011). Text Analysis Methodologies in Corporate Narrative Reporting Research. 23rd CSEAR International Colloquium.

Moore, M. (1995). *Creating Public Value: Strategic Management in Government*. Cambridge, MA: Harvard University Press.

Moore, M. (2013). *Recognizing Public Value*. Cambridge, MA: Harvard University Press.

Morhardt, E.J. (2002). *Clean, Green, and Read All Over: Ten Rules for Effective Corporate Environmental and Sustainability Reporting*. Milwaukee: ASQ Quality Press.

Oevermann, U., Allert, T., Konau, E., & Krambeck, J. (1979). Die Methodologie einer, objektiven Hermeneutik und ihre allgemeine forschungslogische Bedeutung in den Sozialwissenschaften. In: Soeffner, H.-G. (ed.), *Interpretative Verfahren in den Sozial- und Textwissenschaften*. Stuttgart: Metzler, 352–434.

Ortiz, E., & Marin, S. (2014). Global Reporting Initiative (GRI) as Recognized Guidelines for Sustainability Reporting by Spanish Companies on the IBEX 35: Homogeneity in their Framework and Added Value in the Relationship with Financial Entities. *Intangible Capital*, 10(5), 855–872.

Ottman, J.A. (2011). *The New Rules of Green Marketing*. Sheffield: Greenleaf Publishing.

PwC (2014). IFRS disclosure checklist. https://inform.pwc.com/inform2/show?action=informContent&id=1413015612093851 (accessed 26 September 2017)

PwC (2016). https://inform.pwc.com/inform2/s/Management_commentary/informContent/1146055408127572 (accessed 15 February 2017).

Sacer, I.M. (2015). The Regulatory Framework of Accounting and Accounting Standard-Setting Bodies in the European Union Member States. *Financial Theory and Practice*, 39(4), 393–410.

Schaffhauser-Linzatti, M.M., & Ossmann, S. (2017). The Role of Sustainability Information in University Reporting: A Theoretical and Empirical Study. *International Journal of Sustainability in Higher Education*.

Schaffhauser-Linzatti, M.M. (2017). Welchen Beitrag kann die unternehmerische Rechnungslegung zu einer Ethik der Nachhaltigkeit leisten? In: Gabriel, I., Kirchschlaeger, P., & Sturn, R. (eds.), *Eine Wirtschaft, die Leben foerdert*. Ostfildern: Matthias Gruenewald Verlag, 317–335.

Schedler, K., & Summermatter, L. (2011). Mittelfristige Planung von Aufgaben und Finanzen in Deutschland, Oesterreich und der Schweiz. In: *Zukunftsfähige Verwaltung? Herausforderungen und Lösungsstrategien in Deutschland, Österreich und der Schweiz*. Budrich: Opladen, 139–164.

Singh, A.K., & Vasudeva, S. (2013). Does Building Up of Values Matter? An Analysis of Ethical Values of Accounting Professionals and Unethical Reporting Practices in Accounting. *The Global eLearning Journal*, 2(3), 1–25.

Six Swiss Exchange – Swiss Market Index 20. https://www.six-swiss-exchange.com/indices/security_info_en. html?id=CH0009980894CHF9 (accessed 20 October 2016).

Stolowy, H., Lebas, M.J., & Ding, Y. (2013). *Financial Accounting and Reporting*. Singapore: Cengage Learning.

Tassadaq, F., & Malik, Q.A. (2015). Creative Accounting and Financial Reporting: Model Development and Empirical Testing. *International Journal of Economics and Financial Issues*, 5(2), 544–551.

Vienna Stock Exchange – Austrian Traded Index 20. https://www.wienerborse.at/en/indices/index-values/prices- constituents/?ID_NOTATION=92866&ISIN=AT0000999982&cHash=ebc75a963fb1e5c82ec22f9128fd8b93 (accessed 20 October 2016).

Wiemeyer, J. (2013). Unternehmensethik aus christlich-sozialethischer Sicht. *Kirche und Gesellschaft*, 404, 3–16.

Williams, O.F. (2014). *Corporate Social Responsibility: The Role of Business in Sustainable Development*. London: Routledge.

World Commission on Environment and Development (1987). Our Common Future. Link: http://www.un-documents.net/our-common-future.pdf (accessed 15 February 2017).

Index

accelerator functions 83
accidents 6, 7, 122, 124, 146, 147, 148, 152, 155
accountability 24, 57, 58, 67, 94, 104, 257
accuracy of reporting 91, 126, 171, 189, 191, 192, 197, 200, 259
action research 135
advocacy 74, 76, 79, 84
Aerts, W. 7
age, and CSR 228
agency theory 166, 169, **170**, 254
Altuntaş Vural, C. 132
Amengual, M. 129
American Chemical Council 8–9
American International Group (AIG) 242–243
American National Standards Institute (ANSI) 62–63
Analytic Network Process (ANP) 50–51
Andersen, M. 123
Anheier, H. K. 74, 76
appeal processes 68
Apple 126–127
Aragon-Correa, J. A. 144
Arce-Gomez, A. 21
Arvidson, M. 21
ASSET4 8, 10–12
assurance services 172–173
attitudes and beliefs, measurement of 83–84
audit 126, 129, 133, 169, 172, 173, 189, 198, 263, 264
Austria 270–279
awareness-raising 74

balance, principle of (in reporting) 259, 262
balanced scorecard (BSC) 33, 34–37, 38, 40, 50, 73
Bank of England 246
banking, social 206–222
Barraket, J. 19, 20–21
Basel Committee on Banking Supervision 216
baselines 77, 110
Baumann-Pauly, D. 7
Bayer 8

Bedggood, R. E. 21
Beisheim, M. 55, 56, 57–58
Bélanger, J. 6, 7
benchmarks: and auditability 189–190; codes of conduct 123; data envelopment analysis (DEA) 102–121; hotel industry 193; outcomes measurement 199; social impact measurement 26
"benefit-of-the-doubt" ratings 108
Berne Declaration 99
best practice 105–106, 112, 113, 118, 168
Bhopal disaster 5
bias 10, 12, 167
Blank, H. 10, 11
Bloomberg 141
BMW 245
boards of directors 62
Boiral, O. 207
Bondy, K. 130
Bonne, G. 10
bonus-malus systems 241, 246
Boström, M. 54, 56
bottom-up governance 79
Bowen, F. 201n5
brands 122, 125
Bregha, F. 6
broker roles 74
Brown, D. 4, 6, 8
Brown, K. 146
Brundtland Report 90, 260
Bruneel, J. 103
Bucacioc, A. 18, 19, 20, 26
Buchanan, J. M. 256
Burritt, R. 33, 37, 39, 47, 48
business process perspectives 34–35, 39, 46
businesslike goals for social enterprises 103–104
Busse, C. 129

Calderon, J. 180
capabilities 72, 134, 144, 191, 212–213, 217
capacity building 3
carbon accounting 166, 173

carbon dioxide emissions 6, 155, 166–178, 192, 194, 242, 245
Carbon Disclosure Project (CDP) 169–170, 191–192
career development policies 145, 146, 148, 152, 153
Caro, F. 133
Carroll, A. B. 5–6, 14
Carter, C. R. 129, 142, 143, 148
Carter, J. R. 142, 143, 148
causal chains 35–36, 38, 40, 46, 50, 77, 81, 84
Caves, D. W. 110
'Ceres Coalition' 10
charitable principles 89
chemical industry 3–17
Chemistry Industry Association of Canada (CIAC) 5
Chen, C. 105, 106, 107, 108, 113, 118
Cherchye, L. 102, 105, 106, 107, 108, 109, 118
China 126
Cho, A. H. 20
Chong, H. G. 193
civil society 55, 68, 84
clawback compensation schemes 242, 246
Climate Disclosure Standards Board (CDSB) 54, *59*
club good model 4, 7, 8
coalition-building 84
codes of conduct 4, 8, 14, 122–139
codification of standards 59, **61**
coercive isomorphism 168, **170**
Collier, J. 191
commercialization 103–104
commitment-based approaches to compliance programmes 129
common good economy 95–99
common language 21
comparability 78–79, 97, 104, 106, 194, 209, 259, 263
competitive advantage: CSR-washing 192; data envelopment analysis (DEA) 105; efficiency measurements 116; and hygienic factors 41; as motivation for CSR 6; Resource-Base View (RBV) 144; social impact measurement 73, 186; sustainable supply chains 144; and voluntary reporting 257, 264
compliance 44, 58, 79, 122–139
comprehensiveness versus precision in impact measurement 77, 78–79
conflict 84
consensual decision-making processes 58, 64, 256, 261
consensus working groups 57
content analysis techniques 273–279
context adaptability 78
contingency perspectives 154
contractarian reporting 253–268
control-group comparison studies 77

Conzelmann, T. 5
Cooper, D. J. 54, 113
cooperating networks 129
COPOLCO (Consumer Policy Committee, ISO) 92
corporate citizenship (CC) 89–90
corporate foundations 89
corporate social responsibility (CSR): and business ethics 189, 190, 191; and codes of conduct 130; communication about 237; CSR-washing 192; definitions of 89–90, 227; ethical responsibility 272; and gender 228; and the GFC 12; history of development of 5–6; ISO 26000 core concepts 7; in junior managers' project choices 225–239; motivations for 6; multi-stakeholder initiatives (MSIs) 54; public value 269; Responsible Care initiative 3–17; Social Return on Investment (SROI) 71; strategic corporate social responsibility (S-CSR) 89–101, 199; timing of CSR adoption 4, 8, 9–14
corporate volunteering 237
Costa, E. 21, 27, 28
cost–benefit analyses **61**, 71, 94, 107, 253, 263
Cost–Benefit Analysis (CBA) 80, 81, **82**, 83
costs of information 24, 27, 28, 171
counterfactual reasoning 84
criterion-based/purposive sampling 22
cross-database comparisons 10
cross-sectional data 154, 200
Cummings, L. 189
Curbach, J. 89, 90, 92
customer loyalty 37
customer perspectives (balanced scorecard) 34–35, 39, 46

DACH region 270–279
data envelopment analysis (DEA) 102–121
de Giovanni, P. 142, 143, 144, 147, 148, 151
dead-weight effects 71, 74
decentralized production 122, 125
decision-making 73, 84, 227; *see also* consensual decision-making processes
Dees, G. J. 104
deferred compensation schemes 241, 244, 245, 246, 248, 249
deliberative procedures 58, 59, 64
Delmas, M. 5, 7, 105, 106, 108, 113, 118
democratic society 76, 79, 95–97
Depoers, F. 190, 192
Deppe, H.-D. 209
deprivation 78–79
descriptive research approaches 22
developing countries 122, 123, 125, 129, 191
DHL Deutsche Post 245
diagnostic indicators 41
Diaz Guerrero, A. 33, 44, **45**, 46, 49, 50, 51

Dierksmeier, C. 272
difference-in-differences technique 186
Dillard, J. 4, 6, 8
DiMaggio, P. 103
Dingwerth, K. 55, 56, 57–58
disclosure quality 166, 167, 170–174
discourse analysis 79, 84, 273
Discourse Network Analysis (DNA) 79, 81, **82**, 83, 84
dishonest reporting 192
dissemination of standards 68
Donaldson, T. 190
Donovan, J. D. 21
dual objectives, measurement of performance of 102–121
due processes 54, 59, 60, 66–67, 68
Dunfee, T. W. 190
Dyllick, T. 38, 40, 43, 50
dynamic performance analysis 102, 105, 171

early adoption 4, 8, 9–14
Ebrahim, A. 18, 103, 104
ecological impacts: common good economy 95–97; eco-efficiency analyses 50; Global Reporting Initiative 91–92; incentive systems 245; Social Return on Investment (SROI) 72; strategic corporate social responsibility (S-CSR) **93**; sustainability accounting 48–49; *see also* environmental aspects
Eco-Management and Audit Scheme (EMAS) 94
economic sustainability 142; *see also* financial reporting; triple bottom line concept (TBL)
efficiency: efficiency changes over time 102, 106, 111–113, 116–119; energy efficiency 50, 144, 145, 148, 154, 197–198, 215, 242; organizational efficiency 105; relative efficiency measurements 105, 107–119
effort-based approaches to representation 64
Egels-Zandén, N. 126, 134
Eisenhardt, K. 273
Electronic Industry Citizenship Coalition's (EICC) 132
elites 55
Elkington, J. 72, 128, 142, 220n1, 260
employees: career development policies 145, 146, 148, 152, 153; employer selection, and CSR 227–228, 243, 248; health and safety 6, **93**, **124**, 126, 127, **128**, 132, 143, 144, 145, 146, 148, 152–153, 242; humane employment 92, **93**, 124; unions 55, 134; work–life balance policies 145, 146, 148, 152, 153, 193
empowerment 71, 74, 193
endogenous factors 84, 102, 105, 106, 115, 118
energy efficiency 50, 144, 145, 148, 154, 197–198, 215, 242
enforcement frameworks 125, 192; *see also* regulatory frameworks

entrepreneurial private authorities 54
environmental, social and governance (ESG) disclosure 8, 167
environmental and social management control 50
environmental aspects: content analysis techniques 269–283; environmental reporting 49; hotel industry 193–194; incentive systems 242, 248; in junior managers' project choices 226; linked to social aspects 141–165; Natural-Resource-Base View (NRBV) 144; and operational performance 145; and the SBSC 37–51; scientific classifications of 41; social banking 215, 220; Social Return on Investment (SROI) 71, 79; supply chains 128; sustainability accounting 48–49; *see also* triple bottom line concept (TBL)
environmental management systems (EMSs) 44, 128
Epstein, M. 18, 20
Escrig-Olmedo, E. 10
Esteban, R. 191
ethics: business ethics 189, 190; ethical designs of studies 77; ethical universals 189, 190; ethical-driven CSR 4, 6, 7, 243; in financial reporting 269–283; ISO 26000 94
euforia 180–188
European Central Bank 215
European Commission 9, 90
European Union (EU) 18–19
European Values Study 84
Eurosif 10, 246
EuSEF 18–19
evidence-based practices 59, 66–67, 73, 77
experimental designs 77, 180, 228–230
expert-based procedural legitimacy 60–67

fair business practices 94
Fair Labor Code (FLC) 192
Fairbrass, J. 7
Färe, B. R. 110
Fernández-Izquierdo, M. A. 10
Figge, F. 34, 37, 38, 39, **40**, 41, 43, 50
Financial Accounting Standards Board (FASB) 263
financial reporting 65, 92, 169, 171, 179, 187, 254, 257, 263, 269–283
Florida, R. 145
Foerstl, K. 133
Fondazione Sodalitas 18
Forest Stewardship Council 54, 56
forestry industry 56, 90, 228, 260
Fransen, L. W. 56, 57, 58
Free Welfare Associations, Germany 76, 80–85
freedom 272
Freeman, R. E. 258
Friedman, M. 173
future-ranking of sustainability reports 94
'fuzzy' indicators 74

game theory 255
GECES 18, 21
Gemeinwohlökonomie (common good economy) 95–97
gender 228, **231**, 232, 234, 235
general interest product 95
Generally Accepted Accounting Principles (GAAP) 270
Germany 76, 80–83, 228, 240, 245–246, 249, 270–279
GHGP 169, 170
Gibassier, D. 55, 68
Gimenez, C. 142, 143, 144, 145, 146, 151, 152, 153
Givel, M. 5, 6, 14
Glasbergen, P. 57, 64, 68
global brands 122
Global Citizenship 199
Global Compact 192
global financial crisis 12, 15, 206, 214, 242, 246
Global Impact Investing Network (GIIN) 80
global industries 54
global organizations 123; *see also* multinational companies (MNCs)
Global Reporting Initiative (GRI): carbon dioxide emissions 166; content of 257–259; corporate social responsibility (CSR) 227; as guide for content analysis techniques 274–275; hotel industry 191–192; incentive systems 246, 249; limitations of 253–268; Responsible Care initiative 3, 7; strategic corporate social responsibility (S-CSR) 90–92, **93**, 97–98; Sustainability Balanced Scorecard (SBSC) 49, 54, 55, 57–58, 59, 65–66, 68
globalization 89, 122, 256
GLS Bank 217–219
Gobeli, D. 141, 143, 154
Golini, R. 148
Gössling, S. 194
governance: bottom-up governance 79; environmental, social and governance (ESG) disclosure 8, 167; governance gaps 269; multinational companies (MNCs) 125; multi-stakeholder initiatives (MSIs) 56–57; Social Return on Investment (SROI) 78–80; Sustainability Accounting Standards Board (SASB) 62–63
governments *see* policy level performance tools
Graves, S. B. 146
Gray, R. 264n1
Green, J. F. 54
green banking *see* social banking
Green Hotels Global 194, *195–196*
green investments 155
green rents 169
green supply chains 129, 142, 147
GreenEngage 194, *195–196*

greenwashing 3, 172, 173, 207, 225, 243
Grieco, C. 18, 19, 21, 26, 28
grievance procedures 57
growth measures 209–220
Guenther, E. 173
Guidance on Social Responsibility *see* ISO 26000
Guthrie, J. 273

H&M 127–128
Hahn, R. 166, 173
Hahn, T. **41**, **42**, **43**
Hair, J. F. 161
Hallström, K. T. 54, 56
Hamburg Airport case study 33, 44–50, 51
Hansen, E. 37–38, 41, 43, 44, 50
Hart, S. L. 144
Hart, T. 103
Haughton, G. 103
health and safety 6, **93**, **124**, 126, 127, **128**, 132, 143, 144, 145, 146, 148, 152–153, 242
Herz, Robert H. 62
Hilton's LightStay 190, 194, *195–196*, 197–198
Holt, D. 148
Homann, K. 254, 263
Hong, J. C. 125, 129
Hotel Carbon/ Water Measuring initiatives 194, *195–196*
Hotel Footprinting Tool 194, *195–196*
hotel industry 189–205
Howard, J. 3
HP 132
Hsu, W. 129
Hu, A. H. 129
human capabilities and wellbeing 72
human capital 144
human dignity 95–97
human rights 92, **93**, 94, 272, 273, 274, 275–276, 277, 279
humane employment 92, **93**, 124
humane procurement **93**
Hutchins, M. J. 129
hybridity 79, 104, 107, 109
hygienic factors 41
hypernorms 190

IBM 132
impact measurement: barriers to standardization of 18–30; comprehensiveness versus precision 77, 78–79; euforia 180–187; impact modelling 73–74, 78; impacts over time 126; long-term impacts 20, 77, 272; macro-level impacts 76, 81, **82**, 83; micro-level impacts 76, 81, **82**, 83; outcomes measurement 24, 74, 182–183, 199, 200; Social Return on Investment (SROI) 71–88 *see also* environmental aspects; social impact measurement

Impact Reporting and Investment Standard (IRIS) 80, 81, **82**, 83
implementation costs 8
incentive systems 240–252
inclusiveness 57–58, 63, 65–66, 258, 259, 261
indirect effects 153
indirect results, measurement of 182–183
industrial accidents 5, 6, 7, 122, 124, 146, 147, 148, 152, 155
industry best practice frontiers 105–106, 112, 113, 118
industry-level standards 132, 134, 169, 172, 194–197, 200
informal relationships 129, 133
information asymmetries 134, 169, 171, 257
information economics 254
information exchange 129
information management systems 48, 49
information overload 262
information requirements of the SBSC 48, 49
in-house teams 185–186
innovation perspectives 34–35, 74, 144
inside-out perspectives *47*, 49
institutional theory 76, 166, 168–169, **170**, 256
intangible assets 34–35
intellectual capital reporting 269
intensity metrics 172
interest intermediation 76
internal communication 186
internal information systems 48
internal sustainable practices 143–147
internal value-chains 34–35, 39, 46
International Accounting Standards Board (IASB) 263
international case-study design 273
International Financial Reporting Standards (IFRS) 270–271
International Integrated Reporting Committee (IIRC) 54, *59*
International Labour Organization (ILO) 122
international standards 92, 94, 97, 99, 122, 123
International Tourism Partnership 190
investor initiatives 123
IÖW/future ranking of sustainability reports 94
Isnet 22
ISO standards: as authoritative source 67; ISO 14001 6; ISO 26000 7, 92–94, 97–98
issue framing 84
Italy 18, 22, 27

Jaeger, S. 273
Jamali, D. 206, 227, 269
Jarvis, C. B. 148
Jenkins, R. 129, 130, 132
Jiang, B. 133
joint audit 133
joint problem-solving 129

Jorissen, A. 54, 55
judicial review 56

Kahreh, M. S. 228
Kaplan, R. 34–37, 40, 43, 50, 73
Karaibrahimoglu, Y. Z. 12
Kehl, K. 73, 84
key performance indicators (KPIs): ASSET4 10; carbon dioxide emissions 172–173; impact measurement 73; industry specific 169; intensity metrics 172; non-financial reporting landscape 59; pre-test, post-test design 183–185; and the SBSC 47, 48; social impact measurement 184; sustainability reporting 49
King, A. A. 4
knowledge transfer 8
Kolk, A. 56, 57, 58, 130, 132
Koppell, J. G. S. 67
KPMG 49, 141
Kraft, K. L. 228
Krlev, G. 71, 72, 75, 77, 78
Kroeger, A. 186
Kyoto Protocol 166

labour practices: company reputation 225; developing corporate compliance programmes 122, 124, 125, 126, 129, 134; and environmental performance 145–146, 153; financial reporting 275, 276, 277; hotel industry 193; strategic corporate social responsibility (S-CSR) 92; triple bottom line concept (TBL) 143; *see also* employees
lagging indicators 35–37, 41, 43, 46, 48
Lai, F. 148
Lange, R. 244
Laplume, A. O. 191
LBG standard 199
leading indicators 35–37, 41, 46, 48
learning perspectives 34–35, 39, 46, 56, 73, 79
legal frameworks 5, 38, 54, 133, 269, 270–273, 279
legal-driven CSR 4–6, 14, 169
legitimacy: compliance programmes 126; expert-based procedural legitimacy 60–67; input legitimacy 56; legitimacy theory 166, 167–168, 254, 256, 261, 264; moral legitimacy 57, 256, 261, 262; of policy decisions 103; procedural legitimacy 54–70; and social impact analyses 73
Lenox, M. J. 4
Leslie, D. 193
licence to operate 167, 169, **170**
life trajectory projections 77
LightStay, Hilton 190, 194, *195–196*, 197–198
Liket, K. C. 20
litigation-cost hypothesis 169
Liubicic, R. J. 129
Locke, R. 129, 132, 133
longitudinal studies 77, 200

long-term impacts 20, 77, 272
long-term incentives 240–242, 243
long-term measurements 242, 245, 249
Lund-Thomsen, P. 129
Lydenberg, S. 58

Maas, K. 19, 20, 26, 47–48, 49
macro-level impacts 76, 81, **82**, 83
Malmquist productivity index 102, 109–113,
  116, 117–118, 119
management commentary 270–271, 273–276,
  278–279
management control systems 50, 240
management reporting 270–271, 273–276,
  278–279
management tools 40, 186, 187
Mangla, A. 129
manufacturing costs 146, 152
marginalized actors 55, 71
Margolis, J. D. 146
market acceptance 68
market failures 78
market for virtue 68
market-based standards 66–67
market-driven CSR 4, 6, 7, 14
mark-ups/premiums for responsible goods/
  services 207, 227
Marshall, R. S. 4, 6, 8, 145, 152–153
Marz, J. W. 228
materiality principle 253, 261, 262–263
Maxwell, D. 148
Mayring, Ph. 270, 273, 274, 276, 278
Mele, V. 54
Mena, S. 54
mentoring 129
Merkl-Davies, D. 273
meta-analyses 173
metrics: absolute 65; barriers to standardization
  of 18–30; development of 62; Global
  Reporting Initiative 65; intensity metrics 65;
  monetization 21, 24, 71, 74, 75, 81, 104;
  satisfaction metrics 74, 185, 242; selection
  of 21; for social performance 104; socio-
  economic metrics 74, 75; Sustainability
  Accounting Standards Board (SASB) 62; *see
  also* performance indicators
micro-level impacts 76, 81, **82**, 83
Middelkoop, M. J. 6
mimetic isomorphism 168, **170**
mission drift 104
mixed-method designs 84
moderator variables 173
Moffet, J. 6
monetary proxies 74
monetization 21, 24, 71, 75, 81, 104
Montiel, I. 7, 191
Moore, M. 269, 271

moral legitimacy 57, 261, 262
morality, economic theory of 254–255, 263
Morsing, M. 201n5
Mulgan, G. 18, 21, 27
Muller, M. 132, 142
multi-faceted organizations 80–83
multinational companies (MNCs) 122–139,
  189–205
multiple accountability disorder 67
multiple-case (holistic) models 22
multi-stakeholder initiatives (MSIs) 54–70
Muñoz-Torres, M. J. 10
mutual gains 262, 264
mutual support 83

Nachhaltiges Investment 10
narratives 24, 271, 273
Nastanski, M. 54, 55
natural capital reporting framework *59*
Natural-Resource-Base View (NRBV) 144
neighbour relations 44, 46
net impact calculations 74
network density 76
network theory 84
networks 76, 133
neutrality, principle of 55
New Economics Foundation (NEF) 94
NGOs (non-governmental organizations):
  acceptance of standards 68; accountability
  to 192; Berne Declaration 99; compliance
  monitoring 133; market for virtue 68; multi-
  stakeholder initiatives (MSIs) 56, 57; supply
  chains 123; voice of 55
Nicholls, A. 20
Nike 133
non-market perspectives in the SBSC 38–39, 41,
  43, 44–46
non-profits: Free Welfare Associations, Germany
  80–83; social impact measurement 19;
  Social Return on Investment (SROI) 72;
  standardized measurement tools (SMTs) 18;
  value creation 78–79, 83
normative isomorphism 169, **170**
Norton, D. 34–37, 40, 43, 50
NVivo 23

objective hermeneutics 273
observational designs 77
OECD (Organisation for Economic Co-operation
  and Development) 18, 19, 21, 122
Oevermann, U. 273
operations management, sustainable 141–165
organizational citizenship 243
organizational communication 73, 237
organizational development 79
O'Riordan, L. 7
Orlitzky, M. 146

outcomes measurement 24, 74, 182–183, 199, 200
output measurement 74, 182–183, 199
outsourcing 170, 172
oversight committees 62, 63

Pagell, M. 141, 143, 154
Panwar, R. 228
Parmar, B. L. 167
participation: measurement of 74; principle of 54, 55, 56, 63–64
Patagonia 90
Patel, C. 189
payout policies 241–242, **244**
Pedersen, E. R. 123
Peng, D. X. 148
perceptual versus objective measures 155
performance drivers 41, 43
performance indicators: lagging indicators 35–37, 41, 43, 46, 48; leading indicators 35–37, 41, 46, 48; standardized measurement tools (SMTs) 21; *see also* key performance indicators (KPIs)
performance measurement: over time 106, 109–113, 242, 245, 249; and the SBSC 47–50
person-organization fit 225, 248
Pesci, C. 21, 27, 28
pharmaceutical industry 7
philanthropy-driven CSR 6, 8, 89, **104**
Pinkston, T. S. 5–6, 14
plant level 142
plausibility checks 173
PLS-SEM analysis methods 150, 164
Podsakoff, P. M. 184
policy level performance tools 102–121
political advocacy 76, 79, 84
political capital 76
Political Claims Analysis (PCA) 79
Political Discourse Network Analysis (DNA) 81, **82**, 83
political influencing 84
pollution: Hamburg Airport case study 44, 51; Natural-Resource-Base View (NRBV) 144; and operational performance 145; triple bottom line concept 148
post-test measurements 183–185, 230, 232
Powell, W. 103
power resources theory 84
Prakash, A. 3, 4, 6, 7, 8, 14
precision versus comprehensiveness in impact measurement 77, 78–79
premiums for responsible goods/services 207, 227
pre-test, post-test design 184–185
proactive behaviours 44, 46
procedural legitimacy 54–70
process-tracing technique 226
product stewardship 92, **93**
Product Sustainability Assessment 94
production frontier methodologies 105

production theory 209, 212
productivity changes over time 102, 109–113
professionalization 103–104
profit-maximization objectives 105, 134, 173, 211, 212, 231
public comment periods 63–64, 65, 66
public goods 76
public interest balance sheet 95, 97
public relations 129
public value 269, 271
Public Welfare Economy 95–99
publicly available datasets 27
Pullman, M. E. 144, 145, 152
purposive/criterion-based sampling 22

qualitative data: financial reporting 270, 273–274, 278–279; impact measurement 81; impacts over time 126; social impact measurement 20–21, 22–23; Social Return on Investment (SROI) 75, 76
quality of information 126, 166, 167, 170–174, 192, 258, 259, 263; *see also* accuracy of reporting
quality of life improvements 141, 143
Quality of Life (QoL) 81, **82**, 83
quasi-experimental designs 77

Rahman, S. 4
randomization 77
Rangan, V. K. 18, 103, 104
Rao, P. 147, 148, 152
Rasche, A. 58
rating agencies 99
RCTs (randomized controlled trials) 185, 186
reasonableness 262
reciprocity 76
recycling levels 129, 143, 148
Reebok 134
regularity, procedural, principle of 55–56
regulatory frameworks: incentive systems 240, 245–246, 256–257, 269–270; as motivation for CSR 5, 6; private regulation 6; regulatory innovators 54; voluntary codes of conduct 14
relationships 261
religious organizations 76
Rennings, K. 4
reporting: reporting errors 172; reporting requirements 7, 179, 262; and the SBSC 47–48; social banking 207; Sustainability Balanced Scorecard (SBSC) 49–50; timeliness of reporting 259; voluntary reporting guidelines 3, 180, 254–257, 263; *see also* Global Reporting Initiative (GRI); greenwashing; quality of information; sustainability reporting; triple bottom line concept (TBL)
representation, principle of 55, 56–57, 64, 67
reputation 5, 7, 125, 130, 133, 148, 152, 225

resource allocation 20, 26, 73, 103, 144, 261
Resource-Base View (RBV) 144, 154
responsibility principle 272, 274
Responsible Care initiative 3–17
Responsible Supply Chains 122
return-on-capital-employed (ROCE) 37
Reuter, C. 129, 134
reward functions 242–243, **244**
Ribando, J. M. 10
Ricaurte, E. E. 193
risk-based approach to audit 126, 173
Roberts, S. 133
Roberts Enterprise Development Fund 72, 94
Robson, K. 54
Rodríguez-Garavito, C. A. 134
Rogers, D. S. 129
Rogers, J. 58
Roundtable on Sustainable Palm Oil (RSPO) 57
rule of law, respect for 94

SA8000 128
Saaty, T. 50
SABI Database 149
sanctions 4
San-Jose, L. 208
satisfaction metrics 74, 185, 242
scenario modelling 78
Schaltegger, S. 7, 33, 38, 39, 40, 41, 43, 44, **45**,
   46, 47–48, 49, 50
Schapiro, Mary 62
Schepers, D. H. 54
Schleper, M. C. 129
Schmid, K. 244
Schmiedeknecht, M. H. 92, 94
Schouten, G. 57, 64, 68
Schultz, M. 201n5
Schwartz, S. H. 190
scientific standards 185, 186
sector reform 117–118
Securities and Exchange Commission (SEC) 59
self-enforcement 262
self-esteem 75
self-reported data 126, 192
Sen, A. 72, 227, 248
Seuring, S. 132, 141, 142
Seveso disaster 5
share-based incentive systems 242, 248
shared audit 133
shared vision capabilities 191
shareholder value 49
Sharma, S. 144
short-term interventions 77
signalling theory 248
Singhapakdi, A. 228
small and medium-sized firms 7
small and medium-sized social enterprises 25, 55
smart feedback 190, 198–199, 200

social acceptance 57
social accountability systems 128
social auditing 189
social banking 206–222
social capital 76, 80
social cohesion 72, 74, 76, 80
social contracts 167, 254, 262, 263
social control 58
social enterprises 18–30, 179–188
Social Impact Investment Taskforce 74
social impact measurement: content analysis
   techniques 269–283; hotel industry 193;
   incentive systems 242, 248; in junior managers'
   project choices 226; linked to environmental
   performance 141–165; as management tool 20;
   multidimensional 72; online surveys for social
   impact assessment 185; social entrepreneurship
   179–188; Social Return on Investment
   (SROI) 71–88; social value creation
   measurement 18–30, 75; stakeholders 21, 28,
   76, 185, 187; support for 25, 27; sustainability
   accounting 48; Sustainability Balanced
   Scorecard (SBSC) 37–51; *see also* triple bottom
   line concept (TBL)
social justice 95–97, 272–273, 274
social labelling programmes 123
social media 193
social media banking 207–208
social network analysis 79, 84
social reporting systems 179–188
Social Return on Investment (SROI) 21, 27,
   71–88, 94–95, 97–99
social trust 76
Social Value Act 19
social value creation measurement 18–30, 75
social washing strategy 24
socio-cultural sphere 38
socio-economic metrics 74, 75
'soft' factors 33, 34, 37
soft law regulation 54, 133
solidarity 95–97, 236
Souto, B. F.-F. 12
Spain 149
Spitzeck, H. 41
stakeholders: and climate change 167, 168,
   169; coercive isomorphism 168; common
   good economy 95–97; communication to
   173, 271–272 *see also* dialogue withcustomer
   perspectives (balanced scorecard) 34–35,
   39, 46; deception of 192; decision-making
   227; dialogue with 192–193, 199–200, 227,
   261; direct versus indirect 41, 182–183;
   and disclosure quality 173; external
   accountability 24; fuzzy definitions of 260;
   Global Reporting Initiative 91, 254, 258,
   259, 260, 264; and impact measurement 73;
   inclusiveness 57–58, 63, 65–66, 258, 259,

261; involvement-consultation continuum 57; ISO 26000 92, 94; and legitimacy theory 167–168; multiple accountability disorder 67; multi-stakeholder initiatives (MSIs) 54–70; neighbour relations 44, 46; perspective of stakeholders as starting point 41; representation, principle of 55, 56–57, 64; Responsible Care initiative 7; shift to stakeholder perspectives 225; social impact measurement 21, 28, 76, 185, 187; Social Return on Investment (SROI) 81, 94; stakeholder maps 182; stakeholder theory 166, 167, **170**, 190–191, 192–193, 254, 260, 264; standardized performance tools 102–121; and supply chain management 129; sustainability reporting 49, 192–193; and transparency 97; 'unexpected' stakeholders 76–77; value for society not the investor 75; *see also* employees
standardization 78, 180, 191, 194, 200
standardized measurement tools (SMTs) 18–30, 189
standardized performance tools 102–121
standards: industry-level 132, 134, 169, 172, 194–197, 200; international 92, 94, 97, 99, 122, 123; market-based standards 66–67; regulatory innovators 54
statistical matching methods 77
Stechemesser, K. 173
strategic corporate social responsibility (S-CSR) 89–101
strategic objectives: and the balanced scorecard 35–37; common good economy 97; and corporate sustainability 240–241; and CSR 89–101; data envelopment analysis (DEA) 105; and the GRI 262; Hamburg Airport case study 44–47; importance of performance measurement 103–104; and the SBSC 40–41, 43, 49, 50; and social impact analyses 73; strategic core issues 41; sustainability as externalities 38; varying strategic missions between social enterprises 104, 108
strategy maps 34, 46
strong sustainability 8
subjective evaluation 24, 41, 97, 185
subsidy mechanisms 103, 107, 113–114, 118
supply chains: carbon dioxide emissions 170–172; compliance programmes 123–125, 128–130; globalization 122; green supply chains 129, 142, 147; Responsible Supply Chains 122; sustainability reporting 49; triple bottom line concept 142, 144
Surroca, J. 144
sustainability, history of concept 90
sustainability accounting 47, 48–49, 50, 54–70
Sustainability Accounting Standards Board (SASB) 54–70

Sustainability Balanced Scorecard (SBSC) 33–53
sustainability reporting: complete reporting 170–171; and financial reporting 269; future-ranking of sustainability reports 94; and the GRI 253–268; key performance indicators (KPIs) 49; Social Return on Investment (SROI) 78; supply chains 49; Sustainability Balanced Scorecard (SBSC) 33–53; transparency 49; USA 57–70; *see also* triple bottom line concept (TBL)
sustainable development 190–191
sustainable operations management 141–165
Sutherland, J. W. 129
Sutton, M. 256
Switzerland 270–279
systematic reviews 74

Tebroke, H. 209
technological progress 34, 106–107, 111–113, 116–119, 125, 168
Then, V. 73, 74, 75
Thomson Reuters 8, 9, 10
throughput legitimacy 64
timeliness of reporting 259
timing of CSR adoption 4, 8, 9–14
total asset calculations 206
traceability 225, 263
trade unions 55, 134
transparency: common good economy 95–97; CSR (corporate social responsibility) 97, 225; and the GRI 258; ISO 26000 94; multi-stakeholder initiatives (MSIs) 57, 58; and procedural legitimacy 55, 56; and the SBSC 40; social banking 208; Social Return on Investment (SROI) 78–79, 94; Sustainability Accounting Standards Board (SASB) 62; sustainability reporting 49
TRASI database 28
Tria, B. 94, *95*
triangulation of data 22
TripAdvisor Green Leaders 194, *195–196*
triple bottom line concept (TBL): and CSR 227; developing corporate compliance programmes 128; and the GRI 260; hotel industry 189; incentive systems 240, 245, 249; real-life cases 141–165; social banking 206, 208; and the SROI 72
trust games 255–256, 257
trust relationships 76
Tschopp, D. 54, 55
Türker, S. 132
Turner, R. 8

UKSIF 10
UNEP-FI 10
unions 55, 134

unit invariance 106
United Nations (UN): Brundtland Report 90, 260; and CSR 8; Decade of Education of Education for Sustainable Development 180; Environment Programme (UNEP) 90; Global Compact 122; International Covenant on Civil and Political Rights 92; sustainable development 191; Sustainable Development Goals 72; Universal Declaration of Human Rights 92, 122
universalism 190
University of Stuttgart 99
USA 54, 55, 57–68, 246, 249
USSIF 10
Utting, P. 58

values: carbon dioxide emissions 167; circular framework of values 190; core values 191; corporate 23, 71, 80, 91, 94, 236; internal value-chains 34–35, 39, 46; non-profits' value creation 78–79, 83; objectivity of value 21; public value 269, 271; social value creation measurement 18–30, 75
VCI 3, 7, 8
Velasquez, M. G. 189, 190
Vigneau, L. 192
Vogel, D. 14
voluntary codes of conduct 14, 123
voluntary disclosures 167, 169
voluntary guidelines 92, 122
voluntary reporting guidelines 3, 180, 254–257, 263

Waddock, S. A. 146
Wagner, M. **45**, 46, 48, 49, 50
Wal-Mart 141
Walsh, J. P. 146

Walth, A. 244
warm glow theory 26
waste management **41**, **43**, 44, 48, **93**, 144, 145, 148, **196**, 197, 198, 275, 276, 278
watchdog roles 56
water consumption 194, 197–198
WBCSD 166, 168, 170, 171
weak and strong sustainability framework 4, 8
Weber, C. 186
weightings 107–109, 110
welfare regimes 71, 76, 78–80
Wheeler, D. 141
Whirlpool Corporation 124–125
White, A. 65
Wieland, J. 92, 94
Wiggering, H. 4
Wilke, P. 244
Wood, D. 58
work–life balance policies 145, 146, 148, 152, 153, 193
World Bank 12
World Business Council for Sustainable Development 246
World Commission on Environment and Development 90, 271
World Health Organization 67
World Values Study 84
WRI 166, 168, 169, 170, 171

Yin, R. 22, 55
Yousefpour, N. 19, 20–21
Yu, X. 134
Yuthas, K. 18, 20

Zadek, S. 189
Zahn, E. 209, 212
Zhu, Q. 144, 145, 148, 151